Christian Eschatology and Social Thought

Christian Eschatology

and Social Thought

A HISTORICAL ESSAY ON THE SOCIAL
IMPLICATIONS OF SOME SELECTED ASPECTS
IN CHRISTIAN ESCHATOLOGY TO A.D. 1500

BY RAY C. PETRY

PROFESSOR OF CHURCH HISTORY
DUKE UNIVERSITY

NEW YORK   ABINGDON PRESS   NASHVILLE

CHRISTIAN ESCHATOLOGY AND SOCIAL THOUGHT

Copyright © MCMLVI by Pierce & Washabaugh

Library of Congress Catalog Card Number: 56-5372

SET UP, PRINTED, AND BOUND BY THE
PARTHENON PRESS, AT NASHVILLE,
TENNESSEE, UNITED STATES OF AMERICA

TO
MY COLLEAGUES
on the faculty of
The Duke University Divinity School

Foreword

THIS BOOK ATTEMPTS TO PLACE IN HISTORICAL PERSPECTIVE THE SIG-
nificant interaction between the church's doctrine of "The Last
Things" and its teachings on social responsibility. These are reviewed, as they were experienced, together, in the Christian life before the Protestant Reformation. Our Christian hope has recently
dealt all too exclusively with the social scene *or* the ultimate, heavenly community. This study shows that, in historical Christian experience at its best, these eternal and temporal concerns have consistently
been interlaced.

Throughout this work the words "eschatology," "society," and
their related forms are thought of in the large historical context of
Christian life and doctrine. Historically, this has not meant divorced
considerations of the community involvements of earthly society on
the one hand and of the societal regard for the heavenly association
on the other. On the contrary, the conscious and unconscious Christian response to the distinctive claims of the temporal and eternal
societies has set them in a focus of inseparability and causal intercon-
nection. It has been precisely the cumulative modern reversal of
this tendency that has obscured our historical understanding of the
Christian tradition regarding both the eschatological and the social
equations in Christian experience.

Today we have all too little regard for eschatology. Our preoccupation with the problems of earthly society seldom prompts any
thought of eschatological motivation or involvement. To be sure,
we already have some magnificent studies of the eschatological postulates of early Christianity, as we also have learned inquiries into its
social teachings. But these tend, in almost every case, to be specialized investigations of limited periods for one or the other of the
two, that is of the eschatological or the social. Furthermore, they
generally separate matters of philosophical and theological causality
from the consideration of historical-social process and analysis.

This study attempts to see, throughout the entire period of the

7

ancient and medieval church, the equipoise rigorously insisted upon for eschatological and social assumptions. We do not hereby imply that the Church changed at once, from all its previous positions, at the advent of the Protestant era. It is thought wise, however, to end these researches short of the major departures of the sixteenth century from the previous medieval tradition. Books in plenty on related themes have leaped over the pre-Protestant era in almost its entirety. This one will close by necessity where at least some of these started by choice.

The terms "eschatological" and "social" will be viewed as having a large body of normative significance over and beyond the diversified, and often temporary, connotations that have now come to confuse us after nineteen hundred years. I have refused to oversimplify and denature the term "eschatology" by precipitate definitions. The early chapters make quite clear the clarifications and basic postulates for which I accept responsibility. Regarding the words "society," "social," and the like, all easy definitions must also be renounced.

There may well be honest critics after the book's publication, as there were before, who feel that the words "society" and "social" are used too sweepingly, without proper regard for the terminologies and usages now approved among sociological and historical researchers. To this I can make but one reply: The largest connotations of these words are employed here much more because of the Christian rationale that has been associated with them in the past than out of deference to our contemporary canons of delimitation. "Society" and "social" meant bold, cosmic things for centuries of Christians before these same words were delimited by us for purposes of scientific precision in controlled areas of research. It would be difficult for us to prove our right to do what we will with our own words, even if we could prove that they were actually ours. It should be said quite frankly at the very outset that this book reports and interprets historical views which by no means limit the connotations of the words "society" and "social" to human, terrestrial experiences.

Christian thinkers here under study constructed their body of ideas, even as we still do, about ancient words to which they often gave an at least partly independent interpretation. These have now come down to us via such terms as the Greek *koinonia* and the Latin *societas*. These still have mutualizing and corporative meanings not limited to our circumscribed gamut of interpersonal relations. Translated into English, they continue to suggest the larger connotations of "community," "society," "fellowship," "companionship," "associa-

8

tion," "guild," "fraternity," and the like. These words, deriving their Christian meaning from the heavenly corporateness or sociality as the model, impart a distinctively Christian character to earthly associations, which are deemed imperfect copies of the celestial. For these Christian eras here studied, all permutations of social ideas that we now tend to think of as human, suggested, rather, the primary ramifications of the eternal world pressing in upon the earthly one.

These social views, however repugnant or inspiring to the modern man, deduced the primary meaning of society from the heavenly world and applied it judgmentally to all earthly societies. Today we habitually redefine "social," whether loosely or strictly, in terms of earthly society, and we tend, both eloquently and tragically, to refrain from attributing a "social" character to the "heavenly," or to the kingdom of heaven. This book employs the words "society" and "social" in their older and richer senses as still having significant referability to "society" and the "social" in our own age.

Quite obviously, this book cannot claim to have covered with complete comprehensiveness or with equal attention all areas of significance germane to Christian experience. The principles of selectivity and representativeness have definitely been invoked. The study limits itself largely to the Western tradition, though appreciative, if inadequate, attention has been accorded some representative Eastern sources. Large sectors of economics and education together with other topological considerations lack distinctive treatment, not because this could not have been effected, but because it was not deemed feasible under the present organization. In some instances these have been discussed in relation to other categories; in some they have been regretfully omitted, though not ignored. In last analysis, the subtitle is to be remembered as it was set forth—advisedly. The book marks out the large lines of social implication deducible via source analysis from responsibly delimited aspects of Christian eschatology before the Protestant Reformation. In these matters of selective emphasis, as in all other cases where I have profited by much appreciated counsel, I have had to be guided, finally, by my own judgment rather than by others' suggestions. May I have decided rightly in this opportune day of Christ's reburgeoning, universal church!

The debt of gratitude incurred by me is—as so often—utterly unpayable. Neither the full roster of those who helped, nor the description of their various services, can be adequately listed. Among those who must not remain nameless are the following whose services are recorded thankfully without the ascription to them, in any case, of responsibility for what I have finally said or done.

For readings of the manuscript in its virtual integrity, though in an earlier draft, I signalize the services of my colleagues in Duke University, Robert E. Cushman and Howard E. Jensen. For readings and advices over a period of years, almost the whole of the Duke Divinity School faculty is hereby recognized. My gratitude is deeply felt for the assistance of Donn Michael Farris, librarian of the Divinity School, and of his associates, Miss Joyce Lockhart and Miss Doralyn Hickey. My obligation to the combined staffs of the Duke University Libraries is heartfelt. My further thanks to American and European libraries for extended use and checking facilities must stop short of individual designation.

I acknowledge, for its having stood in a position of uniquely valuable assistance, the Duke University Research Council with its senior officers, John Tate Lanning and Walter M. Nielsen.

For stenographic and secretarial services I wish to remember, especially, Mrs. Howell H. Lewis, Mrs. John Davis, Mrs. Donald Roettger, Mrs. Louis Hodges, and Miss Jacqueline Harper. In a distinct category of appreciation for assistance in a crucial period, I remember my niece, Dr. Joanne E. Mertz. To my wife, who has never been anything less than a full collaborator, I must say the least adequate thanks simply because it is to her I owe the most.

The following acknowledgments are made to publishers from whose works I have had generous permission to quote: The Westminster Press for selections from my book *No Uncertain Sound*, copyright 1948; *Theology Today* for my article "Christian Eschatology and Social Thought" in the July, 1948, issue; the Mediaeval Academy of America for my article "Mediaeval Eschatology and Social Responsibility in Bernard of Morval's *De Contemptu Mundi*" in *Speculum*, April, 1949.

RAY C. PETRY

Contents

CHAPTER I

The Problem of Christian Eschatology and Social Thought

TODAY, IN SPITE OF THE CUMULATIVE DISASTERS THAT THREATEN TO end our civilization, few people think calmly and rationally about the dissolution of our world. Eschatology is a term virtually unknown. Its connotations of final things and world's end are still a part of our Hebrew-Christian ideology. But they are decreasingly effective as conditioning forces in our everyday social reactions.

It is frequently argued that these thought-forms lost their validity with the coming of modern science and philosophy. To be sure, they are patronizingly granted a kind of symbolic significance. Customarily, however, they are thought to retain permanence for a few fanatical groups of millenarians only. Even in those communions where eschatological doctrines are still held to be authoritative and applicable to daily life, the historical relationship of last things and social thought is but indifferently capitalized.

More recently, however, the emergence of the atomic threat—for there has been little enough of atomic promise—has posed anew the problem of man's future and his end. During a brief period, after the first atomic disclosures, prognostications were rife concerning the incredibly heightened tempo of human progress now potentially within the human grasp. These glowing dithyrambs have since given way to gloomy predictions, fitting in quite well with the sinister purposes of hypernationalistic politicians, on the ineluctability of further wars. Desperately, and with infinitely greater foreboding, the common man clutches at a fading hope that civilization may, somehow, still survive.

As might be expected, a number of religious enthusiasts now find sudden and unprecedented support for their most frenzied contentions. More than one person not of their persuasion asks whether these wildest predictions may not shortly be translated from the realm of shadowy aberration into the blaze of stark actuality. May not the entire human world come to an irrefragably final end with horrors that even the Revelator dared not conjure up?

Even reputable interpreters of the religious press come forth, on occasion, with articles positing the inevitable and imminent destruction of mankind and treating at length the procedures to be adopted in preparing for the dread event.[1] In some instances the basic Christian assumption that man as a race cannot continue indefinitely in a physical existence on an earthly planet becomes indescribably confused with a wholly arbitrary conclusion: namely, that God himself has no other choice than to terminate man's collective pilgrimage on earth with the very instruments of destruction that science has wrested from unwilling nature. Presumably, and all too presumptuously, we are asked to grant the superiority of man's will to total annihilation, at his own chosen place and time, over God's possibly vetoing purpose.

Before the splitting of the atom, however, and the application of its consequences on an internationally destructive scale, prescient students of Christian thought saw that we could not long escape a rendezvous with some more satisfying doctrine of eschatology than was ours. For generations past, scientists had been suggesting the real, if far-off, possibility of a peremptorily ruptured human life on the planet earth. Philosophers, religious leaders, and countless others had often raised the question as to the possibility of true progress where no adequate reflection on final ends was involved.[2]

[1] Compare the views of W. Fallaw, "Atomic Apocalypse," *Christian Century* (Sept. 25, 1946), 1146-48; (Nov. 27, 1946), 1438-39; and B. G. Gallagher, "Annihilation is Evitable," *Christian Century* (Oct. 30, 1946), 1308-10.

[2] Consult the editorial reassessment of science and religion in *Life:* "Untragic America" (Dec. 2, 1946, p. 32) and "Science: a Mystery Story" (June 23, 1947, p. 30) in conjunction with the penetrating, if brief, examinations of the *Christian News Letter* (Dec. 29, 1943; August 22, 1945; Jan. 9, 1946). Among the standard works on Christian eschatology in relation to science and history see: J. Baillie, *And the Life Everlasting* (New York, 1933) ; R. Seeberg, *Ewiges Leben* (Leipzig, 1920) ; F. von Hügel, *Eternal Life* (Edinburgh, 1913) ; R. H. Charles, *A Critical History of the Doctrine of a Future Life in Israel, in Judaism, and in Christianity* (2nd ed., London, 1913) ; A. E. Taylor, *The Christian Hope of Immortality* (2nd ed., London, 1939) ; and P. Althaus, *Die letzen Dinge* (5th ed., Gütersloh, 1949). Handbooks summarizing Roman Catholic doctrine and literature include J. Pohle, *Eschatology, or the Catholic Doctrine of the Last Things: A Dogmatic Treatise*, edited and adapted by A. Preuss (St. Louis, 1917, 1945) ; H. Hurter, *Medulla Theologiae Dogmaticae* (Oeniponte, 1889), pp. 705-45; A. Tanquerey, *Synopsis Theologiae Dogmaticae* (New York, 1920), III, 644-57; and F. Diekamp and A. Hoffmann, *Theologiae Dogmaticae Manuale . . .* (Rome, 1946), IV, 461-568. A recent treatise is R. Garrigou-Lagrange, *L'éternelle vie et la profondeur de l'âme* (Paris, 1945), translated by R. Cummins as *Life Everlasting* (St. Louis, 1952).

In fact, the more the roseate hopes of a materialistic future unfolded, the more these discerning critics of autonomous human advancement were driven to raise their voices in protest. They saw
quite correctly that the question could not be resolved by any util-
itarian consideration of how close man might be to great achievement, or how late or soon he might be uprooted from the earth. They
clearly divined the historic Christian insight that, not the immediate
state of man's fortunes, but the mandate of the Divine, is the governing basis of human operation.

All, in truth, that the atomic madness has since done to re-create
the inquiry comes with its providing a sense of terrible urgency; plus
the newly emphasized Christian assertion that any time is time
enough to save man, whatever the immediate future in store, if his
view of his ultimate end is unobscured and galvanic.

Now, in the aftermath of war and in the shadow of searing dissolution, the focus of the human animal is sharpened. Again, as so
often in the past, the conventional interpreters of man as a self-suf-
ficient being counsel him to use his "God-given secrets" in the well-
prepared, precautionary interests of the strong for the weak. Beyond
asserting that it is God's will that they be his intelligence officers, his
ordnance, and his custodians of world power, they offer no reconciliation of man's arbitrary national wrath and God's universal redeeming love. According to such a view, the Western world has the rightful duty, to be implemented if necessary by atomic force or hydro-
gen bomb, of protecting for subsequent inspection the ideals of
Jesus the Christ that they frankly disparage as unworkable—in our
time.

But the answer to such a fatal claim in the present crisis is suggested, first, by the thinkers of the past half-century who found their
clue in a clear reshaping of Christian convictions throughout the
ages; and, second, in a canvassing of earlier Christians for their basic
response to God's world and the needs of his people. Here, as always, one may benefit by looking back, not that he may revert in un-
nerving nostalgia to the bygone charms of another age, but that he
may proceed, through the remedying of his own time, to the far-
visioned society of the kingdom supreme.

Fortunately, there have been signs, in the decades past, of a more
sober rethinking of the old patterns of doctrine as they affect both
the expansion and the curtailment of man's corporate existence on
this terrestrial planet. These indications appear to augur no merely
awe-struck cognizance of either the catastrophic or the beneficent

potentialities of applied science. They imply, much more hopefully, a discriminating, if belated, admission that the most fundamental problems of human society must be posed far less to the arbiters of the physical sciences than to the interpreters of spiritual ultimates. In Catholic communions, and in the more conservative Protestant connections, there is a periodic recanvassing of history in relation to the end of time. Even from the centers of a vaunted liberal theology come a tardy recognition of eschatological considerations hitherto stubbornly ignored and a new critical interpretation, as well as a humbler evaluation, of the worths that may have inhered in patterns of social thought long since discarded.

A reputable body of scholars deeply concerned with the spiritual lapses and cumulative inertia of modern religious life supplies a mounting chorus of reaffirmation as to the abiding significance of eschatological doctrines. What is even more important is a not always grudging acknowledgment that Christian social thought has been largely barren aside from the inner vitality of eschatology; and that, contrary to the easy platitudes of some modern scholarship, eschatology has not been lacking in social repercussions of a constructive order. The realization dawns, however slowly, that in the first fifteen hundred years of Christian history, at least, eschatology provided the basic motivation and nucleating matter for Christian social thinking. Dawning, also, is the discovery that the ecclesiastical historian must play his part in reanalyzing and resynthesizing the long ignored intimacy of eschatology and Christian social thought.

Some modern writers, then, find in eschatology a definite, and oftentimes laudable, social propulsiveness. Perhaps no affirmations of this kind can be wholly effective apart from specific and representative writings on the subject. It must be made clear at once that the significance of any group selected will lie, not so much in the fact that they are historians or theologians *per se,* as in the fact that they challenge contemporary disregard of things eschatological where the whole future of the Church and its social obligations are concerned.

Ernst Troeltsch emphatically denied the assertion that eschatology mutilates Christian social thought and practice. It was his contention that Christianity gets its most powerful social impetus from its commitment to the absolute society which lies beyond any and all societies of the present world. He said most succinctly:

The Christian Ethos gives to all social life and aspiration a goal which lies far beyond all the relativities of this earthly life, compared with

16

which, indeed, everything else represents merely approximate values. The idea of the future Kingdom of God, which is nothing less than faith in the final realization of the Absolute (in whatever way we may conceive this realization), does not, as short-sighted opponents imagine, render this world and life in this world meaningless and empty; on the contrary, it stimulates human energies, making the soul strong through its various stages of experience in the certainty of an ultimate, absolute meaning and aim for human labour. Thus it raises the soul above the world without denying the world. This idea, which is the deepest meaning of all Christian asceticism, is the only means by which strength and heroism may be maintained in a general spiritual situation, in which the emotional life is infinitely deepened and refined, and in which the natural motives for heroism are either altogether lost, or else the attempt is made to try to reawaken them on the side of brutal instinct. This idea creates a perennial source of strength for strenuous activity, and a certainty of aim, both of which make for simple health and soundness of mind. All social Utopias, then, become superfluous; over and over again experience teaches that the ideal cannot be fully realized; but this does not mean that the seeker for Truth and justice need lose heart and fall back into scepticism, a temptation to which serious and truth-loving souls are prone, and the effects of which are very manifest among the finer spirits of the present day. The life beyond this world is, in very deed, the inspiration of the life that now is.[3]

Another German author, Rudolph Seeberg, expresses considerable surprise over his discovery that eschatology does not, as popularly thought, become a deterrent for positive social action. Speaking of the eternal refrain, "The end is near," he says: "The most remarkable thing about this is that it has not undermined moral power." He maintains that the very necessity of holding oneself in readiness for the Lord's coming had the effect of enhancing strong moral living at its best. Eschatological consideration did not lead, in the early period of the Church, at least, to laziness and brashness. It conduced rather to vigilance and humility.[4]

When one turns to English authors of even more recent periods, he does not get an essentially different story. Thus the Roman Catholic, Baron von Huegel, never tires of insisting on the primacy of eschatology in all social considerations. This emphasis is to be

[3] *The Social Teaching of the Christian Churches* (New York, 1931), II, 1005-6. Used by permission of the publishers, The Macmillan Co. Cf. his "Eschatologie," in *Religion in Geschichte und Gegenwart*, II, 622 ff., especially 628.
[4] *Lehrbuch der Dogmengeschichte* (Leipzig, 1922), I, 186-87. Cf. J. T. McNeill, *Christian Hope for World Society* (New York, 1937), Chap. I.

found consistently in his works on the teachings of Jesus, as well as in his First Series Essays.[5]

Speaking as a devoted Catholic layman, he represents a point of view far removed from the obscurantism often associated with certain elements in Catholicism and Protestantism, alike. Thus, his interpretations of eschatology shown him to be dissatisfied with many of the flatly dogmatic deliverances of purely traditional theology. What he does most effectively is to reorient the abiding significance of these problems in relation to the changing patterns of different eras and vacillating modes of thought.

One discerns, everywhere, his insistence upon the priority of the heavenly kingdom and the positive social repercussions that follow for present-day society. Thus it is quite inspiring to follow his stress upon the primacy of God and the social dedication to fellow men which derives from it. He deftly relates this emphasis on the problem of Last Things to its vitalizing effect for everyday, terrestrial community.

Dr. von Huegel cites, with approval, Canon Holland's profound observation to the effect that the proximity of Christ's advent "does not weaken but heightens the call to persistent self-purification and uninterrupted service of others." Certainly, von Huegel's own belief is that Jesus' eschatology, his unalloyed dedication to the eternal kingdom, is far from mutilating his social concern in the present; it actually gives the characteristic tone to his daily existence.

From the standpoint of Protestant English scholarship, a similar emphasis is inescapable. Dr. J. S. Whale gives a needed corrective to our modern this-worldliness. He says: " 'Other-worldliness' is the differentia of Christian life in this world." He shows how Neville Figgis built his whole social structure upon the concept of commitment to the heavenly society as being primary and determinative for this worldly order. After a penetrating discussion of this issue, Whale concludes as follows: "Our citizenship is in heaven. Its centre is in God. This is true of original Christianity; this is the unmistakable implication of our Churchmanship, and it has immense relevance to the predicament in which we now are." [6]

Canon Holland of Christ Church, Oxford, incorporated in the Liverpool lecture of 1916 some insights of invaluable proportions.[7]

---

[5] See, particularly, *Essays and Addresses on the Philosophy of Religion, First Series* (New York, 1928), pp. 119 ff., 195-224.

[6] *Christian Doctrine* (New York, 1941), pp. 184-85.

[7] H. S. Holland, *The Real Problem of Eschatology* (London, 1916).

He demolished the ever-recurring charge that eschatology is essentially pessimistic of all that pertains to the present world. His thesis was that there is a real continuity between the present world with its efforts and the world that is to come. Jesus, he insisted, could and did speak with such pertinent reference to affairs in everyday society just because he believed in an intimate continuity between the world to be and the world that was, even now, being summoned into likeness with it. What the Lord wills for this life cannot be severed from his ultimate plans to be realized fully in the eternal kingdom. Jesus' own parables make clear that this kingdom which is *future* in its complete fulfillment is already *present* in its operation and influences. Far from proposing a rigid separation of the future and the present, Jesus is proposing, not another world in which to find refuge, but one whose character and being is even now modifying and reshaping the present organization of life.

The assumption has often been made that one may have a fervent expectation of a second advent or a real interest in the present life—but never both. Canon Holland battles against the contention that one may be motivated by world redemption but not propelled at the same time by world renunciation. It has been tiresomely reiterated that the belief in a catastrophic arrival from without and the faith in grace instilled from within are mutually exclusive. Again, many would say that the believer may register on the side of some transcendent action from without, or he may believe in immanent growth—but he must choose between the two. Now, Canon Holland's real service lies, in part, in his annihilation of these supposed alternatives.

Here, for Dr. Holland, emerges the real problem of Christian eschatology. It consists, strategically, in the very fact that Christian eschatology, with its impassioned commitment to an impending and fundamental change, does not destroy the Christian's interest in the present. The apparent contradictions hitherto noted are found, not to destroy each other in collision, but to reinforce each other in their very coexistence and collaboration. What happens is:

The sense of the imminent end of all things, far from tending to disorder or eviscerate the demands of the moral law or the steadiness of self-control or the urgency of present conduct or the vitality of living interests, actually emphasizes and intensifies these demands. The motives intertwine and the appeals coincide.[8]

[8] *Ibid.,* pp. 16-17. See also pp. 3-15.

Dr. Holland readily concedes the eschatological and even apocalyptic frame of the Master's thought. He levies upon this and the later biblical writings to sustain his major thesis. He notes, as any objective observer must, how the Pauline literature, the crisis documents, and many others insist in the same breath upon the early return of the Lord and the necessity for corporate moral effort in the existing present. Truly, as he says, eschatology plainly intensifies the significance of moral endeavor and heightens the worth of routine service.

As for the belief in impending judgment, this only serves the better to show the direction in which all life is inexorably tending. Catastrophe in the offing by no means vitiates the work of slow growth.[9] Those responses, both personal and social, that pass the crisis test are precisely the ones that have been maturing in the preceding times. Only in looking to the critical hour, and finding what it calls for, can one safely build in the direction of it. Whether the time allotted before the culmination be long or short is, strictly speaking, of minor importance. Already operating under the unseeing gaze of the average observer are the powers and the forces that will one day be summoned into irrevocable and unquestionable openness. On this point Christian history insists with inflexible doggedness. Concerning this, the verdict of history is a clear vindication for heightened action, however inadequate, where ultimate testing is kept in view.

What Jesus so unflinchingly demands and Paul so faithfully reports is just the quality of attachment to the eternal kingdom which alone can provide any real redemptive power in the present society. Canon Holland asserts

that in order to determine your conduct here on earth you must first have secured a pivot in the transcendent world beyond. . . . Out there in that other world take your stand; and then, with this footing secure, you may return upon the life here, and determine its direction, and assert and govern and adapt and correct it, so that it takes on a rational purpose, and serves a coherent end.[10]

So also, true renunciation—the release from the immediate as being the most important—is frequently the best guarantor of service to the present world. Crisis there will be, but it *need* not, and

[9] *Ibid.,* p. 22.
[10] *Ibid.,* p. 26.

historically *does* not, in even a preponderance of instances, rob present considerations of their rightful portion. Seeing issues that must sooner or later come to an inevitable head makes one best prepared to plant his feet and move his share of the load from this time forward.

This constitutes setting one's affections on things above. It does not spell the turning of one's back on things beneath. The corollary in Pauline thought posits the consequent transformation of things beginning here and now in the direction of things subsequent and beyond. For this purpose the early community responded to Jesus' and Paul's admonitions to make the brotherhood of the present answer to the eliciting community of the future. The kingdom of God is not brought in by man. It will come in God's own way and with his unconquerable consummation. It is coming even now, in its present impact upon the belligerent, but already defeated, world that knows it not.

Canon Holland concludes with an emphasis upon the Eucharist as the fusing point and spiritual nucleus for the Christian community. As will be demonstrated elsewhere in these chapters, the Eucharist is the veritable promise of beloved fellowship resustained on numberless occasions "until Christ's coming again." Dr. Holland might have gone on to implement the clear inferences of his unspoken thought. That is, in the eucharistic banquet of the faithful lives the already responsive symbolism of the festive companionship most natural to the kingdom of God.

Dr. Bevan sets forth from England his interpretation of the Greek and the Christian life assumptions.[11] In it he gives several chapters to the problem of eschatology in relation to Christian social thought. A chapter on human progress is followed by one on the problem of eschatology. This may seem to many self-styled moderns a strange collocation of things old-fashioned and quite new. He certainly does not propose to accept traditional dogma at its face value. Yet he is equally stubborn about relinquishing all but the symbolic aspects of apocalyptic values in their larger eschatological setting.

In the conclusion of his study, he lays down certain principles that ought to govern our faith in the abiding values associated with Christian eschatology. These amount, in the main, to a re-expression, in modern phraseology, of the lasting quality of a traditional faith. He holds on to the essentials of a Last Judgment theory. In

---

[11] *Hellenism and Christianity* (London, 1921), pp. 201-25.

his case this assumes, mainly, the form of an individual accounting. However far removed it may be in actuality from the descriptions made available to us in Scripture and tradition, it does reassert the kernel of moral responsibility before God in the light of his total universe.

Again, Dr. Bevan restates the conviction that there is a continuity between the values of this life, all too little realized here, and their further realization in a life to come. Inhering in this statement are implications for the doctrine of rewards for the righteous. But he contends for much more than this. He perceives that any idea of future beatitude must link an expanding personality and a social experience with indisseverable bonds.

Manifestly, "any future bliss must be social. This is implied in the innermost character of the spiritual life. Love itself, the highest of values, implies a society." Perhaps a major factor in the unsatisfactoriness of our earthly condition comes from the limited and oft-interrupted community that we have one with the other. "The idea of a society in which the possibilities of knowing and loving are extended beyond anything we can conceive in our present conditions— that seems to be the essential thing in the doctrine of the Church Triumphant, of Heaven." [12]

Support is lent Bevan's views by the German scholar Dietrich Bonhoeffer. He paid with his life for his Christian social views when confronted with Nazi statism.[13] These positions, to be treated more fully elsewhere, receive their vitality from a similar thesis. For Dr. Bonhoeffer, the community to be realized fully, when the pages of history shall have been forever closed, provides the greatest magnetic pull of socially fructifying character to be encountered in the stream of historical events. A genuinely Christian eschatology thus provides the *raison d'être* and the clue to action for mutuality in this life.

A classic study in the sociology of religion, Robert Will's *Le Culte,* adds further weight to the role played by eschatology in determining temporal social action. It must suffice, here, to state what will receive amplification further on. This monumental work of Protestant scholarship demonstrates, conclusively, how human dedication to an

[12] *Ibid.,* p. 223.
[13] *Sanctorum Communio: eine dogmatische Untersuchung zur der Kirche* (Berlin u. Frankfurt/Oder, 1930).

ultimate society modifies and energizes the corporate activities of the here and now.[14]

In a recent English study of theology (1939) a collaborative approach is made to the ramifying problems of theology, comparative religion, Testamental studies, ecclesiastical history, and related subjects. Dr. N. P. Williams here allocates a place to the pertinent reconsideration of the Last Things.[15] In two compact pages of real insight, the author demonstrates how far removed the conventional problems associated with this subject are from the working assumptions of the average theologian.

He believes that such data as those based upon the authoritarian systems of Thomas and Dante are not likely to be carried over successfully into our own thought-forms; especially where their contentions as to the physical universe are concerned. He is doubtless right in thinking that for most moderns the usual norms of time and place traditionally associated with Jewish-Christian eschatology can have little support on other than a symbolical basis. It is true, furthermore, that certain elements in the conventional eschatology have sprung from a too slavish patterning after particularly apocalyptic passages in Jewish and Christian texts.

It is perhaps not surprising that empiricist theology has

been prone to regard the whole eschatological element in Christianity as outworn lumber, inherited from its Jewish parents, which has no serious value save in so far as it can be regarded as a vivid symbolism of the fact that God's purposes cannot be assumed always to realise themselves by the way of automatic progress and smooth upward evolution, but may from time to time find their expression in unpredictable and devastating catastrophe.[16]

This, however, Dr. Williams feels to be an all too cavalier conclusion. Some there are, such as the intellectualists who hold a position of "critical orthodoxy" informed with the aid of Historical Theology, who will not easily abandon great truths of Christian teaching simply because these come in unacceptable forms of presentation. Thinkers like these will rightly observe the need of a modern eschatology which will not sacrifice the essentials of traditional doctrine but properly discriminate them from the accretions of time and circum-

[14] *Étude d'histoire et de philosophie religieuses* (Paris/Strassbourg, 1925-35), especially III, 39 ff.

[15] Chapter I: "What Is Theology?" in K. E. Kirk, *The Study of Theology* (London, 1939), especially pp. 59-61.

[16] *Ibid.*, pp. 80-81.

stance. It is unfortunate that such serious work as has recently been done in the field has been all too much limited to a group under Barthian and related influences. "It may be the vocation of Christian thinkers, who live in happier surroundings, to elaborate a concluding section of Systematic Theology in a less somber and terrifying vein." [17] If one may question this hope of finding a happier circumstance for evaluation, he may, nonetheless, look forward to a more satisfying interpretation of the truth with regard both to our own credulity and to the historic circumstances attending the growth of thought in such particulars.

It is surely of no accidental significance that one of the younger American theologians of our time should combine a penetrating interest in the social aspects of soteriology with a genuine regard for the problem of eschatology. In his *Social Salvation* (1935), John Bennett considers the profounder implications of sin and evil for social experience; the interdependence of the individual and the group where social salvation is concerned; the oft-debated relevance of Jesus for society; the Church as the agency of social salvation; and—in his next to the last chapter—the search for a social eschatology.[18]

His discussion candidly regards eschatology as an indispensable element in our working theology as well as in our social life today. Apparently aware of the relative disrepute of the very term and its implications for a liberal-minded society, he asserts that "eschatology as such we cannot do without, because it is nothing more than a coherent view of the future which gives meaning to the present moment in which we stand." He observes further that, whether cognizant of the fact or not, liberal theology has had a social eschatology. This has taken the rather naïve form of believing that an ideal social order could be built "as the cumulative result of the efforts of men in every generation." He notes, too, that such a view has not stood the test of everyday experience. Consequently, many people have been left without a satisfactory eschatology—left virtually with none at all. With this experience has come a new sense of need, not only for the term eschatology, but for a working appreciation of the reality it connotes.

Bennett then launches out upon a discussion of what really constitutes progress and its relation to final objectives in the realms of the good life, ethically and socially considered. In his concluding

[17] *Ibid.,* pp. 81-82.
[18] Pp. 141 ff., 177 ff. Compare his article in *Social Action,* IX, 6 (June 15, 1943), 20 ff.

pages, he discusses the intrinsic worth of the present, with proper regard to modern theology as mediated through Barth, Tillich, Brunner, Reinhold Niebuhr, and others. He refuses to have the present removed from the area of significance in man's life. His final considerations, however, deal with "the hope for a consummation beyond history." Here he recognizes the fact that beyond time there may well be an experience quite social in its character which is truly the kingdom of God. He shows himself aware of the social implications of many ideas of heaven, all too often outmoded in expression so far as the present day is concerned. Professor Bennett is correct in his judgment that interpretations of the heavenly vision have been far too much slanted in an individualistic direction. He sees that if the kingdom of God beyond history is finally to become a reality, with the liberty of God's children made actual in an ultimate society, then we shall have "the only equivalent in truly social terms of the old idea of heaven, to which individuals were saved one by one and where, under the influence of mysticism and contemplative philosophy, the *summum bonum* was too often the individualistic vision of God rather than the reign of God in a community." Of course, Bennett does not seem to be properly conscious of the very real sociality that inhered in many of the prevailing views that he stigmatizes by implication. He is content, for the time being, to attribute to Barth and Troeltsch some possible yearnings for an expectation of that which lies beyond history but helps to condition present existence.

Dr. Bennett argues persuasively that this ultimate hope with its anchorage in past history need by no means be an opiate, "though in many forms that is just what it has been. At its best this hope is merely the crown of a Christian eschatology which gives a final security to human values." And he quotes with approval a further section from Troeltsch as to the manner in which such a hope actually conditions present life in a social fashion.

In a concluding paragraph, as in his later works, Bennett becomes more reserved. He knows that whatever the degree of validity attaching to the problem of eschatology, it will be of increasing concern in the coming days. He is sure that we cannot go on dodging the question indefinitely. Beyond this he seems unprepared to go.[19] A colleague, Professor C. C. Richardson, has addressed himself to the larger meanings that may well be derivable from such earlier beliefs

[19] *Social Salvation,* p. 179.

as the Creed affirms regarding the resurrection of the body.[20] Professor Richard Niebuhr and his brother, Reinhold, have encountered aspects of the eschatological problem as they have explored the relation of Christian theology and ethics to the contemporary social scene.[21]

From Switzerland, Dr. Oscar Cullmann is launching a series of studies in French and German that bid fair to speak far more pertinently to the problems of eschatology in relation to social thought than have the previously lauded tomes of Barth and Brunner.[22] Moreover, a series of articles in nearly adjacent fields has recently been presented by M. Goguel.[23] So, also, a number of provocative articles and pamphlets have emerged from various international centers: viz., from Tübingen on death and the hereafter; from Lund on eschatological aspects of Augustine's thought; from Zurich, Neuchâtel, and other Swiss centers on eschatology, law, and ethical considerations; and from America on eschatology and the ethics of Jesus.[24]

Obviously, however, an eschatology befitting our appreciation of abiding Christian values, together with our repudiation of untenable thought-patterns, might well be placed in a firmer context of respectable Christian thought than is now the case. This would make it possible for us to note the manner in which eschatology becomes, not a mere symbol of pious hopes, but a positive incentive from the

[20] "Some Thoughts on the Christian Hope," *Religion in Life*, XVII, 4 (Autumn, 1948), 531-39.

[21] H. R. Niebuhr, *The Kingdom of God in America* (Chicago, 1937) and *Christ and Culture* (New York, 1951); Reinhold Niebuhr, *Faith and History* (New York, 1949), particularly pp. 255 ff.

[22] *Le retour du Christ* (2nd ed., Neuchâtel, 1945); *Christus und die Zeit* (Zurich, 1946), translated by F. Filson as *Christ and Time* (Philadelphia, 1948); also *Christ et le temps* (Neuchâtel, 1947).

[23] "Pneumatisme et eschatologie dans le christianisme primitif," *Revue de l'histoire des religions*, CXXXII, 1-3 (Juil.-Déc., 1946), 124-69; CXXXIII, 1-3 (Jan.-Juin, 1947-48), 103-61.

[24] H. Thielicke, *Tod und Leben: Studies zur christlichen Anthropologie* (Tübingen, 1946); R. Prenter, "Metaphysics and Eschatology in the Sacramental Teaching of St. Augustine," *Studia Theologica*, I, 1-2 (Lund, 1947-48), 5-26; J. Ellul, *Le Fondement Théologique du droit* (Neuchâtel, 1946), notably pp. 71-75; J. Taubes, *Abendlandische Eschatologie* (Bern, 1947). Especially pertinent are the studies of A. Wilder, *Eschatology and Ethics in the Teaching of Jesus* (rev. ed., New York, 1950), bibliography, pp. 215-19, and H. A. Guy, *The New Testament Doctrine of the "Last Things"; a Study of Eschatology* (London, 1948), with its excellent survey of primary and secondary matter. See also R. Shinn, *Christianity and the Problem of History* (New York, 1953) and its strong eschatological focus for the relations of history and contemporary society.

posthistorical future to an enhanced co-ordination of efforts in a socially responsive present. If the abiding values of the Hebrew-Christian tradition are to be preserved, we must take account of the Jewish and the Christian insistence that only through a dedication to a primary order as yet unrealized can come any true progress in the intermediate stages of our lives as they are lived on this earth.[25] If human values inhere in anything more lasting than their own limited tenure, they must derive such worth from a worshipful dedication to God and his eternal kingdom. But if they give themselves in enduring loyalty to a kingdom that is beyond history, and not made by it, they must also feel the benign influences of kingdom community in their socially effective and historically valid present. This is not a thesis to be defended; it is the considered verdict of Christian thought as it has come down to us from the earliest times. The contentions and counterpropositions of Christian thinkers in our own day only give more serious focus to this long-standing article of faith.

Quite trenchant in this regard is the message of a convert from Roman Catholicism to Unitarianism, Dr. W. L. Sullivan. Having turned his back, for the sake of truth, on much that was once sacred but has since been rendered blasphemous, he does not, thereby, cast aside all convictions formerly held. With gathering momentum, he intensifies, even as he reinterprets, his faith in religious ultimates. His valedictory, republished posthumously, emphasizes that the consummately societal character of final judgment and heavenly joy marks out the path that consecrated followers of the Divine must walk in during their earthly associations:

Because a man has to save his soul, that does not destroy the fact that he must save it in a commonwealth of souls, nor the further fact

[25] Not to be overlooked are the researches on Hebrew-Christian eschatology and the teachings of Jesus to be found in such basic studies as those of H. D. Wendland, *Die Eschatologie des Reiches Gottes bei Jesus* (Gütersloh, 1931) ; J. Weiss, *Die Predigt Jesu vom Reiche Gottes* (Göttingen, 1900) ; C. H. Dodd, *Apostolic Preaching and Its Developments* (Chicago, 1947) ; and also his *History and the Gospel* (New York, 1938) , as well as his *Coming of Christ* (Cambridge, 1951) ; R. Otto, *The Kingdom of God and the Son of Man* (London, 1943, rev. ed., 1951) ; T. W. Manson, *The Teaching of Jesus* (Cambridge, 1931) ; and his *The Servant Messiah* (Cambridge, 1953) . Cf. K. W. Clark's "Realized Eschatology," *Journal of Biblical Literature*, LIX, 3 (1940) , 367-83, in relation to Dodd's contentions. W. D. Davies, *Paul and Rabbinic Judaism: Some Rabbinic Elements in Pauline Theology* (London, 1948) , pp. 285-320, is pertinent to the whole discussion of Hebrew-Christian eschatology and the teachings of Jesus, as is his *Torah in the Messianic Age and/or the Age to Come* (*Journal of Biblical Literature*, Monograph Series, Volume VII, 1952) ; cf. Guy, *op. cit.*, pp. 70-85, 103 ff., and its bearing here, also.

that this salvation precisely depends on how he has worked with and for these souls.

When we utter the word soul we do not mean an isolated thing all alone in a private boudoir making itself pretty for inspection on judgment-day. That would be absurd, and the religious sense is not absurd. We mean that how I act on other souls I shall answer for to the Lord of souls. . . . Instead of destroying the social sense I know of nothing that could more heavily charge it with energy, zeal, and love. The social sense is so sacred that its activity is not confined to earth and time; it determines the very judgment of the Eternal.[26]

[26] *Under Orders* (W. Rindge, N. H., 1944), p. 153. Used by permission of Richard R. Smith Publisher, Inc.

CHAPTER II

Historic Principles of Christian Eschatology and Social Thought

A BRIEF GLANCE AT THE MANNER IN WHICH SPECIALIZED NEW TESTA-
ment scholarship bears immediately on the social implications of
eschatology now becomes instructive. This will serve as a fitting
culmination to the representative testimonies of modern thinkers. At
the same time it will prepare the way for a preview, shortly to follow,
in which the historic principles of eschatology and Christian social
thought are to be set in preliminary relief.

Characteristic views of varying types are available in Dr. E. J.
Bicknell's commentary on Thessalonians and Dr. E. F. Scott's
volume on the Apocalypse.[1] Discussion of the Pauline correspondence
with the Christians at Thessalonica introduces enduring first-century
insights. Bicknell is representative of those scholarly modern thinkers
who have no intention of defending the exact world views presented
by the New Testament writers, yet who maintain that certain abiding
worths are to be found in them. He pleads for caution lest the present
world disparage these religious values as belonging to the purely
subjective intuitions of antiquated thought. At the same time he suggests that we discard certain ideas that are clearly outworn.

Thus, in analyzing the significance of the Thessalonian correspondence, the author revives once more the question as to how far the
limitations of Paul and his age seriously damage the religious contentions for which they stand. Even if one holds that a conception of
heaven fully compatible with the world view of Paul is impossible to
a thinker with a twentieth-century perspective, he may still not

---

[1] *The First and Second Epistles to the Thessalonians* (Westminster Commentaries,
London, 1932) and *The Book of Revelation* (London, 1940). W. D. Davies' penetrating
examination of Jewish-Christian documents and their bearing on Pauline studies is a
fuller, more intensive study of Testamental scholarship with large significance for this
study. See his *Paul and Rabbinic Judaism*, especially Chapter X, with its mastery of
the entire literature. Observe, also, the further analysis of Jesus' significance for Jewish-
Christian eschatology in Chapter III of the present work.

escape, too lightly, the challenging perceptions which go beyond the realm of changing, surface outlook. Thus Paul might have had what is to us a wholly untenable view of heaven in terms of location and spatial arrangement; nonetheless, the main burden of his insistence that heaven calls for a closer fellowship with Christ and with one another in Christ "is quite unaffected by any discoveries of physical science." [2]

Bicknell is, furthermore, not of the opinion that we may derive any detailed scheme of eschatology from the Pauline writings. Much less than R. H. Charles, would he attribute to the Apostle any carefully articulated system of thought on this matter. Admittedly, too, there is much of the occasional in Paul's emphasis upon certain interrelated phases of eschatological belief. But this still leaves a large area of question concerning the really abiding quality of spiritual penetration found in Paul and other early Christians; particularly as this relates to the problem of an ultimate world order in its relation to temporal society and the present.

In his note on the permanent value of apocalyptic, Bicknell raises issues which may be more properly assessed in terms of the whole problem of eschatology. He knows how alien these thought-forms are to men of modern stamp. He sympathetically agrees that only the most uneducated can give an unalloyed support to these first-century views as being an exact interpretation of the physical universe. But he, like Scott, insists that values expressed through metaphor and symbol do have significance beyond that which may be immediately attached to them. Certainly one need not commit himself to every vagary of symbolism in the process of seeing some worth represented by otherwise untenable pictures of the universe. So orthodox an interpreter of Roman Catholicism as Pohle concedes this readily enough in his discussion of ancient medieval beliefs regarding resurrection and judgment. [3]

It is increasingly apparent that some leaders of our present era have been all too ready to disparage, not only the particular patterns in which eschatological thought is clothed, but also the significance of the thought itself. If we ask with Bicknell what values there are in apocalyptic—and, for that matter, in a more generally extensive eschatology—we get a forthright answer. He asserts that specific truths find their expression in the somewhat exaggerated thought-

[2] Bicknell, *op. cit.,* p. 47. Cf. Davies, *op. cit.,* pp. 285 ff. for Paul's eschatology in detail.
[3] See *Eschatology,* pp. 49-51, for example.

forms of an earlier day. His remarks are so pertinent that their bearing on the problem of eschatology and the present may be profitably analyzed.

He insists, first of all, that apocalyptic puts God, and not human progress or well-being, at the center of all history and all existence. This has been a lesson particularly hard to incorporate in the progress-bent mind of our era. As anyone may easily observe, the present age likes to think of its ability to conquer all situations in the name of human effort and effectiveness. But the ancient thought-forms declare that God's sovereignty carries with it actions independent of human co-operation. One is forced, on such a basis, to undergo the humbling experience of importuning God for some things that an individual, or even his collective order, cannot achieve. It is in this sense that the cautions of Baron von Huegel, on the Catholic side, and of numerous Protestant scholars, on the other, come into focus.

Again, Bicknell suggests that these eschatological conceptions remind us of the role exercised by divine grace. The kingdom of God, though it may come in part by means of man's co-operation, is not the "crown of a long process of human development, but . . . a sudden act of divine power." This, too, is hard for the vast optimism of a humanistically inclined world order to conceive. But it is one of the most easily demonstrated emphases of the Master himself. The heavenly city from above, about which Paul and the early Fathers speak, is not itself conditioned by, and consummated through, the slow efforts of mankind. If the efforts of humanity are worth anything, they secure their power and direction from the heavenly order that already prevails and that will some day break in upon the existing human society.[4]

This author, like quite a few others, sees the necessity for correcting the one-sidedness of an evolutionary perspective. He realizes how necessary it is for us to appreciate an outlook that goes beyond the sheer instantaneousness and cataclysm of an earlier world view. Like Bosworth and Holland, Bicknell holds that the two ideas of evolution and catastrophe are not in any necessary conflict.[5] Catastrophe has its preparation in slowly moving forces; and, on the other hand, the more gradual phenomena embody qualities of cataclysm. It is pointed out that the Gospel of John shows how the idea of final judgment may be fully compatible with that of present judgment.

---

[4] Bicknell, *op. cit.*, p. 49.

[5] *Ibid.*, pp. 49-50; cf. E. I. Bosworth, *The Life and Teaching of Jesus According to the First Three Gospels* (New York, 1929), p. 246.

The final doom is but the showing up in the light of God of differences that already exist. At the same time, Christianity is committed to a belief in the supernatural, in the sense of belief that the full range of existence is not revealed to our senses. There is a spiritual order beyond and behind this present visible order. If so, then there must be at least the possibility of the breaking through of this supernatural order into the present visible order, with the result that there emerges some act or event that could not have been predicted, some utterly fresh happening. Apocalyptic stresses the existence and the influence of the unseen.[6]

Bicknell indicates how such insights help us to realize the relative significance of past, present, and future. We are reminded that the full attainment of things as they are to be is the secret of the future; and that the future for its part helps, certainly, to condition the present. It is not a simple case of the future's being made up of an accumulation of pasts and presents.

To us who live in space and time, perfection is to be found not in the present, but in the future. The present is to be used in order to forward it. Thus apocalyptic is an antidote to that pantheistic or idealistic view of the world which holds that it is the present world that is perfect, if only we can look at it in the right way.[7]

It is precisely here that Bicknell underscores the significant possibility of God's conquest over evil, a conquest greater by far in its present working than man can possibly know. Where there is a proper consideration of the difference between right and wrong and the faith that right will prevail over evil, the real basis of a true optimism is always present. Even while apocalyptic and eschatology seem to react with complete pessimism about the present state of things, they are in reality committing themselves to a victory that is ultimately sure because it is God's own. "The apparent pessimism of Apocalyptic, as it surveys the present order, is the very ground of an ultimate optimism. This world is not yet the world that God wills it to be." [8] However different the prophets may have been from the apocalyptists at many points, they found themselves in common agreement here. In fact, all found it necessary to declare that a bright future was possible only when present actualities were made responsive to ideals as yet future in their fullest realization.

Bicknell denies that apocalyptic, with its tendency to other-world-

[6] Bicknell, *op. cit.*, p. 50. Used by permission of the publishers, Methuen & Co., Ltd.
[7] *Ibid.*, pp. 50-51. Used by permission of the publishers.
[8] *Ibid.*, p. 51. Used by permission of the publishers.

liness, completely dissipates devotion to present obligation. He observes: "In the teaching of Christ the apocalyptic expectations are in no way in conflict with present duties." Perhaps it is too strong to say that Christ was interested in the world as it now is. It is certainly correct to say that

this life is the testing-ground for a life which is to attain its fullness hereafter. . . . So to in St. Paul, eschatology does not weaken but strengthen the call to present sanctification. Life is to be lived here and now as by those who will have to give an account of it. But the temptation to shirk the ordinary tasks of the present age is sharply rebuked. Christians are to be better citizens, better workmen, better servants because they have already tasted the powers of the age to come, and look for its consummation. So too history proves that men are able to make a better contribution to the present world-order if they sit lightly to it and if their true hope lies beyond. To be wholly absorbed in this world is to miss its true meaning. A right other worldliness is the condition of the truest success and the wisest use of this world.[9]

An interesting comparison with the position adopted by Bicknell in his work on Thessalonians is supplied by Dr. E. F. Scott in his treatment of the Apocalypse.[10] He does not flinch at the conclusion that John presents something related to a philosophy of history and that some such consideration has its proper place. But where the philosophical historian has greatest regard for the past, the Apocalyptist "tries to understand the present in the light of the future." [11]

The Apocalyptist correctly senses the manner in which the future lays hold upon present obligation and activity. Thus Dr. Scott says, interpreting the thinkers of an earlier age, "there is an ultimate goal towards which all the events of today are making, and you cannot properly understand them, you cannot measure their real importance, unless you can relate them to that absolute end." [12] This, by the way, is not so foolish as it may appear to the present-day schematizer of thought. Fancy and imagination no doubt obtruded themselves all too often into the apocalyptists' considerations. But they had an unshakable faith that there was reality in the purpose of God as it affected the present and that they were his instruments in helping bring that will to the knowledge and committed activities of men. If one

[9] *Loc. cit.* Used by permission of the publishers.
[10] *The Book of Revelation* (London, 1939).
[11] *Ibid.,* p. 155.
[12] *Loc. cit.*

33

were to ask them about the end to which all things were moving, in order to have a good basis for understanding the present, he would doubtless receive the reply that Dr. Scott has represented them as giving: "God will finally establish his Kingdom, and all that is happening now has some relation to that end." [13]

With a reply to materialism that is increasingly informing and inspiring, the Revelator values things present in the light of God's ultimate purpose. This is the kind of Christian philosophy of history which alone can destroy the seductive insinuations of imbedded materialism. Otherwise, man must enshrine current life as its own end and accord to future ideals, as yet unrealized, only such validity as they may derive from an accretion of human powers and growth.

A similar and even more striking homage to the internal significance of apocalyptic insight is provided by Dr. Scott's treatment of two worlds in relationship to each other. In the Book of the Revelation it is the heavenly world which is forever drawing forth the earthly one. Earth and heaven are set over against each other. Representing two world orders, they are at once discontinuous and continuous. Separated, they are nonetheless bound together. "The lower world depends on the higher, and exists for the sake of it. In itself it has no meaning, and we can make nothing of it till we know of that world beyond." John was himself assured that "the earthly scene will at last be merged in the heavenly one." [14] As already observed elsewhere, it is the Church's commitment to the fellowship of the saints in heaven, yet to be consummated, that knits them together in earthly fellowship, even now.

Dr. Scott notes the similarity in framework, at least, with the thought of Plato and other philosophers where this problem of the visible and the invisible is concerned. But John is thinking much more concretely than they of the kingdom of God as a state of being in which we shall know communion with God. Throughout, this sense of relationship between the two worlds and the passionate belief that this world serves the intermediate possibilities of the eternal fellowship most loyally is the major contribution of the Revelator. In attempting to interpret the present in the light of the divine future, he necessarily employs symbols which may, perhaps, fail of an accurate character. But he is no mere speculator. He wants to stiffen the present Church in a heroic response to the heavenly community with which it is to be ultimately associated.

[13] *Ibid.*, pp. 156-57.
[14] *Ibid.*, p. 167.

Professor Scott interprets John in this respect as Bicknell would interpret Paul—and as many others would see Christ, likewise—namely, as calling for a long vision and a far view to the future as being the best possible dedication to the present and its corporate necessity. It is, perhaps, not asking too much to demand a further consideration of such values as this in analyzing our own present needs.

If one were to reconstruct, historically, from the representative thought of past Christians, an analysis of our confusion in futures and ends, something like the following would probably have to be said. The Christian, like everyone else, has a future. He frequently accepts it as being, in the main, like that commonly anticipated. This is a departure from the thinking of his early Christian ancestors. They looked for a destiny above and beyond that of the prevailing society. But the average Christian does not know this; or, perhaps, knowing it, he congratulates himself on being thus changed for the better. He is now thoroughly domesticated, at last, in the world of men as a whole.

In one respect, the average Christian is even more like the non-Christian world than he thinks. That is, he accepts the immediate future for his real one. He takes it for granted that this future is largely an accumulation of the past—the world's past. He gives acceptance to the dictum that he is a creature of all that has preceded him; and that his future is, also.

Such a Christian, therefore, is content to face a future that will be more like himself and his past than it will be unlike him and that which has gone before. Some minor changes may be anticipated, but only in the line of a purely natural development from what has previously been. The nominal Christian is careful to propose no very revolutionary departures beyond those of a mounting physical character. And these, of course, can easily be documented to past experience. "Origins" is a big word with him—big enough to be cautious *for,* to be true *to,* and to go slowly *from.* But in his preoccupation with beginnings, such a Christian forgets the fact that Jesus, Paul, and countless others were even more concerned with a future than with a past—the future which proposed to transform all beginnings with a final destiny.[15] These early Christians were certainly not expecting a future manufactured out of any past. They frankly believed that both their present and their past were being shaped and made

[15] *Ibid.,* pp. 168-72.

conformable to what still lay before them. The early Christian, therefore, continued to think of his origins as having been made with an eye to his ultimate end. He looked, therefore, to a future which was unpredictably thrilling; to a certain degree discontinuous with his present and past; and undeniably revolutionary.

His present, of course, reflected this opinion of his future. Naturally, too, he felt called upon to help change that present, at once, in the direction of eternal plans registered from the beginning of the world but not yet completely fulfilled. In his eagerness he did sometimes try to overleap his present entirely, but only when he disregarded the clear mandates of Jesus and the lucid teachings of Paul.

The early Christian and his closest spiritual kin across the ages have continued to insist on a clear differentiation between an immediate future which is merely an accumulation of past happenings and an ultimate futurity beyond time with which God challenges all pasts and presents. For the true Christian knows that he is determined from before far more than from behind. Origins involve merely the place and the time wherein he started, observably, to respond to the kingdom of God. That society, yet to be realized in the future that lies beyond history, is already working among men and demanding their prime loyalty to it in the historical present. Quite literally, as Jesus taught and as Paul said, the Christian must be transformed by the kingdom which is yet to be, rather than conformed to the world which already is, or has been.[16] All of man's history, therefore—the Christian's especially—may be viewed as most significant for what it reveals of direction, purpose, intention, and destiny. Numerous Christians would insist that the historical record describes best what has been, and is now, occurring in response to the eternal solicitation. That is, both past and present respond best when they answer to a divine imperative finally and fully operable beyond the limits of history. The present is not neglected when we start remaking it with the aid of past experience on the pattern of a future design. In fact, the historic Christian position contends that human life becomes more social when it is patterned on an ultimate community, beyond the confines of history, than when it looks backward to a temporally inhibited society set within the limits of history.

Progress merely from behind is petty progress. Such advancement may provide wings instead of wheels, but it is still material. It may

---

[16] Cf. the Beatitudes; Matt. 5:1–7:27, etc.; Luke 9:57-62; 12:22-32; Rom. 12:2.

talk in terms of internationalism instead of localism, but it still depends upon coercion. With it may come bigger wars to end all conflict, but no large or enduring peace. In a world characterized by such development, no destination may be more than sixty hours from any airfield, but the passenger is still planet-bound; the human spirit is still enslaved. In such a world, longer life may be possible; but it will still be flesh and blood. The more of such physical gains we register, the less of anything else an accommodationist Christianity seems to require.

The real trouble is not far to seek. Such progress is not based on truly Christian principles. It looks ahead, but not far enough. The future that it envisages is merely borrowed from the accumulation of past and present. It is only less like them because it is a more bewildering accumulation of them. Man's real future—the future within time, and stretching beyond it, that is reserved by God for him and held out in challenging love to him—is scarcely anticipated at all. The authentic Christian, alone, has the courage and the imagination to look first at the ultimate. He believes that our present, together with that which lies immediately ahead, should respond, at once, to God's plan for the kingdom. He thus anticipates a beloved community which shall someday transcend all things of earth, but which, also, places its demands upon every present society on earth. Only with such an immediate dedication to the divine realm will a proper differentiation of futures be clear. Looking far to the ultimate of all futures, to the eternal realm that succeeds all time, we shall be best prepared for that which lies immediately ahead. And that future which is immediate shall reflect, not only the accomplishments of the past and the designs of the present, but the commands of the far future as well.

Having made such a commitment, we shall find our present standards of progress lazy and inadequate. We shall no longer be content to point out how much better we are than we have been. Our puny arguments that we are children of the past and that we, therefore, bring with us to the future only that which we have from the past will be finally dissipated. For we shall then stand under the necessity and judgment of what we were always intended to be. As Christians we have always been children of the future—the far future. And this is the consideration that has always made Christianity fruitful and unafraid. It is the element, also, that has helped to build a true Christian society in this world, not on the pattern of earthly existence, but after the fashion of everlasting life.

37

If the demurrer be entered that such a reconstruction is fanciful in the extreme and under no circumstances fitting for the worker in historical fields, the issue will have to be firmly joined. Historians have always had as their legitimate province the examination, not only of sterile "events," and of so-called "facts," but, even more justifiably, the observation and interpretative assessment of ideals and convictions that help to alter the human response to the universe.[17] Not only has the above summation of Christian premises sprung fully uttered from the historical records of man's social inclination; it has also constituted a more powerful reagent in the historical process than most political happenings so true to the stereotypes of historical lore. In an era rent by nuclear schism, the church historian, certainly, will do well to look backward for suggestions as to what lies ahead.

Having set in proper focus the vital importance of eschatology as related to social thought, we may now enunciate some basic hypotheses that grow out of primary researches in Christian history. Strikingly conformed to the experience of Christianity in its first fifteen hundred years, these principles may also be found to reside, perhaps somewhat surprisingly, in the substrata of later Christian life and thought. No mere caprices of private speculation or group eccentricity, they represent the historical composite of Christian convictions maintained through the centuries. As here interpreted, they stand detached from the more sensational patterns of ancient world view that have so often been permitted to obscure the essential character of Christian eschatology. Revealed, thus, as the center of an abiding faith rather than on the margins of external structure, they clarify the ultimate motivations for individual and social existence to which Christianity has given rise.

According to the fundamental assumptions of Christian eschatology, attention focuses at once upon two basic orders of life. The first of these is an ultimate one as distinguished from the temporal exigencies of our world and time. This order is necessarily transcendent of all purely human relationships. Its anchorage and point of focus are heavenly rather than earthly. Its point of origin and pattern of progression descend from the divine to the human. As a kingdom of life this community had a social ordering before the beginning of the world. Those of the celestial regions constituted the

---

[17] Consult G. Salvemini, *Historian and Scientist: An Essay on the Nature of History and the Social Sciences* (Cambridge, Mass., 1939); Also R. C. Petry, "The Church and Church History," *Duke School of Religion Bulletin* V, 3 (Nov., 1940), 63-77.

original membership of this first society. This kingdom under God's rule has, therefore, long since had its inception; though it waits for its final consummation upon God's own future.

Opposed to this first order of life—first, that is, in terms of both chronology and significance—is a second, subordinate social life. It is temporary in that it is related indistinguishably with the passing of time. It is terrestrial whereas the other is heavenly. Its interests, when truly normal, have an inevitable, forward reference from the human to that divine society from whence it was derived. But, in its typical development, it is preoccupied with mundane considerations. This second order with its appearance of perpetuity is deceptively pervasive now. All too secure in its obvious recapitulation of the human and the temporal, it may seem to be in control of man's only realizable world. But, according to all representative Christian thought, it is to be supplanted in fact, and likewise transformed and transfigured, by that other society which already is, in part, and which will, at the end of history, be final and complete. As previously stressed, the ultimate order is first, by reason of origins and of significance. Thus it has always been social inasmuch as it has bound together, from the beginning, the Trinity and all of those saints, angels, and heavenly ones working in intimate conjunction with the creative activity of the Deity. And it will, in the reaches of eternity, become the kingdom of Christ and of God. As such, it will include within its power and direction all those having given, and continuing to give, full co-operation with God and each other under the enduring rule of the Father.

The temporary order is, likewise, secondary as to both time and importance. As such it always was, and will always be, socially answerable to the eternal order of life. For it, too, there will come a time of social reincorporation with the enduring kingdom which shall embrace a new heaven and a new earth.[18]

From the very first, both heaven and earth have been destined to a unified cosmic end. The final ordering of life will embody heaven and earth in a new totality where God's will is to be done without

[18] Matt. 19:28; Rev. 21:1; *De Civ. Dei*, XII, 16-20; *Confess*, Bk. XI. For provocative studies on the relation of time and eternity, the cyclical and the linear views of history, see Cullmann, *Christ and Time*, pp. 38-68; R. E. Cushman, "Greek and Christian Views of Time," *Journal of Religion*, XXXIII, 4 (Oct. 1953), 254-65; and Taylor, *The Christian Hope*, pp. 89-95. Apropos the role of the Eternal society in relation to the present order, consider C. N. Cochrane, *Christianity and Classical Culture* (Oxford, 1940), pp. 506-16; and E. Gilson, *Introduction à l'étude de Saint Augustin* (3rd., Paris, 1949), pp. 246 ff.; also Hügel, *Eternal Life*, pp. 87-94.

reservation. The cosmos has always been, and will forever be, socially oriented. Springing from the creative activity of God, all beings have, from the first, been inevitably related to God and to one another. Both the evil and the good are likewise social. Thus the present order is a confluence of those who are to be ultimately triumphant and those who are finally to be defeated in accordance with their acceptance or rejection of God's proffered gift of life everlasting. They have this enduring social reference as regards both their lostness and their savedness. They are conceived of, in their life processes, as going to ends that are both good and bad; but, in each case, constituting a corporateness of righteousness or unrighteousness, of bliss or woe.

In keeping with such patterns of thought, cosmic as well as particular judgment has been thought necessary to the Christian plan of ultimates.[19] Hence, an individual may be regarded as facing a particular consequence now and later, for a series of particular acts. But these same individuals are regarded as sharing in a collective judgment that shall have its consummation at some great assize. It has been peculiarly acceptable to most orthodox Christian thought that such final rendering of accounts should take a definite and dramatically social form. Upon the final assessment, groups of evil beings are thought of as being resolved into a lasting companionship of evil. The good, on the other hand, have their eternal reward as a society of the good, with Divinity, as the supreme good, at their head and in their midst.

Such a judgment, described repeatedly with a variety of literary embellishments through the centuries, has always maintained a predominantly social setting. As before indicated, the conclusion of such a reckoning is an ultimately social purpose or end. Christ coming again in the humanity that once suffered at cruel hands and the Twelve Disciples who assist him constitute a social judiciary.[20] Theirs is unquestionably a social basis of decision. In conformity with Matthew, chapter 25, they pronounce a benediction or malediction in terms of social action on the part of those who accepted or rejected the poor and little ones in Christ's name. Once consigned to right

[19] Matt. 25:31-46; John 5:29; A. Huck, H. Lietzmann, and F. L. Cross, *A Synopsis of the First Three Gospels* (Tübingen, 1936), p. 181; E. Klostermann, *Das Matthausevangelium* (H. Lietzmann, ed., *Handbuch zum Neuen Testament,* 2nd ed., Tübingen, 1927), pp. 204 ff.; Bonhoeffer, *Sanctorum Communio,* pp. 175-76; Althaus, *Die letzen Dinge,* pp. 172 ff.; Pohle, *Eschatology,* pp. 18 ff.; Diekamp, *Manuale,* IV, 501 ff.

[20] Matt. 19:28; *De Civ. Dei.* XX, 30; T. W. Manson, *Teaching of Jesus,* pp. 268-70; Diekamp, *Manuale,* IV, 503.

or left, the judged ones face a social consummation. According to the predominating doctrines of the Church, they await a beatitude or a joylessness that is unendingly and unmitigatingly corporate. That is, they are eternally happy together in God's heaven, or they are forever deprived and without joy in the company of the evil ones.[21]

This separation of two social bodies cannot be said to constitute a continuing duality of life. Whatever the disparities of their ultimate destiny, both societies will be disposed to the triumphant ends of the one undefeatable God. One may, therefore, with St. Augustine, think of those in God's City as constituting the only true fulfillment of unimpaired society. All others are, in a real sense, bound together, not so much by what they have, and are, as by what they lack and fail to be.[22]

The tradition of a time-limited purgatory and of an unending heaven and hell sees in both societies a single significance. They are, alike, born out of God's plan of redemption and of man's acceptance or rejection of it. Whatever they become has final significance only insofar as they realize or fail to find a place in God's own eternal family. The Origenistic system of thought with its "school of souls" looks to continuing judgment and redemption until all beings shall have been brought into ultimate reassociation with God in a single triumphant society.[23]

Even the chiliastic Christian thought-forms, with their varying degrees of radicalism, have a basically positive relation to what one may call the more traditional, normative eschatology. This is true whether one considers the Revelation of John, the fragmentary sayings of Papias, the apocalyptic ideas of Lactantius, or the stigmatized aberrations of Joachim of Flora. Theirs is, originally at least, an attempt to see a foregleam of the cosmic kingdom, with the embodiment of both its earthly and its heavenly aspects already registered, victoriously, to some extent on this earth.[24]

[21] *De Civ. Dei*, Bk. XXI; Althaus, *op. cit.*, pp. 189-90; Pohle, *Eschatology*, pp. 149-54.

[22] *De Civ. Dei*, X, 25, XV, 2-3, XIX, 13, XX, 30; Garrigou-Lagrange, *Life Everlasting*, pp. 117-25; Gilson, *Introduction* pp. 225-42; F. E. Cranz, "*De Civitate Dei*, XV, 2, and Augustine's Idea of the Christian Society." *Speculum*, XXV, 2 (April, 1950), 215-25; Hügel, *Eternal Life*, 93-94; *Essays and Addresses, First Series*, pp. 195-224.

[23] For the pertinent references to the *De Principiis*, especially Books II-III, and other works of Origen, see Seeberg's *Lehrbuch*, English translation by C. W. Hay: *Textbook of the History of Doctrines* (Grand Rapids, 1952), I, 159-60; and E. de Faye, *Origène: Sa vie, son oeuvre, sa pensée* (Paris, 1928), II, Chaps. 14-17, especially pp. 231-48.

[24] Cf. Scott's section on the Millennium (Rev. 20:4–22:5) in his *Book of Revelation*,

This earthly millennium was not, however, originally viewed as an end in itself. For such chiliasts as those mentioned, this terrestrially triumphant society was probably just an ante-way to the consummate heaven-on-earth-and-in-heaven. Originally, perhaps, this chiliastic zone was merely an advance on the final return from a long-term investment. Here was expressed a yearning, optimistic faith that evil is not completely triumphant even in the present inequitable order. At its best, whether in John the Revelator, in Joachim, or in the most positively biblical Anabaptists, this new earthly age of heavenly character is just the vestibule to the ultimate kingdom. Seen in its more positive emphases, even chiliasm is validated by a socially positive responsiveness, at once, to the supremely communal demands and standards of God's cosmic fellowship.[25]

At its worst, as in Münster, among the Millerites, and within certain modern sects, the chiliastic expectation of imminence and earth-timedness has been permitted to obscure the prerogatives of the finally transcendent society. It has ignored Christ's and Paul's warning that the hour is unknown to anyone but God. Too often this has resulted either in waiting for the day or in attempting to force the divine hand. Here has been a literal taking of the kingdom of heaven by violence. And all of this has succeeded only in obscuring or overriding the claims of the ultimate with a bid for some temporal, millenarian victory.

Although nonchiliastic eschatology soon became rather normative in Christian history, no period was to be without its admixture of the more usual with the more apocalyptic forms, as well as the spiritualizing influences of the Johannine literature and Origen. These types of eschatology have often been combined in the same individual, as witness the Gospel and Letters of John, the Revelation, and St. Augustine.[26]

---

pp. 91 ff. and 150 ff. Consult the text of Papias, especially Fragment 1, in the edition of J. A. Kleist, *Ancient Christian Writers,* 6 (Westminster, Maryland, 1948), pp. 105 ff. and the notes, pp. 204 ff. Significant portions of Joachim's *Liber in Expositionem in Apocalipsam* (Venice, 1527) are translated by E. Aegerter, *Joachim de Flore* (Paris, 1928), II, 90 ff., 113 ff., 132-42; cf. "De Articulis Fidei," in E. Buonaiuti, *Scritti Minori Di Gioacchino Da Fiora* (Rome, 1936), pp. 72-80. An understanding analysis of Joachim's work is K. Loewith, *Meaning in History* (Chicago, 1949), pp. 145-59 and Appendix I. See H. Bett, *Joachim of Flora* (London, 1931); also G. La Piana, "Joachim of Flora: a Critical Study," *Speculum,* VII, 2 (April, 1932).

[25] Note the bearing of Scott, *Revelation,* pp. 94-96. Cf. Charles, *The Future Life,* pp. 420-30, on John's Gospel and eschatology.

[26] Note the welter of data and its sympathetic millenarian interpretation in L. E. Froom, *The Prophetic Faith of Our Fathers* (Washington, 1950), I, 685 ff., on Joachim.

These two predominant forms of eschatology, the normative and the millenarian, have sometimes been distinguished as pessimistic and optimistic, respectively. Actually, the pessimistic and the optimistic trends have been found, in varying proportions, in prophetic literature as well as in chiliastic and nonchiliastic eschatology. The prophets were defeatists with regard to immediate hopes for the redemption, as a whole, of a sinful, unregenerate order, though they were presumably optimistic, for at least a remnant, insofar as doom was avoided or transcended in a spiritually revitalized, earthly community. Chiliastic optimism was related in a time sequence with a future millenarian era on earth. But even here, a final beatitude of social character seems to have waited beyond the limits of a chiliastic interlude.[27] Normative, nonchiliastic eschatology was frankly pessimistic regarding the human, terrestrial era; but it was gloriously optimistic for human life in the new age which should have been partially socialized, already, in the present according to the standards of ultimate kingdom life.

In all these forms of eschatology, contrary to general acceptance, there is a large, though varying, emphasis upon social meliorism in the temporal order in terms of response to, and preparation for, the final community. This meliorism never extends to a full belief in the perfectibility of the present world society. It often amounts to little more than a sense of social solidarity on the part of a select group. It is never humanistic in the modern atheistic sense; it is always theocentric or Christocentric. In the pre-Reformation period, at least, it does not habitually accept the challenge to sweeping changes in the structure of the present social order. When genuinely Christian and eschatological, it emphasizes to some degree: (1) Christian social solidarity; (2) a socially minded missionary responsibility; (3) growing social cohesiveness in the Last Days; and (4) passionate concern for the new age and its societal commitments, however late or soon they may come. This is true to some extent whether of the Revelator, Lactantius, Chrysostom, Bede, Francis, Joachim, or Wyclif.

Here, Matthew's Gospel and the Revelation are often set in contrast against the Fourth Evangelist. It is too often held that Matthew is eschatological and apocalyptic; whereas the latest Gospel is de-

---

On the Anabaptists and Münsterites consult F. H. Littel, *The Anabaptist View of the Church* (Berne, 1952), pp. 106 ff. See Rev. 20:4–22:5; *De Civ. Dei*, XX, 7, and Serm. 259 for the double focus in Augustine. See A. Loisy, *Le quatrième évangile* (Paris, 1903), pp. 74, 741-42; De Faye, *Origène*, II, 231-48.

[27] This fundamental differentiation is that of E. Wadstein, *Die eschatologische Ideengruppe* (Leipzig, 1896); cf. Scott, *Revelation*, pp. 92-94.

clared to be nonapocalyptic and even noneschatological. Actually, John, too, is eschatological after his own fashion. He believes, definitely, in two major orders of life. For him, as for the Synoptics, the future one is primary and determinative. It is, of course, social in the ultimate sense connoted by Jesus in his beautiful prayer of consecration. The present order is temporal, but it has an answering response to the eternal community. Judgment has already taken place or is in the process of being realized. Consummation is yet to be.[28]

Ordinarily, and perhaps rightly, the normative, cataclysmic eschatology is held to have no rapport with the evolutionary concept of life. That is, the cataclysm of the Gospels and the more developmental conception of modern times are held to be in necessary conflict. Yet, there may be evolution and growth within cataclysm; and cataclysm may take place within the realm of process. In no case, to be sure, do we have in early Christian thought any sense of biological evolution or sociological development as currently understood. The closest approach to mounting, developmental response is, perhaps, to be encountered in the Hellenistic-Christian philosophy of Origen.[29]

The most significant working conclusions historically derivable from all this may now be stated. Christianity, to the Protestant Revolt, at least—and even now, when properly understood—is primarily eschatological. That is, it believes that there are two orders which are at once discontinuous and continuous with each other. The discontinuity is primary with regard to the priority of the consummated kingdom. In other words, the future kingdom is more *unlike* than *like* the present order. Continuity is real and powerfully active inasmuch as the present order is elicited by, dedicated to, and even now socially responsible to, the final community. The present answers the demands of, and goes forward selectively to a place in, the ultimate corporation of Trinity, angels, and blessed ones.

All origins and ends are cosmic. Human origins are significant because they betoken potential responses to cosmic ends without disregard of past experiences. Human development may be partly consummated through universal upheaval. Cosmic cataclysm may utilize normally human growth and development. Cataclysm is not sufficient

---

[28] Cf. Loisy, *Le quatrième évangile,* pp. 741-42; Charles, *The Future Life,* pp. 420-30; B. W. Bacon, *Studies in Matthew* (New York, 1930), pp. 412-35, in particular pp. 413, 428; F. C. Grant, *The Growth of the Gospels* (New York, 1933), pp. 207-8; B. H. Streeter, *The Four Gospels* (New York, 1925), pp. 474-78.

[29] E. I. Bosworth, *The Life and Teaching of Jesus* (New York, 1929), pp. 245-46; E. J. Bicknell, *Thessalonians* (London, 1932), pp. 49-50; V. Monod, *Dieu dans l'univers* (Paris, 1933), pp. 33 ff., 340 ff.

for cosmic growth; it must be superseded by a working community with an undefeatable fruition. In any case the human-divine present must respond to the divine-human end—or know tragedy!

Disaster results all too surely from putting the human-present aspect first, thus distorting its divinely cosmic origins. The consummation is thereby forced in violent fashion, whether by the Münsterite excesses of the sixteenth century or by the superficial optimism of religious education in the recent "twenties." Calamity is entailed, also, in forgetting that genuine eschatology demands social action, now, in response to the ultimate society. It is a grievous mistake to assert that the repudiation of first-century world patterns dooms the heart of Christian eschatology.[30]

Most tragic is the tendency to ignore the immediate implications of historic Christian eschatology, which are themselves indisseverable from true Christianity. These lessons are: (1) that the present order must be replaced by, not just modified by, a final one; (2) that the present order must grow out of the future more than it grows out of the past or gives rise to the future; (3) that the future kingdom, while served by the known present and past, makes—and is not made by—the present and the past; and (4) that the social present is under the demands of the social future. The society of the existing order must be patterned, now, after the community of "that other" order.

The hope for a full recovery of Christian vitality in an exhausted world lies, therefore, in the revived appreciation of a valid Christian eschatology. An intimate acquaintance with its historic principles provides the best protection against the historical distortions and spiritual perversions that masquerade unchallenged in the name of genuine Christian teaching. A discriminating reappropriation, by the Church, of the eschatological premises upon which its very life depends is the surest possible guarantee of renewed Christian ministry to world society.[31]

---

[30] Bicknell, *Thessalonians*, pp. 49-51.

[31] R. Shinn, *Christianity and the Problem of History* (New York, 1953) seems to be aware of this in the very organization of his material. Compare with this his "The Christian Gospel and History," in J. A. Hutchinson, ed., *Christian Faith and Social Action: A Symposium* (New York, 1953), pp. 23-36, especially 34-35.

CHAPTER III

The Response of Temporal Society to the Eternal Kingdom

1. In the Thought of Jesus

THERE CAN BE LITTLE DOUBT THAT THE KINGDOM OF GOD COMES FIRST in all of Jesus' teachings. It is the preoccupation of his whole existence. This assumption is not based upon any arbitrary collection of recorded statements. It is possible only because it alone fits into the range and character of his whole being.[1] In spite of controverted passages, one may derive clear expressions of Jesus' feeling about the kingdom.[2] It was, first of all, thought of as the ultimate of all societies. To what precise degree he thought of this community as having already been inaugurated is not wholly clear. He evidently believed that it was already in existence to the extent that the Father had even now surrounded himself with some of his creatures who would reign with him forever. At some undisclosed time, known only to God, still other beings would be joined to him in keeping with the consummation which he had planned from the beginning of the world.

Jesus did not concern himself primarily with the numerical extent

[1] K. Müller, *Kirchengeschichte* (3rd ed., Tübingen, 1938), I, 59-67; S. J. Case, *Jesus, A New Biography* (Chicago, 1927), pp. 419-41; H. Lietzmann, *The Beginnings of the Christian Church* (London, 1937); Hügel, *Eternal Life*, pp. 62-66; Luke 12:22-31; Matt. 6:25-33; Matt. 8:19-22; Luke 9:57-62.

[2] Critical guidance in texts and interpretation is available in H. Lietzmann's *Handbuch zum Neuen Testament* with E. Klostermann, *Das Matthausevangelium* (2nd ed., Tübingen, 1927), and his (with H. Gressmann) *Das Lukasevangelium* (Tübingen, 1919); also D. W. Bauer, *Das Johannesevangelium* (Tübingen, 1925). Always useful for parallel Greek Texts is A. Huck, H. Lietzmann, and F. L. Cross, *A Synopsis of the First Three Gospels* (Tübingen, 1936). Particularly helpful for running commentary on parallel texts is *The Mission and Message of Jesus: An Exposition of the Gospels in the Light of Modern Research* by H. D. A. Major, T. W. Manson, and C. J. Wright (London, 1937), especially Book II, "The Sayings of Jesus," pp. 301-639, by T. W. Manson. See also Manson's *The Teaching of Jesus* (Cambridge, 1945), especially chapters VIII and IX. Throwing continuing light upon the whole is W. D. Davies, *Paul and Rabbinic Judaism*, notably Chap. X. Cf. J. Héring, *Le royaume de Dieu et sa venue: étude sur l'espérance de Jésus et de l'Apotre Paul* (Paris, 1937).

of that fellowship which should one day constitute the divine realm. Whether or not he thought of this society as being located somewhere in the heavens above, in the renewed earth beneath, or in some combination of the two, is not clarified by the documents that we have at hand. The far more important consideration—the one with which Jesus was pre-eminently concerned—is clear. The kingdom existed already, in part, and would someday be completely fulfilled as a new world order. This would result in the renovation of the whole universe in terms of a new heaven and a new earth. Such an order would come only with the more or less cataclysmic discontinuance of the prevailing framework of things. However much inconvenience might result to the present way of man's life here below, all human beings must stand prepared to surrender their whole experience to a new social-individual continuum on the basis of God's transcendent will.

It is in this sense that Jesus speaks about the kingdom of God as being first. He means to say, literally, that the everyday concerns of those who follow God's will are to be intimately related to a planned economy of the universe which God has conceived from the beginning of time and which he is even now working out to its consummation. It is to this pattern of social behavior that the followers of Christ are to conform themselves. Jesus has come to reveal its outlines, sufficiently, to his disciples to make possible their adherence to it. Since they are being informed as to its character and its demands upon them, they are to begin living at once according to its requirements.

Jesus does not temper the claim upon his followers of a wholly sacrificial devotion to that which is not yet generally visible to the eyes or the minds of men. He exacts a declaration of loyalty to a kingdom not fully seen. Those who come after him must make themselves perfect even as the Father in heaven is perfect. Not that they must attain to deity. Rather must they order their lives according to the community which God is currently setting up in the universe as the model of all social relations. Strictly speaking, man's reaction to God's will does not materially alter God's plan. His will is immutable. It does matter in the life of the person whether or not he aligns himself with the divine behest.

Jesus insists that one must give himself to this seemingly impractical way of life without reservations. No other loyalties to family, traditions, or personal livelihood dare come first.[3] There is not the

[3] Matt. 10:37-38; Luke 14:25-27; Manson, *Mission and Message*, p. 423; Cross, *Synopsis*, p. 51; Klostermann, *Matt.*, p. 92.

slightest suggestion that man will be permitted to make his habitual social responses the measure of his loyalty to the new society. It is fatal to think of entering the kingdom of God on the basis of what men have previously done and been in terms of world society. The order is just the reverse. God has determined the way in which his creatures shall live together. The subsequent history of their associations, together with current and later practice, are to be criticized and redeemed in terms of a social plan which is actual in God's own design but still future to the experience of men. Since they are to live according to that which has not yet fully been, they must have a revelation of its nature and demands. Jesus is precisely that revealer. He has come to lay down the standards and to clarify the procedures by which human life is eventually to be governed. Failure on man's part to live in accordance with God's plan cannot defeat God's will. Such refusal can mutilate the healthy prospects of man's development in the universe.

It is worse than futile to think of Jesus' revelation of God and his kingdom as having application solely to the individual person. God's plan for men is a unified one. From the very beginning, it has envisaged persons in relationship to each other. It sees human beings as realized persons on the basis of their final companionship with each other. They have no independent existence apart from this cosmic unity of life. When they shall have realized this more fully, they shall have put themselves in a position to be unified persons in terms of an integral humanity. This, too, it is the burden of Jesus' ministry to reveal. No more important point can be made with regard to Jesus' teachings than this: His whole emphasis upon the sacredness of human personality is to be interpreted in the light of man's relationship to God and neighbor. No one has any value whatsoever aside from God. A unified person is unthinkable unless he follows devotion to God with service to his fellow men. Jesus never labors this conception. He takes it for granted throughout his teaching that one who is a vigorous personality is invariably so in relation both to the divine and to the human. One cannot become an individual aside from a social relationship. One cannot be truly social without consequent manifestations of a rebirth in individuality.

The problem here referred to is one in which an old antagonism forever reasserts itself. The social is stubbornly set against the individual, and the individual is almost perversely held to be in contradiction to the social. If there is any truth at all in the gospel of Jesus, it is the insistence that there can be no true individuality without a social experience and that there can be no social experience which is not made up of participating individuality. There is a sense in which society gives rise to the individual, just as units are composed of persons. The criticism of many writers on Jesus' teachings —namely, that one must not look for social expression in any of his thought—is particularly beside the point. However one may wish to stress the importance of distinctive personality, one cannot afford to hazard the suggestion that such may be found aside from other personalities.

The more he studies the teachings of Jesus, the more one sees the value of emphasizing the polarity of the social and the individual. Jesus' whole thought about the kingdom of God is an immense clarification at this point. Jesus starts with a divine society out of whose created energies man comes. He places every man as a person in relationship to that society. This indicates the way in which one becomes supremely personalized when he participates in social experience. Any purely collectivist interpretation which surrenders the individual for the group or any purely individualistic note which denies the validity of anything other than the personal must finally be discarded as a working solution. Jesus finds reality in the group and in the individual as they inhere in each other. The person comes to realization in the sociality of God's kingdom. The more he believes in that kingdom as a working community of life, the more he discovers what he was created to be in terms of individual fruition.

It is on the basis of these working assumptions that Jesus proclaimed unalloyed devotion to the kingdom. This reign has begun to be and will become, completely, the fullest realization in companionship of men with God and with each other. Since this is the basic prerequisite for all effective living, it must have the unreserved allegiance of all who would live completely and happily. When men put their hands to the kingdom as to a plow, they move forward into an exacting future. Looking back for any other purpose than to see the direction from which they have come, they are recreant in their primary loyalty to the beckoning, future society. "No man, having put his hand to the plough, and looking back, is fit for the kingdom of God." One centering attention upon the dearness of a relative or fellow human being has lost major contact with God, who gave being to all of these beloved individuals. God has willed that all of these since the world began may have opportunity to come into a heavenly kingdom. So long as they proceed on his terms, they are welcome to enter.

Scholars have discussed exhaustively the exact meaning which Jesus attached to the kingdom of heaven. Some have insisted that there is no necessary connotation of social experience in Jesus' thought about the kingdom. He simply means, they say, that God will rule absolutely over those submitted to him: that is, the kingdom is the realm of God's rule. But the realm of God's rule actually means nothing aside from people who are to be ruled by God.[4] Thus it is that the kingdom becomes the community of those among whom God's will is done. Those who see in advance the full blessing of submitting themselves at once to the loving disciplines of a divine Father, become, even now, members of his society. But there will come a day in the history of the world—or, rather, at the end of that history—when all obstacles to their union with him will be removed. Then their willing subordination to his eternal plan will be joined to the working association of their fellows around the throne of God. The whole section of the Beatitudes—that beautiful passage on the qualities of life that make men happy or blessed—has special point in this connection. Jesus says that those are supremely happy who exemplify, now, the qualities that are to be characteristic of their abiding fellowship in the presence of God.[5]

One characteristic of the eternal kingdom will be its all-inclusiveness with regard to groups, personalities, and representatives summoned out of different ages in the world's history. In describing the characteristic outline of the eternal society, Jesus recalled quite logically the place that will be given in it to the patriarchs, the prophets, and others of their kind. From the beginning of time there have been those who looked forward to an experience, not yet clear, which would enfold them in a common mutuality based on submission to the divine. Jesus indicates that many will come from various parts of the earth and sit down in the convivial assembly of the redeemed. Among them will probably be some not of the generation of Abraham, Isaac, and Jacob. All will certainly have passed the rigorous test of conforming their wills to God before they shall have been invited through God's banquet door.[6]

---

[4] Charles, *Future Life*, pp. 84-86, 134-36, 365-71; G. Dalman, *The Words of Jesus* (Edinburgh, 1902), p. 94. See, in his *Die Worte Jesu* (2nd ed., Leipzig, 1930), II, 75 ff., a whole series of word studies on the Kingdom, the future age, and eternal life. M. Goguel, *The Life of Jesus*, translated by O. Wyon (New York, 1933), pp. 562 ff.

[5] Matt. 5-7; Luke 6:20 ff.; Charles, *Future Life*, pp. 378 ff., 84-86; Manson, *Teaching*, pp. 294-95; Manson, *Mission and Message*, pp. 338 ff.

[6] Luke 13:22-30; Matt. 8:11-12; Isa. 49:12; Mal. 1:11; Manson, *Mission and Message*, pp. 416-18; Charles, *Future Life*, pp. 84-86, 134-36, 365-71; Klostermann, *Luk.*, pp. 508-9.

Clarification of human values was not always easy for Jesus when dealing with people so thoroughly committed to the world's view of things. He found difficulty in describing the kind of deeply humble experience that re-creates the eternal fellowship. There came to mind, most helpfully, the living parables found in children themselves. He insisted that something of the selflessness and candor so characteristic of childhood at its best would be integral with the very heart of kingdom experience. Not the peevishness and sullen recalcitrance so typical of childish moods at unhappy times, but the willingness to speak one's inner heart and to grant whole-souled commitment to the objects of love, were the qualities which Jesus sought to inculcate in his followers.[7]

One of the many vexing questions that confront the student of Jesus' teachings is the problem of comparative ranking in the eternal order. Did Jesus believe that some would stand above others in positions of authority and leadership? This query is not easily answered. Such suggestions as those forthcoming from Luke 22:24-30 would indicate that, perhaps, he granted the possibility of such marks of superior and inferior placement. Perhaps he was speaking only in terms of functional divisions of responsibilty. In any case, he makes clear the basis on which people will assume leadership in the kingdom of God. They will follow no pattern of dominance and submission. In their world the standard of service and social responsibility will be supreme. Jesus' action at the Last Supper is emblematic. He takes upon himself the character of a servant and performs the most menial tasks in their behalf. However glorious may be the experiences that characterize the heavenly company, there will be ample opportunity to give and to receive. Each will have as his continuing mission the service of his fellows in Christ's name.[8]

Jesus is certain that the final society of the kingdom will be constituted by those who have accepted a definite call to the beloved community. He does not mean to imply that God has deliberately shut out any who would come into it. But from the very beginning of the world, he has determined what the character of this ultimate companionship shall be like. Only those, therefore, who understand the qualities of life there demanded and who make preparations ac-

---

[7] Matt. 18:2-4; 10:12-15; Manson, *Mission and Message,* pp. 498-99; Klostermann, *Matt.*, p. 147.

[8] Luke 22:24-30; Manson, *Mission and Message,* pp. 629-31; W. Manson, *The Gospel of Luke* (The Moffatt New Testament Commentary, 1950), pp. 243-45 (cf. Mark 10: 42-45; Matt. 19-28; Isa. 53); Klostermann, *Luk.,* pp. 575 ff.; Cross, *Synopsis,* p. 187.

cordingly will be able to come in. The Those who will accept God's free graciousness sufficiently to follow humbly God's eternal plan for his blessed company will fulfill the requirements of an elect people. They will be carrying out the provisions of successful social experience demanded by the Father of all created beings.[9]

The very nature of the kingdom of God as Jesus conceived of it was communal in its major aspects. The highly varied figures of speech that he applied to it were never intended to serve as a definition. These parabolic utterances were thrown out in the hope that men might come to experience something of the moving spirit that was at the very heart of the kingdom. In that association with God, complete submission to his will was to be of paramount importance. Repentance for one's sins and throwing oneself upon the divine mercy were necessary prerequisites for entrance. Once having come into the circle of God's beloved, however, the major conviction to be registered was a sense of the divine love which would go out to all the Father's children. The result of such an ineffable experience would be happiness of the fullest sort.[10]

Nevertheless, in the very nature of things, happiness in the kingdom would be like that of children sitting down to a parental table spread with all the necessities of life. This would be a society at its best. Those who fed at the Lord's board would sustain to each other the intimacies known only to a family. It is peculiarly fitting, therefore, that the metaphors which Jesus frequently uses in describing such a society have as their center the character of banquets and other like occasions of corporate fellowship. At the expense of complete accuracy, Jesus even suggests that there will be eating and drinking— experiences inevitably associated with human ways of conviviality.

One of Jesus' parables interpreting the kingdom as the great community recounts the familiar story beginning, "Blessed is he that shall eat bread in the kingdom of God." One may justifiably see in this more than a contention for the sovereignty of God. There may be deduced from it the communal character of the eternal kingdom. According to one interpretation, invited guests are, first, the righteous Jews. Jesus himself is the servant announcing the feast to the would-be banqueters. But the original guests withdraw their

[9] Matt. 25:34; Manson, *Mission and Message*, pp. 542-43; Manson, *Teaching*, pp. 265 ff. and Reference Index, p. 346; Klostermann, *Matt.*, pp. 204 ff.

[10] A. Loisy, L'évangile et l'église (3rd ed., Bellevue, 1904) , pp. 41-42; Hügel, *Eternal Life*, pp. 62-66.

first acceptance. They put temporal before ultimate things, earthly before heavenly treasures.

At this juncture Jesus the servant, at the divine behest, invites the maimed and the *déclassé*. As the first group may be the religious aristocracy of the Jews, so these last may be publicans and sinners. After these are brought in, there is still room for others. The servant now hears a surprising order: "Go out into the highways and hedges, and compel them to come in, that my house may be filled." Insistent hospitality and not actual compulsion is, of course to be understood; God's purpose goes beyond Israel. Here is the corollary to the prophetic doctrine proclaiming the universalism of the eternal rule.[11]

It may well be, as one authority suggests, that if people do not enter the Kingdom, it is because they are disinclined. No mechanically operating predestination decides who shall, and who shall not, come in. This does not make man's entry his own private affair. The two basic emphases of Christ's teaching, according to this point of view, are, simply, that no man enters uninvited by God, and that no man remains without, unless he so chooses. This is to say, a man cannot save, though he can damn, himself.[12]

At all events, in the above passage Jesus is stressing the fact of kingdom communality based on repentance and submission to the divine will—from all quarters where repentance and poverty of spirit are to be found. This obviously includes poor despised Jews and Gentiles as well. The banquet is a real community of the poor and the humble.[13]

The fact cannot be contested that Jesus thought of the eternal kingdom as being composed of those whom God would save beyond any merits of their own.[14] No one could be worthy to gain for himself, all unaided, a place in this most happy society. One must be invited by the Father, who would then make possible kingdom entrance. No one might glory in his having worked out the right to share in this ultimate fraternity. The special significance of such parables as those involving equal pay to laborers having worked on widely varying scales of time is to be understood at this juncture. It is perfectly justifiable for God to pay latecomers as much as those who have been employed all day. In each case God responds out of his own mercy

[11] Matt. 22:1-10; Luke 14:15-24; Manson, *Mission and Message*, pp. 420-22; W. Manson, *The Gospel of Luke*, pp. 172-74; Gross, *Synopsis*, p. 161.

[12] Manson, *Mission and Message*, p. 422.

[13] *Loc. cit.*; W. Manson, *The Gospel of Luke*, p. 174.

[14] Matt. 16:1-20.

and not in terms of any right that has been won by the laborer. Those who are given the eternal award of continuing fellowship with God and his children are alike in one major particular: none of them would be in possession of this great social experience had his admission depended upon his own worthiness. Such righteousness as these manifested consisted solely in their acceptance of God's magnanimity extended to them without regard to their own merits. Thus Jesus reminded his followers that God sends rain on the just and the unjust. Repentance alone is the key to entrance across the portals of the eternal kingdom.[15]

Perhaps the most baffling constant in the midst of all the world's variables is one simple insistence of Jesus. This is his startling contention that his followers cannot, any more than other men, be righteous of themselves; or good in the sense of meriting anything at God's hands—let alone salvation. Their only distinction from non-disciples is their realization that of themselves they possess no claim to consideration. Nothing they are or do is warranty for any divine recognition. All other men present some virtue, however meager or imposing, as leverage upon God's favor for their lives. Christ's followers, alone, need worry not at all; for all that they need is laid up for them against their asking. It is forever subject to their call. One astoundingly simple condition has to be kept in mind. They must always remember that they deserve nothing; then they are on the best possible vantage ground to request all that they truly require. Always, upon asking, they discover that God has anticipated their necessity and made provision for it. Followers such as these are the best—indeed, the only true—representatives of the kingdom at work in the world. What God is doing for them, he wants to do for all who will receive his free offering. The root meaning of the kingdom society is the fellowship of those who understand this principle of God's grace given without regard to merit; claimed with a full sense

[15] Matt. 20:1-16; Manson, *Mission and Message*, pp. 510-12. One may query Dr. Manson's assertion that "the parable cannot be made to support the thoroughgoing Pauline and Lutheran doctrine of salvation by grace alone" (p. 510). His remarks on p. 512 regarding verse 16 permit the inference, at least, that the kingdom is not something to be won or lost on the basis of humanly calculated works or merits. Note C. H. Dodd, *The Parables of the Kingdom* (New York, 1936), pp. 122-23. Cf. A. Nygren, *Agape and Eros* (New York, 1932-39), Part I, pp. 61-65. Perhaps one should remember with Lietzmann, *Beginnings*, pp. 65 ff., that the New Righteousness has its own peculiar reward. See Davies, *Paul and Rabbinic Judaism*, pp. 221 ff. Cf. Klostermann, *Matt.*, pp. 159 ff. Compare Luther's "Predigt am Sonntag Septuagesima," 24 Jan., 1529, Evang. Matt. 20, *Werke* (Weimar, 1904), XXIX, 37 ff.

of its unmeritedness by any man; and passed on to all who will unite with them in its joyful reception as the one and only thing needful.

Not what his followers *will* into existence, but what, in glad faith, they *accept* as God holds it out to them, becomes the measure of their life-fullness, together, and individually. Any vaunted freedom to determine what they shall have, be, or do, is an illusion of an activist humanism. They have not the liberty to defeat God. They possess only the dubious opportunity to turn aside awhile from their birthright. Free to be exercised is one stubbornly guarded privilege. They may, if they will, summon God's overriding salvation into evermore resourceful planning. The character of the kingdom community they cannot determine. The reception of its riches is theirs to welcome. This they evidence by offering their wills to the divine solicitude of the kingdom—a kingdom predestined of God for their heritage from the beginning of the world.

What seems, therefore, at first glance, to be an invitation from Jesus to commandeer the kingdom through working for the poor and despised, becomes, in truth, something wholly different. Men do not effect the kingdom for themselves by their kindness to the lowly. Their acceptance of the divine *agape* as it works in their own unworthy selves results in their proving themselves sons of the kingdom. This they do by their identification with God's least. When they learn how God saves men, they know how they are to be saved. There remains only the necessity of their entering, with the humblest of all the earth, the vanguard of those who claim the eternal heritage of God's gracious lovingkindness. They reach the kingdom through the narrow way of God's *agape* as it lives and is revealed in Christ.

The kingdom, then, is not something that they win by deeds sufficiently good, or a favor they enjoy because of moral superiority, however slight, over someone else. It is not something they win at all. Goodness and superiority of their own they have not.

Yet the kingdom is apparently promised Christ's followers, in the words of Matthew (25:34 ff.), by virtue of deeds done for the Master in the persons of his least. A closer scrutiny, however, reveals a profound truth: these seeming acts of supreme virtue sufficient to guarantee eternal reward, are, in reality, testimonies in themselves to something far different. The ministry to the naked, hungry, homeless, and universally despised is but the passing on of God's *agape*. It is not the means of gaining kingdom entrance except as it is the final consequence of being in a great succession; the tradition of those who help transmit to others the same fatherly beneficence in which their sure election to the Beloved Community rests.

It is easy enough to be a party to costly error at this point. One may readily confuse, on the surface, the working of the divinely gracious initiative and the Christian's active acceptance of that free gift in a faith that reveals its objects through the works of answering love.

In the centuries after Jesus, the difference often appeared slight between meritorious works, humbly offered for the laying hold on heaven, and the joyous testimonies of contrite souls sure that God alone, as revealed in Christ, could save. Consequently, many a penitent soul floundered about in a morass of despair. He did this, even as he sought to bring gifts worthy of divine acceptance. And so he struggled until, in moral anguish, he lost every offering in the slough of despond; every oblation, that is, except his own final capitulation as one wholly unworthy of any favor. Then, again, he seized in faith, alone, through importuning fear, upon a love that had never forsaken him; one that would never let him go.

At intervals thereafter, he might be subverted by a resurgence of activating will or prideful self-esteem. Even then, he would the more readily drop back into the pit of his own digging and lay hold the more fervently upon the love that his faith had preserved in unforgettable memory. And, however battered and debauched he might be by his own wandering outside the walls of the kingdom city, he would the surer come safely into the company of that great kingdom. Such as these, therefore, have nought but their penitent submission of all wilfulness laid at the Lord's feet to make them ready, once more; prepared for a place in supremely corporate beatitude at his banquet table of the Father's love.[16]

The only incumbents of the kingdom, in fact, are people who take the hard way through the narrow gate. They are selected for kingdom association by their uncompromising loyalty, not to present social claimants, but to the ultimate order. Disciples do not make of their nominal human bonds of acquaintance the sinews of an eternal society. They manifest their readiness for such social experience by giving it their unreserved service in the present.[17]

Jesus nowhere conceals his belief that relatively few persons will meet the standards of the divine kingdom sufficiently to be admitted into its fellowship. This selectivity, however, is based, not upon

[16] Lietzmann, *Beginnings*, pp. 65-68; Nygren, *Agape and Eros*, pp. 61-65.

[17] Matt. 10:37-38; Luke 14:25-27; Manson, *Mission and Message*, p. 423; Klostermann, *Matt.*, p. 92; *Luk.*, pp. 515 ff.

some arbitrary principle of exclusion, but rather upon the difficulties which many will feel in meeting the requirements of the divine fellowship. Thus, there are individuals who may be self-excluded because they reject the terms of repentance and humility which God inexorably imposes. Many are called, but few chosen. Jesus speaks of the way that leads to the kingdom as being straight and narrow. God will not bar ingress to those who are prepared to come into the eternal companionship on his terms. But he will refuse access to those who prefer the diversion of broader and more appealing ways.

The position of the Pharisees is apropos in this connection. Jesus is reported as having upbraided them sternly, upon occasion, for having closed the door to the kingdom upon many who were prepared to follow its dictates. Some were not ready to make the sacrifice of self-importance which kingdom acceptance required. Nor would they proffer the keys of the kingdom to any who would come in without their assistance. They not only made their officiousness a bar to their own inclusion, but they imposed it, likewise, upon those who would humbly accept God's terms. In effect, they refused to enter the kingdom themselves and became the means of closing its gates upon others, also.

Jesus is asked: "Are there few that be saved?" He replies, "Strive to enter in at the strait gate: for many, I say unto you, will seek to enter in, and shall not be able."

Man cannot come in unless God invites him; but, having been invited, it is up to man to enter. And this is on God's not-too-easy terms. Quite possible to man, they are not lightly met. One must repent, and that before the door is shut. Here is a note of urgency and irrevocability not at all conducive to casual unconcern. Having squandered their opportunity, the self-excluded need not blandish the Lord with reminders that they shared a former social engagement with him. Not some superficial, incidental association, previously, but the repentance necessary to guarantee lasting association in the kingdom is in order.

Those who enter joyously into the final commonwealth come on the kingdom's terms, not their own. There, many who have been last shall be first, and many who have been first, last. Members of the kingdom are not admitted because of their claims upon Christ, but rather upon his recognition of them as being the kind for whom the kingdom was designated.[18]

[18] Luke 13:22-30; Manson, *Mission and Message*, pp. 416-18.

Jesus had no illusions about the peculiarity of the kingdom as viewed by conventional society. It was definitely not the kind of assembly toward which the world's "great people" would gravitate. Why should any outstanding man of wealth and position clamor for admittance to a company distinguished only by its glad reception of God's unmerited graciousness? Yet this was exactly the circumstance that Jesus anticipated for all his followers. They proceeded on the living assumption that their fellowship would be that of people who had but one thing to recommend them to the divine mercy: namely, their sense of unworthiness and their contrite acceptance of the terms laid down by the Father for those who would live with him in unselfish dedication to himself, first, and then to each other.

But Jesus did count upon the exhilarating prospect which this would hold forth for the truly humble of earth. Those who prepared in meekness and unassuming service for a life of mutuality would wish nothing better than the opportunity to live with their fellows in God's presence forevermore. Seen from such a viewpoint, the kingdom of everlasting life would be worth every sacrifice required, in the present order, of those who anticipated membership in the future society. If, then, one hoped to be enrolled in this vast community of love, one must immediately renounce all other supports of wealth, position, and self-importance. Here was the pearl of great price for which one would gladly sell all else in the joyous hope of possession.[19]

It would be folly to suppose that Jesus was fundamentally ignorant of the age-old inertia that welded people to the ancient order. It is a natural tendency of human beings to hold on to things with which they are familiar rather than to commit themselves to the fearsome unknown. Perhaps Jesus was ruminating in this vein when he remarked the propensities of those preferring old wine to new. In any event, Jesus consistently advanced the claims of the new world over the old.

Long before twentieth-century versions of the New Order, Jesus was proposing a radical reversal in the priority of things. He advocated nothing less than complete loyalty to the future as over against the past. Traditions, in and of themselves, must cede to demands levied upon the existing order of God's kingdom. That reign was to

---

[19] Matt. 5:1-3; Luke 6:20 ff.; Matt. 13:44-46; Manson, *Mission and Message*, pp. 338 ff., 488-89; R. P. L. de Grandmaison, *Jésus Christ* (Paris, 1929), III, 371 ff.; Klostermann, *Luk.*, p. 441; Lietzmann, *Beginnings*, pp. 66-67.

have its triumphant fulfillment at the end of history. Paul realized the significance of Jesus' contention when he insisted that the followers of Christ must be transformed by things above and beyond, rather than conformed to things having been and already ensconced in the *status quo.*

Jesus, and Paul after him, would be satisfied with nothing less than the challenge of all things that are, and have been, by the things that must be. These, Jesus well knew, are the things of God, which must judge and determine the things of man. In the reorientation of God's universe, nothing less than a totality of life under God's rule could be held up as a standard for intermediate stages in the development of Christ's followers. Two orders of life there were: the old and the new; the way of flesh and the way of spirit; the house of Satan and the house of Christ. Loyalty must be sharply defined. Minds must be made up irrevocably and in terms of concrete action. One must be for God and Christ; or against them.[20]

On no account is the citizen of this commonwealth to be thought of as one lacking in righteousness. His own rightful inclusion in this community is not based upon any independent goodness that must compel the divine admiration. It is sorrow for sin committed and acceptance of forgiveness freely granted that constitute the new Christ-standard of uprightness.

The righteousness described by Christ in Matthew 5 and Luke 6 is adjudged superior to that of the Pharisees. Here, the new law is placed over against the old *Lex Talionis.* A new criterion of behavior, where enemies and friends are both involved, now emerges. It has been insisted that the kingdom of God in the Old Testament be defined as the regenerated community in which the divine will should be realized. The argument that the sovereignty of God is to be equated with the kingdom concept remains inadequate. There is a sense in which the kingdom community conditions the blessedness of the individual. The kingdom character is in essential contrast to the "worldly and political expectation of the Jews." The new realm of which Christ spoke was a *"community in which the divine will was to be realised* on earth as it is already in heaven, and into which the individual could enter only by abjuring all self-seeking individualism. In this aspect the kingdom appears as the common good

[20] Luke 5:37-39; Luke 11:17-23; Matt. 12:25-30; Manson, *Mission and Message,* pp. 546, 377-79; W. Manson, *Luke,* pp. 57-58, 138-40.

of man." [21] So the kingdom is the highest good, as the parables of the hidden treasure and the goodly pearl clearly indicate. Of all such goods, life comes first. There is, here, the distinction that

life is the good of the individual, but the kingdom that of the community. By entering into life the individual enters into the kingdom. We have thus the perfect synthesis of the hopes of the individual and of the divine community in Christ's kingdom of God.[22]

Those who enter the kingdom of God do, undoubtedly, form a community—the heavenly kingdom—over against the kingdoms of this world. The men of the world go one way and those of Christ, another; just as the Jews received the old law, so Christ's new Israel receives a new law. This is the way of Jesus. It is his own individual and social standard of life now and hereafter. Thus, Jesus' moral teaching does not emerge as some new ethic, an interim kind, for instance. It is simply an integral part of his kingdom concept. Here is the kingdom-way in which God's will may be applied on earth as well as in heaven. It is the pathway wherein the citizens of the heavenly kingdom may demonstrate their obedience in dedicated conformity to his will.[23]

The bearing of a conjunction of ideas assembled from leading scholarship can now be readily assessed.[24] The kingdom is a community in which God's will is to be realized. It is to be both present and future; and the divine will is to be the immediate and lasting concern of the new law and the new righteousness. Consequently, this completely social experience of the consummated kingdom must be entered into in heaven and on earth by men who act like the citizens of such a kingdom. In these later connections we may observe the socializing character of the divine love in all who follow him. This Godlike *agape* is part and parcel of the new righteousness. It is the penitent, enemy-loving poorness in spirit that the Beatitudes proclaim as the way to the kingdom and its joyous, corporate life.

A recent study maintains resourcefully that Jesus sets up no

---

[21] Charles, *Future Life*, p. 370. Used by permission of the publishers, A. & C. Black, Ltd. See W. Manson, *Luke*, pp. 66-70, on Luke 6:27-36 and Matt. 5:38-48; F. C. Grant, *The Earliest Gospel*, pp. 244-49.

[22] Charles, *Future Life*, p. 371. Used by permission of the publishers.

[23] Manson, *Teaching of Jesus*, p. 295.

[24] Of particular importance are the studies of Manson, *Teaching*, pp. 275, 301, 305, etc.; Grant, *The Earliest Gospel*, Chap. XI; Lietzmann, *Beginnings*, pp. 62-66; Loisy, *L'évangile*, Chap. II; Grandmaison, *Jésus*, I, 347-98; Goguel, *Jésus* (2nd French ed., Paris, 1950), pp. 460-78.

ethic in opposition to the Jewish one. That which prevails is a "deepening, spiritualizing, renewing, 'fulfilling' the old." [25] An eschatological, but not exclusively apocalyptic, frame of reference for Jesus is contended for. It may be true, moreover, that Jesus' "ethics has no concern with the secular relations of man, but only with men as members, or potential members of the kingdom of God." [26] That is, purely secular problems must give place to a seeking, first, of God's kingdom. Such a consideration is manifestly involved in the problem of the tribute money. God is sovereign; he comes first, and Caesar gets what is his—in any case, not much!

No, according to the prevailing secular temper—that is, "in our modern sense of sociological utopianism"—Jesus' teaching was not social;

but it was something vastly profounder, a religious ethic which involved a social as well as a personal application, but within the framework of the beloved society of the Kingdom of God; and in its relations to the pagan world outside it was determined wholly from within that beloved society—as the rest of the New Testament and most of the other early Christian literature takes for granted.[27]

We may grant that

it was a social gospel they proclaimed, yes—but only as the gospel of the coming Reign of God over all the earth, and as the new *Halakah*, the description of "life in accordance with the sayings of the Lord" who was God's final Messenger to his elect. It was no message of social reform, no blueprint for a perfect human society, save in the ultimate sense that the Kingdom of God is to take the place of all earthly societies, when "the kingdom of the world becomes the Kingdom of our Lord and of his Christ." [28]

The kingdom, then, will be made up of the group of truly righteous. This righteousness, however, is not any attainment of their own. It is, as Habakkuk would say, the uprightness of those who live by their faithfulness. These are the ones who are genuinely repentant and, as such, have no lasting stakes in the present aeon. They are dedicated ahead of time to the final society. They are the

[25] Grant, *The Earliest Gospel,* p. 248.
[26] *Ibid.,* p. 250.
[27] *Ibid.,* p. 251.
[28] *Ibid.,* pp. 251-52; cf. Manson, *Teaching,* pp. 305 ff

community of men committed to the doing of God's will on earth
as it is in heaven.

One may believe that, in some degree, the parable of the vineyard
describes the state of true penitence, not of selfish merit, that charts
the way to the eternal beatitude. That is, those who truly repent and
confess their utter worthlessness are the only ones who have an opportunity to qualify for the acceptance of God's free grace.[29] The
most startling effect of this—the effect often missed—is that no society of the present age is so truly socialized as this final interpene-
tration of men who acknowledge freely their sole dependence on God
for true kingdom membership. And in this context there is point to
the frequent insistence that the kingdom is really the realm of God's
sovereignty. As already indicated, however, this confraternity under
divine sway is characterized by mutuality and joyousness at their
best.

Jesus had no intention of misleading his followers into some vacu-
ous attachment for an even more vague society of the future. Having
tried consistently to make clear the antecedent claims which attached
to a kingdom not yet fully realized, he proceeded to make its standards operative immediately in the everyday life of his disciples. The
qualities which would insure their entrance into the kingdom were
easily discernible. They might check themselves by a very simple
test. If they were to have fellowship in God's consummated reign on
earth and in heaven, they would even now love as he loved and forgive as he forgave. As sons of the Father in heaven, they would follow
the standard of perfection which he laid down. They would love
enemies as well as friends. They would extend their ministrations to
those who were evil as well as to those who were good. They would
live in the present world, which was not to endure, according to the
standards of that ultimate world to which there would be no end.[30]

Jesus reveals the kingdom, also, in terms of a sovereign ruler who
can be great enough to empower the importunities of his children for
admission and then grace his own responsiveness with the gift of
entrance. The kingdom of God, the end-desire of all desires, may be
entered by knocking. With a magnanimity unparalleled among

[29] Luke 6:20-26; Matt. 20:1-16; Lietzmann, *Beginnings,* pp. 65-68; cf. Grandmaison,
Jesus, I, 373 ff. See note 15, above.
[30] Luke 6:27-36; Matt. 5:38-48; W. Manson, *Luke,* pp. 66-70; T. W. Manson, *Mission
and Message,* pp. 341-47; Manson, *Teaching,* pp. 52 ff., 306; Klostermann, *Luk.,* pp.
442 ff.

human fathers, the God revealed by Christ bestows the best possible of all gifts upon those who sincerely ask them.

Pictured here is a household of divine love in which all come alike to the Father's house through trusting in his love and throwing themselves in confidence upon his expanding mercy.[31]

It is no accident that Jesus so frequently utilizes the terminology associated with household and family. The God whom he reveals and to whom he directs the loyalty of his followers is the sovereign of the universe; he is equally the Father of all mankind. No better figure could be utilized than the one springing out of the association of children and parents. When one thinks of the ways of the household, one reflects upon everyday experiences that dignify and ennoble children and their natural brotherhood. It is in this fashion that Jesus describes the eternal company as being a close-knit brotherhood. He resourcefully portrays the manner in which the kingdom of God will evince the prime characteristics of responsible intimacy. If there is to be any unity in life, it must come through disciplined love. Jesus envisages the heavenly fellowship as it discharges the obligations of brotherhood under the most auspicious circumstances of divine benevolence.

Clearly, Jesus will not be content in the Last Days with mere assertions of loyalty. Saying "Lord, Lord" will not prove one's dedication to the eternal kingdom. One must, rather, keep the commandments of God and his Son. This will mean dedication in the most costly areas of life. Naturally, those will be joined together in perfect harmony who stand ready to make every sacrifice called for by kingdom fellowship.[32]

Jesus' delineation of the kingdom leaves no doubt as to the response that will characterize his followers during their passage through temporal society. The kingdom of God the Father is the ultimate in societies. Those yearning to be its citizens later will pattern upon it, in un-self-conscious fidelity, the conduct of their citizenship in the temporal world. Saved by God's unmerited grace, they will move among all men as brethren; transmitting, to these, the forgiving love that has been freely accorded them.

Jesus is, therefore, dedicated to a community supreme—the kingdom of God. He places this eternal social order over against the present temporal society. He has no desire to modify the present one,

---

[31] Luke 11:9-13; Matt. 7:7-11; Manson, *Mission and Message*, pp. 373-74; W. Manson, *Luke*, pp. 136-38 (on Luke 11:5-13).

[32] Matt. 7:21; Luke 6:46; Manson, *Mission and Message*, pp. 352, 468, 515.

as such. He reveals God's purpose to replace it with the eternal order, beginning at once. He has no intention of rectifying the present situation in terms of social reform such as the modern world usually advocates. Yet he by no means withdraws from this existing state of society either by despising it or by inaugurating some type of interim procedure. What he proposes is a kingdom life beginning now among his followers on the basis of the only standard by which they may be safely governed. Not waiting for some future circumstances of ideal proportion, Jesus demands that they employ in their everyday, earthly experience the attitudes and reactions that God makes normative for those called to his everlasting fellowship.

Demonstrably enough, the whole root and outreach of Jesus' ethic is governed by an eschatological source. Nonetheless, this ethic is more social, not less so, because of its ultimate ground. Since a new world order is to be in operation eternally, not on the plan of man's envisaging, but of God's, the present order of things must be changed, at once, in the direction of the future demand. Present social experience must respond without delay to the only type of enduring community which God has in mind. In other words, God's will must be done on earth as it is in heaven. The life enjoined is that of utter faithfulness to God's forgiving love, fully redemptive for all believers, and not some legalistic priority for the privileged or the powerful. The perseverance of two mutually opposed kingdoms, one temporal, the other eternal, must soon cease. Unity growing out of God's eternal provision must hold sway. God's will must be done on earth as in heaven because there is coming into existence, even now, a universe in which all life shall be renovated and made answerable to the divine order.

Christ's followers may pray, "Thy kingdom come. Thy will be done in earth, as it is in heaven," only when they are prepared to live in a world which has no duality for them. Having been called to a community in which this shall be eternally true, they are even now under the necessity of thinking and acting in accordance with its fullest demands upon them. They are men more and more perfectly conformed in the present to God's will as it shall be consummately realized in the future. They are even now to let their lights shine among men in such wise that others may be attracted to the origin of this divine radiance. Having accepted an invitation to the eternal banquet through grace, they have the joyous opportunity of inviting others to share that supremely social experience with them. They have this opportunity in terms of their own repentant lives, which shall teach others the way of penitence and everlasting fulfillment. By putting another and final order first in their own lives they may lead others to do likewise.

Thus a kingdom which has, as yet, only partial fulfillment in the easily observable world of affairs may have a thoroughly socializing effect upon that world. Others may decide to glorify the God who can work such changes in men's experience. They may utilize the divine grace, in accordance with the example that Jesus provided, to live the way of perfection; that is, to proceed according to the standards of the eternal kingdom in the here and now. If so, they, too, accept the requirements of the new law of Christ, which is the love of enemies and the forgiveness of detractors rather than the hatred of foes and consideration for friends alone. This will carry with it, in substitution for pagan dominance, the motive of vicariousness and renunciatory service. Thus does the acceptance and retransmission of *agape,* that freely flowing, unmerited *love,* transcend the limits of ancient liberality and self-orienting charity.

Insofar as frail human beings respond to this social regrouping on the basis of kingdom standards, they, too, may help to make ready the way for the divinely inaugurated and God-sustained order of triumph. In the process of such commitment—and without any self-conscious desire to do so—they may contribute to the radical amelioration of existing conditions in the present social order. As the by-product of their devotion to an eternal way of life they will inevitably regard the present with a new concern for the welfare of women, children, the weak, and the oppressed. Through reacting out of the spirit of humble ministry to the least of God's creation, they take the one final step calculated to place them within the ultimate brotherhood. They insure the promise of the eternal society by having made their own selfish considerations ancillary to the requirements of needy people everywhere. In so doing, they will have cemented their lives with Christ in an enduring ministry characteristic of the everlasting kingdom. It is not strange that Jesus is quoted as having said that the Father will place at his right hand those who have served the naked and the lowly in the name of his Son.

It should be noted, however, that the kingdom is socially significant, not because it anticipates a primarily human revolution in society as it now exists; but because it predicates the primacy of a wholly other order which has, nonetheless, a real continuity with existing social experience. As such, it effects changes in Christ's followers, immediately. Because of this fact, it has repercussions in those who observe the dedication of his disciples. Great damage can be done to the whole concept of the kingdom as Jesus accepted it, if one insists upon making the final test in terms of the existing order of life. Once having assumed that God's order comes first, one may point out confidently, as Jesus always did, that life in this immediate sphere of action is modified and redirected without dalliance or equivocation.

Jesus permitted no easy misunderstandings regarding the character of loyalty to the kingdom. The kingdom was the rule of God. Such a rule was resulting already in an uncalculating love proceeding from him, without discrimination, to all mankind. Those who discovered through Christ's revelation of him the character of that love made no reservation in their own response. Within the natural limitation of their human weaknesses, they sought to love him as he first loved them. At this point they discovered the inevitable relation of love for God and love for men.

Jesus had brought into meaningful connection the old Deuteronomic insistence that the first commandment is love of God and the second, like unto it, is love of fellow human beings. Once Jesus' disciples glimpsed the possibilities of love already manifested in Christ's own sacrificial being, they realized, also, something of the unfetteredness of the divine concern for the human creation. Men having given themselves with finality to the kingdom of God's beloved could retain no selfish exclusion from the affairs of their brethren. An old contention often lost sight of is here brought into play once more. The only effective service of a humanitarian nature must originate outside any regard for that which is purely human.

Only a man or woman who is totally dedicated to God is a safe ministrant, in love, to those for whom God has given his own Son. Jesus habitually emphasized the close communion between himself and the Father as a further symbol of God's desire to reconcile the world unto himself. Presumably, Jesus sought first to show the full nature of the kingdom of love in order to convince men how much their presence in it was desired.[33] The only way for his disciples to realize their own participation in the coming kingdom was to make habitual, among all those whom they met, such love as that with which God had first loved them. Jesus did not conceal from them the probable results of their re-expressing such divinely engendered af-

[33] Luke 10:25-28; Mark 12:28-34; John 3:16; Manson, *Mission and Message*, pp. 551-53; Grant, *The Earliest Gospel*, pp. 231-52; W. Manson, *Luke*, pp. 130-32; Bauer, *Das Johannesevangelium*, p. 54.

fection. It might cost them the conventional supports of life; even as it was to cost him his mortal existence. But it would give them joyous peace of mind such as that with which Jesus, even now, was overcoming the world.

It is significant that once Jesus brought a measure of conviction to his hearers concerning the kingdom, he immediately required of them a repreaching of it to the world.[34] Not only was his gospel centered about the necessity of repentance in the face of an imminent change in world order; he also laid upon his followers the necessity of a like proclamation. It was no more possible for them than for Christ to speak such words of warning while they continued on the prevailing assumptions of a this-worldly society. Once they glimpsed the social character of the eternal kingdom, they sensed, also, their part in its propagation. Socialized on the basis of their own new experience, they had necessarily to extend to their fellow beings the same gracious opportunity to which they had been invited. This meant that they must relay to the world about them—and increasingly to society at large—the new standards of corporate conduct by which men must live. They could not count the cost to themselves when involved in such a mission. No disaster that might overcome their physical persons had any chance of touching the integrity of their immortal lives. To live eternally in the company of God and his chosen, they must live without reserve on the bases of ultimate fellowship. Such is the way of true blessedness, now and later.

The real beatitude is, then, a social one; not because it springs from a temporal anchorage, but because it proceeds from an eternal one. The partial rejoicing which is already in existence springs from the eternal happiness which is yet to be. But it is just because the poor in spirit are the kind of people who give precedence to the eternal society that they are to be supremely happy; that is, to possess the kingdom of God. And because they are such kingdom people, they are already a corporation of life approximating that which will find maturity in the fully realized community. This accords well with Jesus' parables on those who go into the banquet before the sons of the kingdom—that is, the proud ones; and with his sayings on the banquet spurned by the proud and accepted by the humble.

The abiding characteristic of true Christian social thought is that it is not co-ordinated with the present society as the true center of

[34] Matt. 10:1-16; Mark 3:14-15; 6:7-13; Manson, *Mission and Message*, p. 471.

reference. Because of this, alone, kingdom-destined men can give the present its true, socializing impact. For this cause they gladly let their lights shine that others may be led to the Father's realm whence all saving grace proceeds.

The sense of the two orders of life and their proper relation is here strongly implied. If it be said that Christian eschatology takes priority of interest from the social past or present, let the argument be granted! The Christian knows that both past and present have their full significance only when viewed in the light of the future. To be truly productive, the present social order must respond to, and be broken into, by the future and eternal one. This was Christ's view— and that of his true disciples, also, when they were in an understanding mood.[35]

It is evident that such an eschatological consecration by the lowly in heart gives to them, now, a kingdom character of communal life and mutuality that cannot escape having immediate social consequences. This is the whole bent of Christ's life and teachings. Not thinking primarily of contemporary social change, he insures it by demanding a precedence of devotion to the eternal society and its standards. Consequently, the joyousness of his followers is in part actual, even as it grows with anticipation. And those so blessed have a togetherness which their exclusion from the company of some men, for Christ's sake, cannot make sad or dissatisfied. Yet felicitous as the lot of those committed to God's eternal kingdom undoubtedly is, their happiness now is deprivation itself in contrast with the ecstasy to be.

"Blessed are ye that hunger now: for ye shall be filled. Blessed are ye that weep now: for ye shall laugh." "The contrast between the present and the future lot of the godly is that between a famine and a feast." [36] Frequently in Jewish and Christian imagery the future good time is likened to a feast or banquet. In Matthew 5:6 the reference is not to a literal famine. Hungering and thirsting after righteousness has its fitting amplification in Luke's meaning. This righteousness surpasses the mere alignment of human conduct with divine standards. It is man engaged in fulfilling God's will, and God seen in the process of bringing his acts of gracious mercy to fruition. In

[35] Luke 6:20-26; Matt. 5; Manson, *Mission and Message*, pp. 338 ff.; Lietzmann, *Beginnings*, pp. 65-68.

[36] Luke 6:21; Manson, *Mission and Message*, pp. 338, 339; Klostermann, *Luk.*, pp. 441; W. Manson, *Luke*, pp. 63-65.

such a double fulfillment, those who now experience life's frustrations will find complete satisfaction.[37]

This contrast of present versus future recalls the natural opposites of "weeping and laughter, sorrow and joy." It also suggests the state of homesickness among the saints who pine for God's kingdom. Their joy must wait on its coming.[38]

This sharpens the point of Luke 6:20. Discrimination between the various orders must be ever more nicely appreciated; the present must seem unsatisfactory at best; the future must pull agonizingly upon the follower of Christ—else he is not a true follower. But if such a disciple truly thirsts, he will be filled at last. In the meantime he will continue to yearn, and to do the will of God with those of his kind. In such fashion he will be allowing his light to shine so that all may see, if they will, and become kingdom men, also.

Obviously, the disciples will convince others, not by virtue of their own humanly attained goodness, but by showing in themselves what God's redeeming power can achieve through the receptivity of fallible men. Thus, in portraying now the kingdom life, they become socializers of the present in the only adequate way possible. They help others, in accordance with Paul's injunction, not to be conformed to the present but to be transformed by the future.

The standards and bases of such socializing response to the world's present need are laid down in the New Law. It is this law, however, that requires the loving, not only of friends, but of enemies, also.[39]

Perhaps it is only human to assume that the attempt to follow such an absolute ideal would change the whole character of "civilized" life. But is it to be assumed that such life ought not to be changed? [40] Passages like Luke 6:32-36 and Matthew 5:45-48, though possibly embodying certain modifications of Jesus' original statements, do preserve an unalterable authenticity. That is, they stress the enduring separation of the kingdom society from that of the world's social behavior. Just loving those who love him leaves one squarely on a worldly, Gentile basis of social experience. It is customary for sinners to reciprocate among themselves; and to exclude all but those moving in their immediate area of friendship. But this is an insufficient basis for the associative life as conceived by Jesus. One thing, and one thing only, creates a new social order on the

---

[37] Manson, *Mission and Message*, pp. 339-40.
[38] *Ibid.*, p. 340; Phil. 3:20.
[39] Cf. Matt. 5:17-20, 43-48; Manson, *Mission and Message*, pp. 445 ff.
[40] Loisy, *L'évangile*, p. 68; *Les évangiles synoptiques* (Haute-Marne, 1907-8), I, 593.

plane of the kingdom: namely, the love of enemies as well as friends. This treatment of people, good and bad, with unmerited love—just as God sends rain on the worthy and the unworthy—makes men sons of the Father which is in heaven.

Manifestly, the ultimate society is here interpreted as judging and replacing the social standards of the temporal world. Those who put the ultimate community first come under the immediate demands of the eternal society. The question is not, Will the world hold such individual action to be practicable? Of course it will not! The question for Jesus' followers is: Do you prove, now, your part in the kingdom society by action which is indubitably that of God's sons?

Such replacement of the present order by the divine one starts at once. Now is the day of salvation; after this the judgment comes. In the consummated kingdom no such opportunity will continue to be offered those outside. Being perfect as the Father is perfect is equivalent to making his social-individual standards operative now in a hostile world. This the follower must do, insofar as he is able, whatever the consequences.

Again, the disciple has no right to speculate lugubriously as to the chances of ideal conduct in a realistic world. One is to go ahead "never despairing." [41] In other words, such followers must trust in the triumph—late or soon—of the divine community over the human one. But, win or lose, the divine order is their sole guide and objective. The highest reward offered them, and the only significant one, in fact, will be their own inclusion in the corporate sonship of the eternal ruler and Father. But to be so included, they must believe in, apply, and trust, its social-individual standards—now.

Going on such assumptions may well change the structure of any social order. Even thinking about them may inaugurate some far-reaching departure, however unanticipated. The motivation is, once more, that of dedication in calm faith to God and his kingdom. The individual and social reaction toward men, with whatever humanitarianism may be involved, grows out of an antecedent devotion to the Divine.

Significantly, too, this is a clear case of kingdom social patterns being made the determining element in temporal social relations for those who put the kingdom first. This is "not mere imitation of a divine standard set up, so to speak, in heaven. It is the reproduction, in daily life and in relation with other men, of something which has

[41] Manson, *Mission and Message*, pp. 345-47; W. Manson, *Luke*, pp. 67 ff.

come down to earth and touched our own lives." That is, both the motivation and the power are first God's—and then, ours.[42]

Jesus is forever widening the gap between those responding to the kingdom and those following the pattern of temporal society. These two societies are fundamentally different. Naturally, they elicit diametrically opposed reactions. Nations of the world put first the concerns of the day, with all their legitimate but secondary appeal. Kingdom men, however, will seek God's kingdom before everything else.

However foolish this quest may seem, success will come. For God, not man, brings the kingdom which is the perfectly consummated society. In the meantime, the kingdom response of his disciples is clearly and immediately required.

Again, the answer to those who say that such a course is not practical is: You mean that you put the present order first. For the Christian, no reaction to present society is practical which does not eventuate from a superior loyalty to the ultimate community.[43]

Jesus never doubts the eventuality of the impending conflict that must flare up between the householders of God and the vassals of Satan. Satan, for his part, is not so foolish as to precipitate civil war in his own ranks. A divided house or kingdom is sure to fall. Satan is guarding his all-demanding community against God's all-requiring society.[44] Obviously, Satan is not against himself. If Christ exorcises demons, it is by God's power, in defiance of Beelzebub. Satan has no place for Christ.

Jesus is not in league with Satan. His purported exorcism of demons is evidence of the realm of God in operation. It is a sign of the triumphant warfare of God against Satan's kingdom. Jesus is the channel of his royal power. Jesus and the kingdom of God struggle with and defeat Satan and his kingdom.

This warfare permits no detached observation. Everyone fights on some side. He is with Christ on God's side or else he is aligned with Satan. The fact that each body of allegiance is a unity so long as it is a kingdom at all—a kingdom divided against itself cannot stand—makes the issue one of a given social order. Satan and, perhaps, the world are set over against God and those who support his empire.

---

[42] Manson, *Mission and Message,* p. 347.

[43] Matt. 6:25-33; Luke 12:22-31; Manson, *Mission and Message,* pp. 403-5; Klostermann, *Matt.,* pp. 62 ff.; Klostermann, *Luk.* 498 ff.; W. Manson, *Luke,* pp. 154 ff.

[44] Matt. 12:25-30; Luke 11:17-23; Mark 3:23-30; Manson, *Mission and Message,* pp. 377-79; Cross, *Synopsis,* p. 67; W. Manson, *Luke,* pp. 138 ff.; Klostermann, *Matt.* p. 108 ff.; *Luk.,* pp. 488 ff.

Thus, attachment to the burgeoning kingdom of God and of Christ demands a showdown of participation at once. In such fashion is the kingdom already come. The victorious new order is, even now, in operation. The only question is: Who are for and who are against it?

As elsewhere, the question is not whether we have sociality or individuality, but what kind of each we shall have. Both kingdoms—that is, Satan's and God's—have a unifying force. Satan's, with its pattern of domination imposed upon an all too quiescent temporal order, seeks victims from among its supposed beneficiaries. But Christ's kingdom draws Christ-empowered men to a struggle that redeems and blesses the despoiled ones in a unifying, triumphant order.

Consequently, in aligning themselves with Christ, the sons of the kingdom bring the socializing power of their heavenly resources without delay to the aid of all humankind. Being for or against Christ's kingdom, and being for or against Satan's, is the basis for final judgment. Here is the evidence for the grouping of men into separate orders at God's right and left hand.[45]

Just what manner of men the supporters of God's kingdom really are is dramatized powerfully in Jesus' analysis of true greatness. He cites the fact that the kings of the Gentiles hold lordship over them, but that in his company it is not so. As for him "that is greatest among you, let him be as the younger; and he that is chief, as he that doth serve." Ordinarily the one sitting at meat is the greater. But Jesus, who now serves, rather than being served, is undoubtedly the one who has the true priority. He, in turn, appoints them unto a kingdom even as "my Father hath appointed unto me; That ye may eat and drink at my table in my kingdom."

Thus the character of the future kingdom casts the role of its disciples in the present society. The way of the world is here set aside in a way of life that is one of serviceability rather than privilege. Jesus may possibly be implying the existence of ranks of leadership in the ultimate community; but, if so, it is a leadership for service,

[45] Matt. 25:31-46; Manson, *Mission and Message*, pp. 540-44; Klostermann, *Matt.*, pp. 204 ff.; Manson, *Teaching*, pp. 245 ff., "The Final Consummation." On the relation of eschatology, apocalypse, and judgment in the thought of Jesus and of Paul, see Davies, *Paul and Rabbinic Judaism*, pp. 99 ff., as also Chap. X; R. Otto, *The Kingdom of God and the Son of Man*, translated from the German by F. V. Filson and B. L. Woolf (London, 1938); Goguel, *Jésus* (2nd French ed., 1950), pp. 460 ff.; J. Héring, *Le royaume de Dieu et sa venue;* also C. H. Dodd, "Eschatology and History," *The Apostolic Preaching*, pp. 79-96.

not for special consideration.[46] In the community of Christ's followers, where the leader does not sit in domination, but stands in service to all—and even washes his disciples' feet—the social character of a new way of life is fully evidenced.

Since his followers have shared temptations, trials, and numerous vicissitudes, they are, likewise, to share in his consummated glory. God gave this kingdom to Jesus; he now gives a share of it to his disciples. They shall share the joy which is represented by feasting at a table. They share privileges and responsibilities suggested by the figure of men enthroned in judgment upon other souls. By inference, at least, the way to prepare for a part in such a kingdom is to participate in a mutuality of service here below.

What, specifically, Jesus intends his followers to do is perfectly clear: the kingdom being at hand, the disciples are to heal the sick, serve those in want, both spiritual and material, and otherwise perform their functions as advance products of the divine kingdom. Starting at home, those preaching the kingdom are to exemplify its logical concern: namely, a sacrificial ministry to needy men. "The Kingdom is the future breaking into the present, and manifesting itself in the things which the disciples are to do in addition to their preaching." [47]

Perhaps it will be said that no temporal reconstruction of the present order is intended. Possibly not! But a truly social reordering on the ultimate basis of the kingdom, is. This parallels Jesus' insistence that he does things kingdomwise which surprise John the Baptist and render him, greatest in this world though he is, less than the least of the kingdom's little ones.

For Christ came to heal. His mission was to save the lost; that is, those needing a doctor. The charge that Jesus' teaching lacks social point is, perhaps, best refuted by the fact that his whole passion was to seek and save the lost, the sinful, and the repentant. For these, God's banquet waited. For these, who were truly poor in spirit, the erstwhile "sons of the kingdom" would stand aside.[48]

---

[46] Luke 22:24-30; Manson, *Mission and Message*, pp. 629-31; W. Manson, *Luke*, pp. 243-45 (cf. Mark 10:42-45; Matt. 19:28) .

[47] Matt. 10:5-8; Manson, *Mission and Message*, pp. 471-72; Klostermann, *Matt.*, p. 86.

[48] Matt. 21:28-32; Manson, *Mission and Message*, pp. 514-15; Lietzmann, *Beginnings*, pp. 65-68.

CHAPTER IV

The Response of Temporal Society to the Eternal Kingdom

2. In the Thought of the Early Church

JESUS' FOLLOWERS FOUND IT DIFFICULT ENOUGH, DURING HIS EARTHLY association with them, to envisage the kingdom as he taught it. Shocked and numbed by his death, they may well have surrendered for a time any belief in the new world order that he preached. With the dawn of the resurrection faith, however, their rudely dissipated hopes were revived. Their once confused loyalty to the kingdom began to be clarified and augmented as they waited expectantly for Jesus' reappearing in the vanguard of the new age.

Early Christian literature reflects a growing, if somewhat altered, contention for the supremacy of the new world order over the old. There is, for many Christians at least, a strengthening of the faith that if Jesus is to be rejoined in any enduring social experience, he must be rediscovered in terms of a new world which will wholly replace, or at least absorb, the present earth and all its environs.

It cannot be denied that, with the passage of time, some Christians felt themselves growing restless at Christ's failure to reappear. Had not he, himself, encouraged them to believe that his return would come in the very lifetime of those who had seen him leave the earthly scene? Such a tradition may have been fostered through the Church's own amplification of Jesus' teachings. But there had been good reason in any case for them to expect a reasonably early return of the Master. And the fact that after long years he had still not returned caused no little discouragement and confusion to some members of the Church. Many of them had, apparently, forgotten Jesus' own insistence that he himself knew not the day or the hour when the kingdom of God would come. What he had stressed was the necessity of one's finding a motivation in the future for all activity in the present, however long that present might endure.[1] When Paul and others like

---

[1] See the argument and documentation of Chapter III.

him called this all-important fact to the attention of Jesus' later followers, some comfort and renewed hope must have come into their lives.

Nonetheless, it should be admitted that quite a lot of disillusionment and some basic modifications probably entered Christian thought about the future kingdom. Some historians have gone so far as to imply that with the development of the early church as an established organization the expectation of a new world order became less and less operative in the Christian rationale. One must concede that there was probably some outright repudiation of the eschatological hope as the motivating element in everyday routine. Surely the mere fact that generation after generation passed on without the promised return must have had considerable effect upon the thought-forms that became increasingly dominant in Christian circles.[2]

When this has been said, however, a remarkable phenomenon emerges with all the greater clarity: However modified the future hopes of Christians might be, those expectations having fundamental reference to a new world society still provided the actual basis upon which Christian social life continued to rest. Whatever revision was needed as to the likely time of Jesus' Parousia, the belief in his new advent not only maintained itself but also secured new support in the passing of the years.

More and more, the faithful learned a lesson which Jesus had long sought to incorporate in their consciousness: that is, the actual time at which the new order will come is not a major concern of the Christ-follower. His major obligation is ever to be ready for the day when it shall break upon the earth. This was the reminder that Paul found it imperative to bring repeatedly to the Thessalonians' attention.[3] Significantly enough, this same warning was coupled with Jesus' own teaching: namely, that the world of Christian brotherhood in the hereafter, of which his disciples long to become parts, must be the determining ideal for the society which they themselves help to set up on this earth.

Apparently, Jesus' old teaching about the eternal order's placing its demands upon the present society never lost its force completely in the lives of his followers. It is true that these later disciples, living as they did in areas far removed from the original Jewish sphere of

---

[2] Davies, *Paul and Rabbinic Judaism*, pp. 285 ff., summarizes the situation via Dodd, *The Apostolic Preaching and Its Developments*, pp. 68-72.

[3] I Thess. 5:1-11; 4:13-18, etc.; Davies, *Paul*, pp. 289-91.

influence, frequently brought in an admixture of ideas which must have sounded strange to the older members of the Christian community. John's Gospel, although it continued to speak of another world as determining the life of temporal society, utilized conceptions and a vocabulary that seemed far removed from those of the Synoptic Gospels. But in the Last Gospel, as elsewhere in the prevailing literature of the early centuries, the same cardinal emphases persisted. A world somehow related to the existing society, in God's own time and way, would one day come to replace that society. Although still waiting for its fulfillment upon God's own plan and will, the kingdom as the basic reality in the universe was the deciding factor in the conduct of Jesus' followers.[4]

The mere fact that days and years could, and did, pass by without the colossal upheaval which Jesus himself had anticipated did not fundamentally shake the faith of truly Christian disciples. If, after a short period of time, they found it wise to readjust their expectations to the infinite possibilities of God's own plan, they felt no evident humiliation at their own inability to set correctly the ultimate day and hour. And once having reballasted their conviction that the new world would surely come, they might easily nurture such a living faith, though the centuries themselves multiplied.

One thing they sensed far better than they could say: Jesus himself would return to usher in, for God the Father, the blessed society of the redeemed. And when he came, those only would be ready for his reappearing who had looked unfalteringly to that day in the long hours and sacrificial mutuality of their existence on earth. The lodestar of their very lives would have appeared, long before, to promise the fulfillment of their social-individual blessedness in the triumphant society. Having reached the era decided upon by God as the one most appropriate for the ending of all time, they would have made the best possible use of his earth, and all of its fellowship available to them, as anticipatory preparation for the perfect commonwealth of heaven.

Seen in this light, the attitudes and reactions of the early and medieval centuries are not at all surprising. Not only did they refuse to give up the vital belief in the distinguishing characteristics of the two orders of life as Jesus had taught them; they continued to follow, if sometimes afar off, his basic admonition to be ready for the

[4] See Dodd, *Apostolic Preaching*, III, "Paul and John," especially pp. 65 ff., on the modified and refined eschatology of John, with which compare Charles, *Future Life*, pp. 420-30.

everlasting association which lay in the future by following in the present the pattern of God's own kingdom society. This remained at least nominally characteristic of the period which lengthened into the centuries of the Protestant Reformation, itself.[5]

The Apostle Paul stands definitely at the head of those who, after Christ, taught the primacy of the eternal kingdom in the considerations of the temporal society.[6] Wherever he preached, he proclaimed the Great Day and the necessity of readiness for it. His hearers experienced plentiful confusion as to the details of Christ's second advent. The Apostle felt called upon in both of his Thessalonian Letters to exhort Christ's followers on this point. No expectation of an early return was to leave them supinely indifferent to the claims of their brother men. However long or short might be the interim between their own day and the Lord's return, they must live in a community of corporate thought and action befitting those who were called to the superabundant society of the future. None could be ready to live with the Master then who were not already following the pattern of his social life among the brethren.

All of Christ's followers, those having passed on and those still in the flesh, were to rejoin their Saviour on the Last Day. In the meantime, they must prove themselves ready for admission to the kingdom by maintaining their unity with God and Christ in the spirit of Christian *koinonia*. Because they awaited the replacement of the present order by the one that should ultimately triumph, they must neither slacken the reins of discipline nor reduce the mutualizing activities of their temporal community. Paul reminded his brethren ceaselessly to what a great consummation of brotherliness they were called. It was for this corporate glory in Christ that they were summoned as participants from the beginning of the world. Making ready to enjoy it to the full, they must assume a responsible ministry of peace and goodwill that their own day so much needed. To that end, let mutual love increase and the service of fellow men abound! [7]

[5] The characteristic features of medieval eschatology as delineated in Wadstein, *Die eschatologische Ideengruppe,* and R. C. Petry, *Francis of Assisi* (Durham, N. C., 1941) Chap. V., and to be analyzed in the succeeding chapters of the present book, present outlines still quite discernible in such works as Bonhoeffer's *Sanctorum Communio,* Althaus' *De letzen Dinge,* etc.

[6] Paul's eschatological perspective with its deviations from, and reinforcements of, Jesus' thought is ably presented with full literature by Davies, *Paul,* particularly in Chap. X, "The Old and the New Hope: Resurrection," pp. 285-320. Cf. Héring, *Le royaume;* H. A. A. Kennedy, *St. Paul's Conceptions of the Last Things* (London, 1904).

[7] I Thess. 1:1-10; 3:11-13; 4:11-24; II Thess. 1:4–2:16; Charles, *Future Life,* pp. 438 ff.

The correspondence with the Corinthian brethren is rooted, like that of the Thessalonian Epistles, in this fundamental problem of the eternal kingdom. When Paul, in chapters 12–14, considers the versatility of human endowment and the corporateness of the mystical body, he is drawing upon no mere theory of political or social science. Here, as elsewhere, his conviction of sonship in God's kingdom gives him the sure clue for all answers to those who would know how to live with the brethren. The unity which Christ brought to his headship of the brotherhood had come from the oneness of the Father. The elect group which Christ had founded is one day to become incorporated in the city of heaven. Only those who live now under the species of the eternal society can play their part in its reciprocating experience of love.

It is with reference to such an end-product in social life that Paul pronounces, not only his beautiful encomium on Christian *agape,* but also his whole credo of universal life.

The brethren at Corinth have been endowed with every gift necessary to their pilgrimage toward the heavenly country. Though their vindication waits upon the final day which shall usher in their eternal fellowship, they are to proceed, at once, to live its life on earth. No hope centered on the temporal existence can be matured in joy. The end of history may even now be in sight. The kingdom of God and his Son must be not only their primary belief but also their ever-vigilant concern. Let them move toward its happy fulfillment in a dedicated society of brotherliness! [8]

Every Letter that Paul writes to his Christian friends is full of his preoccupation with the new world that is yet to be. Because of this fact—by no means in spite of it—he enjoins upon them a type of conduct in the existing society that shall prove their allegiance to their future city. Only those who live under the inspiration and within the community of Christ are to be found worthy of a place in the happiness of the kingdom: "But the commonwealth to which we belong is in heaven, and from it we are eagerly awaiting the coming of a savior, the Lord Jesus Christ" (Phil. 3:20, Goodspeed). [9]

It is this citizenship in heaven, out of which Christ himself, the elder brother, has come and to which all his followers will return with him, that is the pattern of the true Christian life. Within it is found every incentive to an improved social experience in this

---

[8] I Cor. 1:4-9, 30; 3:10-15; 15:19-28; Davies, *Paul,* pp. 291 ff.; Charles, *Future Life,* pp. 445.

[9] Davies, *Paul,* p. 319.

present world. No one who for a moment forgets the character of his eternal Sonship with the Father can join with Christ in his kingdom. In order to be incorporated in that community, one must live in the present world the life of harmony, truth, and light. Such transformed experience, with its social and individual qualifications and results, is the closest approximation possible, in time, to the ultimate society of the redeemed.

In his Letter to the Romans, Paul advances the inclination of life which he feels should be characteristic of every Christian. Looking forward to the future by which all life must be governed, he calls for a commitment to God's will rather than a conformity to the ways of earth. "You must not adopt the customs of this world but by your new attitude of mind be transformed so that you can find out what God's will is—what is good, pleasing, and perfect" (Rom. 12:2, Goodspeed).[10] In logical continuity with this thought is Paul's further insistence that one must immediately find his responsible place in the community of those who are to realize the fellowship of Christ in God. This permits no excessive estimate to be placed by any individual upon his own merit or station. Just as the Corinthian Letters point out, each will find his life's meaning in a division of labor within the spiritual corpus of the Lord.

Gifts, each properly apportioned to those who shall have the opportunity of employing them, are not to be arrogated selfishly to the person in question. Love such as that which proceeds from the Father himself is to be manifested by each toward others in the brotherhood. Out of this consecration to final values there will naturally follow a new and joyous devotion to the needs of those who live around them. The wants of God's people are to be supplied. Even persecutors are to be blessed and not cursed. Harmony is to be everywhere in evidence. A hungry enemy is to be fed. Evil is to be overcome with good.

Paul concludes with a discussion of the varied duties and obligations of social life; involving as they do the responsibilities of government and the claims of mutuality that are most fully in keeping with the Golden Rule. The motivation for social conduct of such high order is immediately traceable, in Paul's thought, to the new order of life that is impending:

All this especially, because you know this critical time and that it is

[10] Charles, *Future Life*, pp. 461 ff.

time for you to wake from your sleep, for our salvation is nearer to us now than when we first believed. The night is nearly over; the day is at hand. So let us throw aside the deeds of darkness, and put on the armor of light. Let us live honorably, as in the light of day (Rom. 13:11-13, Goodspeed).

Nothing could be more consonant than this with the behavior of those who have been called to participate as fellow heirs with Christ in the society of completed glory. Any suffering encountered on the way to that consummation must seem as nought when scrutinized in the light of human destiny. There is no doubt in the Apostle's mind as to the experience—so fully socializing in its every contour—that draws the faithful toward it even now. It is this experience not yet fully realized to which the whole Christian life is tending. This is the future to which one must be wholly conformed; none dares to make himself a craven copy of that which has, in the past, determined human responses. Those elected to likeness with the Son must discover from the celestially eliciting community now awaiting consummation the nature of the association which is to characterize their brotherhood in the present hour. And in the molding of their lives after that future experience there is no time for dalliance. The Christian's life must be lived, at once, in accord with the transforming new order that is in God and Christ.

Controverted as the authorship of the Ephesian Letter may be, this does not alter the Pauline stamp that remains fixed upon the correspondence. Making allowance for certain inconsistencies of literary figure found within it, one is confronted with the same appeal to unity of life that Paul transmits to the brotherhood in his Letters. Looking over the shoulder of the writer, one feels a welcome to join in God's secret plan, for the whole race, which has been put upon the divine records from the very beginning of the world. From the creation itself God has willed "that everything in heaven and on earth should be unified in Christ" (Eph. 1:10-11, Goodspeed).[11] Through union with him, his followers become marked with the seal of the Holy Spirit. This is a prefiguring of the inheritance by which they are to come into full possession of, and to be fully possessed by, the Lord Christ Jesus. Through him, also, they are to be raised to the joyous companionship which shall be theirs throughout eternity. As fellow citizens of God's people and members of his fam-

[11] Charles, *Future Life*, pp. 461 ff.

ily, they will experience, even in this life, a sociality approximating that of the eternal kingdom.[12]

The whole theme of the book known as First Peter may be paraphrased as follows: You are called to a social experience that is an everlasting community. Prepare for it, therefore, by every kind of solidarity which is within your power. Be alert, instant in response to the needs of others, and mutually supporting in your temporal obedience to the beckoning fellowship that socializes from the beyond.

As befits a work written in a period of testing, this piece of pseudonymous writing stresses the disciplinary character of the Christian life on earth as a fit preparation for entrance into the eternal kingdom. Those who are called of Christ must be given to a holy destiny even as he is holy. They are to be as living stones built into a spiritual house. Sojourners and exiles here below, they are directed to make their passage to the eternal family secure through ministrations to the brotherhood. Suffering even as Christ suffered, they are all to be united in the fellow feeling of brotherly affection. "For this is your vocation"—First Peter would say—"to bless and to inherit blessing" (3:9, Moffatt).[13]

Believing as he did that the end was near, the author could but call upon his fellows to stand ready for entrance into the great city of the beyond. They must keep steady, then; maintain their composure; be always in prayer; and never fail, whatever the difficulties encountered, to minister to each other in love. Judgment will come; but, for those who are faithful, it will be but the first step in the final dissolution of things earthly and the unchallenged establishment of blessed community for all those united in Christ. To that end, presbyters and all other officials, as well as the humblest of Christ's followers, must put on the vestments of humility and serve one another. Social alertness in the world that now is can be the only true preparation for a participating share in the world that is to be hereafter.

First Peter envisages Christ's people as an elect race who are born to a heavenly inheritance that cannot be approached, in its perfect solidarity, by any human institution. As a consecrated nation, a people who belong to him, they are called from darkness to light. Once no people at all, they are now God's own. Even as they wait for the

---

[12] Eph. 1:13-14; 2:19-22; cf. Will, *Le culte*, III, 43-44, on the Pauline eschatology.
[13] I Pet. 1:16; 2:4-5; 2:9-12; 3:8-12; 4:7-11; Charles, *Future Life*, pp. 443 ff.

transformation which shall come, they must live the life which he has entrusted to them as followers of his enduring society.[14]

The Letter to the Hebrews, like First Peter, regards disciplined Christian association on earth as the chief prerequisite to the complete solidarity of the eternal kingdom. Those who have an eternal inheritance awaiting them cannot think of finding in the existing order any abiding home. The author boldly says, "We have no permanent city here on earth, but we are in search of the city that is to come" (Heb. 13:14, Goodspeed).

All such citizens of the eternal metropolis must regard their present life as one of pilgrimage in which faith preserves them for the approaching consummation. Foreigners though they may be to the present age, they cannot reach the heavenly commonwealth which God has prepared for them unless they manifest the communality of life which is to be characteristic of the heavenly republic in the future. Thus they must let love for the brotherhood continue. Alertness to the needs of all those around them must prove their sonship in the abiding future. Christ will reappear to save his followers. But those who believe in his advent must make ready for him by a reciprocity of love. This is the only means by which they may anticipate the coming of the Great Day. The visible world is already waxing old. It is to be replaced and renewed within a universal framework which shall preserve the kingdom in perpetuity. Those who make ready by thoughtfulness and helpful ministry to all in need are truly going out to meet him who must surely come in triumph.

A crowd of witnesses already bends down from the heavenly battlements to spur the present followers of Christ in the running of their race. Faith in the justice of God and his familial provision for them has led these patriarchs and apostles on the heavenly way; those who now live must surround each other with brotherly concord as they follow in this celestial train. Fully surrendered in hope and faith to the promises of one who is completely trustworthy, they have only to arouse each other to rivalry in love and good deeds. The more imminent the Great Day, the more crucially important it is that they neglect not, as some do, their meeting together and encouraging each other.[15]

The first-century work known as the Great Apocalypse is, by all odds, the most striking of the crisis documents in the history of the

[14] I Pet. 2:9-12.
[15] Heb. 12, entire; also, 10:23-25.

early church. Undue attention has been accorded the peculiarly chiliastic imagery with which its later chapters are suffused. Regardless of the particular form of eschatology which it represents, it mirrors accurately the same concern with the ultimate kingdom that other early and medieval literature evinces.[16] It is of secondary significance, in this connection, to argue the effectiveness or inadequacy of the apocalyptic eccentricities in this work.

True, John the Revelator is bent on showing that there will be a millennial reign on earth. This, as Dr. R. H. Charles and other authorities have pointed out, is not the typical form which Christian eschatology was to preserve in its more orthodox phases. Perhaps, as Dr. E. F. Scott suggests, the writer's primary concern was to envisage the great beatitude in the heavenly realm that lay beyond the time of the millennium. The work, when properly studied, seems to support this view. It is altogether likely that the author exaggerated his treatment of the millennial interlude for a particular reason: namely, because he wished to show that evil on this earth would not be completely triumphant, even in the days before the final kingdom had been consummated.[17]

When this has been said, however, a trenchant fact still remains inescapable. From the beginning of the work, John is placing a premium upon loyalty to God's kingdom as the measure of victory for all people who call themselves Christians. A cosmic struggle begun in heaven and continued on the earth will have its ending in God's triumph on earth as in heaven. Those who dare to believe in the victory of the Lamb may themselves become victorious. Whatever they may suffer—and John seems to think that most, if not all, Christians may have to surrender their temporal existence under the persecution of the Roman state—true Christians may be assured of immortal life together with those who have been slain before them; that is, if they will but remain undivided in their loyalty to the cause of Christ.[18]

Anticipating as he did the blows of fortune which emperor-worship as a Roman imperial cult might lodge against the Christian fraternity, John was concerned with one thing only. He would have the followers of Christ remain true to the standards of the Father's enduring world. Because of this, the prophet and seer—seeing, from before, the

---

[16] See the emphases of Scott, *The Book of Revelation*, and the foregoing chapters of this present work.

[17] Scott, *Revelation*, pp. 166-72; Charles, *Future Life*, pp. 403-12.

[18] Rev. 2:10-11; 3:10-13, 21: 12:10-12. Also chapters 20–22, inclusive.

events which were yet to occur—held up before the gaze of the faithful the triumph that was even now guaranteed by the Almighty. In the light of the sacrifices which Christ had made, and many of his saints with him, John could not foresee any easy way out for others of the faithful. They must conceive of their brotherhood as a corporate existence including all those having gone before and those yet to be. As such, they must give every indication of common purpose that would show on earth their dedication to heaven. Meanwhile, God in his own good time would bring victory to their banners.[19]

Consequently, John admonishes the seven churches of Asia to be alert in anticipating their common duties and discharging their corporate responsibilities. Only thus can they be worthy to come through the fiery trial and be reassociated in the Father's kingdom with the Lamb that was slain. Seeing in vision those who have already come triumphant through their martyrdom, John calls those who are yet to meet their test unto an unshaken witness that shall reunite them with all the blessed. God has always reigned triumphant in heaven. He now purposes to send his heavenly city down on earth for a thousand years to be a foretaste of the society that shall one day reign supreme over a completely renovated and purified universe. Only after this earthly trial and millennial aftermath can the heritage prepared for all Christians from the beginning of the world be experienced in its fullness. In the meantime, all must look to it—however far the view—as the motivating standard of their present lives. That standard, too, must be conceived as a fully social experience out of which the truest personality of each shall emerge.[20]

There is a double focus in the Apocalypse. Even during the millennium, men will not have entered the fully celestial order. But at the very outset, as reported through the devices of apocalyptic imagery, John was admitted into the heavenly realm. With the aid of divine prevenience he was permitted to see things both earthly and heavenly. He therefore traces in their time-transcending significance events as they have come to pass in vision and will unfold in heaven and on earth.

It is noteworthy that John saw enacted, first, the struggle on the heavenly plane. Satan lost on that field of battle as he will again in the last ages of the world:

Not only is the earthly struggle consequent on the heavenly one, but all that happens in it is controlled from Heaven. . . . In a larger sense,

[19] Rev. 21:7-8; 7:9-10; 12:10-12.
[20] Rev. 1:1-3; 7:1-17; 16:15-18; 22:12-15.

the earthly sphere is brought into relation to the higher one. Earth and Heaven are set over against each other. They are separate, and yet they are linked together. The lower world depends on the higher, and exists for the sake of it. . . . John seeks to impress on us that the earthly scene will at last be merged in the heavenly one. The Church is conscious of its helplessness. It finds itself in this world of time, subject to weakness and poverty and the assaults of brutal enemies. But it must look upward and beyond. It belongs to that company of God's people who are now triumphant. It has fellowship with them even now, and in the end will be united with them in the higher world.[21]

This is vital. Here in a millenarian treatise we have the final focus on the final order; that is, on the heavenly kingdom, not on the intermediate, earthly-heavenly millennium. The millennial concept itself indicates that God will come, even on earth. But the goal lies always beyond the millennium. The whole motivation is derived from the ultimate society of the victorious, ever-suffering saints. It is significant that John shows the end at the beginning of the drama. He sees the future as it will impinge upon, control, and recondition the present.[22]

The millennial factor—which is often regarded as being less than orthodox—thus takes a definitely reduced place. The emphasis here, as in the nonchiliastic, normative eschatology, falls upon the future, eternal society that gives character and communal vitality to those now suffering and overcoming in the present, temporal society.

The millennial reign is significant here, as in other apocalypses, only because it gives a foretaste of the eternally conquering society. The New Jerusalem, or heaven on earth, does but prefigure the even fuller society, which is the heaven of the Godhead and of the saints on earth as in heaven.

In the Revelation, as now arranged and as traditionally interpreted, the souls of the martyred dead, alone, were resuscitated in the first resurrection; then followed the thousand-year reign with Christ; after which Satan was released, fought with God and his people, and was destroyed. Following this came the second resurrection—that of all the dead—and judgment proceeded out of the books that were opened in the presence of all.[23]

Then, "I saw a new heaven and a new earth. . . ." Whereupon God

---

[21] Scott, *Revelation*, pp. 166-67. Used by permission of the publishers, Charles Scribner's Sons and Student Christian Movement Press.
[22] *Loc. cit.;* also pp. 168-70.
[23] Rev. 20:4-15.

came to dwell with his people. Everything was made new and the overcoming ones were given life everlasting. Others proceeded to the death which they had merited by their failure to support the true church.[24]

So the traditional account ends, with paeans of victory for the society which reigns in God's bright fellowship forever. To be sure, John spends most of his time on the millennial age. But his goal is the eternal city. He knows little more of it than that which is said about the New Jerusalem, and that is little enough. Whether or not certain modern commentators are right in distinguishing sharply between a heavenly city coming down out of heaven and another which is supreme over heaven and earth, there is still manifested in the Apocalypse both a continuity and a discontinuity of orders. There is a world comparatively earthly and one in heaven that is the New Jerusalem. In any case, the New Jerusalem is let down out of heaven, and earthly society is transformed by it.

One may readily agree that over and beyond his apocalyptic imagery John

is seeking to express the truth which lies at the heart of all religion. . . . Over against this visible order there is a higher one for which, as spiritual beings, we are meant to live. . . . For John it is the Kingdom of God, the state of being in which we shall have direct fellowship with God. . . . It was impressed on him that everything in man's life must be related to this higher order of things, which is the real one.[25]

However much the Christian in a given era may be tempted to believe that reality inheres in the obvious, he must always be called back to the realization that the data of the present mean nothing aside from something that is beyond the present and within the as-yet-unrealized future.

Before you can understand the present, you need to see the future, in which the present will be unfolded. Before you can truly account for some visible thing, you must have the sense of a higher reality, which in some way it represents.[26]

The foregoing analysis seeks to focus our attention on an indisputably Christian conviction: That which concerns us most in the

---

[24] Rev. 21:1-8.
[25] Scott, *Revelation*, pp. 168, 169. Used by permission of the publishers.
[26] *Ibid.*, p. 169. Used by permission of the publishers.

present order has its end and objective in an order that rises transcendent to, though in direct relationship with, our own. It is precisely this necessity of seeing our partial world in relation to the eternal whole that the apocalyptic writer insists upon. Since the eternal purposes of God have their realization beyond the time of which we are a part, they come to us out of the future, signaled to us from the unknown. But it is the consummation which that unknown shall reveal to us that holds, within itself, the realization of God's will as it has been from the dawn of time. Quite logically, therefore, in order to live in the present world as God would have us live, we must inquire penitently and prayerfully as to what he would have us be in this world and in the eternity that lies ahead. Again one may sanction the conviction that:

> In the Book of Revelation, therefore, everything turns on the idea of a vital connection between the two worlds. From the misery and confusion which he sees around him, John looks beyond. He interprets all the present events in the light of a divine plan of which they are a part, and which will come at last to its fulfilment.[27]

Furthermore, John is not speculating wildly. He has a major objective always before him. This is the determination to nerve the Church in a period of persecution for a stand which will be worthy in the present of its membership in the eternal community of the saints. John has one concern for the Church and every individual who claims a share in it on earth. This is that they shall realize their bond with the heavenly community whose ultimate victory he has already seen prefigured. To be sure, those to whom he speaks will have to accept in faith the promised outcome. He himself has been vouchsafed a preview of the end which is already conditioning the intermediate activities of time. He knows—and calls upon all Christians to believe—that the persecution which is now coming upon them is only a small part of an even greater conflict which was waged first in heaven and is now about to be resumed on earth. In the earlier stages of that conflict Satan was ejected from the intimacy of God's companionship. Even though the Great Enemy may prevail for a time, his end is sure. The order which he stands for is already in fateful collision with that of Christ. The victory which will come to Jesus' banner is beyond doubt.[28]

[27] *Ibid.,* pp. 170-71. Used by permission of the publishers.
[28] Rev. 12:1-17; 21:1-8; 22:12-17.

Herein lies the significance of John's hearing a voice from the kingdom world which speaks words of encouragement, warning, and criticism to the seven churches. Here is, from the very beginning, a call for temporal response to an eternal order. Communal responsibility alone will bring the Church, and every person on earthly pilgrimage within it, to the heavenly fulfillment.

Suffering and death have known their bloody gamut before and will repeat it again. But as Satan was defeated in heaven, so he will be defeated and finally ejected from the earth itself. John has just seen what is to him proof positive of this fact. It is his principal duty to transmit to the faithful his own conviction which will make them ready to pass their own tests victoriously.

His book begins with a view into a future community as yet all too unfamiliar. It ends with a picture of the beatitude, or at least its preliminary phases. However lacking in accuracy as to the times and seasons foretold his predictions may have been, his basic presuppositions have been supported by history itself. Persecution did eventually come, even as he had known it would. Who will say that his vision of the future did not have a major part to play in preparing men for their present, then and thereafter? He was indeed "conscious of a higher order to which everything in the end will be subject."[29]

It should be noted that, although there is a marked difference between the Johannine eschatology and that of the Synoptics, there does exist a specific eschatological character in the former as in the latter. There are commentators who would so spiritualize the highly mystical Gospel of John as to divorce it almost entirely from any final consummation. Actually, John, as well as the other Gospels, has a marked sense of the divine unity out of which the community of the kingdom proceeds. This becomes, in turn, the conditioning element in the universe which leads the individual creature to eternal life. When the Christian loves the community of his brethren on earth with the love that originated in the divine community, he prepares himself for a final return to an all-socializing experience in the consummate future. In this process of reorienting himself to an eternal order, he becomes a true person in the present order. This is demonstrated, alike, in the Gospel and in the Letters of John.

Charles observes that although the kingdom is seldom mentioned, the concept is frequently found in John's writings.

The divine gift of eternal life, as the good of the individual, can

[29] Scott, *Revelation*, p. 172.

only be realised in so far as it brings the individual into vital union with the divine community, which is none other than the kingdom.

He proceeds, with reference to specific passages in the Johannine Letters, to show that

eternal life and the kingdom are correlative and complementary thoughts in the fourth Gospel. The indispensable evidence of this life in the individual is his love to the community. He who possesses it not has no divine life as an individual; he neither comes from God nor knows Him.[30]

Thus, within a pattern that is strikingly different from the first three Gospels, the author of the last preserves an even more refined suggestion as to the differentiating yet relating qualities of the two orders. In his Gospel one is as definitely reminded that an eternal order of things will replace the present, as he could ever be by Mark, Matthew, and Luke. And the suggestion is perhaps even more powerful that the final life of the blessed in everlasting joy is a community experience. True, one may anticipate that final experience in some measure by acting now on its eternal principles. But it will eventually reign supreme. Then, when time has given way to eternity, love as it is fully known and practiced by the members of the Godhead will become the transforming environment of all others who love and are beloved of God. Looking forward to such a fully social experience, all of Christ's brethren may well begin to practice a community of life in this world which shall be at least approximately related to fulfillment in the eternal community. It is in such a context that Jesus is represented as praying the Father that the brethren on earth may be one as he and the Father are one in heaven.[31]

The little books of Timothy and Titus belong, in all probability, to a period later than Paul. However much they incorporate ideals and conceptions that draw upon the Pauline influence, they surely reflect an organizational emphasis subsequent to his immediate lifetime. In them is found the typical Christian regard for a future out of which a new order is to come; and which, in coming, shall replace the regnant forms of social procedure. Although generations may already have passed away since Christ predicted his early reappearance, the old motivation which finds its anchorage in the eternal world is still to be observed.

[30] Charles, *The Future Life*, p. 426. Used by permission of the publishers.

[31] John 17; W. Bauer, *Das Johannesevangelium*, pp. 196 ff.; Loisy, *Le quatrième évangile*, pp. 798 ff.; Charles, *The Future Life*, pp. 422-31.

Christ's own injunction, and that of Paul who followed him, to be ready for a new order of life, however imminent or far removed it may be from the present, is here clearly reflected. Christians are to live, as always, firmly grounded in the corporate aspects of the faith until the reappearance of Christ. The Great Day may have been long deferred; but, as in much later times, its coming is definitely considered an article of a practicable creed. God's chosen are still to live as under the spell of the great Last Day. Only if they endure shall they reign with him. Trials and tribulations innumerable may intervene before that time comes. But the Christ, who will judge the living and the dead, will make his decision on the basis of life as it is lived before the second Advent. Godly living in this world is to characterize the community life and the personal conduct of all who wait for the glorious appearing of God in Christ on the Last Day. Those who are to claim their heritage, then, must make their investment in it secure, now.[32]

Representative teachings drawn from uncanonical literature reflect views similar to those of New Testament authors. At the end of the first Christian century, a certain Roman bishop by the name of Clement reproduced the major outlines of Paul's correspondence with the Corinthian brethren. The same passion for unity is apparent in his various letters. A generation, at least, has elapsed since the writing of the earlier Apostle. It is not strange, therefore, to find reflected in this work the organizational development of a later Christian stage. Actually, Clement is concerned that his Christian fellows at Corinth find in association with their bishop the means of a new unity in Christ.[33]

Clement's whole position, however, is instructive as to the way in which he leans upon the time-honored eschatology to give bearing and vitality to his social urgency. Knowing as he does that all Christians value most their membership in the kingdom of heaven, he naturally uses this leverage to secure productive social effort among the brethren. After admonishing the Corinthians to find a new unity in love and co-ordinated effort centered in the bishop, he concludes: "Thus have they done and will do, that live as citizens of that king-

[32] I Tim. 6:11-16; II Tim. 3:1-17; 4:1-8.

[33] F. X. Funk, ed., *Patres Apostolici* (Tübingen, 1901), I, 98 ff.; J. B. Lightfoot, *The Apostolic Fathers* (New York, 1890), Pt. I, Vol. II, pp. 5 ff., 271 ff.; K. Lake, *The Apostolic Fathers* (Loeb Classical Library, Cambridge, 1949), I, 8 ff.; B. Altaner, *Patrologie* (3rd ed.; Freiburg, 1951), pp. 73 ff.; B. Steidle, *Patrologia* (Friburg i/B, 1937), pp. 11 ff. See the recent critical edition by C. C. Richardson, in *Early Christian Fathers* [The Library of Christian Classics, I] (Philadelphia, 1953), pp. 33 ff.

dom of God which bringeth no regrets." [34] It is not an accident that he stresses the necessity of living even now as citizens of a kingdom yet to be realized in its fullness.

In another connection he calls upon the men at Corinth to realize once more how responsible they are for a solidarity unknown to animals, the solar universe, and indeed to other men. He seems to be inciting the Christians of Corinth to such social concord as shall be worthy of those who seek a place in the eternal kingdom. He adds, "Look ye, brethren, lest His benefits, which are many, turn unto judgment to all of us, if we walk not worthily of Him, and do those things which are good and well-pleasing in His sight with concord." [35]

In an eloquent passage, Clement outlines the program of Christian unity which is in keeping with the standards Christ imposes upon his kingdom brethren. The Christian, he thinks, looks forward to a special portion with those who shall be blessed of God. This is the joyous inheritance which every Christian has a right to anticipate. But he has that right only in terms of such co-operation as shall transform a selfish individualism into a humble, penitent mutuality.

Let us clothe ourselves in concord, being lowly-minded and temperate, holding ourselves aloof from all backbiting and evil speaking, being justified by works and not by words. . . . Boldness and arrogance and daring are for them that are accursed of God; but forbearance and humility and gentleness are with them that are blessed of God.[36]

Among the fascinating documents of the second century (*ca.* 130-40) is one purporting to have been written by a certain Barnabas. It is obvious that we are not here dealing with the companion of St. Paul. In fact, one of his chief preoccupations seems to be the necessity of proving all things Christian highly superior to their Jewish counterparts. In the course of his long and frequently involved references to Scripture—all interpreted in highly fanciful allegory—he comes upon the inescapable problem of the Last Days. Here, he is not at all loath to exploit the old writings for his own particular ends of Christian interpretation. This is his usual tendency.[37]

[34] Cor., 54; tr. of Lightfoot, *Apostolic Fathers,* I, ii, 299; Lake, *Apostolic Fathers,* I, 100, 101.

[35] Cor., 21; tr. of Lightfoot, *op. cit.,* I, ii, 283; Lake, *op. cit.,* I, 46, 47.

[36] Cor., 30; tr. of Lightfoot, *op. cit.,* I, ii, 287; Lake, *op. cit.,* 58-61.

[37] *The Epistle of Barnabas;* Funk, *Patres,* I, 38 ff.; Lake, *The Apostolic Fathers,* I, 340 ff.; Steidle, *Patrologia,* p. 281; Altaner, *Patrologie,* pp. 38, 59 ff.; J. A. Kleist, *Ancient Christian Fathers,* 6 (Westminster, Md., 1948) : P. Quasten, *Patrology* (Utrecht, 1950) , I.

It is natural that Barnabas should call upon Jewish literature for authority to support his belief in the Last Days. He is not hard-pressed for proof-texts. But he is sobered by the thought of the responsibility which is thus imposed upon his Christian compatriots. However bizarre the tenor of his work may appear, it is modified throughout by an extremely social perceptiveness. He is primarily concerned that his fellow Christians act upon assumptions growing out of loyalty to God's eternal society. Furthermore, he brings home to his associates the necessity of their living at all times so that they need not be afraid of the Last Days' catching them unaware.

His frank assessment of the relationship between history and the eternal society brings his book most sharply into focus.

We take earnest heed in these last days; for the whole [past] time of your faith will profit you nothing, unless now in this wicked time we also withstand coming sources of danger, as becometh the sons of God.

Barnabas puts greatest possible stress upon meeting crises of the present world order in the light of the eternal standards of conduct. He continues:

that the Black One may find no means of entrance, let us flee from every vanity, let us utterly hate the works of the way of wickedness. Do not, by retiring apart, live a solitary life, as if you were already [fully] justified; but coming together in one place, make common inquiry concerning what tends to your general welfare.[38]

A solitary life, as Barnabas well knew, was frequently inadequate to an individual's meeting the stark realities of life. Jesus had labored to show his followers the indispensability of brotherly interaction in the development of true personality. And he had placed the center of vitality for the present social experience in the resources of God's eternal kingdom. Barnabas, whatever his many faults, was clear at this point concerning the fuller meaning of the Master's injunction. He was sensitive to the necessity of each individual soul's building a temple to God in unselfish co-operation with other like souls. He knew quite well that each person must assume his own share of responsibility in preparing for the awful day of Judgment.

The Shepherd of Hermas (*ca.* 150) continues to be in many respects a highly baffling literary piece. Needless to say, there is no

[38] Ep. IV, 9-14; tr. of the *Ante-Nicene Fathers* (New York, 1899), I, 138-39; Kleist, *op. cit.*, pp. 41-42.

complete agreement on all the connotations associated with its various symbols. It is not too much to say, however, that its eschatological sensitivity involves, in typically Christian fashion, a true sociality.[39]

Not only is there a marked tendency to look forward to the future society of God's kingdom; there is also a clear premium placed upon dedication to that kingdom in terms of service to the present world society. Just because the Judgment is coming in all its stark irrevocability, Christians, above all other men, are called upon to discharge in the routines of everyday life their stewardship owed the ultimate society. Therefore, all classes and stations in society are to have regard for all others in terms of a social ministry which shall finally be assessed and rewarded at the Judgment Day. The rich are to aid the poor; the poor are to pray for the rich. Mutuality is to be given its most intensive application within the long perspective of the grand reckoning.

Above all, Christians are exhorted to remember that such citizenship as they have in the present world is but temporary and intermediate. "You know that you, as the servants of God, are living in a strange country, for your city is far from this city." [40] Obviously, a false evaluation of primary loyalties may easily result in tragic loss. If one acts on assumptions conformable, mainly, to the affections of this human city, he will, in the very nature of the case, fail of his responsibility to the citizenship that is beyond. And, having formed an attachment to the present world, he will find himself decreasingly capable of commitment to the greater of the two societies. It is, therefore, the law of God's great city that must become the governing and guiding principle of the Christian's life. He must, even as Jesus said, decide which master and which society he will serve. No double attachment will here be tolerated. One cannot live according to the laws of the purely human commonwealth and hope to be received into God's country. By the same token, one must be prepared to travel with the lightest equipment possible while on pilgrimage to the final realm. By so doing, he will not barter the standards of the eternal kingdom for convenience in the present world order. "Take heed," says the pastor, that "you who serve the Lord have Him in your hearts" and "do the deeds of God." [41]

[39] Lake, *Apostolic Fathers,* II, 6 ff.; Altaner, *Patrologie,* pp. 63 ff.; Steidle, *Patrologia,* p. 284; Seeberg, *Lehrbuch,* I, 186-87.
[40] *Similitude,* I, 1; Lake, *Apostolic Fathers,* II, 138, 139 ff.
[41] *Sim.,* I, 7; Lake, *op. cit.,* II, 140, 141.

All individuals who find the true meaning of personality in such unequivocal commitment to the divine society will be correspondingly aware of their current social responsibilities. They will, as Christ admonished, be perfect according to the standard of God's heavenly rule. It is not strange that those of such a faith should be much concerned about ministering to widows, looking after orphans, practicing hospitality, preventing injustice, and otherwise consolidating their Christian citizenship. The writer is convinced that, next to one's loyalty to the Divine, nothing is better than these things. Whoever walks in such paths, lives according to God.[42]

Like the *Didache* and *Barnabas*, each of which discusses the two ways of life and death, *Hermas* analyzes the constituency of the heavenly kingdom in terms of negative and positive traits. Significantly enough, those who refrain from antisocial activities on the one hand, and those who give themselves to constructive deeds of community life on the other, shall be enrolled in the kingdom of life. Those who would be counted among the elect of God must act now after the fashion of those who were called from the beginning to share in the final beatitude. There will come a time when one may no longer produce fruits worthy of those who serve in the Lord's vineyard. Now is the time to contribute to the necessity of the saints and to regard the needs of one's fellow men. Like the author of the Revelation, *The Shepherd of Hermas* is emphasizing the necessity of positive social action, whatever the disadvantages that may appear in the way. Even though the most malign forces of the universe loom up before them, God's servants must in the present world follow the lead of their Master while in passage to his realm.[43]

The *Epistle to Diognetus* is a distinguished vignette of early Christian literature.[44] Representing, possibly, the later decades of the second century, it phrases in beautifully Johannine language the relationship of the temporal Christian community to the kingdom above and the more visible world below. By this time, apparently, Christians were often looked upon as being remiss in their duties to the society around them. It is true that Christianity as a whole had not immediately developed any large sense of responsibility for the reclamation of mankind generally. Nonetheless, it would be wholly

[42] *Mandate*, 8; Lake, *op. cit.*, II, 102-7.

[43] See the foregoing references, also *Sim.*, II; Lake, *op. cit.*, II, 142 ff.

[44] Lake, *Apostolic Fathers*, II, 348 ff.; Kleist, *Ancient Christian Fathers*, VI, 127-34, 210 ff.; Steidle, *Patrologia*, p. 31; Altaner, *Patrologie*, pp. 102-3; H. I. Marrou, A *Diognète* (Sources Chrétiennes, Paris, 1951); Richardson, *Early Christian Fathers*, pp. 205 ff.

unfair to stigmatize the Christian group as having no interest beyond itself. Properly enough, the Christian community placed first its responsibility to the society of God, as it would one day be realized in heaven and on earth. Following Jesus' own injunction, the *koinonia* proceeded to cement its comradeship with the brethren who composed this inner core of kingdom living. The redemptive energies available to the world, without, must certainly come from a vitality engendered by this spiritual corpus.

The special concern of the *Epistle to Diognetus* is that fellow Christians affirm the major allegiance out of which their whole life stems. The author does not want them to be thought lacking in normal human interests and activities. He stresses how much they have in common with mankind, generally. In fact, they behave in the time-honored ways that are common to men everywhere and in all periods. Nevertheless, there is a fundamental difference in their own and the world's reactions to the society of which they are both a part. Whereas most human beings are oriented in temporal society as if it were the source of their existence and the end of their lives, the Christian makes no such mistake. He knows that nothing purely human can give substance to his abiding affection. He and his fellows can never be the "advocates of any merely human doctrines." However much they may appear to be related to an earthly association, they realize that the society from which they stem is an eternal, and not a purely terrestrial, one. Thus, "they pass their days on earth, but they are citizens of heaven." Regardless of the activities which seem to bind them in common humanity to other human beings, they are ennobled and rededicated to human life in terms of a distinctive commitment: their allegiance to an eternal kingdom. Actually, the social ministry which they exercise among their fellows, as well as in the world without, is given power and catholicity by their having sprung from, and their being on pilgrimage to, the eternal community.[45]

An authentic note is sounded when the writer says: "What the soul is in the body, that the Christians are in the world." Whatever is of value in the Christian ministry to temporal society gets its leavening power from that community which is beyond all things human. And though Christians may be confined in the world as in a prison house, yet, in their passage to a better world, they give to this social

[45] *Ep. Diogn., V;* tr. of *The Ante-Nicene Fathers,* I, 26; Lake, *op. cit.,* II, 358-61; Kleist, *op. cit.,* pp. 138-40; Marrou, *op. cit.* pp. 62 ff.

life about them something of the zestful liberty of that greater community which shall be theirs.[46]

Christ, himself, who was cocreator with God the Father, came to earth as the servant of all those who were cast down. In this capacity, he fulfilled the functions of one loving rather than judging. But, admittedly, he will come again to judge; and he will decide men's fate by the criteria of suprahuman social ministry which he himself exemplified. Whether or not he receives men into his kingdom as his own kind will be determined on the basis of their service to him and his.

It is literally impossible for men to *deserve* incorporation by the kingdom of heaven. But God will *give* that kingdom, for Christ's sake, to those who truly love him. However impossible it may seem that men should receive such complete beatitude for such a paucity of effort on their own part, the astounding fact remains: whoever loves God and his Son with the love which these manifest will serve fellow men in such fashion as to be worthy of an invitation from the Divine to come up higher. Their worthiness will come, not from themselves, but from within their selfless ministry to those whom God and his Son so dearly loved. Love makes it possible for one to imitate the example of the divine goodness. However surprising this may seem, man can be an imitator of God. Obviously this cannot be accomplished in a self-seeking spirit contrary to God's majestic character. Only in service to neighbor may one really discover the deep mysteries of God's universe. He will discern that the only basis of a genuine society consists in unequivocal loyalty to the heavenly realm.[47]

The Apostolic Constitutions—in their present, composite form an Eastern product of around 375—are made up of materials drawn from different centuries and varying circumstances of the Church's early life. Obviously enough, certain parts of the work recapitulate portions of earlier pamphlets such as *Barnabas*, the *Didascalia*, and the *Didache*.[48] This work, however, depicts with particular usefulness the mounting problems of early Christian existence. According all too little attention to the many sections with eschatological im-

---

[46] *Ep. Diogn.*, VI, 1 ff.; tr. of Lake, *op. cit.*, II, 361 ff.

[47] *Ibid.*, X, especially 4; Lake, *op. cit.*, II, 373.

[48] Altaner, *Patrologie*, pp. 43-44; Steidle, *Patrologia*, pp. 269-71. Text in F. X. Funk, *Didascalia et Constitutiones Apostolorum* (Paderborn, 1905), 2 Vols., especially Vol. I. Cf. B. S. Easton, *The Apostolic Tradition of Hippolytus* (1934); J. Muilenburg, *The Literary Relations of the Epistle of Barnabas and the Teaching of the Twelve Apostles* (Marburg, 1929). Cf. Richardson, *Early Christian Fathers*, pp. 161 ff.

port, we make several generalizations borne out by the obvious facts.

There is no less an emphasis here upon the sense of impending judgment than one finds elsewhere in early Christian literature. Here, too, there is marked alertness to the issues of the Last Things. This necessitates manful Christian regard for the social obligations of everyday life. Whatever the irksomeness of the long routine, one is committed to the necessity of being ever ready for the Lord's return. When he does come again, the Master will bring with him his saints, the company of which each follower of Christ longs so much to join. The only sure way that one may take his place in that happy band is by making "this present world . . . a place of combat to righteousness." [49] Here, as elsewhere, the author is responding to the eliciting character of the heavenly world as he puts his hand to the tasks of mundane experience. Like the writers of other Christian manuals, the authors and compilers of *The Apostolic Constitutions* joyfully anticipate the time when all the faithful shall be gathered into the house of God. But this lays a specific obligation upon everyone who dares aspire to Christ's heavenly brotherhood. If he would be found ready at the Judgment Day to enter therein, he must give a social accounting of his own life, worthy to be read and approved in the last age of the world.

Occupations as diverse as teaching the Holy Scriptures to the young and arranging fitting marriages for those of the right age belong in this category of eschatologically motivated social endeavors. These and similar injunctions scattered throughout the work proclaim, not only an ancient piety acclimated to Christian beginnings, but also an institutional shrewdness accentuated by later, organizational development.[50]

Lactantius (d. *ca.* 303) is usually thought of as one of those Fathers who put such emphasis upon the millennial reign as to be relatively unconcerned either with the ultimate society that follows after it or with the social present that precedes it. But what has already been said concerning the larger chiliastic interest in the eternal future and the temporal society is pertinent here. The author is noticeably concerned with the Judgment and what follows immediately upon it. He occupies himself, also, with the present society as it should be modified by devotion to an even more ultimate future. He feels that all hope of life and salvation is to be placed in dedication to God. Of course, earthly things are to be scorned in favor of the

---

[49] *Ap. Const.,* VII, 33; tr. of ANF, VII, 472.
[50] *Ap. Const.,* VII, 11, 31-32, 38, 41.

heavenly, with vigilant preparation for the Day of Judgment. But in proper anticipation of the new world each one is to train himself for a mortal existence of justice, self-restraint, and virtue. This he is to do that he

may hold fast innocency, may be of service to as many as possible, may gain for himself incorruptible treasures by good works, that he may be able, with God for his judge, to gain for the merits of his virtue either the crown of faith, or the reward of immortality.[51]

Basil of Caesarea (d. 379) was a man of deep community interest, both in monastic life and in his episcopal mission outside. His *Rules* show a decided preference for cenobitic existence, or the common life of monks, as over against the eremitic experience. Throughout his busy career he was characterized by a devotion to man's true community, the heavenly Jerusalem. But this eventuated all the more in a sensitized response to the temporal world, toward which he felt a growing obligation.[52]

In the ninth homily of his famous *Hexaemeron,* so influential in the making of the medieval mind, he emphasizes Philippians 3:20. In Pauline fashion, he calls upon man to distinguish himself from purely terrestrial animals, with their downward gaze, by turning his head upward to the celestial society:

Raise thy soul above the earth; draw from its natural conformation the rule of thy conduct; fix thy conversation in heaven. Thy true community is the heavenly Jerusalem; thy fellow citizens and thy compatriots are "the first-born which are written in heaven." [53]

How well Basil translated his affection for the new city in heaven to the new city on earth is witnessed by Gregory Nazianzen in his panegyric on the Saint. The philanthropic proof of Basil's love for the heavenly brotherhood is here described as coming to fruition just outside the Caesarean metropolis. In this place of ministry to

[51] Bardenhewer, *Geschichte der altkirchlichen Literatur* (Freiburg im/B, 1914), II, 525 ff.; Lactantius, *Institutionum Epitome,* 68 (73), *Corpus Scriptorum Ecclesiasticorum Latinorum* (Vienna, 1890), XIX, 761; tr. is that of ANF, VII, 255; cf. E. H. Blakeney, *Lactantius' Epitome of the Divine Institutes* (London, 1950), Epilogue, pp. 123-24.
[52] Bardenhewer, *Geschichte,* III, 130 ff.; W. K. L. Clarke, *The Ascetic Works of Saint Basil* (London, 1925), 2 Vols.; M. M. Wagner, *Saint Basil: Ascetical Works* (Fathers of the Church, 9; New York, 1950).
[53] *Nicene and Post-Nicene Fathers* (NPNF) 2nd Ser. VIII, 102. Used by permission of the publishers, Wm. B. Eerdmans Publishing Co.

suffering humanity, the benevolence of the wealthy was placed at the disposal of the sick and defeated. According to Gregory this project of Basil provided the most wonderful evidence of all, that man's earthly life could be made approximately conformable to the heavenly brotherhood. This was "the short road to salvation, the easiest ascent to heaven." Thanks to the generosity of many, inspired by their leader Basil, that most hideous of all diseases, leprosy, was treated with true Christian humanity. This early hospital demonstrated that Christ, the head of all men, was no longer to be dishonored by the disregard of his afflicted members. Gregory is, perhaps, not exaggerating the effects produced by such devotion to temporal society in the name of heavenly community. The result "is to be seen, not only in the city, but in the country and beyond, and even the leaders of society vie with one another in their philanthropy and magnanimity toward them." This, thinks Basil's friend, is the imitation of Christ by cleansing leprosy in deed, and not by word only.[54]

Among the early Christian preachers who distinguished themselves for social theory and even more significant social practice, none surpassed the eloquent John of Antioch, called Chrysostom (347-407). The mass of writings which he has left the world are a tribute to the social sensitivity with which he faced the problems of his day. Thus he may be consulted as a significant leader in the thought of those Christians who felt that to be followers of Christ they must, necessarily, minister to all those whom Christ loved.[55]

Chrysostom should, therefore, be approached for his beliefs about the Last Days and future kingdom as they affect the Christian's everyday life. Surely, one who talked with such a desperate sense of urgency about the need of ministering to one's fellow man could not have failed to stress the ultimate society out of which all such ministry stems. Such expectations are by no means disappointed. In the organization of relief measures with which John sought to alleviate human suffering, and in the exhortations which he addressed to those Christians whom he thought capable of helping in such social service, the eschatological motivation shines clear and direct.

[54] See the Panegyric on St. Basil by Gregory Nazianzen, 63; NPNF, VII, 416; Altaner, *Patrologie*, pp. 248-60; Steidle, *Patrologia*, pp. 116 ff.; 111 ff. On the "New City" see Ep. 94 in the Loeb edition and translation of Basil, II, 149; Theodoret, *Hist. Eccl.*, IV, 19; Sozomen, *Hist. Eccl.*, VII, 34.

[55] Altaner, *Patrologie*, pp. 278 ff.; Cayré, *Patrologie* (Paris, 1944), Vol. I.; A. Puech, *Histoire de la littérature Grecque Chrétienne* (Paris, 1928-30), Vols. II and III; Bardenhewer, *Geschichte*, III, 324 ff.

Chrysostom centers his entire social program in the gospel. There is in his humanitarian consciousness no slightest regard for man as a being apart from God. Likewise, he has no concern for some purely humanistic solidarity detached from the great society of the eternal beatitude. Consequently, his social concern rises out of his dedication to the heavenly kingdom. Because of consecration to the eternal society, the life of his people in the world of today must respond to the fuller life of that beloved community, tomorrow.

In a homily on Matthew he voices this eloquent plea:

Let us show forth then a new kind of life. Let us make earth, heaven; let us hereby show the Greeks, of how great blessings they are deprived. For when they behold in us good conversation, they will look upon the very face of the kingdom of heaven.[56]

Chrysostom is under the firm impression—even as Jesus himself was—that the present may be most effectively served by turning its attention to that which is beyond. The preacher astutely analyzes the difference between the social motivation of the pagan world and that of the Christian. He finds the leverage of every true Christian's life in the future; therefore, he exhorts his people to supply a type of present action that the pagan, with his commitment to the temporal world, cannot experience. Happily, the good lives of Christ's followers will become in a truly corporate sense a reflection of the heavenly kingdom. And it is Chrysostom's conviction that, when the outside world sees this Christian life burgeoning in a fashion that is gentle, unenvious, and socially responsible in every degree, the outer society will, itself, be mightily impressed. Was it not Jesus who declared that his followers must, by letting their lights shine, convert others to the way of perfection as it is in the Father? So, too, Chrysostom represents the heathen as saying:

If the Christians are become angels here, what will they be after their departure hence? if where they are strangers they shine so bright, how great will they become when they shall have won their native land!

Perhaps he is somewhat naïve when he concludes:

Thus they too will be reformed, and the word of godliness "will have free course," not less than in the apostles' time. For if they, being twelve,

<hr/>

[56] Hom., XLIII, 7 (Comm. on Matt. XII, 38-39); NPNF, 1st Ser., X, 277-78; R. C. Petry, *No Uncertain Sound* (Philadelphia, 1948), p. 70; J. P. Migne, *Patrologia Graeca*, 57:463-64.

converted entire cities and countries; were we all to become teachers by our careful conduct, imagine how high our cause will be exalted.[57]

If Chrysostom's congregation listened with even a moderate degree of interest, it could not avoid several observations. Obviously, he was calling for a type of missionary action which was thoroughly congruous with the very essence of Christianity itself. Furthermore, he was interpreting that missionary experience as being both an obligation and an opportunity growing, logically, out of the very heart of Christian social life. In keeping with this, he was reintroducing the sequence that Jesus himself established: to find the means to a new solidarity among the faithful which should be capable of changing the character of everyday life, one must seek the power and direction of the eternal kingdom itself.

With a zest and power of persuasiveness that are characteristic of the preacher at his best, Chrysostom solicits a specific commitment to this missionary program on the part of everyone who denominates himself a Christian. He is thoroughly alert to the possibility that some may wish to excuse themselves from such a responsibility on the grounds of familial duties. They may interpret him as calling for a type of action—both individual and social—that only the unmarried or otherwise detached person could hope to accomplish. Chrysostom hastens to correct any such misimpression. There is no person who can avoid the clear mandate to serve people in some capacity. The preacher makes no demand that his hearers desert the accustomed lanes of everyday routine; he asks only that they pursue their legitimate activity in the way of Christian virtues. Such virtues will indeed be the means of lighting the candle that shall shine before the whole world.

Whatever the Christian's capacity and opportunities may be; whatever his age, sex, or vocation; whether he be free or unfree as the temporal world regards him; he can, in any case, transmit the socializing power from above to the world of which he is a part. Such a responsible opportunity can be denied by no one who truly loves the Lord Jesus.[58]

Chrysostom shares the ever-continuing and passionate interest in the Dominical prayer.[59] The sermon which he bases upon it is, like so many of his works, filled with a deep concern for his fellow man regarded in the most far-reaching fashion. When one addresses him-

[57] NPNF, 1st Ser., X, 277-78. Used by permission of the publishers.
[58] *Ibid.,* p. 278.
[59] Hom., XIX, 6-7 (Matt. 6:1 ff.) ; NPNF, 1st Ser., X, 134-35.

self in prayer to the Father in heaven, he is not relegating God to the heavens as if he were limited or imprisoned there. Rather is he withdrawing the one who prays from earthly things below to the concerns of Divinity above.

Once more Chrysostom is turning his gaze to that future which lies beyond time; and to the very heart of that future as the source of all-empowering action in the world of men. Following the Christ, one prays not to a Father who can be arrogated to oneself, but to the common Father of all those who look to him. By this very token, all those who supplicate God, their common Father, become deeply involved in the welfare of all those who have such paternity. Such a sweeping dedication can mean that the worshiper will find himself cleansed of invidious hatred, the sense of superiority, and all the arrogance that the jealous-hearted are prone to exhibit. All of those praying in the Father's name are placed anew in the circle of his kindness and love. Thus, the corporateness which comes down from the heavenly Fatherhood is transmitted in each day's association to all those with whom the Christian comes in contact. Each man, whether he be subject, ruler, soldier, philosopher, or barbarian, shares in the one true nobility which common sonship of the one eternal Father gives.

Having such a Father in heaven inevitably carries with it the sense of being lifted up from purely earthly things to the affairs of heaven. But it also remands each of the faithful to the common task of showing his heavenly nobility within the commonplace world. One cannot be a son of the eternal Father without seeking to hallow his name. And such glorification cannot be better rendered than through the exemplary command which Christ himself enjoined. "Let your light so shine before men, that they may see your good works, and glorify your Father which is in heaven" is the logical assumption of those who recognize their place in the eternal society. Such a course of action inevitably fosters the children's part in the kingdom which God himself is to bring.[60]

For to pray "Thy kingdom come" befits one who calls himself a child of God. Such a one is "not to be rivetted to things that are seen, neither to account things present some great matter; but to hasten unto our Father, and to long for the things to come. And this springs out of the good conscience and a soul set free from things that are on earth." But this is by no means to argue that one is relieved of the

[60] *Loc. cit.*

necessity of ministering to the people and with the things that are on earth. This life is not to receive more than its due. It will receive that which is to be given it if one properly understands how it may best be redeemed in the light of the eternally perfect, future society.

Actually, one must never forget the third petition of the Lord's Prayer: "Thy will be done in earth, as it is in heaven." Only as we long for the things to come and hasten toward the kingdom that shall be, will we be earnest in

showing forth the same conversation as those above. For ye must long, saith He, for heaven, and the things in heaven; however, even before heaven, He hath bidden us make the earth a heaven and do and say all things, even while we are continuing in it, as having our conversation there; insomuch as these too should be objects of our prayer to the Lord.[61]

What stronger impulsion for social action can be found than this which Chrysostom so patently derives from the power-giving society of the kingdom? He sees no reason why the truly Christian body of Christ is to be kept from heaven, even while it lingers here below. Of course, no complete consummation is thought to be possible before the kingdom fully comes; "but it is possible even while abiding here, to do all, as though already placed on high." From such a motivation, so personalizing in its corporate environment, there must ensue a fully rounded impact on the world of mankind that lives in the temporal sphere. The order of God as it will be some day fully experienced, and as it is already being reflected in the Christian body, cannot fail to give a new exterior to the present order of life.[62]

In a real sense, such an anchorage in the world beyond will give stability and firmness to the present life in all those phases where continuity with the future is possible. It may truly be said, furthermore, that in this respect "there will be no difference between things below and above, separated as they are in nature; the earth exhibiting to us another set of angels." Such fulsome language doubtless has the same focus as Paul's own admonition to be transformed by things above rather than to be conformed to things below. The effect of such a view upon the world as it is, cannot fail of a large measure of transformation in the light of what must and shall be.

So it was that Chrysostom found inspiration for present social

[61] *Loc. cit.* Used by permission of the publishers.
[62] X, 135.

ministrations as he awaited the Last Days of the world. Seizing upon the Master's own reminder, he called upon his people to make ready now, by acts of kindness to the least of men, for a favorable verdict in the Last Judgment. It is in keeping with Chrysostom's whole emphasis that he should give homiletic expression to the terms upon which men should be approvingly accepted or irrevocably rejected by Christ in the evening of the world. In great cities such as those where Chrysostom preached, ample opportunity was at hand every day for the authentic Christian to befriend the needy. It must have brought Matthew 25 sharply home to John of Antioch's hearers to be told that what Christ demanded of his followers in his name was not some impossibly heroic episode but a truly selfless ministry of simple, unassuming character.[63] They were admonished to remember that, in the Judgment Day, Christ would make his decision, not upon the basis of what his disciples had done to or for him immediately, but in the light of the would-be follower's response to the humblest who asked in His name. Upon some thoroughly unostentatious action taken almost unconsciously might depend one's inclusion in the house of the Lord and the kingdom of the eternal. Few have told better than Chrysostom the way that should lead to such endless delight in the company of Christ, the Father, and all his saints.

[63] Hom. LXXIX, 1-2 (Matt. 25:31-41) ; NPNF, 1st Ser., X, 474-77.

CHAPTER V

The Response of Temporal Society
to the Eternal Kingdom
3. From the Outset of the Middle Ages
Through Bernard of Cluny

IT WILL PERHAPS BE PROFITABLE TO ANALYZE MORE AT LENGTH THE constituent elements which, growing out of the ancient Christian culture, entered into the fabric of medieval social thought. There is, at the outset, the inevitable consideration of two sharply differentiated orders of life. No medieval man would deny his consciousness of one world in which he lived and another in which he sought ultimate citizenship. Quite naturally, the present order of existence figured more prominently in his daily calculations. Untrained and thoroughly unsophisticated as most men and women of the period were, they speculated with but limited range upon a world wholly beyond them.

This is not to say, however, that they denied the reality of that which was to have its clearer manifestation in the future. Their working philosophy took into consideration, not only the possibility, but also the overmastering probability, of such a world. Furthermore, they heard on every hand the Church's insistence that the less visible of their two worlds was the more real and the more completely social. Eschewing any highly involved arguments, the priest emphasized the primary significance of the heavenly society.

When one goes beyond the premises just laid down, he finds certain other factors which are very much in the minds of medieval thinkers. One of these stresses the relationship sustained between neighborly associations of the known world and the even more socializing activities of a future community. Jesus had declared that the society yet to be was the final determinant in the conduct of the present life. He depicted this with a starkness that seemed almost savage to the average churchman of the Middle Ages. Consequently, at quite a number of points, the typical medieval leader modified the rigidities of Christ's social and individual demands. Perhaps the net effect of all this was to make less immediate and less sweeping the claims of the eternal on the temporal society. It would be erroneous, however, to think that the result was a complete removal of the prior claims made by the heavenly kingdom on the earthly association. As a matter of historical record, the greatest medieval leaders continued to draw in large degree upon the social motivation of the impinging future for guidance in the direction of present-day conduct.[1]

Typically enough, the strongest emphasis upon the new world took the form of exhortations to the faithful to be ready for the fateful day of Judgment. Placing stress in this fashion upon the dividing line of history and eternity had the effect of drawing people's attention to two different social orders. In this fashion, the average medieval man was called upon to subject the corporate activities of his present world to the judicial scrutiny of God and Christ, who would determine the place of each soul in the kingdom of heaven.

When the Judgment came, it would be an unequivocally social experience. Unlike the individual judgment, which came to each person at the time of his physical death, this great occasion would call upon all human beings created since the beginning of time to stand together for a final examination.[2] The divine sentence would give some individuals incorporation in the blessed society; it would condemn others to the everlastingly miserable companionship of evil beings. Not only would the process of judgment involve all mankind; it would be carried out by groups of individuals held worthy of being associated with Christ in the passing of sentence upon others. When the decision had finally been arrived at, individuals would be sharply divided into corporations of those hopelessly evil and those gloriously redeemed.

The future, designed from the beginning of the world for those who were to reign with God, was definitely cast in terms of a society. In fact, it would constitute the quintessence of social experience. The very difficulty with which medieval writers labored their descriptions of its ineffable joys is largely occasioned by their attempt to

---

[1] See representative documentation of this thesis in previous publications by the author such as *Francis of Assisi: Apostle of Poverty* (Durham, 1941), Chap. V, and "Medieval Eschatology and St. Francis of Assisi," *Church History*, IX, (1940), 54-70. Consult also E. Wadstein, *Die eschatologische Ideengruppe* (Leipzig, 1896).

[2] *Petri Lombardi, Libri IV Sententiarum* (Quaracchi, 1916), II, 994 ff.; Liber IV, Dist. XLIII, cap. 1, ff.; cf. "De judicio particulari" and "De judicio universali," pp. 470 ff. and 501 ff., in Diekamp, *Theologiae Dogmaticae Manuale*, IV.

analyze the unimaginable. Social experience on the new plane of living would so far outstrip any known kind of companionship as to dwarf all powers of expression with regard to it. The medieval preacher was always exhorting his parishioner to realize that the only possibility of living in the fullest fellowship of the future is to make ready for such companionship insofar as one is able in the present. The manner in which the medieval priest suggested this to his people was often gravely different from the parables by which Jesus had sought to inculcate the great truth. Jesus' teachings were definitely, and sometimes sadly, adapted, modified, and even distorted. That they continued to exercise an unmistakable influence was a real tribute to the intensity and uncompromising quality of the originals.[3]

The major social fact for the early and medieval church is this: No terrestrial sociality has meaning apart from the corporate finality of the coming Judgment, and from the new society that is inaugurated with it. All natural societies are held to be secondary and amenable to the dictates of the supernatural kingdom. The cogency of this argument as it is expressed throughout pre-Reformation times is patent.

Seen in medieval perspective, the Last Days will precipitate a shift from one order of life to another; but the pertinence of the coming catastrophe is that individuals and human society as a whole must now prepare for the corporate judgment which shall usher in the invincible community of heaven. This may not, in the Middle Ages, result in the complete equalization of demands laid upon all individuals. It may not affect primarily the classes and strata of society as they were then organized. But it does bring natural society under the dictates of supernatural community.[4] One may enumerate at length such individuals as Francis of Assisi, Innocent III, Roger Bacon, Catherine of Siena, and others who would not think of attacking the existing social organization but who would certainly summon it to the bar of kingdom judgment. They would surely say that one cannot enter the beloved community, hereafter, without

[3] Reflections of this are easily discernible in H. R. Patch, *The Other World According to Descriptions in Medieval Literature* (Cambridge, Mass., 1950) and in St. John D. Seymour, *Irish Visions of the Other World: A Contribution to the Study of Mediaeval Visions* (London, 1930). Cf. Taubes, *Abendlandische Eschatologie*, especially Chaps. II and III.

[4] E. Troeltsch, *The Social Teaching of the Christian Churches*, translated by O. Wyon (New York, 1931), I, 303-4; O. Schilling, *Die Staats-u. Soziallehre des Heiligen Thomas von Aquin* (Munich, 1930).

taking a specific part in the process of social amelioration here and now. One may justly criticize the medieval neglect of adequate social programs for world betterment; one cannot safely ignore their developing consciousness of social ultimacy. The manifest failure of their social thought to seek and achieve a fundamental transformation of Christendom can best be analyzed following a more detailed interpretation of typical source literature.

Augustine is, of course, distinguished for his contribution to Christian social thought in eschatological setting. He penned one of his greatest works to depict the characteristics of "the two cities." As he himself declared in *The City of God* and in his later *Retractations,* he believed in the complete ultimacy of one city only—the City of God.[5] However, in this human scene, men were constantly frustrated by their inability to distinguish between the two cities, one of God and the other of the Devil. These would remain comingled in part until the all-revealing Day of Judgment.

The Bishop of Hippo pointed out to his people the necessity of watching for distinguishing signs. In so doing he called upon them to build their lives according to the standards of the ultimate rather than those of the temporary world order. He made clear his own devotion to the City of God. However much the predestined community during its pilgrimage on earth might be mixed with the citizens of another community, it had its final destiny in the kingdom beyond. Augustine admonished all men to follow the behests of the ultimate city as it made its demands upon them in the temporal realm.[6]

There are two loves, he pointed out, just as there are two cities. Of these, one is holy and the other unholy, or worldly. One is social, the other private. One concerns itself with the common utility and the requirements of fraternity; the other considers the common life

---

[5] Augustine's characteristic attitude to the two orders is found in the *Retractationes* as in the *De Civitate Dei,* itself, both edited in the *Corpus Scriptorum ecclesiasticorum latinorum* (CSEL), Vols. XXXVI and XL (Pars 1 and 2). For the *De Genesi ad Litteram,* XI, vx, 2, see CSEL, XVII, Pars 1, pp. 347-48. Note particularly *De Civ. Dei,* XI, 1, XIX 28, 1, 4, XXII, 30. Cf. *Enarratio in Ps.* LXIV, 2, MPL XXXVI, 773. Consult Gilson, *Introduction à l'étude de Saint Augustin,* pp. 225 ff.; Altaner, *Patrologie,* pp. 364 ff. Cf. H. Rondet *et al., Études Augustiniennes* (Paris, 1953), pp. 99-160.

[6] *Enarratio in Ps.* LI, 6; MPL 36:603-4; *In Ioannis evangelium,* Tract. XXVII, 11; MPL 35: 1621. Admirable source selections on "Jerusalem and Babylon" are available in E. Przywara, *An Augustine Synthesis,* pp. 265 ff. Cf. M. Pontet, *L' exégèse de S. Augustin prédicateur* (Paris, 1944), pp. 447-553.

only as it gives opportunity for domination. One city is tranquil, the other turbulent. One is pacific, the other seditious.[7]

In all of these parallels, Augustine is but trying to focus the disparity between the two social groupings as they become gradually if vaguely apparent to the Christian. However they may overlap, temporally, these societies are ultimately to be separated. One will proceed to a conjunction with the good angels in the kingdom of God. The other will find its partnership with evil angels in eternal fire.

Here, as in related writings, Augustine implies that the only city that shall have full, lasting sociality is God's own. Now, in order to achieve this ultimate community with the blessed, one must place his life in the keeping of those standards and ideals which grow out of that ultimate society. Augustine believes that the kingdom of God in its earthly phase must respond to the eternal kingdom as it shall finally be realized. By implication, at least, those who observe the life which is holy, social, devoted to the common utility, tranquil, and pacific, are following, in the temporal society, the solicitations of the ultimate kingdom. Continuing, Augustine observes that the City of God, even on earth, requires the unselfish consideration of fellow men; it does not tolerate social exploitation. Such ruling of neighbors as is required is directed to their good, not to selfish overlordship. Good and not evil, and justice rather than injustice, are the desired ends in the service of which the pilgrim city moves to its eternal homeland.[8]

No one was more aware than Augustine of the powerful motivation for the temporal world that was provided in the character of God's completed city. He was disinclined to leave the eternal city in the future. He declared repeatedly that the best means by which the present may be transformed is a dedication to the City of God as it will one day be, in heaven. Actually, the double character of the twofold society on earth would one day be clarified. When the Judgment Day should dawn, men would clearly see the distinguishing qualities of each society and depart into their appropriate realms of bliss or woe. One society, and the one only, would be preserved in full communality—that one which should know full membership in the body of Christ and his saints.[9]

Augustine was well known for his passionate devotion to the ideal

[7] *De Genesi ad Litteram*, XI, XV, 20; CSEL, XVIII, Pars 1; pp. 437-38; Przywara, *op. cit.*, p. 266.

[8] *Loc. cit.*

[9] *De Civ. Dei*, XV, 1, 2, 4; XI, 1; XXII, 30.

and practice of peace. He derived this from the pattern of eternal order, which he then interpreted in terms of its effect upon the existing habits of mankind. Although he was quick to point out the major discrepancies between the consummate life of peace in the hereafter and the very weak approximation to it found on earth, he did not fail to utilize the motivating power that came from the eternal to the temporal. Thus he started with simple examples of peace found within the human soul and proceeded to wider areas of civic harmony. He recognized that ultimate peace must be reserved for heaven. Such vitality and diversity as he attributed to pacific life within man and among men, he derived from the ultimate powers of the kingdom of God. And in the pursuance of better Christian living, possible on this earth, he directed human minds toward the fulfillment of their most cherished ideals in the celestial company.

In the treatment of peace found in his classic work *The City of God* he discusses, first of all, the peace that is found within the body. It comes, he says, from the well-ordered composition of the parts. That peace which is experienced within the rational being is brought about by the well-ordered repose of the appetites. Thus ideas and actions must be in good accord if one is to live the life of reason. When soul and body are brought together in wholesome relationship, an animated spirit results. Such peace as may be found existing between mortal man and his God proceeds from well-ordered obedience and faith under the rule of eternal law. Men know peace among themselves only when their hearts are united in a life of order. Those of a common household live at peace when each respects his rank and function in relation to that of others. The state can experience true peace only when its citizens are united in a common bond by reason of which each commands or obeys as befits his station. The peace of the celestial city, in its turn, consists in that joyous mutuality of the blessed with God and with one another, wherein the most perfectly ordered intimacy of united hearts is perpetuated. Thus universal peace is the tranquillity of order. But order, itself, is possible only when there is assigned to each component member the function which it should discharge in relation to others both like and different from itself.[10]

In the rather extended treatment of his ideal, which, of course, he hopes to find actualized to a large degree in human society, Augustine makes numerous digressions which do not concern us here.

[10] *Ibid.,* XIX, 13.

But his conclusions are of fundamental significance. He does not anticipate that man will give expression, on this earth, to a life of social perfection. But he does believe that present society should move toward a realization of that order which is already being revealed through the overcoming kingdom of the future. As a result the mortal who makes best possible use of opportunities given now will have even greater ones in the future. He will enter into the peace of immortality; he will come to know the glory and the honors which are in keeping with this peace. These he will enjoy in heaven's shared felicity. Those, on the other hand, who have badly used their earthly resources will not only have squandered them here, but will also have deprived themselves of those indescribable benefits which belong to eternal comradeship.

Augustine feels keenly the wide disparity between everyday peace as it may be known among fallible men and the perfected concord of heaven. He reserves the use of the term in its widest connotation for the description of celestial order. But he continues, nevertheless, to press for an earthly approximation in Christian mutuality of the balanced fruition of eternity. This has the result of laying upon temporal society the impress of ideals and the standards of action which are born out of a world beyond. True, like St. Paul, St. Augustine may permit social alleviations that fit all too loosely within the absolutism of Jesus; but, like Paul also, he never completely forgets that the Christian is obligated in the present life to a transformation from above rather than to an accommodation from below. Christians build, even while on earth, upon the foundations that are heavenly. The individual, together with his group, must respond to an order transcending the one in which he now lives. Augustine is never happier than when he is calling temporal society to make its Christian response to the eternal world—from which its life comes and to which it must return. After all, the purpose of God in begetting man from within a primal unity was to prepare him for a part in an everlasting community.[11]

A sermon often attributed to Augustine is a further delineation of representative views.[12] The occasion is one of dedicating a church,

[11] *Ibid.,* XII, 27; XIX, 13; Przywara, *op. cit.,* pp. 211 ff.
[12] "On the Dedication of a Church (II)": Sermon CCCXXXVII. On the Saints, MPL 38: 1475-78. Translated in R. C. Petry, *No Uncertain Sound* (Philadelphia, 1948), 14:90-94. For the corpus of Augustine's Sermons, see D. G. Morin, "Sancti Augustini Sermones Post Maurinos Reperti," in *Miscellanea Agostiniana: Testi E. Studi* (Roma, 1930), I; A. Kunzelmann, "*Die Chronologie der Sermones des Hl.*

with proper cognizance of both its physical and its spiritual attributes. Building a church constitutes a good work which is to be appreciated in terms of the faith and charity of those who have contributed to the construction. But the pastor reminds his people of something even more important than establishing a house of worship: namely, the building of that great church which is to be consummated in heaven, within the range of things spiritual, and beyond the mutability of material joys and limitations.

To this latter concern the preacher more specifically addresses himself. It is appropriate to prize the goods of earth and time; one needs all this to be alert to those internal buildings, raised only with the aid of the divine hand. God is certainly not unmindful of the good services performed by his faithful in the erection of spatial dwellings. Even more does he assist them in becoming a part, themselves, of his eternal dwelling place. He stands ready to make possible their entrance into the construction of his temple where, through faith, hope, and charity, they will become living stones. More literally, in the process of thus becoming such living stones, they will be formed by faith, established by hope, and united by the bonds of charity.

It was in order to construct this edifice that the Apostle Paul, that wise architect, proposed as the foundation, Jesus Christ himself. Here was the stone, sovereign and angular, of which St. Peter had spoken: the angular stone rejected of men but chosen and honored of God. The exhorter reminds his hearers that in joining themselves to this stone they find peace; in supporting themselves upon it they find stability. It is at once the *fundamental* stone because it serves as the rule of life, and it is the *angular* stone because it unites his followers. Building his house on such a foundation, man may feel himself prepared to face with all security every temptation in the world. Nothing can move or destroy him.

Once more reverting to his comparison between the earthly and the heavenly structure, the homilist reminds his people that just as this visible house has been built to unite them externally, so the edifice which is none other than themselves is constructed in order that God may inhabit it spiritually. Did not the Apostle say: "For the temple of God is holy, which temple ye are"? Thus, the faithful construct a temple externally with earthly materials; but they raise an interior temple by means of holy lives. This temple now to be dedi-

---

Augustinus" in *Miscellanea Agostiniana*, II, 417-520. Cf. Altaner, *Patrologie*, p. 383, for later literature; also Steidle, *Patrologia*, p. 180. See Pontet, *op. cit.*

cated—the one made in time and with earthly materials—comes in the present. The second one will find its dedication at the end of the ages when earthly bodies shall have been made incorruptible and crowned with immortality. Men can well afford to put into such a building, regardless of all the hardships and sufferings that it may entail, every effort looking toward the eternal joy. In the end, God will inhabit the spiritual dwelling in the very midst of the saints. There will come a time when in full joyousness the Lord will say: "Come, ye blessed of my Father, inherit the kingdom prepared for you from the foundation of the world." No human tongue is capable of describing the transports of joy and the certain tranquillity that will then characterize blessed men in the community of life with the heavenly Father. It is, of course, the desire of all Christians to inhabit this dwelling place. In fact, those who come into God's house do, thereby, themselves become the house of God. As the Psalmist had suggested, God inhabits his own and they are of themselves his dwelling. The full vision of his face in complete companionship with him and all his children is the goal of their present pilgrimage.

Having laid down in the first three divisions of his sermon the manner in which the future glory of the heavenly associations calls forth present unity and reciprocity of life, the preacher now moves more directly to the central thesis of his homily. In a brief but eloquent exposition of Colossians 3, he calls upon those who would be united in the celestial brotherhood to build their foundations in heaven. "Courage then, my brethren," he says; "if you would be raised with Jesus Christ, seek the things of heaven, where he is seated at the right hand of God; have a taste for the things above and not for those here below."

The homilist reminds us that it is in the heavens that Jesus Christ, our foundation, has been placed. For this cause we orient our dwelling in his direction. Building earthly habitations, in which the materials tend always to descend by virtue of their own weight, men habitually place the foundations below. For us, on the contrary, who are building for a spiritual world, the foundation stone is placed above, in order to attract us toward it by the weight of charity. We need to remember all the more, therefore, to work out our salvation with fear and trembling. For it is God himself who, by his own will, works in us the will to accomplish.

The preacher admonishes us, therefore, to be about our tasks. Since we are established in Christ as living stones which are to enter into the building of God's own temple, we can do no less. Before we can become so, we must stand ready to go through whatever process of quarrying and polishing that life and its privations may entail. It is only thus that we may be properly prepared, with the aid of good works, to merit the joyousness of eternal repose in an intimate companionship with the angels.

The author realizes, and strives to bring the realization to his hearers, also, that the physical dwelling which we now construct will not remain; our bodies, with the aid of which we raise temporal structures, are themselves mortal. But we go to a house which God has built—one not made with human hands, eternal in heaven. And it is there that, by a process of the divine transformation, we shall emerge from the Resurrection with bodies celestial and forever enduring. Even now, however, as we see Him indirectly, and as we move toward that eternal society, we must employ good works which are not themselves eternal but which lead us to that everlasting life. The very building of the physical edifice now being completed is such a work. In the process, however, of exemplifying temporal good works, we are on the way to obtaining the eternal recompense. As we lay down foundations within our hearts, built as it were on the teachings of the apostles and the prophets, we are already helping to raise the unassailable walls of the future habitation.[13]

Benedict of Nursia (d. 542), the cenobitic legislator of the West, does not labor the theological concept of the ultimate kingdom. But the prologue, like the conclusion, of his Rule, makes it clear that true mutuality is indispensable to kingdom entrance. The body of his work is largely given over to a flexible, yet inspiring, interpretation of the manner in which worship of the Divine conduces to Christian reciprocity in a renunciatory fraternity. Benedict could not possibly know of the larger repercussions in social life that his rule was to engender in later centuries. There is little reason to believe that he even thought of himself as the legislator for an order. But in him, as in Basil, a dedication to ultimates had its sure eventuation in widespread social influence.[14]

Gregory the Great (d. 604) was an ardent admirer of St. Benedict. He paid his filial regard, not only in the second book of the *Dia-*

---

[13] NUS, 14:93-94.

[14] *Regula*, Prol. et concl.; on the rule and its various editions see the definitive work of Don P. Schmitz, *Histoire de l'ordre de Saint-Benoît* (2nd ed., Maredsous, 1948), I, 15-40, and U. Berlière, *L'ordre monastique des origines au XII* siècle* (Paris, 1924), pp. 36 ff.

logues and in the establishment of monasteries after the Benedictine plan, but also in the monastic mission to the English.

Whatever else one may say about the highly credulous Pope, we must admit that Gregory's own conception of social responsibility is keenly alive. Worn down by heavy responsibilities on every side and convinced that the end is near, he does not waver in his service to the people around him. He is another striking evidence that a sense of impending judgment need not paralyze temporal effort. In fact, one discovers in his commentaries on Kings, his *Moralia*, and in his homilies on the Gospels how much his expectation of the Last Days heightens his social responsiveness to the present. The Lombards threaten Rome itself; plagues descend upon the populace; rivers overrun their banks. The wrath of nature seems to portend the vengeance of the great Judge. And Gregory is too human not to voice his near-despair. But he goes on his wonted way of routine service to every cause that demands his attention. Like the good bishop and pastor that his *Pastoral Rule* commends, he is the embodiment of ministry to the specific requirements of innumerable people. Though cast down, he is yet lifted up to the vision of the eternal city. And, like Basil and Benedict, he lifts his flock with him.[15]

The Abbot Columban (d. *ca.* 615) was a stern Irish missionary and monastic lawgiver. In a truly remarkable document addressed as a letter to Pope Boniface IV, he makes the impending end of the world and the beginning of a new cosmic order the occasion for a sweeping exhortation.[16] He beseeches the Holy Father to watch over his flock in the perilous times that now precede the Last Day. His constant refrain is vigilance: "Vigilance, I say, papa, vigilance; and again I say be vigilant." He lays upon the Pontiff his own mantle of sober responsibility for souls, without whose care salvation itself may be lost.

[15] See the *Morals* in the translation of Charles Marrott in the edition of J. H. Parker (Oxford, 1844) ; also *Morales sur Job, livres 1 and 2* (Sources chrétiennes, Paris, 1952). The *Liber Regulae pastoralis* (MPL 77:9-128) is translated by J. Barmby in NPNF, 2nd Ser., XII (2nd part), 2 ff. Consult his *In primum regum expos.*, MPL 79:288-98. A useful translation of the *Dialogues* is that of O. J. Zimmermann and B. R. Avery, *Life and Miracles of St. Benedict* (Collegeville, Minn., 1949). Cf. Schmitz, *Histoire*, I, 41 ff. Gregory's balancing of the active and contemplative life is admirably translated in passages selected by Dom C. Butler, *Western Mysticism* (2nd ed., London, 1951), especially pp. 176-85.

[16] Ep. 5, MPL 80:276-77. Cf. the literature cited in M. Manitius, *Geschichte der lateinischen Literatur des Mittelalters* (Munich, 1911), I, 181 ff. See, further, the references in G. K. Anderson, *The Literature of the Anglo-Saxons* (Princeton, 1940), p. 242; cf. L. Gougaud, *Gaelic Pioneers of Christianity* (Dublin, 1923).

The Pope should know that it is his duty to declare the truth, however unpalatable, in the face of whatever mendacity he may encounter. Let no wiles of evil men deter him from exercising his pastoral function in this grievous time. Let him remember that the blood of the saints will be required at the hands of the pastor. How can he be less than a true preacher of the word and an unremittingly vigilant pastor of the flock when so much is at stake? In pressing home his point the Abbot fills his columns with references to the writings of Paul, the Apocalypse, and other scriptures of the Old and New Testaments. All point alike to the impending Great Day. All call for wariness and responsible ministry on the part of the shepherd to the flock committed to his care. The language with which Columban calls upon Boniface to arise and prepare for the final accounting of the world has a decidedly Pauline flavor.

The Venerable Bede (d. 735) was a benediction to his own day as he has been a glory in the history of the Church. His loving service to it was such that his memory has been preserved in the ritual itself. Firmly imbedded in the Breviary for All Saints is a sizable portion of the sermon for that occasion still generally attributed to him.[17] This remarkable homily has pertinence for the problem of eschatology in relation to social thought and life. Not only does it place emphasis upon the Church as the supremely eschatological institution which works among men; but it also emphasizes the drawing power of the eternal world upon the social experience of the faithful. It is this latter emphasis that is of immediate and most practical concern. In speaking to faithful Christians on the occasion of All Saints he holds up before their eyes the great reward of heavenly companionship. Much of his sermon is concerned with delineating the character and making warmly personal the fellowship appeal which emanates from that experience of glory. The obvious motivation for good life among his fellows in the world below is the desire to join the citizenship which is in heaven:

Now, therefore, brethren, let us enter the way of life; let us return to the celestial city, in which we are citizens, enrolled and inscribed. . . . Let us consider, therefore, the felicity of that heavenly habitation, in so

[17] See the "Breviarium in Festo Omnium Sanctorum": Die, Nov. 2; cf. J. M. Neale, *Mediaeval Preachers and Mediaeval Preaching* (London, 1856), pp. 2-9. Cf. Bede's *Opera Omnia*, ed. J. A. Giles, in the *Patres ecclesiae Anglicanae* (London, 1843), V. (Homiliae) LXX; NUS 17:108-9. On Bede's career and significance see E. S. Duckett, *Anglo-Saxon Saints and Scholars* (New York, 1947), pp. 217-36; Anderson, *op. cit.*, pp. 225 ff., and notes, pp. 248 ff.

far as it is possible to consider it: for to speak the truth, no words of man are sufficient to comprehend it.[18]

The labors of earth must give rise to a place in the companionship of heaven. Perhaps the kingdom of heaven does suffer violence. One may make his way in, as it were, by force, without winning the disapproval of the Father. This is possible, however, only if one gives rise in the present world to such characteristics as are those of the heavenly community. With those having gone on who now await a glad reunion, the faithful on earth may well press forward to their portions in the eternal city. The saints, having completed their pilgrimage to their country, have left easily discernible footsteps; those who will follow in them may come also to their society.

Another sermon attributed to Bede bears close resemblance to the one on All Saints.[19] For him there is no time like the present for making ready to receive the future. He loves to cite the exhortation of Jesus that all those who would be his followers must ever be ready to join him in his eternal kingdom. The only way to be ready for the great Judgment event is to live always in watchfulness and utter probity of life. When Christ comes to divide the sheep from the goats; when he places the nations over against each other in terms of righteousness or wickedness; then shall he announce not only his decision but the basis of his final assessment. And Bede knows no better word than Christ's own which says: "Verily I say unto you, Inasmuch as ye have done it unto one of the least of these my brethren, ye have done it unto me."

Therefore, my brethren, I beseech you, that they who are in the habit of good works would persevere in every good work; and that they who are evil would amend themselves quickly, before sudden death come upon them. *While therefore we have time, let us do good to all men,* and let us leave off doing ill, that we may attain to eternal life.[20]

St. Boniface, Apostle to the Germans (d. 755), is credited with a Sermon "Of Faith and the Works of Love." Even in its present form, it gives an intimate picture of the manner in which the true Christian may relate his heavenly aspirations to his current social actions. Faith, love, and works are treated in terms of the Beatitudes, with their emphasis upon patience, mercy, and peace; as well as in terms

---

[18] Neale, *op. cit.*, p. 4.
[19] "A Sermon for Any Day," Neale, *op. cit.*, pp. 14-16.
[20] *Ibid.*, p. 16.

of loving God and one's neighbor. Boniface tries to produce sound living among his rude hearers by appealing to the laws of heavenly concord:

Teach your children to fear God: in like manner, also, exhort your family, and all your neighbours, to do good works, lest any one should be lost to God through your negligence. . . . Invite those that are in enmity to concord. . . . *Judge thy neighbour righteously.* . . . And the Lord saith that the man shall dwell in His tabernacle—that is, in His kingdom—*who hath not taken reward against the innocent.*[21]

Continuing in this line of education which he hopes will enable his parishioners to follow the heavenly pattern of society, Boniface calls on his people for further fruits of the good life. The burden of his theme seems to be: Seek the Church as the house of prayer. Avoid gossip; give alms; be hospitable to one another. The Lord will surely say in the Judgment, "I was a stranger. . . ." Boniface points out that all those who are in pilgrimage are virtual strangers on earth. Each one can well afford to think of the others in terms of the far land to which they travel. If the Christian is to hear favorable words from the Master on the Last Day, he must visit the sick, minister to widow and orphan; give tithes; fear God and honor the king. He will surely not forget to know the Lord's Prayer by heart, "because in it every necessity of the present and future life is briefly and fully summed up." Of course all Christian men and women will pay proper regard to the fasts and feasts of the Church. They will not disregard the privilege of participation in the body and blood of their Lord. In the sacrament of the altar Christ gives them, ever and anon, the food from heaven which shall sustain them on their way to the promised land.

Continuing, Boniface says: "These, my beloved brethren, are the works of faith, which ought to be observed in common by all Christians; and whosoever will not be a partaker of them in this world, can never be a partaker of the kingdom of God in the world to come." The manner in which the eternal kingdom may be capitalized for social motivation is here aptly demonstrated.

Following hard upon the foregoing materials is a good section on the Judgment and the social joys of heaven which are to follow. At its conclusion the preacher says: "If ye persevere in these works to the end, [He] will also give to you, as to his own children, the eter-

[21] *Ibid.,* pp. 22-27, especially p. 23.

nal and heavenly kingdom, that ye may be, as the Apostle says, *heirs of God and joint heirs with Christ."* [22]

The works of Cynewulf (*fl.* 750) are a literary treasure. They are no less significant because of the theological conceptions which they embody. Nothing that Cynewulf wrote is more effective than his famous work on *The Christ*.[23] And within this remarkable production he gives a high place, indeed, to the consideration of world's end and the kingdom which lies beyond.

The whole context of judgment is an awesomely social one. Deeds and thoughts formerly hidden in the bosom of each, now have their heralding in the presence of all. The closely guarded secrets of the individual—the modest good deeds locked away in the closet of God's faithful and the nefarious schemes hatched in sinful hearts—now become the focus of earth's last convocation of all humankind.

Each token by which those at God's right hand are known to others—and by which they know themselves—to be the chosen of the Lord's eternal city reflects the corporate aspect of life in the present; as it figures, also, the existence that was before and shall be after this life. With dramatic starkness Cynewulf gives his version of Matthew 25; with a heavy stress on fateful deeds and thoughts. The multitude of the pure chosen ones called by Christ himself to be his right hand—as also "the sinful horde on the left hand"—have already made sure their respective places while on earth by way of their attitude to fellow men. To the blessed at his right hand "the high-king of heaven shall say":

Now with friends receive ye the Kingdom of My Father, that was prepared for you in winsomeness before all worlds, blessedness with bliss, bright beauty of home, where ye with well-loved men may see true weal of life, sweet heavenly joy. This have ye merited since joyfully ye received with gracious heart wretched men, the needy of the world; when in My name they humbly craved your pity then did ye grant them help and shelter, unto the hungry bread, clothes to the naked, and those that lay diseased in pain, enthralled of sickness, their souls ye softly stayed with love of heart. All that ye did unto Me what time ye sought

[22] *Ibid.,* pp. 25, 26.
[23] Cf. the edition of C. W. Kennedy, *The Poems of Cynewulf Translated into English Prose* (London, 1910), pp. 190-94; also his *Early Christian Poetry Translated into Alliterative Verse* (New York, 1952), pp. 268 ff. Consult Anderson, *op. cit.,* pp. 123-32, and notes pp. 148-49; M. M. Dubois, *Les éléments latins dans la poésie religieuse de Cynewulf* (Paris, 1943).

them out with kindly love, ever strengthening their souls with comfort. Wherefore in blessedness with My beloved long shall ye reap reward.[24]

Hrabanus Maurus (d. 856) was one of the most learned men of the ninth century.[25] Monk, churchman, and controversialist, he plunged into all the deep-flowing currents of his age. His scholarship is not so much original as recapitulatory. Its emphases, however, are solidly indicative of the prevailing thought of his times. His sermons are not, in the main, highly inspiring, though some of them, like the one entitled "On Baying Against the Moon," are lively broadsides against the more superstitious beliefs of the people. In these homilies, however, particularly the ones on the Easter occasion and the Advent season, he is motivated by a strong eschatological devotion to the inculcation of Christian social virtues.

His commentary on First Thessalonians is especially noteworthy for its interpretation of Christian solidarity on the part of those who await the resurrection and the judgment of the faithful. For him, as for the earlier apostle, eschatological focus and social activity belong in inseparable combination. Christians are not those who sleep like other men when their alertness should be consolidated in preparation for the Last Times. They are, rather, dedicated in anticipation of the coming Judgment to the common utility of their fellows.

Maurus' comments on Chapter 5 are thoroughly oriented in the Pauline doctrine of Christian society and unity as the proper response to eschatological demands. He proceeds after the model of the earlier leader to enjoin meditation and action in the present life suited to the guarantee of corporate blessedness in the future. Rejoicing always in the expectation of the promised happiness, the true followers of Jesus render, not evil for evil, but good to all, in everything. In this work, as in his treatment of Second Thessalonians, Maurus draws heavily from his store of patristic erudition. Even though his thought is not characterized by scintillating innovations, his emphasis upon the response of the temporal society to the eternal kingdom is effectively implemented.[26]

Wulfstan, next in rank as an early preacher to the eminence of Aelfric, became Bishop of Lincoln around 1001 and later served as

[24] Kennedy, *Poems*, pp. 193-94. Used by permission of the publishers, Routledge & Kegan Paul, Ltd.
[25] See Manitius, *Geschichte*, I, 288-302; E. S. Duckett, *Alcuin Friend of Charlemagne* (New York, 1951), pp. 311-12; see the *De clericorum institutione* (MPL 107) discussed by Manitius, *Geschichte* I, 296 ff.; cf. the *Sermones*, MPL 110.
[26] MPL 112:555-60 ff.; Com. on I Thess. 4:9 and 5.

Archbishop of York. His death in 1023 ended a fruitful ministry.[27] One of his homilies is occasioned by the incursion of the Danes about 1014. He opens his address with the words: "Dearly beloved, understand the truth: this world is in haste, and drawing nigh the end." Convinced as he is that the sad state of affairs now plaguing Britain is one of the signs of antichrist, he is concerned to notice how his people play into these evil hands. But this circumstance is not of recent origin. For years the Devil has had all too easy a time with those who show little faith toward one another, however trustingly they may speak. Injustices are rife, with few who care enough, and think enough, to seek a remedy. The preacher knows that national sin is all too prevalent; and to that corporate iniquity he traces the unhappy state now being suffered. With homiletic fire and directness, he declares that any relief that comes must be better deserved at God's hands than anything yet seen. Wulfstan is sufficiently great to tell his people without qualification that their misery is justly deserved and the cure derivable only from God by way of their own improved actions.

With a striking effectiveness that shows how international and timeless is the appreciation of temporal response to divine community, Wulfstan continues in his admonitory way. Reminiscent of Salvian, he implies that crimes not to be tolerated among the heathen have here been perpetrated in a Christian land. Among the pagans nothing brought for idle sacrifice can be diverted to selfish uses. The English, however, despoil both "the inward and the outward of God's house." All too brusque for acceptable preaching is the minister's analysis of causes and cures. Almost modern is his catalogue of the social sins that are rampant. God's laws decline. The laws of the nation also lapse. Sanctuaries deteriorate. The poor and the defenseless are victimized as a customary procedure. Justice is distorted. Free men's rights are violently torn away as are also those of even less fortunate beings. In short, God's statutes are hated and the ways of instruction sneered at. With unerring finger the preacher places the blame and assesses the loss, which "will be common to all this nation, unless God save us."

How many modern preachers would dare indict their people with the phrases that follow? Evidently the attacks of the Danes are held to be petty in comparison with the internecine malice and depravity of the English themselves. The rights of kin for the protec-

---

[27] See K. Jost, *Wulfstanstudien* (Berne, 1950), and Anderson, *op. cit.,* pp. 340 ff., notes pp. 353 ff.

tion by those of their own blood are forsworn. Neighbors are roughly used. The faith toward God and man is sadly breached. The acme of all disloyalty comes in a man's betraying the soul of his lord— in plotting against his very life. Not only kings and lords, but sponsors and godchildren, also, have been slain throughout the nation. Holy places, far from being honored as sanctuaries of refuge, are torn down in the process of obliterating those who fly within. Christian folk have been sold into slavery with what appears to be customary alacrity. Certainly God records all this against the country.

Can it actually be that Wulfstan is speaking literally when he excoriates the sale of children by parents for a price? The minister warms to his subject with the insistence that even worse things afflict the nation still. This being the case, it is certainly not strange to find a thrall escaping from his lord and seeking refuge from Christendom among the Danes. This may involve yet more complicated sins if the escaped thrall later fights against his erstwhile friends.

No wonder that the affairs of state go so badly and that the English are starved for victory. Sea robbers have become so boldly successful that they can take on English Christians at the ratio of ten to one— not because the pirates' hearts are so pure, but because the English are so full of sins and rightly deserted by God. Things have become so bad that the once proud Englishman has to stand in humiliating impotence while his wife or daughter is violated before his very eyes. Plainly God's wrath is at work upon those who so richly deserve it. Every sin in the social category is described by Wulfstan, who finds in these the real cause of English decline. In fact, the distinctive quality of the entire sermon is the sense of communality that runs through it and the inflexible insistence that corporate unrighteousness spells corporate doom. People now take delight in boasting of evil deeds. They are ashamed of such virtues as may crop up in them unawares.

The time is all too short in which to seek salvation. But each and all should do what is possible. Loving God and his laws, and keeping the promises of baptism both in word and work, are still not impossible. How completely Wulfstan draws upon the empowering character of socializing eschatology for reform in his own depraved society is clearly revealed in his closing words:

Let us often meditate upon the Great Judgment whither we are all bound, and save ourselves with zeal from the raging fire of hell-torment, and secure for ourselves the glory and gladness which God has prepared for such as work His will upon earth. May God help us. Amen.[28]

One of the starkest representations of social decay, approaching world's end, and impending judgment to be found in medieval literature is that advanced by Bernard of Morval, who wrote about A.D. 1150, during the period of Peter the Venerable, his abbot at Cluny, 1122-55.[29]

Bernard's major work, *De Contemptu Mundi*, lay for more than four hundred years after its writing until it was first printed. Thereupon, its fleeting appearances in different languages were almost uniformly followed by rapid excursions into obscurity. Some extracts from the first book were printed in 1849, from sources still not clear, by Archbishop Trench in his *Sacred Latin Poetry*. Upon these, with apparently no firsthand perusal of any manuscript or full text, J. M. Neale, the colorful translator and versifier, based his famous paraphrases on "Jerusalem the Golden."

With an indifference reflected by his public as to the total balance and significance of the work from which Dr. Neale drew his panegyric "On the Heavenly Country," he brought out versions in 1851-59 and thereafter which appealed powerfully to the imagination of English readers. Such continued interest in Bernard of Cluny as was maintained until 1906 owed its perseverance in the main to reprintings, with slight modifications, from these early renderings by the versatile Dr. Neale. In three issues of the *American Journal of Theology* for that year, S. M. Jackson presented, with brief editorial comments of his own, the prose translation of the entire *De Contemptu Mundi* made by Henry Preble. The translator's basic Latin text was, it seems, that of the Rolls Series edition by Thomas Wright.

By 1910 Dr. Jackson had completed his examination of virtually all known manuscripts and printed editions of the poem then in existence. He published an annotated bibliography of these, with Preble's translation of the *De Contemptu* and other works attributed to Bernard. This work still remains of great value even though later textual studies make the inadequacy of the translation based upon Wright's edition increasingly apparent.[30]

[28] "Sermon to the English," ed. H. S. Cook and C. B. Tinker, *Select Translations from Old English Prose* (Cambridge, Mass., 1908), pp. 198-99; NUS, p. 123; Anderson, *op. cit.*, pp. 341, 354-55.

[29] See the detailed notes of R. C. Petry, "Mediaeval Eschatology and Social Responsibility in Bernard of Morval's *De Contemptu Mundi*," *Speculum*, XXIV, 2 (April, 1949), 207-17. Note M. Manitius, *Geschichte*, III, 780-83.

[30] S. M. Jackson and H. Preble, ed. and tr., *The Source of "Jerusalem the Golden,"*

Although Preble's continues to be perhaps the most, if not the only, usable English translation of the entire work, an excellent recent edition of the Latin text with introduction, full notes, and manuscript variants provides the basis for a new appreciation of Bernard's major work. This 1929 edition by H. C. Hoskier not only shows in parallel columns how blithely Neale skipped about in his selections and how freely he rendered Bernard; it also demonstrates how pale and colorless Preble's prose translations frequently are. Best of all, Bernard's poem, freed from the grosser errors of previous editors and translators, stands forth, perhaps for the first time, in its true light. It is critically, yet sympathetically, evaluated in proper historical perspective as the genuinely social concern of a courageous soul for a world order sadly in need of redemption. The poet's addiction to ridiculous distortions does not essentially alter this verdict of the work.[31]

Evidence that Bernard really intended, as his preface hints, to make his prophetic denunciations the necessary prelude for a more constructive process of evoking Christian social cohesiveness in a decadent civilization is discernible from the faulty, but by no means despicable, presentation of Jackson and Preble. From the reconstructed text of Hoskier the fuller stature of Bernard, as fearless social critic and proponent of responsible social action, is more clearly observable. For him, as for many other medieval eschatologists, a primary attachment to the perfect community of heaven made him ostensibly scornful of temporal society and yet strangely sensitive to the Christian's responsibility for leadership within it.

Anyone who reads, carefully, this poem on the contempt of the world must agree that there is in it much that is flagrantly unfair. Bernard's most relentless critics, however, have sometimes been considerate enough to judge his exaggerations in terms of a literary effusion not wholly answerable at the bar of modern historical criticism. Even so, one is likely to miss the full significance of his work unless the total sweep of his conception is taken into account. One should not, of course, attempt to alter the obviously medieval complexion of his thought. Bernard has little hope for any considerable extension of human history. He clearly believes that man's "golden age" is in the past. He not only exaggerates the evils of current so-

---

Together with other Pieces Attributed to Bernard of Cluny (Chicago, 1910); hereafter abbreviated as SJG; T. Wright, *The Anglo-Latin Satirical Poets and Epigrammatists of the Twelfth Century* (2 Vols., London, 1872).

[31] H. C. Hoskier, *De Contemptu Mundi* (London, 1929), hereafter abbreviated as DCM.

ciety, but ascribes them all too frequently to unilateral causes. As is customary, even among the literary leaders of our own day, sexual perversions play altogether too heavy a role in his account. His attacks upon womankind as a whole are as unwarranted as they are unchristian. At times it seems as if Bernard's sole concern was to describe with obvious relish the descent of all humanity into merited destruction. Surely, no era could have been so full of wickedness, unrelieved by the slightest trace of redeeming virtues, as that which the contemporary of Peter the Venerable and Bernard of Clairvaux holds up to our startled view.

Nonetheless, we may well remind ourselves that Bernard of Cluny, who is, himself, belabored by undiscriminating critics, cannot fairly be expected to subside into any mold that will fit the modern man. His thought-forms, stubbornly fixed in their major outlines, are also devoid on many occasions of any great versatility in treatment. Granted, then, that Bernard was convinced of man's best days on earth as already past. Let it be admitted, also, that he did not expect any great change to be brought about in human society because of his or any other prophet's thundering. Certainly, he would be the last to believe that some sudden change of human nature could be occasioned; or that such a rightabout-face could avoid the dread Judgment so surely in the offing. All of this may seem to permit of one verdict only: Bernard was merely a diseased monk with no concern for his fellow men and with the single desire to make their remaining days on earth as abject as possible. This, however, is obviously a greater distortion, for those who know the Middle Ages, than Bernard's own foreshortenings.

Quite another conclusion is unavoidable for those who discern the actual current of Bernard's conviction. His real passion is to disclose the attitudes and courses of action which a true Christian must exemplify in a realistic world of evil and disillusionment, whatever his chances of altering the existing status of affairs. In reality, moreover, the monk of Cluny is not so thoroughly pessimistic as he sounds. Regardless of the flat statements interspersed throughout his work, he does believe conditions may be ameliorated, if only within rigidly prescribed limits. True, the social order is not expected to yield itself to any basic reordering of life on this earth. But men may, if they choose, improve their relationships with each other and so insure a better status in the life to come. This may be termed selfish and unbalanced. Perhaps it is. But it also incorporates insights from the established pattern of Christian thought: that is, man finds his best motivation for the improvement of his own and other people's lives, not in some superficially sentimental response to the whims of his fellow men, but in genuine obedience to the larger demands of the eternal kingdom of God.[32]

It is instructive to discover that in a large portion of Bernard's work there is just this eliciting quality of the eternal fellowship at work in his consideration of temporal society. What has so often been stigmatized as gullible acceptance of a ridiculously material heaven is, in reality, something far different. Not unlike the poetic fantasies of Peter Damian is Bernard's picturing of "Jerusalem the Golden" as the acme of human-divine fellowship. Similar, also, to Damian's thought is Bernard's insistence that only in aspiring to that far-off citizenship is there to be found a true reason for establishing harmony among the pilgrims of this earthly life.[33]

And because, as he says, "The hour of doom is at hand; the times are out of joint," he must also cry, "Let us awake." [34] Bernard clearly seems to derive satisfaction from his anticipation of the terrors that will shortly overtake the damned. But it is libelous to insist that he has no other concern. He is mainly absorbed with the prospect of stabilizing the character and preparing the defense, against every form of evil, on the part of those who may yet prove themselves worthy of a place in the heavenly beatitude. Bernard's enemies and indifferent defenders have satirized his preoccupation with heaven and his gratification over the just deserts that will overtake others in hell. But they forget that he considers the joys of heaven the best reason for living a good life on earth and the pains of hell a very real deterrent against sampling the questionable delights of evil.[35]

If Bernard brutally says that after the Judgment once dutiful children will no longer be concerned with the sufferings of their parents, thereafter doomed to eternal torture, this may be because he honestly feels that there will come a time when the good shall no longer be capable of sorrow; and the wicked shall no longer be permitted to make the innocent pay for the guilt of others. In any case, his work is full of the pressing invitation to Christians to prove, by their earthly life in service to other people, their right to be adjudged worthy, in the Last Day, of inclusion in the blessed company.[36]

[32] DCM, I, 1-21 (1-2); III, 835-914 (98-101).

[33] DCM, I, 111-54 (5-6); S. H. Hurlbut, ed., *The Song of Peter Damiani on the Joys and Glory of Paradise* (Washington, D. C., 1928), pp. 14-17; DCM, p. xii; I, 265-66 (10).

[34] Tr. of SJG, I, 105; Cf. DCM, I, 1 (1).

[35] DCM, I, 19-22 (1-2).

[36] DCM, I, 97-100 (4); I, 655-718 (23-25); 145-50 (6); 393-94 (14).

Suppose one grants Bernard's near-obsession with the joyous society of heaven. Suppose, further, that one attempts to understand, sympathetically, his justifiable disillusionment with the decay of social responsibility seen on every hand. Does it not, thereupon, become easier to appreciate his reasons for invoking the Last Judgment as the real and impending circumstance that must bring the present life into closer accord with the ultimate community? Viewed from this standpoint, Bernard's analysis ceases to be a merely ludicrous overstatement of social evils for the purpose of highlighting monastic virtues.

The manner in which Bernard vacillates between a description of ineffable social joys in heaven, a pitiless exposure of social evils on earth, and a focusing of all eyes upon the Judgment Day, inevitable for all, thus becomes understandable. Heaven, indeed, will be a companionship beyond description. Every aspect of sanity in mind and body will there be in evidence. The fruits of a good life, with its human weakness redeemed by the divine mercy, will now have won for the celestial inhabitants a beautiful existence free from unhappiness of any kind. This will be a paradise that shall serve as the true country of all its citizens, a heavenly congregation with complete enjoyment of its Christ.[37]

Like his famous contemporary of Clairvaux, the monk of Cluny could not fail to exalt this city of Zion as the ultimate community to which every human eye should turn. Far beyond the maudlin sentiments so often attributed to the medieval poet, Bernard thinks of heaven as exercising a drawing force upon those who are still in pilgrimage. If such a prospect of fellowship and joy will not serve to galvanize the energies of men on this earth, what can there be that will? If, furthermore, leaders in any age need an incentive of more than purely personal character to nerve them to unselfish leadership in their own age, what can possibly exceed the rewards held out from heaven to those who serve their fellow men?

Basically no different, Bernard is merely more eloquently vocal than hundreds of his literary contemporaries in stressing such points. If Jesus himself said (Matthew 25:35) that men should be judged at the last accounting on the basis of their response to the needs of his humble ones, he must have been making this same point. Bernard is not slow to emphasize this. The modern skeptic pretends to be horrified at the inhumanitarianism of authors such as he. How can he

---

[37] See, especially, DCM, I, 25-384 (2-14).

possibly look with such cold unconcern upon the anticipated sufferings of those judged guilty and sent away into everlasting torment! But it must be remembered that the modern world has its own forms of unfeeling disregard for multiplied thousands of innocent women and children caught in the vortex of war's destructiveness. Bernard simply could not think of anything more important to him and his fellow men than avoiding hell and arriving at heaven. That being the case, he made no attempt to alleviate the savage realism of the Judgment scene.

Furthermore, his second and third books are not merely a requiem on the good days of a perfect order that is past—though they may seem to be just that. There is much verifiable truth in his attack on the various social diseases that infected the whole body politic in his day. The passages in which he indicts culpable civic leaders, clerical worthies irresponsive to their people's cry, and even the defective guardians of home life, are by no means foreign to the picture drawn in the pages of other reporters.[38]

The poet of Morval cannot check his vituperation of social evils any more than the leaders of our day who feel a deep sense of responsibility in the midst of obvious perversions can maintain a craven silence. But he does manage to end on a constructive note. In the Last Days some will be found worthy. No one knows when those days will come, though Bernard obviously thinks them near at hand. Those who would be saved then must stand firm now. Little as they may hope or even desire to alter the established façade of society, they must at least stand together as Christians, living, in the present age, such a corporate and individual life as will merit the Master's approval. Who knows? Perhaps even Bernard of Morval was not so hopeless as he seems. The only begotten Son of the Father could still effect redemption. Let the holy generation "stand firm in goodness with hearts burning for the skies." They could at least pray the Christ of piety to

crush out the scandals, forgive the sins; build up the good, destroy the rest, blessed King. . . . Grant us to mourn the bad, and take the good; grant us of thine, grant us thyself. Give us back the golden age and primeval strength, we pray. Direct us now, take us to thyself hereafter, lest we perish.[39]

[38] Notably, Hildegarde of Bingen and Bernard of Clairvaux. Cf. DCM, p. viii; Letter 340 of the edition of B. S. James, *The Letters of St. Bernard of Clairvaux* (London, 1952), pp. 459-60.

[39] SJG, III, 171; DCM, III, 893-94 (100); III, 907-14 (101).

Bernard's work *On the Scorn of the World* may not be social in our way of thinking; it is replete with surgical criticism and healing suggestions for the renovation of his day.

Bernard's description of the heavenly fatherland with all its social joys is found in Book I. There, also, is his major interpretation of Last Days and Final Judgment. It is not illogical that Books II and III should be given over mainly to an indictment of temporal society; that is, if any portion of human society in the temporal order is to respond properly to the eternal kingdom and so come safely through the awful Judgment.

Book II is inaugurated with Bernard's favorite exposition on the "golden age" that is past. However unacceptable as a historical thesis, this section is illuminating for Bernard's ideas of individual and social virtues that make a people great. Of course, his ideas have an unmistakably monastic orientation that evokes little sympathetic response in the modern world. Nonetheless, this bygone age that he apparently thinks impossible of recapture and still yearns for was, according to him, one of peace, goodly patriarchs, hard-working farmers, and decently propagating families. Order, honesty, and hard effort won their reward. Gambling and the obsequious worship of gold were banned. Lust was forsworn, and people entered into marriage with sober expectations of producing a godly race. The proper age for attaining fatherhood Bernard confidently reports as having been forty years or beyond. The pastoral virtues were the ones Bernard clearly favored and, in turn, ascribed to the ideal past. Shared resources and the elements of a Christian communality likewise characterized this era as he saw it in nostalgic retrospect. Frugality, deference of youths to elders, and simple pleasures were the golden mean.[40]

All too obviously, this race passed away. Bernard's is quite otherwise. Wealth in goods and all the things of the world is now the predominating concern. *Mundus*, the word originally meaning "clean," is still the word for "world"; but this world is no longer pure—far from it! Restlessness, evasion, and vicious passions characterize it now. Bernard says that he can mention only a few of its vices —about two books' worth to be exact! His Latin must be given modified translation at times to placate English prudery. He reminds us unnecessarily that his story has in it much that is not nice. He warns of his bent for didactic satire and hyperbole. But it is all for a

[40] DCM II, 1-50 (38-39); II, 51 (39); II, 49-64 (39-40); II, 73-74 (40); II, 50-73 (39-40); SJG, II, 131.

good purpose: so that evil may be spurned, the heart raised to wisdom, and a redeeming sense of individual and social responsibility ingrained.

One may be inclined to cavil at Bernard's plea that he weeps as he cries out, "grieving to weep and put forth such a song!" But may he not be sincere in the main? He is not devoid of the prophetic frenzy that calls upon the Lord's spokesmen to limn the outlines of probable doom so that the worst reality may be avoided. In any case, Bernard now excoriates at length the evils characterizing his age. For it is an age of corporate guilt, not merely the doings of isolated individuals, that rouses him to the prophet's fury. Wealth is panted after. Right is little pursued. Inner purpose and outer acts coincide in evil deed. Peace is forgotten. Lust is enthroned. Anti-Christians befitting the leadership of antichrist marshal their hosts everywhere. An ordered society gives way to a rabble's will.[41]

Bernard's strictures on the Church and its failures are the bitterest of all. The harmony of brethren is gone. The good leader who accepts the burden of his people's direction is nowhere in evidence. Reformers who crusade for the betterment of morals are no more. "Who brandishes the sword of his tongue and strikes a blow at guilt with it?" It is Bernard's conviction that the whole race, the entire social order, is the veritable embodiment of sin.[42] All ages go astray.

The bishop, who should be the reverend leader of his flock, is the first to lead his people from the path. He and his subordinates make their places of leadership an excuse for victimizing their people. Stern to the humble, they are craven before robbers. The priest continues the sad story. The cleric reads and knows what he ought to do. He promptly does the opposite. The soldier is the embodiment of everything his profession is supposed to repudiate. The nobility is overweening in its pride and unrestrained in its arrogance. The tax officer connives in the evasion of the rich man's return and drives the poor into the ground. Men of business innovate new frauds everywhere, all the time. The farmer gets all he can, conceals his rightful tithe, and gives thought to no one but himself. Bernard pretends that to continue in the same vein will be simply to repeat and "to serve up a stale dish." [43] But he has more to say. Pontifical leadership, once the symbol of social integrity, now reflects the fundamental instability of a tottering order. The one commissioned to bridge the sea of this

[41] DCM, II, 94-130 (41-42); II, 180-224 (44-45).
[42] DCM, II, 225-33 (45); SJG II, 134; DCM, II, 234 (45); II, 237-38 (46).
[43] DCM, II, 240-46 (46).

world to the land of Zion becomes the thoroughfare conducting all men down the fiery river of the lower world. Preoccupied with riches and the status they confer, the pontiff, like all others, scorns to be a bridge for souls.[44]

The bishops know how to invoke the canons for their own best interests. Royalty is no better. Tyranny grows apace. Church and empire have both betrayed their corporate trusts. Schisms abound.[45]

Perhaps, even as Bernard suggests, it is fruitless to go on. But it is unwise to dismiss these attacks as the tirades of an embittered man. Consecrated leaders contemporary with Bernard agree with him all too well. Other records, too, bemoan clerical preference for affairs of business and the soldier's life to "the sacred repose of the clergy." And when the cleric goes the downward way, none can outdo him in the vicious implacability with which he intimidates and destroys the people. The judge, too, fills his niche in this race of civic prostitutes. Chicanery and extortion are daily practices in country and in town.[46]

Woman comes in for more then her share of vituperation. This is an old story among medieval chroniclers. Bernard's data are not new —only more skillfully spread about. Not all the vices attributed to womankind are without foundation in Bernard's age, but the manner in which he follows Jerome's diatribes against the oft-maligned sex shakes somewhat our confidence in Bernard's more estimable evaluations.[47]

Presumably, also, other ages have witnessed prurience and the diseased untimeliness of adolescent desire. Doubtless in Bernard's day there were fathers ready to give bad instructions to their children as well as sons and daughters full of surprising lessons as yet unlearned by their elders. But the whole noxious tale, so fully, and it seems so willingly, told by our narrator, has a purpose hardly ascribable to sheer scandal-mongering. Bernard seems sincere in his major contention that grief, not joy, predominates in his telling; and that this whole record of bloated ecclesiasticism and civic irresponsibility must be cleared away if the terrors of the Final Judgment are to be hurdled. How can men make ready for a share in eternal bliss if temporal leadership habitually leads them into the ditch? Book II, like Book III, is not simply a public airing of viciousness. It proclaims a man, however unbalanced in his evaluations, who does

[44] SJG, II, 135; DCM, II, 261-70 (46-47).
[45] DCM, II, 271-84 (47).
[46] DCM, II, 291-385 (47-50).
[47] DCM, II, 386-600 (51-58).

care for his people and who does wish their betterment, now, as the guarantee of their eternal place among the blessed. All the digressions and inconceivable duplications of Bernard's strange welter of scriptural and classical materials cannot obscure this basic point.[48]

Book III gives yet further lessons in the analysis of public vice. Lawlessness, endless ambition, a power-mad people and clergy, and a confused mentality are everywhere rampant. In every center of public and episcopal life, it is the worst, not the best, who rule. True pastoral virtues receive nothing but sneering patronage.[49]

What is needed is not further mouthings on the part of nominal Christian leaders, but priests who lift their people upward and bishops whose examples are a trumpet call to Christian orderliness. "Words need action, action words, order labor." [50]

Ever and anon the interesting fact slips out: Bernard is not beyond all hope for his people. It is worth while for the religious leader to live as he preaches and for every responsible person in public and spiritual affairs to set a socializing Christian example. Interspersed with periodic outbursts against newly remembered crimes of popes, kings, and peoples, are stubborn appeals to collective and personal justice. Anticipating the implacability of the Last Judgment, Bernard satirizes the social evils of his day. Against such a background he raises the cry for social righteousness.

<hr />

[48] DCM, II, 601-974 (58-70), for mounting indictments of blighted unity.

[49] DCM, III, 1-854 (71-99). The ambition and venality of churchmen, reaching their apogee in the Roman pontiff, are indicted here with a directness and bitterness hardly surpassed. Cf. III, 345-48 (82). How different from the King of kings, the crucified Christ, who repudiated all wealth, honors, and kingdoms in order to be a true shepherd of his sheep, are the hierarchs who fatten themselves on Christ's flocks in his name (III, 499 ff. [87 ff.]). The remedy lies in Rome's hands. Let her return to Peter's commission (III, 658 [93]). Let Rome and papacy show forth once more the order of old in ministry to the righteous and the oppressed (DCM, III, 687 ff. [94 ff.]).

[50] SJG, III, 161.

CHAPTER VI

The Response of Temporal Society to the Eternal Kingdom

4. From Hildegarde of Bingen to the Later Middle Ages

THE MEDIEVAL PROPHETESS, HILDEGARDE OF BINGEN (D. 1179), IS distinguished for the penetrating social insights that are to be found throughout her *Visions* and *Letters*.[1] She is outstanding for her colorful imagery and her trenchant observations on the world of time in relation to God's eternity. Her sense of the impinging otherness of the future world is expressed by way of constructive criticisms on the total structure of existing society. Like her contemporaries, Bernard of Cluny and Bernard of Clairvaux, she has no hope for anything approximating a modern transformation of the temporal order. But she freely confronts every class of society with its obligations for mutual service within social life as it is now ordered. It is not surprising to hear her blaze forth in fearless denunciation, even as she sings the occasional praises, of outstanding rulers. Nor should it startle us to learn her expressive comments on both the good and the bad within clerical and monastic associations. Everywhere the quality of prophetic egotism is apparent. She speaks with such finality, not because she utters anything by her own unaided reason, but because she surrenders herself as the Lord's spokesman to the divine afflatus.[2]

In Book I, Vision 1, of her master work, the *Scivias*, she contends that it is the heavenly world which empowers humanity in its tem-

---

[1] Available in MPL 197:145 ff., and 383 ff. See M. Boeckeler, ed. and tr., *Wisse die Wege, Scivias* (Berlin, 1928). An English translation is *The Life and Visions of St. Hildegarde*, by F. M. Steele (London, 1914). A helpful sketch is that of J. de Ghellinck, *L'essor de la littérature latine au XII*e *siècle* (Paris, 1946), I, 195-99. Cf. Manitius, *Geschichte* III, 228-37; W. Preger, *Geschichte der deutschen Mystik im Mittelalter* (Leipzig, 1874), I, 16-37.

[2] *Scivias*, I, 1; Steele, *op. cit.*, p. 132.

poral setting for a life that will be worthy of ultimate beatitude. It is impossible to convey in a brief statement the scintillating character of her symbols. Her scenes and figures, majestic and awe-inspiring as they are, shift with such rapidity, and the nuances of her thought are shaded so delicately yet outlined so starkly, that nothing but prolonged quotation can do justice to them.[3]

Nonetheless, in the course of her first vision, she represents the Lord as speaking to her in a penetrating voice and saying:

O man! fragile dust of the dust of the earth, and ashes of ashes, cry aloud and say concerning the entrance into incorruptible salvation: Forasmuch as those who are learned and see the inner meaning of the Scriptures, but wish neither to tell it nor to preach it because they are blind and tepid in preserving the righteousness of God, open to them the lock of these mysteries, which they timid ones conceal in a hidden field without fruit.[4]

Hildegarde is, therefore, bidden to write from such an abundant fountain and with such mystical erudition that these recreant ones "may tremble at the profusion of [her] irrigation, who wished [her] to be considered contemptible on account of Eve's transgression." [5]

This stern condemnation of those who might have been expected to speak the Lord's will and word but who evaded their social obligation to the Lord's people now becomes the occasion for Hildegarde's further exposition of her own prophetic function. She prepares to demonstrate that, however frail she may be in her womanly capacity and just because she is so little in the sight of the Almighty, she has become the veritable instrument for the heavenly Judge's voice. From the center of divine life itself, she has been commissioned to stand up and cry aloud, saying:

These things are manifested to thee by the strongest power of Divine help, because He Who governs every one of His creatures powerfully and benignly, pours forth Himself in the light of celestial illumination, upon those fearing Him and walking in His gentle love, in a spirit of humility, and leads those persevering in the way of righteousness, to the joys of the eternal vision.[6]

This is, apparently, Hildegarde's way, not only of stigmatizing

[3] Cf. the Judgment scene, *Scivias* III, XII: MPL 197:726-30; Steele, *op. cit.,* pp. 168 ff.
[4] I, 1, MPL 197:386; Steele, *op. cit.,* pp. 131-32.
[5] MPL 197:386; Steele, *op. cit.,* p. 132.
[6] MPL 197:386; Steele, *op. cit.,* pp. 132-33.

the pusillanimous representatives of religious life in her own day, but also of stating the desired response of all human leadership to the heavenly community. God, ensconced in the brilliance of kingdom blessedness, is too bright for purely human eyes to look upon. But, loving as he is, he projects a soft, winglike shadow which serves in its protective character as both a chastizing and an admonishing influence. From out this shadow there is revealed to man the justice of true equity. Furthermore, those who dare to answer the heavenly call to their human responsibility on earth find themselves, like Hildegarde, dynamized beyond their own puny resources for a redemptive mission to others. Having learned, like the prophetess, their own littleness, they are in a fair way to discharge the heavenly purposes of spiritual benediction to those around them. This is true "because the gazing into the kingdom of God in humility before Him, fortified by the fear of the Lord, and with the clearness of a good and just intention, trains in men earnest endeavour, and divine stability." [7]

Nothing could say more eloquently than this how passionately Hildegarde believes that the most energetic ministry to humanity in her own day must proceed from a far-off, yet confidently perceptive, view of the ultimate kingdom of God. Those who thus gaze into the kingdom itself for the signs of their prophetic ministry do well to proceed in wholesome fear and humble devotion while they wait for the divine fulfillment of their powers. The Divine, for his part, is so magnanimous in all of his terrifying greatness that he submits himself in the midst of all his riches to a voluntary renunciation for the sake of his creatures. An electric dynamis proceeds from him in comforting and virtuous strength and is conferred upon those who see his will for themselves and are receptive to his plans for them in the service of fellow man. For God, knowing the weakness of men, is able to honor the slightest and the most latent potentialities of human beings for his own benign purposes.

The prophetess closes her section on temporal responsiveness to the eternal kingdom with a clear interpretation of that most reprehensible weakness to which she so often addresses her criticisms. Here, as in her letters and other works, she is as free as God's servants must always be to denounce injustice, the iniquitous failure to remit debt, and all manner of carelessness "in the wonderful things of the works of blessedness." As for the one who renders himself a free agent of

---

[7] MPL 197-387; Steele, *op. cit.*, p. 134.

the eternal kingdom in the temporal world, "he who works the works of salvation running in the way of truth, he obtains a fountain of glory, in which he prepares for himself, both in heaven and on earth, the most precious riches." [8]

Here, as so consistently in the visions concerning the responsibilities of religious leaders in days just preceding the Final Judgment, Hildegarde is free to invoke the divine censure. Like her Old Testament prototypes, however, she is happiest when pointing the way by which humanity may safely respond, in the midst of human associations, to the incomparable beatitude of their royal fatherland.

In a collection of twelfth- and thirteenth-century homiletic treatises there is a work entitled "Concerning Eight Vices and Twelve Abuses of This Age." [9] This document emphasizes the commonplace medieval view of the vices and virtues. There is the customary attempt to exorcise the sway of the vices and to inculcate the virtues. Life in the hereafter is a constantly recurring theme. This is capitalized as a reason for not giving too much place to things that are earthly when so much is at stake in terms of the heavenly. Such a virtue as liberality is inculcated in the hope that one will remember the origin of the goods which he gives as alms and that he will be aware, likewise, of the use that God wishes made of his largesse.

We the faithful are admonished to remember that "our abode is not here, but in heaven." The conventional weighting is also placed upon a relative disregard for things as they *are* in the light of God's plan for things as they *will be*. But this does not mean that one is to be unconcerned about the character of the life that he lives with his fellows. The virtue of charity is made up of "true love to God and to man; . . . but let us do alms as he hath taught us, for love to God, and not for praise; so that our Lord may ever be praised in our good works, and that vain-glory be ever despicable in our sight." Every man ought to live in humility with meekness toward God and men, since none knows the hour of his transition to another world. It is comforting to know that "we may through God's help overcome the devilish sins through warfare, if we keenly fight; and finally obtain for ourselves the everlasting honour ever with God himself, if we strive for it now while here." [10]

Anticipating such a glorious eventuality, and entertaining godly

[8] MPL 197:388; Steele, *op. cit.*, pp. 136-37.
[9] R. Morris, ed., *Old English Homilies* (Early English Text Society [EETS 29.1], London, 1868), pp. 99 ff.
[10] *Ibid.*, p. 106.

fears of the dread alternative reserved for one who does not soberly regard his duties toward God and man, the homilist proceeds to outline the major abuses of his day. These vices are of a predominantly social character. And the author thinks of them as bringing "harm to all mankind if they . . . hold sway." Just as they involve the marring of man's social and individual sense of responsibility, so their opposites are enjoined, by inference at least, as the antidotes for viciousness. Obviously such correctives must grow out of a fundamental dedication to God's eternal kingdom as it shall be consummated in another world. Only then can society be protected against the grievous ills that proceed from wise men without good works, old men without piety, young people without obedience, rich folks without charity, women without purity, rulers without virtue, and Christians without duly ordered concord.

Good social life lived under the benediction of God's own eternal society requires consecrated leadership. How far can a bishop be excused who is negligent in the correction and rule of his people? Who, if not those in responsibility, shall answer for the defection of undisciplined youth, the irresponsible rich, and the quarrelsome body politic? Certainly parents shall not go free of accountability for their children. The rich man who does no alms and hides his good powers earns for himself hell-torment, not a place in the beloved society. One need not be rich in this world's goods to receive strangers, visit the sick, comfort the sorrowful, lead the blind, support the infirm, or otherwise minister to his fullest capacities. No more can a ruler, out of cowardice or disinclination, excuse himself for failure to hold his people under discipline. Nor can he justify negligence in his ministry before God for the welfare of his commonwealth. Quarrelsomeness the Lord cannot abide. No one can be contentious and assume for himself the title of Christ's follower. Only those who walk after the Christ in simplicity and humility—in peace and concord— can be called the children of God. There is no point in addressing God as our Father unless we lay claim to our heavenly inheritance through stripping ourselves of all discord and strife.

Whether one be rich or poor, eminent or lowly, wise or childlike, he must forever remember that he is given some measure of responsibility for his fellows. To the kings and princes of the Church an especial share of responsible ministry is committed. "If the king will with carefulness observe these aforesaid precepts, then shall his kingdom be prosperous in this life, and after this life he shall go to the eternal life for his piety." Likewise, a bishop is given to his people for their aid and direction and not as a victimizer of their helplessness. What he owes to them in the name of the Lord is sobering conduct and a continual instruction in the Master's way. The way of truth and eternal life as it is in Christ Jesus is the lone road by which all men may come to the heavenly Father. Only those who dwell in full consciousness of his scrutiny may hope for a share in the eternal inheritance.[11]

Naturally, one of the favorite themes of all homilists in the early and medieval periods was the prayer of our Lord. The versatility of treatment accorded it speaks well for the spiritual imagination and the intellectual ingenuity of the Christian centuries.

One such treatment of the *Pater Noster* is found in a medieval homily of the twelfth or thirteenth century.[12] Reflected clearly is the faith in the eternal kingdom and its drawing influence upon the social and individual experience. The sermon begins in the customary fashion by calling attention to the Father in heaven. The preacher is theologically and socially oriented toward the whole universe when he directs his parishioners to this primary source of all life and truth. All human life is focused toward the future world which is God's—without regard to space or time. The homilist next apostrophizes the love which should come out of one's reverential passion for the Divine. From it there should proceed the love of fellow Christians. Just because God is the creator and center of the abiding kingdom which is yet to be, and because he wishes his followers to be reunited with him, he directs them all the more to Christ's injunction regarding love of neighbor. Charity and disregard for selfish whims, as Jesus taught, best guarantee that love for man which follows upon the love for God and his kingdom.

Directing his whole life toward God and the neighbor who shall be loved as oneself, the Christian is impelled to pray, "Thy kingdom come." "His kingdom," says the author, "is this middle earth, earth and heaven, and each abode; over all is his great might." His sovereignty is over the whole universe and over the totality of created things.

For man, however, God reserved a special destiny. "He made man in righteousness, in the form of his own likeness." This is the reason that he distinguished the human from all other beings:

[11] *Ibid.*, pp. 114, 116.
[12] *Ibid.*, pp. 55 ff.

> All deer (animals) and fowl of flight
> He made to stoop adownright [downwards].
> Man he loved and cared for well,
> And therefore his face upward he wrought;
> That was all for a good skill [reason],
> If that understand ye will.
> Face upwards he him wrought.
> He would that man of him thought,
> That he should love him with thought [in his mind]
> As the Lord that him wrought.[13]

How could man possibly have ignored this joyous promise which God had entertained for him from the beginning? Certainly, men should pray every day to be the recipients of such kingdom blessedness. "God grant us thither to come, and ever with himself to dwell!" The end of such petitions leads toward a companionship with God and all his company in the celestial dwelling that is to be forevermore. That is the reason why his followers are now on pilgrimage:

> He will be our Father and we his sons,
> For him is all our journey,
> That is our country and our kingdom,
> With him to dwell in heaven.[14]

But before such fellowship can be joined by those who are here below, they must not only pray but also give themselves wholeheartedly to insuring that God's will may be done on earth as it is in heaven. Making this prayer come true means that each of God's followers must "act towards all men with right and skill," in conformity with the divine plan. For this reason man ought to know how important is his feeding upon the bread that is both temporal and spiritual. Without God's grace, and the doctrine of his truth firmly implanted, one may neither save himself nor minister to others. Yet, contribute to others he must! And from his fellow men he must solicit that same forgiveness which he owes to them. In no other way can he continue to follow the Lord's commandment and

> Love [his] fellow Christian day and night
> As [him]self, and that is right.[15]

[13] *Ibid.*, p. 58; Lines (Ll.) 87-98.
[14] *Ibid.*, p. 60; Ll. 113-16.
[15] *Ibid.*, p. 64; Ll. 199-200.

It is difficult for the preacher to see how anyone could possibly be unreconciled with his brother and still dare to offer up this Dominical prayer. Neighbors are to be loved for God's sake. Truly, no one may come into the final kingdom unless he be prepared to love God and serve his fellows forever.

Pierre of Blois (d. 1204) was much admired in his day for his vigorous preaching and his useful correspondence with a variety of church leaders. His letters are full of good advice to those who have recently assumed responsibilities of high office in the Church. As such, they draw their sobering reminders of social obligation from an ultimate sense of duty. Peter warns his readers against the temptation to forget final accountability. Leaders in the Church are intended, as good pastors, to spur their people to renewed Christian life and activity.[16]

This emphasis is definitely supported in one of his sermons, the third for the Advent season.[17] Based upon Philippians 3:20, the theme emphasizes for the Christian that his commonwealth is, indeed, in heaven. That eternal community to which he moves by way of the great Judgment is a stern, yet happy, invitation to a righteous life in the present world; one that is individual and social. Pierre believes that the expectation of future testing and fulfillment best serves to correlate existing social action.

One of Pierre's homiletic efforts, denominated a "Country Sermon," treats of "Christian Fear as the Stepping Stone to Christian Love." [18] His point is the old, but essentially sound, one: The fear of future judgment may condition a wholesome response, by way of Christian love, to the blessedness of the saints which lies beyond. For these saints, even while they were yet in the flesh, lived above the body. While yet men, they prefigured the life of angels, even as Chrysostom had counseled his brethren to do. Those people are thrice blessed who thus look forward to their ultimate citizenship in the holy country. In so doing they rise above their fears to a love that shall be characteristic of the heavenly fatherland. It is their very yearning for the corporate life beyond that motivates their temporal effort. With their eyes on the severe Judge and strict Ex-

---

[16] Petri Blessensis, *Opera Omnia*, MPL 207. The "Epistolae" are cols. 1 ff., and the "Sermones," 559 ff. See, especially, Ep. XV, cols. 51 ff. and XVII, cols. 62 ff.

[17] J. M. Neale, *Mediaeval Preachers and Mediaeval Preaching: A Series of Extracts* (London, 1856) , pp. 196 ff.; cf. MPL 207:568 ff.

[18] Serm. LXV: "Ad Populum," MPL 207:750 ff., especially 752-53; cf. NUS, 32:173-74; Neale, *op. cit.*, pp. 201-2.

aminer, they are preserved from human futility and worldly error. There is no more profitable way of progress than this straight and narrow entrance. For it leads directly into the eternal country.

Of all the medieval men who considered the totality of created things in the light of the Creator's will, perhaps none proceeded with more devotion to the balance of things temporal and eternal than did Vincent de Beauvais (d. 1264).[19] He was certainly not the first to adopt the encyclopedic approach to the problems of life and knowledge. Earlier prototypes had included Bishop Isidore of Seville and the much more recent Bartholomew, the Englishman. Each of these in his own way had brought together a plethora of information sometimes all too little bound by any central theme.

In a fashion reminiscent of Isidore's great work, but going far beyond it, Vincent continues his discussion of everyday human problems with a conclusion that relates them to the ultimate objectives of the divine life. The French iconographer, Mâle, reminds us that Vincent cannot conceive of his work as being finished when he has merely recounted the history of the world to his own time.[20] A Christian knows the future by faith in God's revelation. He knows that the world will come to the end of history, and that the Judgment will follow. This will be succeeded by the consolidation of the good and the lasting incorporation of the damned. Vincent therefore requires an epilogue for his *Historical Mirror*. In it he proceeds to deal with matters more purely speculative, in a fashion closely related to what has gone before. Thus the signs of world's end, the prophecies of Joachim and Hildegarde, the advent of antichrist, and other phenomena popularly associated with the Last Days are given their proper place. He continues with a discussion of the Resurrection, the Final Judgment with its sentences, the tortures of the condemned, the renovation of the world, and, finally, the glorification of the saints in community with the angels and the Trinity. He gives ample discussion to the happiness of the saints and to the grades of honor which shall be known among them. All of this comes in the epilogue to his *Historical Speculum*.[21]

Now in all of this discussion, Vincent nowhere treats the exact manner in which the final disposition of mankind becomes a

---

[19] Cf. E. Mâle, *L'art religieux du XIII° siècle en France* (4th ed., Paris, 1919).

[20] See his (*Epilogus*) *Speculum Historiale* (Douai, 1624), cols. 1323 ff., and Mâle, *op. cit.*, pp. 428-29.

[21] See Vincent in relation to other medieval thinkers in Petry, *Francis of Assisi*, pp. 88 ff., and "Medieval Eschatology and St. Francis of Assisi," *Church History*, IX (1940), 58.

motivating element in present social experience. But the implications of such a relationship are present throughout his various works.

Coming to De Beauvais's book on the education of noble children —and, in particular, their preparation for social responsibilities— one is reminded of the fact that society is never, for Vincent, a completely secular phenomenon.[22] It is true that he quotes passages from classical authors and the Christian Fathers in rather sporadic fashion. But the materials that he takes from Cicero, Epicurus, and the Roman poets are so placed within the framework of Christian social thinking as to constitute a virtually Christian orientation. Over the entire welter of quotations and pious wishes he sprinkles a generous allotment of scriptural text. The result is a curious weighing of human social obligations upon the divine scale of life.

Vincent's thought on social duties results in an admonition to take a definite part in normal, wholesome ways of friendship and peace; this is best designed to lead one to a happy and useful life. It matters little that the author draws his quotations from so widely varying a source of supply. The book of Wisdom may point out how much better it is that there be two, rather than one. Bernard of Clairvaux is called upon for confirmation as to the advantages and obligations of mutuality. Cicero had discoursed at length upon the values of friendship and the necessity of human reciprocity. Only thus could one discharge the duties of Roman citizenship. Paul, in his writings to the Romans and to the Thessalonians, had counseled his Christian brethren to support each other in the ways of discipline and preparation for better life. In Galatians, he had insisted that each have regard for the other if he would fulfill the law of Christ. The net effect of all this was to set up worthy goals and motivations for social participation on the part of young and old. In so doing, one would not merely incur obligations for his fellow men, but he would certainly find the fullest measure of happiness. Like his own contemporaries, Vincent took pleasure in emphasizing the necessity among Christian brethren for a life of responsibly divided labors in the service of the common body, spiritual. Augustine and Seneca, alike, had stressed man's being associated with his fellows if he were to move toward the fulfillment of his destiny as God had previsioned it.[23]

De Beauvais, in concerning himself with the history of the tem-

---

[22] *De eruditione filiorum nobilium,* ed. A. Steiner (Mediaeval Academy of America, 1938).

[23] Cap. XXXII, particularly.

poral world and its everyday affairs, felt the magnetic lure of a great society transcendent to history. In reality, he could no more escape than could Thomas Aquinas, from the stock conclusion of the Christian Middle Ages: namely, that every man must be a whole person or none at all; that a life begun on the human plane must be continued into a superhuman area of life; and that the natural life of the race must be continued within a supernatural sphere. Thus, one of the most important contributions of Vincent lay in his having bound together, so closely, an account of the world's history and a relaying of the popularly accepted speculations about the society that was to surmount the end of time.[24]

It is in this connection that the historians of art and iconography have found Vincent's work so stimulating to their thought. Mâle, for example, has felt no hesitation in proclaiming Vincent's work to be representative at its very center of medieval Christian art. It is because this Dominican brings together so harmoniously, and so unconsciously, the factors of human existence and divine destiny that he can so readily delineate the theological implications to be found in the great architectural structures and other art forms of the medieval period. To have able interpreters of Christian iconography uncover some of the eschatological springs that welled up in medieval art is as edifying as it should be commonplace. What is striking —and perhaps untenable at times—is the manner in which Mâle builds his whole exposition of iconography about the system implicit in Vincent's *Mirror*.[25] Summoned to life from this encyclopedist's pages and graven in the cathedral imagery of glass and stone is that eternal unity for which man's soul cries out and in whose quest he pursues his communal pilgrimage. Whether from the plates and text of M. Bréhier or Professor Morey, however, one may see the irrefutable evidence that world's end was the theme that lay most compellingly upon the collective medieval consciousness. To look at the tympanum of any great episcopal church was to see the layman's book opened wide; it was to resolve upon a place with the sheep at the Judge's right or to run the supreme risk of joining the goats at his left. And the decision called for was one necessitating temporal investment through service, however humble, to the Lord's least.[26]

[24] E. Gilson, *La philosophie au moyen âge* (3rd ed., Paris, 1944), pp. 325-26, unnecessarily depreciates the encyclopedists in favor of the standard theologians. Mâle properly associates them.

[25] Mâle, *op. cit.*, pp. 415-29.

[26] Particularly useful for iconographic studies are L. Bréhier, *L'art chrétien* (Paris, 1928); C. Morey, *Medieval Art* (New York, 1942); C. Enlart, *Manuel d'archéologie*

The thought of mendicant leaders was steeped in eschatological doctrine. Especially was this true of the Franciscans and Dominicans. Francis of Assisi was so thoroughly grounded in the basic presuppositions regarding Last Things that he built his whole responsiveness to the needs of man upon it as a foundation. In clear and unscholastic terms he transformed what was often a dormant emphasis into a living article of belief. All of his admonitions, his beautiful poetic compositions, and his *Rules* are full of the appeal to answer the pressing human cry for assistance with a dedication to God's eternal kingdom. His whole conception of renunciation as it related to Christ, the Bible, the Church, and spiritual community leaps into being from this source.[27]

A like emphasis, though expressed more nearly in the language of the schools, is to be found in the writings of the devoted Bonaventura (d. 1274) and the signally successful preacher, Anthony of Padua (d. 1231).[28] The work of the former follows the outlines of systematic theology and conciliatory administration. The hortatory effectiveness of the latter is now represented to us largely in terms of inadequate sermon outlines. Even here, however, the pivotal significance of the eternal world in conditioning temporal reaction is too obvious to be ignored.

In an even more systematic way, the two great *Summas,* as well as a variety of other writings of Thomas Aquinas (d. 1274), preserve an identical stress.[29] Not only the more flexible treatments of the Lord's Prayer and the commentaries on the Pauline writings, but also his expositions of the Laws bear out this point. In his discussion of the manner in which men are directed by the divine law, he shows how their ultimate, common destiny is the most effective conditioner of temporal mutuality. Particularly should those who have a common end know the union of affection. Since men are directed by God to one common last end, which is true happiness, they "should be united together by mutual love." Being by nature a social or politi-

---

française depuis les temps mérovingiens jusqu'à la renaissance, 3 Vols. (Paris, 1902-16). L. Gonse, *L'art gothique* (Paris, n.d.). Note the theme of "Last Judgment" in cathedral iconography according to Mâle's *L'art religieux du XIIe siècle en France* (3rd ed., Paris, 1928), pp. 406-19, as well as in his work on the thirteenth century.

[27] Consult R. C. Petry, *Francis of Assisi,* especially Chap. V, pp. 86-102.

[28] See the *Breviloquium* of Bonaventura, *Opera Omnia,* V, 20 ff.; especially, pars VII, "De statu finalis iudicie," pp. 281 ff. See E. E. Nemmers, *Breviloquium by St. Bonaventura* (St. Louis, 1947), pp. 217 ff.; cf. Neale, *op. cit.,* for sermon outlines of Anthony.

[29] Convenient translations of the *Summa Theologica* and the *Summa Contra Gentiles* are those of the Dominican Fathers.

cal animal, man needs the assistance of his fellows in attaining this common goal; that is, the supremely social beatitude. Since he is properly directed to divine things, man naturally requires the regimen of life that best guarantees his progress heavenward. The same divine law that causes men to apply themselves to divine concerns leads them to love one another. This is the way of productive mutuality.[30]

As a *social* animal, man feels his need of his fellows as no other animal can. No individualism of any sort whatever can here suffice. Let him learn from the divine law of the eternal kingdom how he may most rationally behave toward his fellow beings. Subordinated as all men are to the one Father, and his eternally ordered harmony in the universe, it is most fitting that they learn the ways of temporal response in this life to the great society that draws them on.

Theirs is a community or commonwealth under God. The divine law is put at their disposal that they may be assured of instruction, first, as to proper behavior where God is concerned and, second, of right conduct where their fellow pilgrims are involved.[31]

In the lives of medieval people nothing bulked larger than the consideration attached to the experiences of the liturgical year. The seasons of the time, the lives of the saints, and the traditional moralizings of the average preacher were well known to them. One who earned the eternal gratitude of many parish priests for his arrangement of saints' stories in accordance with the ecclesiastical calendar was Jacobus de Voragine (d. 1298). It is not strange that at the very outset of his discussion on the various Advent occasions he should stress the prevailing eschatology of the Middle Ages. His treatment of the Lord's advent is not characterized by any spectacularly original excursion. He does distinguish four diverse comings: (1) Christ's first appearing in human nature and flesh; (2) his advent in the heart and conscience; (3) his appearance which comes at death; (4) that of the Last Judgment. It is with particular reference to the fourth that our author's remarks are addressed.[32]

[30] Note, for instance, the *Contra Gentiles* III, ii, 117 and 129; cf. *Opera Omnia*, XII, 409-40, 422 ff.; Dominican Fathers, Chap. 117, pp. 99-100; Chap. 128, pp. 125-26. For the great section on the Laws in the *Summa Theol.*, see Ia IIae Qq. 90-108, particularly Q. 99, a. 4.

[31] *Contra Gentiles* III, 117, 128; *S. Theol.*, Ia IIae Q. 100, a. 5 and concl.

[32] In the Caxton edition (by Ellis) of *The Golden Legend* (Temple Classics, 7 Vols., 1900-22), the treatment of the four Advents is I, ff., with emphasis on the Last Judgment, I, 12-25. Cf. the superior translation by Ryan and H. Ripperger, *The Golden Legend of Jacobus de Voragine* (New York, 1941), 2 vols.

Following the Church's seasons, Jacobus finds plentiful opportunity to stress the glory of the saints which shall follow upon the Lord's last coming. All the usual tokens which shall precede the Judgment in the days of antichrist are traditionally interpreted. Jacobus seems concerned, more than anything else, with the signs and spectacles which shall usher in the Last Day. But this is, after all, only a superficial fascination with externalities. Like all those of his time, he is primarily given to the means of spiritual exhortation. He exhorts all the faithful to make ready for the time of Judgment, after which no sentence may be revoked. Since no verdict may be appealed from the great King and Judge, all should live now and constantly pray that they "may in this holy time so receive him that at the day of judgment [they] may be received into his everlasting bliss."

Inasmuch as Voragine's hagiographical efforts were directed toward the unifying of the Church's seasons with the lives of the saints, it is not hard to understand how such admonitions consolidated the place of the blessed in living conjunction with Missal and Breviary. As all commentators on the service books of the Church have pointed out, the entire preoccupation of the Church in the Advent season is quite literally with the reappearing of the Lord. It follows that Voragine's *Golden Legend,* or book of Readings on the lives of holy ones, should, at the very beginning, deal with sacred endeavors in connection with which those of holy destiny had run, so nobly, their human course.[33]

Few men of the medieval period had as much to say as John Wyclif (d. 1384) in criticism about the Church of which they were a part. So much was this the case that some authorities have styled him a modern man uniquely detached from his medieval mooring. Nothing could be farther from the truth. John Wyclif belongs as definitely to the Middle Ages as a man could. The fact that he departed in a number of instances, and on some specific doctrines, from the timeworn platitudes of his day by no means proclaims him a renegade from the prevailing faith. What he did attempt to achieve was a reincarnation in the Church, which he so much loved, of the ideal which he imputed to Christ, its true founder. In so doing, he found it necessary to castigate quite sharply the hierarchy which had come to rule with all too heavy a hand. But in attacking the prevailing system of organization, together with its personalized greed and victimization of the common people, Wyclif was by no means desert-

[33] Ellis, *op. cit.,* I, 24-25.

ing the great principles of the medieval credo. Least of all was he repudiating the basic pattern of devotion to an eternal world as the best possible motivation for social service in the present community of faithful Christians.[34]

Giving special cogency to Wyclif's teaching and preaching was the forthrightness with which he reproclaimed his attachment to the eternal society as Jesus had envisaged it. In an age all too much compromised by its sense of material convenience, Wyclif proposed a radical set of innovations in the procedures of church and state. If necessary—and he was increasingly convinced of such necessity—he believed that the Church should be divorced from material increment of practically every kind, so that it might set its heart anew on the things that are beyond this world. It was his growing conviction that no loyalty to the present society as it existed could possibly fit men for association with God and his saints in the heavenly realm. A new dedication on the part of fourteenth-century men to that world which was beyond all centuries was required to renovate the present in terms of the future. At this point, it is significant to note that he was not content with the crystallized stratifications that characterized society in his day. Small wonder that he impressed many people in high places as being about to shake the very foundations of things held sacred. It is quite possible, also, that he had no program of social reconstruction adequate to the strain imposed by his negative criticism of the existing order.[35]

Actually, Wyclif was advancing nothing less than the proposition that people of all kinds, great and small, should be held up to the leveling gaze of Jesus of Nazareth. In looking once more upon this Lord of penitence and sacrificial ministry one might discover afresh "Godde's Law" and the way into his eternal kingdom. If those in places of leadership were to aid in such a reorientation of life, they must rediscover the gospel. And if they learned anew the meaning of that gospel, they must set about at once preparing for the Judgment

---

[34] A typical expression is found in Sermon LXXIX on Mark 13:33, NUS, 49:251-53, via T. Arnold, *Select English Works* (Oxford, 1869-70), I, 261-62; 264-66. Cf. J. Loserth, ed., *Sermones* (London, 1887), I, p. vi, n. 1, and pp. vii ff.; R. C. Petry, *Preaching in the Great Tradition* (Philadelphia, 1950), pp. 106-12; J. E. Wells, *A Manual of the Writings in Middle English 1050-1400* (New Haven, 1926), pp. 465 ff., 841, and supplements. Note H. E. Winn's excellent *Wyclif, Select English Writings* (London, 1929) and H. B. Workman's authoritative, two-volume *John Wyclif* (Oxford, 1926).

[35] The relation of Wyclif to eschatology, gospel-preaching, and reform tendencies is stressed in R. C. Petry, "Emphasis on the Gospel and Christian Reform in Late Medieval Preaching," *Church History*, XVI, 2 (June, 1947), 84-86; also *Preaching in the Great Tradition*, pp. 106-12.

which it proclaimed. Briefly stated, that gospel demand called for co-ordinated preparation on the part of preachers and teachers, rich men and poor men, popes and princes, and scholars and peasants. This alone would make each individual ready, in connection with every other, for a place in the eternal world—if God so willed it.[36]

Mirk's *Festial* (*ca.* 1400, 1420), a work very well known in the later Middle Ages, is typical of much preaching upon the accepted themes of the Church.[37] In the regular cycle of the liturgical year there occurs the usual emphasis upon the Lord's Prayer. Mirk, however, gives to his treatment a freshness and an originality rarely found in such a discussion. His whole section is enlivened by a high sense of Christian community, growing out of a vigorous concept of the Last Things. This is particularly true of his treatment involving the *Pater Noster*, the *Adveniat Regnum*, and the *Fiat Voluntas Tua*.

Use of the English tongue is advocated for enlisting the full understanding, where Latin does not—this, too, in the light of the common man's need to banish the seven deadly sins and to lay hold on the grace of God as the Lord's Prayer provides. When, in the English, one says, "Our Father," he acknowledges that all are God's children; that they are brethren and sisters in God; and that if they abide in love, charity, and peace, each with the other, all shall know his common fatherhood. Here is a truly social motivation proceeding out of the freely operating heavenly concord. Furthermore, Mirk declares:

> If you live thus, then ye be brethren and sisters to our Lord Jesus Christ, God's son of Heaven, and shall be with him citizens in the Kingdom of Heaven, and the Father of Heaven is glad and fain of you, and taketh you to him as for his dear children, and have great liking for to hear your prayers.[38]

Quite obviously, ingress to the eternal kingdom and association with God's children is conditioned upon acting, now, like the brethren and sisters of Christ, who is the true Son of the kingdom. In this way his children on earth may act like the Father's own. The way to become brethren and to participate in the citizenship of the everlasting city is the way to God's prayer-hearing favor: this is the cultivation of

---

[36] NUS, 52:258-60; 49:251-53. Consult Wyclif's *De veritate sacrae scripturae*, cap. 20-21, R. Buddensieg, ed. (London, 1906), II, 137-38, 143-73; also his *Opus evangelicum*, caps. 13-14, J. Loserth, ed. (London, 1865), I, 42-46.

[37] Ed. T. Erbe (EETS, ES, 96.1, London, 1905); Wells, *Manual*, pp. 301, 807.

[38] *Festial*, "Oracione Dominica," p. 282; LI. 24-29.

love, charity, rest, and peace, each with the other. Hereupon, says Mirk, we have the right to raise humble hearts to him, saying: " 'Our Father that art in heaven, thy name be hallowed.' Praying thus, you pray for all misbelieved people, willing that all shall come to the faith that you have, leaving all other gods for him." Now this is but another way of saying that true worship of God puts the Divine and his kingdom first, so that the bond of community is even more closely knit with all mankind: "And thus you hallow God's name, showing that we be in full charity to your Father, God in heaven, and to all his people. And thus ye loveth your neighbor as yourself, willing him to come to the joy of Heaven as ye hope all to do." [39]

This placing first of God and his eternal order is, as Jesus said, the best way to serve all brother men, the world over. In praying to God, "Thy name be hallowed," man slays the foul pride that would set him apart and make him aspire to Godhead itself, or reduce him before the malicious wiles of Lucifer. In slaying such pride man sees God, high and lifted up, with all men in a common order of loving obedience beneath him.

"Thy kingdom come" rightly focuses the Christian's preference for the heavenly realm over the lure of the earthly one. Herewith the two orders assume their proper place in life's hierarchy of values. A fervent desire to come to the Father's kingdom in heaven, and the yearning to see him King with whom they shall be associated in everlasting bliss, shows that they are genuine children of his. Thus, covetousness, by which men would trade the true heaven with God for a heaven in this world, is finally annihilated.

The third prayer now becomes pertinent: "Thy will be done on earth as it is done in heaven" is the petition of those who put God's will first, as good children always do. They show, thereby, their proper obedience to the Father and their due respect for each other, the younger to the elder, and "so each one to the other in the degree that God has set him in; as angels do each one to the other in Heaven, so that the lower degree doth worship and reverence to him that is in higher degree without any simulation." Prayer is made to God for meekness and grace to show proper regard for each one— the lower to the higher for love; the higher doing reverence to him that is lower out of great meekness of heart; each one helping the other in need; each one glad of the other's good fortune and sorry for any misadventure that may befall him. Eventually the foul sin

[39] *Ibid.*, p. 282, L. 29—p. 283, L. 4.

of envy is slain—that envy which sets itself against everything companionable and serviceable in human relationships.[40]

Needless to say, such a concept of sociality has no stake in social revolution or democratic forms of organization. Stratification such as one finds in the Thomistic scheme of things is here readily apparent. But it should be remembered that medieval eschatology rarely does more than cement the type of social experience in vogue at the time. It stresses mutuality within God-ordained stations of life. Yet, social it is; and this by way of gaining the heavenly realm whose strata of merits are neither questioned nor resented.[41]

One of a number of medieval works entitled *The Mirror of the World* was translated in the later Middle Ages by William Caxton.[42] Like its predecessors, it is largely a consideration of the physical world, with some theological speculations as to the cause and final end of the universe. In the second chapter the author is treating the subject "Why God Made Man in His Own Image." He concludes that God's reason for creating the world was sheer magnanimity. He did not do it for his own betterment, or from any felt need on his part. Charity and kindness were his only motives. Consequently, he wished others to share with him "of his weal and goodness," each creature participating according to his nature.[43]

In a note appended to the text, our attention is called to the purported work of Augustine *On Loving God*.[44] According to this text, the sole cause of created beings, heavenly and earthly, was the goodness of the Creator, the one true God. Out of his graciousness, he willed that others participate in his own beatitude, the eternal blessedness. The significance of the whole reference and its apparent original is that God, himself, in his very creative act graciously designed the eternal world, not only for his own enjoyment, but that others might be sharers in it. In the succeeding chapters the author of the *Mirror* is fascinated with the remarkable creativity manifested by the Creator in his development of the whole universe. But such is his interest in the beatitude that shall come after the end of history that he returns at last to the joys of the kingdom. Drawing upon imaginative reconstructions which, he frankly admits, cannot

---

[40] *Ibid.*, pp. 283-84.
[41] Troeltsch, *Social Teaching*, I, 303-5, 262 ff.
[42] O. H. Prior, ed., *Caxton's Mirrour of the World* (EETS, 110, London, 1913).
[43] *Ibid.*, p. 12.
[44] *Ibid.*, p. 12, n. 1, as attributed by the author to Augustine, *Liber de diligendo Deo*, cap. 2, MPL 40:849-50.

do justice to the fellowship of the eternal world, he tries to limn the joys of the society which shall be God's own. In conclusion, he counsels every man to make well-considered use of his brief time in this world of trouble and sorrow. None knows the hour of death's coming.[45]

The writer is not explicit to any large degree as to the social character of those present activities that shall help to gain man his entrance into the kingdom beatitude. This is partially owing to his primary amplification of the curious structure of the material world. But the interest that he professes at the very beginning, as well as at the end where God's ultimate plans are concerned, provides a contextual meaning that is quite clear. He proposes no alteration of the prevailing social structure of his day; he does exhort his fellows to live in all areas of life so that they may properly begin, continue, and complete their course and thus attain the blessed glory in heaven.[46]

The Middle Ages had frequent recourse to Augustine for its interpretation of God's unifying purpose in the universe. The *Lay Folks' Catechism* and the work edited by Caxton on *The Mirror of the World* were but two of the many which returned, by way of Hugh the Victorine and Peter Lombard, to the sentiment of the Carthaginian bishop. They utilized the probably pseudonymous work, *On Loving God,* to buttress their argument that God had planned from the creation of the world to make men the inheritors of a blessed community with himself.[47]

In all the medieval conceptions of eternal life, a prominent place was made for the eliciting powers of this eternal society as it acted upon men in their social-individual responses within the world of time. Augustine, himself, in numerous authentic works declared the unity and omniscience of God in creating man out of the energies of the very Godhead to a society with the Godhead. In *The City of God* he declared that, from the very beginning, God anticipated a faithful people who, called by his grace to divine adoption, purified of their sins, and justified by the Holy Spirit, "would be associated with the holy angels to enjoy the eternal peace." [48]

Like those of the Middle Ages, some commentators within more

---

[45] *Mirrour,* cap. 24, p. 183.
[46] *Ibid.,* p. 184.
[47] On the *Lay-Folks' Catechism, The Lay Folks' Mass Book* (EETS, 118, 71, etc.), and the like, see Wells, *Manual,* pp. 355-56, 818 ff.
[48] XII, 22; *In Joan. Evangelium,* Tract, XXVI, 17; MPL 35:1614.

recent times have derived from the African bishop a sentiment true to him and the millennium that followed him:

Live now in that faith and holiness, in that peace of Jesus which makes a present heaven of this earth; as being a true citizen of that heavenly country; then at length shall the Lord's legacy of peace resolve itself into the New Jerusalem, that Vision of Peace which will be glorious, eternal, and perfect.[49]

[49] J. M. Ashley, *St. Augustine the Preacher* (London, 1877), pp. 186-87.

CHAPTER VII

The Ecclesiastical Community
as Servant of the Eternal Kingdom
in the Temporal World

1. Jesus, the Kingdom, and the Church:
Unity in Duality

THE PROBLEM OF WHAT JESUS THOUGHT AND SAID ABOUT THE CHURCH
is controverted beyond any likelihood of general agreement. The
more outright insistence that he dramatically made Peter the reposi-
tory of his ideals and the basis of his consciously planned organization is open to serious reservations.[1]

Jesus' larger significance, however, cannot be seen apart from his
constituting the heart of a fellowship which eventuated in the
Church. Nor can his founding of that Church in its most distinctive
aspects be successfully challenged.[2] As shown in a previous chapter,
Jesus' whole life and teaching are meaningless apart from his devotion to the kingdom.[3] Dedication to the eternal order, itself supremely social, was the key to all the relations which he sustained with his
disciples. Loyalty to the kingdom of God determined the social reorientation of his followers. With much of the life-abandon of their
Master, who had felt himself to be God's unique spokesman for and
revelation of the kingdom, they became the agency for the eternal
in the temporal. While the old order lasted—and its duration was immaterial so far as their total self-surrender was concerned—they were
the society engendered and moved from beyond which permeated the
conventional world with a new ethical leaven. How much time

---

[1] Even the early documents permit widely varying interpretations. See J. T. Shotwell
and L. R. Loomis, *The See of Peter* (New York, 1927) ; also E. Giles, ed., *Documents
Illustrating Papal Authority A. D. 96-454* (London, 1952) ; C. H. Moehlman, *Protestantism's Challenge* (New York, 1939) , p. 119; J. H. Nichols, *Primer for Protestants* (New
York, 1947) , pp. 39-40.

[2] R. N. Flew, *Jesus and His Church* (New York, 1938) , especially Part I.

[3] Chapter III.

elapsed before they began habitually to describe this reality in terms of Jesus' founding is not known. By the time they had begun to do so, they had already made social history; this was by reason of the one who had lifted them out of themselves into a new corporate loyalty.

Eventually, they began to re-examine their relation to their founder in terms of his earliest words and acts. But by that time, what they had become in terms of him was almost inextricably mixed with what they remembered and interpreted him as having said. Their language and his became increasingly hard to separate. In truth they were not mainly interested in doing so. They chose to believe that what they were, thought, and did constituted but the logical outcome of what he had first willed for them.

Thus the task of saying how much and at what points a difference exists between his actual teachings and the ones attributed to him becomes a difficult one. What is apparent through a haze of critical problems is that the Church's sayings were essentially true to his own. Most significant of all is the fact that the company into which he implanted his passionate consecration to the Father's kingdom began to regard itself as being, in a real and incontrovertible sense, the servant of the eternal in the temporal.[4] The more Christ's followers became impaled on the sharp alternatives of loyalty to this world or another, the more they proclaimed that they were at the same time *in* this present order but not *of* it. However compromised with alleviations and institutional convenience their original loyalty to the kingdom became, they continued to insist that they were, first of all, the body of Christ. They thought of themselves as the living society enspirited by the eternal kingdom at work, if not at home, in the current world.

It is difficult, then, to say in what degree Jesus thought of the Church as an independent institution of his own founding. Matthew 16:18 may be more significant for the views of the later church than for his own. Nonetheless, Jesus thought of his followers as a called-out community serving in the present world. So long as the world of time endured, they were to proclaim the coming, and follow the constitution, of the eternal world.

Specifically, Jesus may well have felt, as the Synoptics and John

---

[4] Note the bearing of such treatises as those of Clement of Rome, *The Letters of Ignatius*, *The Didache*, *The Letter to Diognetus*, and others edited by C. C. Richardson, *Early Christian Fathers* (Library of Christian Classics, I; Philadelphia, 1953). Cf. G. Bosio, ed., *I Padri Apostolici* (Turin, 1940, 1942), Parts I-II.

suggest, that he was, himself, the heavenly bread of the eternal kingdom, which should nurture and preserve the community of his faithful ones until they came to reign with him everlastingly in the new age. What he is purported to have said on the occasion of his last supper with the disciples is wholly credible. They were to serve as the corporate embodiment of his saving ministry until he ate and drank with them anew in the triumphant kingdom.[5]

The socializing character of such eschatological views could easily have precipitated the communal life attributed to them by later writers. The Gospel of John is by no means devoid of eschatological significance. The prayer of consecration in chapter 17 depicts the magnetic unity of the heavenly company as it fashions after its own likeness the society of those still in the world. Those for whom Jesus prayed were the very ones who might well remember their eternal heritage prepared from the beginning of time.[6]

Undeniably, the later church interpreted its functions as those of a society on earth responding to a heavenly world. A number of New Testament passages germane to this view probably have direct connection with Jesus' own thought. Thus the burden of the Sermon on the Mount, as recorded in Matthew 5 and Luke 6, has a socializing propulsiveness derived from an ultimate community. Mark 12 and other like sections stress the kind of repentance which, alone, will admit seekers after God's eternal kingdom to membership in the celestial commonwealth. Luke 4, which rests upon Isaiah 61, is concerned to show that Jesus felt a responsibility to the poor and downtrodden. He, like Isaiah, perhaps anticipated some immediate changes in earthly society because of the new world that was even now breaking its way into the present order. Mark 16:15-20 gives expression to a missionary ideal which is surely not foreign to the larger outreach of Jesus' thought and action; it, too, inheres in the very nature of crisis urgency, joined to calm assurance, with which Jesus encouraged all his faithful to anticipate the coming kingdom.

Indeed, as Matthew 10:6-12, 26-33 clearly indicates, the complete self-abandon with which a follower gives himself to the impending kingdom will determine his status before the Father in heaven. One cannot fail to apprise his fellow men of world's end and still have a secure place in the society that shall finally rule. Matthew 12:25-30 demonstrates that the final destiny of Jesus' followers is to be de-

---

[5] Matt. 26:26-29; Mark 4:22-25; Luke 22:17-20.
[6] Cf. Matt. 25:34, and the previous references in Chapter II, nn. 25, 28.

termined on the basis of their undivided commitment to God's realm. Unequivocating service is to express itself in the present world, without delay. Matthew 25:34-46 is consistent with Jesus' emphasis that the new standard of greatness which is to apply in the kingdom is to become operative at once among his followers. They are to be little or great in terms of their absolute submission to the needs of his least.[7]

It may be conceded that the early church read into Jesus' teachings certain connotations that were not originally there. One may well be skeptical, however, of the view that the Church originated at a later period the idea of a society drawn from above that was even now socializing and personalizing the present.[8] In order to make effective, for however slight a period, the socializing character of the kingdom, Jesus had to transmit its social quality to a community. The Church—whether or not founded by Christ as a carefully articulated organization—grew out of the *agape* experience which he made definitive in the familial association with his followers.[9]

The consistency with which the early and medieval Fathers refer to the Church as the social instrumentality of the heavenly kingdom is striking, to say the least. One may pick at random a few of the more significant designations. Thus, Walafrid of Fulda thinks of the Church as the introit and the vestibule of heaven.[10] Lactantius recognizes no true cult outside it.[11] Where God cannot truly be worshiped, salvation cannot be effected. Gregory the Great gravely denies to those beyond God's Church any share in the eternal heritage.[12] Jerome shares this view.[13] Frequently encountered is the patristic idea that God has been, from the very beginning, the fostering creator and supreme governor of the Church; and that he has foreseen it and designed it for his own purposes to the end of time. He will then incorporate it into his eternal society. This conception is developed at some length in St. Hilary of Poitiers, by Prosper of Aquitaine, in Gregory the Great, and by Anselm. The same theme runs throughout the thought of the Middle Ages—whether in the impassioned

---

[7] Mark 9:34-50; Luke 22:15-31.

[8] Ch. Guignebert, *Jésus* (Paris, 1933) , pp. 486-87.

[9] Flew, *Jesus*, pp. 80-122, particularly.

[10] *Glossa ordinaria*—Lib. Levit., cap. VI, vs. 16; MPL 113:312 D.

[11] *Div. Instit.*, IV, 30; MPL 6:542.

[12] *Moral. in Job*, Lib. XXXV, cap. VIII (VII) ; MPL 76:755 ff.; *In primum regum expos.*, Lib. I, MPL 79:46. Cf. Aug., Sermo CXLVI, MPL 38:797.

[13] *Com. in Ezech.*, Lib. II, cap. VII, MPL 25:71.

poetry of St. Francis of Assisi, the noble visions of Dante, or the mystic exultation of Ruysbroeck the Admirable.[14]

The concept of the Church as being in itself a community that joins the eternal and the temporal world is basic throughout the Church's literature. A favorite interpretation depicts the Church as it molds the lives of human beings on earth while preserving eternal foundations in heaven. This is far more than a seemingly awkward figure of speech; it is characteristic of Christian theology in the whole period under consideration. It is possible—yes, even indispensable—for an earthly society to rest upon a basis that is wholly transcendent of the terrestrial. This is the Fathers' main contention when they say, "The church is always stable and indefectible because its foundations are above in heaven." [15]

The Fathers were often quite resourceful in the designations which they applied to the churchly institution. Many of these terms had special reference to local associations of Christians. The word "Church" itself had been used by Paul to indicate both a local community of the faithful and an all-comprising society of Christians—as occasion demanded. But in its larger sense—the one never far removed from the mind of the early and medieval Christian—the word "Church" had relation to a corporate vocation. This calling had come from God himself, and it looked toward a final incorporation in an eternal assembly. Those who were members of the Church were the ones described in the Gospels as having had prepared for them from the foundations of the world an abiding inheritance in the kingdom of God.[16]

Prevailing interpretations of the Church's character and function made it easy for the Christian to think of the ecclesiastical institution as being ancillary to the eternal society while living in temporal community. The very thought of the Church as being in some sense both heavenly and earthly made feasible its designation as the servant of

[14] Hilary Poitiers, *Ex Opere Historico frag.* II, 1, MPL 10:632; Tract in CXXXI Ps. 14, MPL 9:736; Prosper of Aquitaine, *Psalmorum AC ad CL Expositio*, Ps. CXIX, MPL 51:317 ff.; Greg. *In prim. reg. expos.* Lib. III, nos. 9-10, nos. 17-18, MPL 79:153; Anselm, *De Fide Trinitatis*, Praef., MPL 158:261; Francis of Assisi, *Expositio super orationem Dominicam*, in H. Boehmer and F. Wiegand, *Analekten zur Geschichte des Franciscus von Assisi* (Tübingen, 1930), pp. 48-49; G. O. Karrer, *Saint Francis of Assisi, the Legends and Lauds* (New York, 1949), pp. 266-68. Cf. J. Ruysbroeck, *Adornment of the Spiritual Marriage*, ed. C. A. Wynschenk Dom (London, 1916), Bk. II, Chap. 45, pp. 109-10; *Book of Supreme Truth*, Chap. III, pp. 227-28.

[15] St. Augustine, *Enarratio in Ps.*, XXIX, 10; MPL, 36:223. *Enarratio in Ps.* LXXXVI; MPL 37:1103; Sermo 76 (a), MPL 38:479.

[16] Matt. 25:34.

the eternal community in the temporal society of the faithful. When, therefore, the Church was referred to as the assembly of the faithful, it had attached to it, not only the characteristics of the human institution, but also the qualities of life to be associated with people who had an abiding and mutual beatitude. Members of the early church and those of the medieval period, also, were scarcely offended on being referred to as a heavenly company. The description which fitted them most was not one attaching to their temporal character, but much more to their ultimate destiny. Likewise, such a term as "household of faith" conveyed the idea of an intimacy which should be that of members under one roof; in this case it betokened those living already in faithful anticipation of a more joyous domicile in the future. To be reminded that they were a family of God was the highest spiritual compliment that members of a Christian body could accept. But this in turn carried with it an inspiring suggestion: They had been born from the creative powers of God's unifying life unto a social redemption. The divine plan would finally restore them to an everlasting portion in the kingdom of heaven.[17]

Such literary usage assumed that the Church anticipated a heavenly destiny that would be consummately social. The fact that it was described in its interim capacity as being an assembly, a company, a household, a family, a coetus, a city, a corpus, a tabernacle, a domicile, a congregation, or any one of the infinite variety of like terms only indicated the more the ultimate significance attached to the Church's life.[18] The Church aspired to the characteristics that these terms connoted, even while it was on its temporal pilgrimage, because it would realize these qualities fully when it had entered into the everlasting kingdom. The burden of patristic literature, at this point, was to encourage faithful Christians on earth to reproduce in some measure the heavenly outlines of their felicity and mutuality.

Augustine fulfilled a particular mission in focusing the attention of Christians upon their twofold incorporation. In a fashion often since copied, he fixed the imagination of the faithful upon the close parallel between the heavenly and the earthly societies. Fortunately, he emphasized the continuity that existed between them, even while he clearly pictured the discontinuity that maintained.

[17] For a series of names, definitions, cognomens and their specific contexts, drawn from diverse sources, early and medieval, see the index volume, MPL 219:667. Cf. the useful *Elucidatio in 235 tabulas Patrologiae Latinae* (Rotterdam, 1952), under "Ecclesia," pp. 31-32. Of fundamental importance is J. C. Fenton, "Scholastic Definitions of the Catholic Church," *The American Ecclesiastical Review*, CXI, 1 (July, 1944), 59-61.

[18] MPL 219:668 ff.

There was, to be sure, a great separation between the joys of earthly society and those of the supernal community. But he led his Christian brethren on to anticipate things heavenly by cherishing some of the real goods already foreshadowed in mortal associations. Without being traitorous to the heavenly kingdom he could emphasize the joys of this world as a foretaste of things unimaginably greater, and yet to come. The net effect was not to limit expectation to the contours of the terrestrial, but to lift the eyes of the Christian in celestial expectation, even while he sought to surmount things good but evanescent.[19]

The saints must necessarily have a greater love for the eternal city than the affection borne by the denizens of Rome for their city. Surely, it was not only to recompense the virtues of the Romans that their empire had become so glorious. It was, rather, to serve as an example to the citizens of the eternal city while they were on pilgrimage here below; and to make them consider properly what kind of love they must manifest for the heavenly country if they were to surpass the devotion of the Romans for their state.[20]

The principle employed by the Fathers in evolving definitions of the Church is also operative in the description of its characteristics. The analysis of ecclesiastical character has inevitably to do with social qualities. These social meanings, however much they may be related to temporal experiences, have no lasting significance aside from their eternal conditionings.

Thus the typical Christian thinker habitually described the Church in terms of its unity.[21] The *ecclesia* was held to be, ideally, a oneness in Christ. It was always being exhorted to realize such a unifying power. Few, if any, Christians hoped to secure an actuality, however approximate, on the basis of any purely human experiences. They reverted to the heavenly unity, proceeding from the Trinity, to find the pattern and the abiding hope of their earthly institution. Christians were not admonished to build a heavenly unity out of their laboriously perfected humanity. The earthly church, with all of its limitations and tragic failures, was asked to look upon the perfection of its eternal end. The oneness of the triune Godhead, and the perfect concord with it of the saints already in glory, was made the pat-

---

[19] Consult the key source readings in Przywara, *Augustine Synthesis*, pp. 246 ff.; 265 ff. Cf. Augustine's *Catechizing the Uninstructed*, caps. 20-21, NPNF, 1st Ser., III, 304-5.

[20] *De Civ. Dei*, V, 16.

[21] See under XI, i, "Unitas," MPL 219:677-78.

tern for daily living on the part of those who were journeying to the promised land.

Sanctity was another characteristic generally imputed to God's Church.[22] Christian teachers and preachers hastened to explain that they entertained no foolish expectations of infallibility and sinlessness on the part of any group of human beings in this world. Those who were of the household of faith were urged, nonetheless, to remember that they lived for holy ends and that they were in the process of being made ready for an association which God would empower with his purity and oneness. In Paul's time all too many people had been glad to arrogate for themselves a reputation for holiness far removed from the quality of their everyday lives. He had warned them to make their daily living conform ever more closely to the definitive standards laid down by Jesus. Furthermore, he had been quite specific in his declarations that these criteria could not be interpreted in selfish fashion. Those who dared to anticipate a lasting community with God in the future must serve him in the present as one devoted body of Christ. The final unity upon which they patterned their temporal society must preserve their dedication to a holy way of life.

This required, in turn, that the Christian faith be thought of increasingly in catholic or universalizing terms.[23] One might conveniently refer to a church at a given place; but he could not conceive of God's Church as being limited to any place or time. This sweeping quality the Church attributed to the all-pervasiveness of the divine purpose. God might have varying plans for different groups and individuals. But he left none of these out of his final accounting. His Church would be gathered from all the earth, from the beginning of time, and beyond the ending of time, into the kingdom which he had prepared. One thing, alone, gave authoritative perspective to the share of all Christians in catholic life; this was the fact that they had been destined from creation itself to be associated with all others of their kind in the heavenly world. The worship of the Church was admirably designed to remind the faithful Christian of this all-important fact.

As the Christian looked about for the basis of his security and stability in this world, he was encouraged to seek for it in another. He was forever being told that the Church on pilgrimage, which fought the evils of the present age, was to be welcomed into the triumphant

[22] II, "Sanctitas," MPL 219:678-79.
[23] III, "Catholicitas," MPL 219:679-80.

society that transcended all periods and localities. It was that eternal world which had given the Church militant to earth. The Lord God had supplied the foundations for the temporal Church in the apostolic stability which Christ had brought from heaven and committed to Peter and the Apostles.[24]

When the medieval liturgy of the mass repeated the all-inspiring words of commission, which it interpreted as being the beginning of the Church among men, it reminded all the faithful that Peter's strength was from above and that his victory was sure. The Church and those who became associated with it were given their share in that enduring potency. No better sign of promise was theirs than the authority which they had for banding themselves together, under Peter and his vicars, in Jesus' name. Looking to the author and finisher of their faith, they found the basis and the end-product of their association together. They need have no fear as to the value of their society among men so long as they remembered to hold it on the course of the Apostles' choosing. The pillars of heaven were their support; the ship of Christ was their secure transportation; the heavenly food was their guarantee of everlasting life. Their protection for life together in this world was their present incorporation in the everlasting life of the eternal order. Such were the sentiments that the medieval church deduced from the plasticity of early Christian thought and brought to institutional fixity. The medieval formulation is hardly debatable at the point of its having sensed correctly the Church's most uninterrupted tradition. Pursuant to it, the Church accepted its commission to live corporately in this world according to its predestined heritage in the future community.[25]

If one were to select a term most intimately descriptive of the developing Christian regard for ecclesiastical life under the shadow of divine approval, he might well hit upon the designation of "family." [26] Carrying out the long-standing association so sacred to the Jewish tradition, the Christian, too, loved to think of his comrade-

---

[24] IV, "Apostolicitas," MPL 219:680. In relation to the above, see Art. 9 of Thomas Aquinas on the Creed as edited and translated by J. B. Collins, *The Catechetical Instructions of St. Aquinas* (New York, 1934), pp. 48 ff.; *Op. Om.*, XXVII, Opusc. 1, pp. 222-24.

[25] Petry, *Francis of Assisi*, Chaps. V and VI particularly. Consult the *Elucidatio: Patr. Latinae*, under "Cultus," p. 26; "Missae sacrificium," pp. 54-55, etc.; cf. MPL 219:666-86: "Index de ecclesia."

[26] Note the multiplicity of references to "conjux," "Domus dei," "Filia synagogae," "Haereditas dei," "Mater omnium Christianorum," "Paterfamilias," "Sponsa," etc. in MPL, 219:667-72. A pertinent study is J. C. Plumpe, *Mater Ecclesia* (Washington, D. C., 1943).

ship with his fellows as being after the pattern of children in relation to a loving parent. Many of the references to the Church that bear such intimate connections are doubtless casual and of no special significance. But a deep undercurrent of warm, loving regard for the Fatherhood of God and the brotherhood of man was woven into many of the ablest discussions of the Church's character and function. Attention was frequently called to the fact that a purely natural association of human beings ought to have characteristics in keeping with a common, natural brotherhood. Such commentators frequently went on to point out how transcendingly familial should be this society of those who had God for their father and the Church for their mother. They did not forget to emphasize the fact that such a family stemmed from heaven itself and would have its most gratifying reward in the consummation of the eternal household.

The figures which appealed most to the Christian imagination were doubtless those in which the heavenly associations were depicted as following the outlines of a family reunion. Jesus' own parables had been full of such suggestions, and Christian theologians enlarged upon these pictures endlessly. In the homilies associated with the liturgy, as in the sermons to men and women variously circumstanced, the exhortations were most uniformly appreciated when they pointed out the similarity between the human tenderness of the earthly family and the loving concord of the heavenly. Bishops and other responsible churchmen who tried most honestly to bring their parishes into keeping with the Christian ideal made ready capital of such ideas. The Church was consistently represented as a great family on pilgrimage to its eternal home. Those who lived in it most companionably while they were in passage to heaven would be giving the best evidence that they were destined for inclusion within the Lord's household.

A point of vantage in the Church's calendar was its customary pictorialization of the divine family as having a place within it for saints who had already passed on and for the faithful who lived in such fashion as to merit a share within it. All of these might hope to sit down at the Lord's table when they had finally been judged worthy on the Last Day. The Church was undoubtedly at its best when it could appeal to humble Christians to live a wholesome family life on earth as preparation for membership in the heavenly family. All the severity of a disciplinary parent as well as the tenderness ascribed to the Saviour and his virginal mother had a powerful effect upon the emotions and, at least, upon the potential actions of good Catholics. Countless mothers in the Middle Ages looked hopefully upon the faces of the Mother Mary and her son because in them they discerned a familial tenderness that was unsurpassable. All that the word "father" connoted became most beautifully effective on those occasions when the Church, as a universal family, raised its reverent gaze to the Father in heaven.

Many a good medieval Church Father made his most eloquent plea in terms of the Lord's Prayer. Then, indeed, one might say, not selfishly, "My Father," but, rather, as one of many children, "Our Parent, who art in heaven." In so doing he would be reminding all Christians of the ineffable experiences that would be theirs, finally, in the Father's house. Meanwhile, the Church, in the persons of those commissioned by God and his Son, would transmit the Father's requirements to his obedient children. Living according to his law in the present would be the glad duty of those who hoped to come to his household in the future.[27]

A difficult problem throughout Christian history has been the proper clarification of the relationship existing between the kingdom of God and his Church. One approach to the kingdom considers it as the fulfillment of the divine purpose here in this world,

uniting all things by the power of love, and fulfilling all righteousness. In so far as love and righteousness are present within the Christian church, the kingdom is found in that measure in the church. Inasmuch as the Christian fellowship is an imperfect manifestation of that love and righteousness, the kingdom cannot be identified with the church.[28]

Furthermore, "because God's kingdom is to embrace all creation in an ultimate unity, it presents to the church its greatest moral challenge." Here the Church is thought of as receiving a special commission from the already existing Kingdom, and as being given from the divine kingdom the hope and divine resources with which to discharge its obligations to the world at large. But the warning is apropos that "no achievement of Christian unity can be a substitute for the kingdom of God, even though all increase in Christian unity is a part of the coming of that kingdom." [29]

However far removed this may be from the conclusions of specific

---

[27] Cf. Chrysostom, "On the Lord's Prayer," with "De Oracione Dominica," *Mirk's Festial* (EETS, ES 96.1 London, 1905), pp. 282 ff.

[28] An unofficial memorandum of the Chicago Ecumenical Discussion Group: "The Ethical Reality and Freedom of the Church"—unpublished, mimeographed work, p. 3.

[29] *Loc. cit.*

thinkers in the Middle Ages, it does correspond to the early and medieval view that the Church on earth must serve as the servant of the eternal in the temporal. The Church's earliest experience would welcome the sentiment that

the church is the servant of the kingdom of God. The kingdom of God is the consummation of the church's common work and fellowship. It is in common devotion to the will of God to all men that the church finds the surest way to unity. . . . But in neither the consecrated individual nor the community of the faithful is the kingdom of God fully realized, though we have an earnest of its coming.[30]

It is hazardous for any group to identify the kingdom and the Church—under whatever figure—however often Augustine and others may do it. As one interpretation phrases it, "The kingdom of God is the consummation of the Church's common work and fellowship." Furthermore, it is the kingdom which occasions the Church, gives it power on earth, and preserves a heavenly incorporation of it within the eternal realm.[31]

How intriguing early and medieval Christians found this unity in duality to be is evidenced on every hand. More usually than not, the Church is thought of as being placed in time for the purpose of doing the eternal kingdom's will. So the *Didache* says, "Remember, Lord, Thy Church, to deliver it from all evil and to make it perfect in Thy love, and gather it from the four winds, sanctified for Thy kingdom which Thou hast prepared for it." Nostalgic for its final welcome into the ultimate society, the Church cannot forswear its function of leavening the world's life with the salvation offered by Christ.[32]

Clement of Alexandria (d. 215) sees in "the earthly Church . . . the image of the heavenly" and so derives new motivation for the Master's prayer "that the will of God may be done upon the earth as in heaven." Unity, forgiveness, and the ministry of love are the hallmarks of the community that prefigures on earth the solidarity of the celestial world. The Church, after the likeness of eternal unity, enjoys a unified heritage. Its function is to summon to itself, according to the Lord's will, all foreordained to a portion with the just.[33]

Ambrose (d. 397) considers the manner in which the Church be-

[30] *Ibid.*, pp. 3-4.
[31] *Ibid.*, p. 3.
[32] *Didache*, X; Translation of ANF, VII, 380.
[33] *Stromata*, Bk. IV, cap. 8; ANF, II, 421 as quoted; MPL VII, 1278.

comes the means of conferring eternal life, even as womankind serves to propagate the physical life of man. Again, the Church is for him the "torcular," or wine press, of the eternal fountain by which the fruit of the celestial vine is made to flow.[34]

Augustine (d. 430), in a mood reminiscent of Origen (d. 251), declares that Christ's committal of the heavenly keys to Peter is to be interpreted as bestowing all such rights upon the Church in its totality. When Jesus said to Simon, "Thou art Peter . . ." and gave him, forthwith, the means of opening the kingdom of heaven to all who should be associated with him, he literally made the Church the agent of the eternal society operating in the temporal. Furthermore, he specifically indicated that the Church's business on earth was to gather together into a community, on the pattern of the eternal, the conventicle of the saved. These would then be eternally associated in the supernal heritage.[35]

Matching this sentiment in his *City of God,* Augustine utters the praises of the saints' habitation. This city is above, but it begets citizens below where it sojourns till the time of its ultimate reign. From the glorious City of God, celebrated by the holy angels, comes the invitation to men to join in the heavenly citizenship. "Social?" asks Augustine. "How could the eternal city have beginning, or develop, or attain its proper destiny if the life of the saints were not social?" And his countless writings record his faith in the earthly church as the community most responsive among men to the mutualizing purposes of the eternal kingdom.[36]

Hrabanus Maurus (d. 856) was one of those theologians and preachers who helped make real to the ninth century the eternal function of the Church in the temporal world. He saw in the Passover of Christ a symbol of the heavenly kingdom and the salvation of the world.[37] The Resurrection mirrored forth to him and to those who heard him that final renaissance of all human beings. This was to be followed by eternal judgment and everlasting disposal to endless woes or everlasting joys. In a famous Easter sermon which he preached, Hrabanus rises to the heights of spiritual suggestion regarding the eternal beatitude and the manner in which the Church should con-

---

[34] *De spiritu sancto,* Lib. 1, Prol., MPL 16:732.

[35] *De doctrina Christiana,* 18; MPL, 34:25; Sermo CCXCV, ii, 2; MPL 38:1349; Przywara, *Augustine Synthesis,* pp. 224-25.

[36] *De Civ. Dei,* XIX, 5; XV, 1; X, 25; XV, 3.

[37] Manitius, *Geschichte,* I, 288 ff.; A. Ebert, *Histoire générale de la littérature du moyen âge en occident* (Paris, 1884), II, 137-64; G. Schnürer, *Kirche und Kultur im Mittelalter,* II, see index.

duce to that happy end. To this kingdom, conceived of in terms of its eternal character, Maurus grants a twofold entrance:

> For there are two gates,—the gate of Paradise, and the gate of the Church. We have entered first by the gate of the Church,—that is, by Faith and Baptism: in which if we shall faithfully remain, and do good works, after the end of this life we shall enter the gate of Paradise.[38]

Thinking of holy Church as God's own divine agency, Hrabanus denominates it the House of God. From it no Christian soul wishes to be excluded. By good daily living each will seek a part in the Church's great family. Entrance may thus be gained to the "kingdom of the everlasting Father, to whom she bare us as the children of adoption." In the full character of Christian fellowship that shall one day encompass all his saints, each Christian should strive to live now in the world as his Church shall lead him.

St. Anselm (d. 1109) is, of course, well known for his allegorical interpretations of the Scriptures. Commenting on Matthew 14:22, he says: "In this lection, according to its mystical interpretation, we have a summary description of the state of the Church, from the coming of the Saviour to the end of the world." Thus the Lord's constraining his disciples to get into a ship symbolizes his commitment of the Church to the government of the Apostles and their followers. This going before him unto the other side is interpreted as a bearing

> onwards towards the haven of the celestial country, before he himself should entirely depart from the world. For, with his elect, and on account of his elect, he ever remains here until the consummation of all things; and he is preceded to the other side of the sea of this world by those who daily pass hence to the land of the living; And when he shall have sent all that are his to that place, then, leaving the multitude of the reprobate, and no longer warning them to be converted, but giving them over to perdition, he will depart hence that he may be with his elect alone in the kingdom.[39]

The preacher takes full advantage of mystical phrasings and conceptions. But his belief in the Church as providing the means wherewith Christ administers entrance to the saving realm is thoroughly apparent. The celestial kingdom, toward which the Lord points the

[38] Neale, *Mediaeval Preachers,* pp. 38-41, especially p. 40.
[39] *Hom. III, in Evang. Matt.,* MPL 158:597-602; Neale, *Mediaeval Preachers,* pp. 80-82; NUS 25:136-39.

way, and into which he welcomes his saints, is no mere figure of speech. At the end of the world when he shall return to gather his saints from the ends of it, he will reascend to heaven with all his beloved members that comprise his body mystical.

With these sentiments of Maurus and Anselm, Bernard of Clairvaux (d. 1153) was in full agreement when he lauded Mother Church. Even now, though in a place of exile, she has heavens of her own. These are spiritual men through whom she rains down from the eternal realm the word of salvation.

As the bride of the Lord, this Church, catholic and apostolic, transmits to men the saving grace of Christ himself. Conforming herself already in the fervor of her devotion to the unity of her heavenly Spouse, the Church calls humanity to join her in the consummate fraternity of that future glory.[40]

A fragment from a sermon of St. Anthony the Paduan (d. 1231) shows how that alert preacher could play endlessly on the theme of the Church's doing the kingdom's will. Like the parts of a ship—its mast, rudder, anchor, and oars—are the Christian virtues. The mast is emblematic of a united faith in the Church; the rudder symbolizes a loving brotherhood making straight for a secure harbor in the congregation of the saints; the anchor denotes the stability of a divinely operating mercy; and the oars bring the ship to its eternal port. So are the ship and its parts reminiscent of the way of charity and love by which the Church leads men through temporal ministry to a safe haven in the eternal heritage. The ship is, as Bonaventura would say, the means by which men ride out the storms of life.[41]

Later in the thirteenth century William Durand of Mende (d. 1296) produced, in a work *On the Divine Offices,* a series of observations on the Church's divine-human character. In Book I, Chapter 1, he had noted the term "convocation" as a likely designation for the Church. This he felt to be appropriate because "it calleth men to itself." He reminds us that the Church militant is often called Sion "because, amidst its wanderings, it expecteth the promise of a heavenly rest." On yet other occasions it may properly be thought of as *"the tabernacle of God,* because this present life is a journey, and a

---

[40] See, especially, *Serm. in Cant.* XXVII, no. 12; Eales, *Works,* IV, 175; MPL 183:920.
[41] "Christian Virtues Compared to the Parts of a Ship," Neale, *Preachers,* pp. 236-37. On Anthony and his preaching see R. M. Huber, *St. Anthony of Padua* (Milwaukee, 1947), pp. 45 ff., 72 ff., with three of Anthony's sermons in the original Latin, pp. 200 ff. Cf. L. F. Rohr, *The Use of Sacred Scripture in the Sermons of St. Anthony of Padua* (Washington, D. C., 1948), p. 52, n. 66; *In Dom. V Post Pentecosten,* I, 291b ff., *Sermones,* ed., A. M. Locatelli (Padua, 1895).

progress to a lasting Country." Continuing with the various parts of the physical edifice, Durand draws analogies with their spiritual counterparts. Thus, the open court of the building signifies Christ, "by Whom an entrance is administered into the heavenly Jerusalem." "The towers are the preachers and the Prelates of the Church," who constitute her bulwarks and defenses. In yet other connections the preachers are thought of as sustaining beams. The qualities of the watchful preacher are suggested by the ever-vigilant cock.

Durand, as an aggressive reformer and a good liturgist, had ample opportunity in his book to symbolize both the more immediate and the more remote aspects of the Church's life. His references to its parts as a building and to its qualities reflected in its constituency are wholly pertinent to the ultimate destiny which it serves among men.[42]

We may now summarize, with special indebtedness to Professor Robert Will, some of the more important characteristics of the *ecclesia* as it relates the duality of world orders to its unity of life in Christ Jesus.[43]

Because there are two orders of life, so widely different and yet so closely related, the Christian must forever be aware of the temporal and the eternal. It is especially incumbent upon him to think of the eternal community as possessing qualities and a perfection never ascribable to human society here upon the earth. But Jesus, and those who followed him, continued to stress the necessity of bridging the gap which exists between the two orders. If it be true to say that there is discontinuity between them, it is no less fair to point out that there is a measure of continuity. And the sequence is such as to make the temporal society follow the dictates and accept the invitations of the eternal.

Here the twofold character of the Church itself becomes highly applicable to the discussion. For there is a sense in which the Church is, at one and the same time, both eternal and temporal. The ecclesiastical community, therefore, becomes the logical medium by which the world of the eternal and the world of the temporal are related in one continuing, if forever heightening, experience. The Church, when thought of in terms of its eternality, conveys the mandates of the kingdom to the Church which is on earth. The Church eternal,

---

[42] J. M. Neale and B. Webb, eds., *The Symbolism of Churches and Church Ornaments,* a translation of the first book of the *Rationale Divinorum Officiorum* (Leeds, 1843), sections 2, 4, 6, 8, 9, 20, 21, 29, 31, 22; pp. 17-18, 20-22, 27, 30-31, 27-28.

[43] The following pages, to the end of the present chapter, follow closely the argument of *Le Culte,* III, 294-300.

likewise, transmits to the Church temporal the powers of the kingdom. Thus the Church serves the kingdom, both in heaven and on earth. The Church on earth in the course of responding to the Church which is in heaven becomes the servant of the kingdom. The temporal church is, in the midst of making such a response, the redeeming element in the whole world of men.

According to this view the Church may be described in Augustine's terms as a "body permixed." It is a dual phenomenon. As a community it is at once a concrete collectivity and an ideal reality. It partakes of qualities at once representative and virtual. It is both visible and invisible; a human organization in a divine institution. It is a sociological aggregate and a transcendental totality. Here is a historic grandeur evolving in time and a Platonic city reposing in eternity. Thus it appears both militant and triumphant; a deposit of the faith and an object of the faith; a means of grace and an end in itself.

The Church in terms of its empirical character may be thought of as a natural institution involved in sin and error. As such it falls under the judgment of God. In the words of Galatians 1:14 and Acts 15:39, God now conceals the true Church under the weight of sins, disputes, and scandals. That the Apostles, themselves, failed to obtain concord in the Church is apparent. For this Church, conceived of as a terrestrial institution, suffers the contingencies of physical life and material things. It has an evolution in time, a history. Jesus, himself, in order to organize the Messianic forces of a future kingdom established the historical foundations of a terrestrial church. By his very choice of disciples he set up the core of a new Israel, placing Peter in a position of primacy. The parables of the discarded fish, for instance, suppose a compact church of which the eschatological prolongation will correct the empirical contingencies.

In Matthew 18:17 one is invited to see the ecclesiastical constitution in embryo. After the physical disappearance of the Lord, the Church is formed; those who would be saved from within a perverse generation undergo baptism. The Word is announced; bread is broken; a whole tradition grows up which draws for its sustenance on the memory of the risen Lord. New churches group themselves around that of Jerusalem of which James, Cephas, and John are the main supports. A clerical tendency makes its appearance. Paul enlarges the field of Christian life and activities. A growing multiplication of functions is represented in a ministry dealing with the cult and the cure of souls. More and more signs of communication

169

between bodies religiously and economically motivated are now discernible. The problem of literature, finances, and mounting institutional involvement is apparent. Not only growth, but a new confusion of purposes and methods finds expression.

Seen thus from its earthly side, the Church follows very much the course of other secular organizations. In part buried beneath the prevailing customs of the time, it still diverges sharply enough at certain points to encounter hostility and persecution. Its weaknesses are much in evidence. But it has its strength, likewise. In the body of its human membership there are found living faith, a sacrificial spirit, and frequent exhibitions of mutuality. In all of its activities one may discern the living suggestion that though it remains human, it draws upon something that is divine.

An equally clear-cut interpretation of the Church's transcendent aspects might be provided. Within that which is merely apparent and terrestrial, there is a power which is from above. The Holy Spirit, as the day of Pentecost indicates, becomes the constitutive force of the Church that is on earth. This Spirit is the power within the Church which is beyond the things of earth. Yet we must remember that we are here dealing not with two churches but with two aspects of the same Church.

One may defend the position that the Church is the Holy Spirit in its terrestrial actuality. From the Spirit proceeds the vital unity and the mystic supraindividuality that the Church of earth knows. By God's Word, which he dispenses and makes explicit, the Spirit engenders the faith of believing individuals; and by the Word, the Spirit creates the supernatural organism which will receive particular individuals unto itself. For this Word is incarnated in Christ. He has promised to dwell at the heart of his Church until the end of the world. It is the continuing presence of Christ which communicates to the Church environed by this world the supernatural reality of a heavenly Jerusalem.

The Church recognizes, in the voice of the Spirit, the voice of the Lord, himself. For the Spirit communicates to the members of the Church the living echo of his gospel; and the Spirit guarantees to them the mystic presence of the glorified one. Thus, it has been said that "the church is, 'after a fashion,' the sensible halo of the Spirit of the Lord raised to the celestial glory." By means of the Spirit, Christ and the Church comprise a single whole. So intimate is their correlation that the Church may not be found where Christ is not, and Christ is not where the Church may not be found. He is the sole builder of the Church and its angular stone. He is its supernatural head. For this reason the New Testament refers to the Church as the Church of Christ, the Church of the Lord, and the Church in Christ. If the Church is this supernatural organism of which Christ is the Spirit, then the work of the Redeemer will find itself actualized in it.

The foregoing views celebrate the redemptive sociality of the Church. The ideal of world-wide salvation postulates a social grandeur which takes in all areas and times. Fortified with its great universal mission, the Church judges the world; for however much it may be established *in* the world, it is, by virtue of its metaphysical grandeur, also as little *of* this world as Christ himself. Nevertheless, it promises to that world all the fullness of salvation available in Christ. And in such ministry to the unsaved it will serve, not only as a socializing institution, but also as the very consolidation of the life of Christ on earth as it will be in heaven.

"But," one may ask, "how do these transcendent qualities of the Church harmonize with its empirical nature?" For we cannot forget that the Church, in its terrestrial life, is plunged into sin and error. The New Testament, however, does not falter in designating the members of the *koinonia* as saints. This is not because it thinks to exalt them by reason of any moral infallibility. Rather does it qualify them, in terms of their association in the Church, as God's elect who, freed in principle from earthly cares, find themselves in a state of grace. The Church surrounds with an atmosphere of sanctity from on high those sinners who confide themselves to it. This metaphysical sanctity absorbs the moral indigence of the empirical Church.

It has already been observed how much of woe and tribulation the Church experiences here below. But is that not to be expected on the part of the spouse of Christ, who was himself subjected to so much suffering and sorrow? Martin Luther, for example, sympathizes with the Christian desire to find in the Church the pure, undefiled dove of the Lord. So it is, in effect, Luther thinks; but he knows, too, that the Church in the world must, like its Master, suffer scandal and loss. Perhaps these tribulations are a genuine sign of its communion with Christ.

Previously mentioned, also, have been the sensible phenomena which constitute the exterior image of the Church: its worship, doctrine, and constitution. These figurations, however imperfect they may be, are, nonetheless, the symbols of a superior reality.

It is the Church's business to gather together the personal aspirations of the faithful; but this, too, the Church does by virtue of the impulses of divine grace. Whatever power operates in and through the Church is a creation and extension of the divine work—God making use of the whole group in order to seize and save the benighted.

The Church as a temporal phenomenon is irrevocably involved in a relativism which goes with things ephemeral. Here again, however, the ongoing work of the historical Jesus, in conjunction with the life of the glorified Christ, gives to his Church, in which he is always present, a dignity and a power which are beyond and above things temporal. Taken in its larger aspect, therefore, the Church appears as the congregation of those who, here below, see as in a glass darkly; they are, nonetheless, the assembly of the first-born inscribed in heaven. In the twofold Church that is, in reality, one society under two aspects, time and eternity embrace each other.

CHAPTER VIII

The Ecclesiastical Community
as Servant of the Eternal Kingdom
in the Temporal World

2. The Ecclesiastical Hierarchy Patterned After
the Celestial Hierarchy

THE EARLY AND MEDIEVAL CHURCH SOUGHT THROUGH THE CONCEPT of hierarchy to establish ecclesiastical equilibrium between the eternal kingdom and temporal society. The Church delineated among men a social ordering patterned after the heavenly world. Its functions in the human sphere recapitulated, approximately, the gradations from highest to lowest revealed by the celestial world.

Thus, in the course of serving the eternal kingdom in the temporal society, the Church developed its human hierarchy after the heavenly one. Even as the primal unity of heaven was thought to proceed from the Trinity, through the graded ranks of angelic choirs, and thence to man, so the ecclesiastical hierarchy was held to issue from the holy pontiff through archbishops, bishops, priests, deacons, and the minor orders, to the laity itself. Just as the life impulse of all community secured its derivation from the Godhead—increasingly thought of in its triune oneness—so it returned through all the intermediaries of the common life among men, upward through the angelic ranks, and back to the unity that sent it forth. All manyness comes from oneness; and to the oneness of this perfect unity in Trinity all manyness returns for its ultimate association. So argued the theologians of the Church.[1]

This thought, with all of its hierarchical implications, is a com-

---

[1] See "Hierarchia" in the *Elucidatio . . . Patrologiae Latinae*, p. 40. Invaluable references are those of MPL 219:687 ff.; 218:1218 (XXXVI); *De reg. prin.*, I, 2, 3, 12; *De Mon.* I, 15-16; O. Gierke, *Political Theories of the Middle Age*, translated by F. W. Maitland (Cambridge, 1900), pp. 9 and 101-2.

monplace of the Middle Ages. A few leaders will suffice to illustrate its consistent application throughout the pre-Reformation era.

Ignatius of Antioch (d. *ca.* 117) is well known for the significance which he ascribed, at an early date, to the monarchical functions of the bishopric. He conceives of this functionary as mediating to the Church on earth the divine powers of the heavenly world. In effect, he thinks of the Church in the person of its bishop as representing in temporal community the socializing characteristics of the heavenly community. For him, the bishop spends his life communicating to the common weal. He does so, "not of himself or through men, nor yet for vain glory, but in the love of God the Father and the Lord Jesus Christ."

In fact the Church, itself, and all of the services that it renders are made possible only through the bishop and his ecclesiastical subordinates. One who thinks of the Church aside from the bishop is not truly serving the *ecclesia* or its heavenly headship. A valid Eucharist is to be held solely "under the bishop or one to whom he shall have committed it. Wheresoever the bishop shall appear, there let the people be; even as where Jesus shall be, there is the universal church." One may not lawfully baptize or hold a love feast aside from episcopal permission. But an approval granted by him is found well pleasing to God, also. It is a simple measure—almost too simple—that Ignatius proposes: all Christians may find unity and community with divine blessing in adherence to the bishop and those under his direction.

Ignatius himself does not hesitate to call upon the Christian community to define its repentance and vigilance in terms of both God and the bishop. "He that honoreth the bishop, is honored of God; he that doeth aught without the knowledge of the bishop rendereth service to the devil." [2]

Cyprian, Bishop of Carthage (d. 258), is fundamental in the thinking of early and medieval Fathers.[3] However much his theory of the episcopate may occasion embarrassment for some later interpreters, his call to unity through the bishopric remains a powerful one. In his treatise *On the Unity of the Church*, he shows the eliciting quality of the eternal kingdom as it draws upon the temporal

---

[2] *Philadelphians*, 1; Lightfoot, *Apostolic Fathers*, Pt. II, Vol. II, Sec. 1, p. 559; *Smyrnaeans*, 8-9; Lightfoot, *Apostolic Fathers*, Pt. II, Vol. II, Sec. 1, pp. 565-66; Richardson, *Early Christian Fathers*, pp. 74, 84, 108, 115, 127. G. Bosio, *I Padri Apostolici* (Turin, 1943), II, 163-201.

[3] Altaner, *Patrologie*, pp. 142 ff.; Bardenhewer, *Geschichte*, II, 442 ff.; Steidle. *Patrologia*, pp. 72 ff. The *Opera* are edited in CSEL III, Pts. 1-3.

world through the services of the mediating *ecclesia*. He derives the Church's genesis from the heavenly world and the unity of the triune Godhead. From this center of the ultimate kingdom there come the strength and the direction for the Church's unifying efforts among all men. If the Church on earth, responding to the hierarchy of God the Father, Son, and Holy Spirit, will but copy the celestial pattern of *koinonia*, it will be enabled to serve in the Last Days as the propagator of the kingdom heritage. Everything depends, however, upon the manner in which the earthly church, remembering the order of its heavenly derivation, coheres about the bishopric.

Once more, hierarchical leverage is secured from Christ's commission to Peter. Christ, the true head of the Church, came down in reconciling ministry from the celestial harmony of Father, Son, and Spirit to provide a link from the world above to the one beneath. He founded his Church and bestowed upon it in the person of Simon Peter the keys to the eternal kingdom itself. Following his resurrection, Christ gave an equal power to all his Apostles and bestowed upon them an equal responsibility to feed his sheep. In the beginning, however,

that He might set forth unity, He arranged by His authority the origin of that unity, as beginning from one. Assuredly the rest of the apostles were also the same as was Peter, endowed with a like partnership both of honour and power; but the beginning proceeds from unity.[4]

Subsequent interpolations at this point seek to establish the special primacy that tradition later ascribed to Peter. Cyprian, for his part, insisted upon a shared episcopacy secure in its inviolable integrity of the many in one. His symbol of one man's receiving the commission in the name of the whole Church continued in vogue, even when much greater claims for Roman headship were added to it.

In Section 5 of the *Unity* Cyprian delivers one of his most eloquent perorations upon the invigorating efficacy of the bishopric, "each part of which is held by each one for the whole." There follows a panegyric upon the unified Church spreading forth into multitudinous fruitage; purveying the one light in many rays; branching out from the one great tree; "but [with] one strength based in its tenacious root;

---

[4] For a good edition of the *De cath. eccl. unitate*, see E. H. Blakeney (London, 1929). The translation here quoted is that of A. Roberts and J. Donaldson, Edinburgh edition, ANF, VIII, 1, 377 ff. See *De cath. eccl. unitate*, 4; ANF, VIII, 1, 380.

and since from one spring flow many streams, although the multiplicity seems diffused in the liberality of an overflowing abundance, yet the unity is still preserved in the source." [5] So the Church, pervaded with the heavenly light of God, illumines the whole world; yet this one light, however diffused, is never marred in its efficacious unity. The Church, with an outflowing of the divine graciousness, transmits from realms eternal the saving ministry indispensable to the temporal world.

For this reason, therefore, the unity and communicating powers that descend to the whole Church from the one interpenetrating episcopate dare not be violated in their integrity. This Church which is the spouse of Christ cannot be adulterous. She recognizes but one home and but one marriage bed. "She keeps us for God. She appoints the sons whom she has born for the kingdom." Separation from the ecclesiastical community is an act of adultery. This involves separation from the Church's promises—from the eternal heritage that it is her privileged service to bestow upon the faithful. "He can no longer have God for his Father, who has not the church for his mother." Can anyone believe "that this unity which thus comes from the divine strength and coheres in celestial sacraments, can be divided in the church, and can be separated by the parting asunder of opposing wills?" [6]

The foregoing (Section 6) leads inevitably to the metaphor of Christ's seamless robe. The sacramental unity here set forth is symbolized in the garment of the Master: "That coat bore with it an unity that came down from the top, that is, that came from heaven and the Father, which was not to be at all rent by the receiver and the possessor." Naturally, he has no chance of possessing Christ's garment "who parts and divides the church of Christ." [7]

Nor can anyone hope to attain unto the eternal kingdom except through the Church of Christ that shall reign there throughout eternity. Only through the unity and coherence of a properly ordered Church, faithful to the episcopacy in the temporal realm, can one arrive at this ultimate community. No more can an individual or a group cohere in this life-giving body of the eternal in the temporal who despises and forsakes the leading of God's priests. Even the lapsed may find their way home to the kingdom if they will but subordinate themselves to the disciplinary redemption of Christ's Church. Others,

[5] *Ibid.*, 5 (381).
[6] *Ibid.*, 6 (382).
[7] *Ibid.*, 7 (383).

however ostensibly immaculate, will fail of the kingdom if they choose to ignore or try to divide its one instrumentality on earth. It behooves all Christians—looking to the consummation of the Last Days—to be watchful in unity and good works. If they do so, they may indeed "reign with Christ in His kingdom as servants that watch." [8]

Father Anger, in his discussion of the Church as a hierarchical society, has provided a modern commentary on the position of Cyprian just set forth. He demonstrates how completely the Church's views since Cyprian's time recapitulate through the intervening Fathers this doctrine of hierarchical procession. Throughout the Middle Ages, whether in Augustine, Gregory, Lombard, Aquinas, or Cusa, the claims of the eternal kingdom upon temporal society were thought of as being issued by the Church—the Church which recapitulated in its earthly ordering the hierarchy of the heavenly. All the munificence and saving powers made available through the sacraments to sinful humanity were thus thought of as emanating from the divine hierarchy and descending through ecclesiastical hierarchs to the laity beneath. [9]

Thus, the earthly church was interpreted throughout the Middle Ages as being ruled after the pattern of God's own order. And those writings which clarified the various steps in the progression from the lower to the higher were greatly utilized and commented upon. One of these—and a powerful one at that—was the corpus of Dionysian writings.

Controversy has long raged over the identity of the Dionysius in question. Generally speaking, the writer of the *Divine Names, Celestial Hierarchy,* and *Ecclesiastical Hierarchy* is held to be, not a companion of St. Paul, but, in all likelihood, a fifth-century author. He is generally referred to by scholars as the Pseudo-Dionysius. Not only is he removed from the circle of the earliest Christian life, but his work is also definitely centered in the Neoplatonic tradition. As such, he is held by many to have introduced a doubtful quality into the pure Christian stream of experience. Whatever the prejudices entertained with regard to the implications of his work, he must be regarded as a signal influence throughout the Middle Ages. Not only did he introduce a highly mystical note into medieval theology; but he also had much to do with the direction of medieval thinking on a

---

[8] *Ibid.,* 14 (388-89) ; 17 (391) ; 19-26 (392-98) ; 27 (398).
[9] *The Doctrine of the Mystical Body of Christ According to the Principles of the Theology of St. Thomas,* tr. J. J. Burke (New York, 1931), pp. 170 f.

universe ordered to divine ends. The net effect of his rather intricate system was to outline the method and procedure of reaching the highest from the most lowly creatures, and of coming to the lowest from God himself. Grouped beneath the area of divine persons, within the varied classifications of the angels, as also among Christian men, Denys saw a carefully graded system of hierarchies.[10]

The Areopagite started logically enough with a fully reverent consideration of the Trinity and the manner in which fullest unity was preserved within its communicative diversity of persons. Out of this divine life there sprang all goodness and beauty as they were mediated to the orders of the heavenly hierarchy, beneath. These sets of hierarchs, for their part, distributed from the highest to the lowest the gifts that came from above. Through the lowest of their own rankings, especially, they communicated the divine life and wisdom to the earthly hierarchy which Dionysius calls the ecclesiastical.

This whole series of hierarchies has the effect of bringing to mankind through symbols, oracles, and other sacred emblems the reality of the divine experience insofar as it can be revealed via the angelic hosts. On the human plane, the Church through its liturgy as it is administered by the ecclesiastical hierarchs becomes the instrumentality of lifting men to the realms above; and of making them communicants, finally, in the life of God himself. Throughout his work, Dionysius leaves the implication that the ecclesiastical orders are to respond, not only in symbolic fashion, but also in life impulses, to the heavenly orders. It is this significant influence which becomes so pervasive in all medieval thought.[11]

From the ninth century on, translators and paraphrasers such as Hilduin and John Scotus Erigena, together with many other medieval commentators of later periods, place increasingly large emphasis upon the Dionysian literature. Even those who base their hierarchies more directly upon the thought of men like Augustine and Gregory continue to reflect the Neoplatonic influences of Dionysius, however

[10] A good brief introduction to the problem, as well as the texts, is contained in M. de Gandillac, *Oeuvres complètes du Pseudo-Denys l'Aréopagite* (Paris, 1943), pp. 7-64; with select literature, pp. 61-64. An incredibly meticulous work is that of Dom Ph. Chevallier, *et al.*, *Dionysiaca: recueil donnant l'ensemble des traductions latines des ouvrages attribués au Denys de l'Aréopage* . . . (Paris, 1937), 2 Vols. See R. Roques, "La notion de hierarchie selon le Pseudo-Denys," *Archives d'histoire doctrinale et littéraire du moyen âge*, XVII (1949), 183-222, and XVIII (1950-51), 5-44; likewise Mario Dal Pra, *Scoto Eriugena* (2nd ed., Milan, 1951). The *Mystical Theology* and *The Celestial Hierarchies* are edited by "The Shrine of Wisdom" (1949).

[11] On the text and interpretation of the Hierarchies see Gandillac, the *Dionysiaca*, Roques, etc., above.

indirect those influences may be. Moreover, in writers such as Thomas Aquinas a most traceable line of influence springing from Denys is always at hand.[12]

Thus the manner in which the Church on earth, in the person of the pontiff, first, and other hierarchs under him, responds to a heavenly hierarchy is given exposition in Aquinas much after the fashion of Dionysius. The extent to which Denys modifies medieval thought-forms, even in the days of Hilduin, who preceded Scotus, is easily traced in scholarly researches. It is instructive to follow in Peter Lombard the various lines of authorship reflected from Augustine, Gregory, Abelard, and Hugh of St. Victor; with occasional references to Dionysius himself. Proceeding to Thomas Aquinas, one discovers that the previous outlines have been incorporated with both direct and indirect indebtedness to the Areopagite. In last analysis, the whole medieval structure does reflect the imprint of the Neoplatonist in practically every commentary upon the orders of life terrestrial, celestial, and supracelestial.[13]

In this complicated problem of hierarchy, the Church plays its part as the instrumentality by which the divine will is mediated through celestial ordering to human beings. In spite of his highly intellectualized conception of the heavenly realms, Dionysius gives a reverently comprehensive treatment of the manner in which the Eucharist as the heart of the liturgy and the hierarchs within the ecclesiastical community serve the eternal purpose. He likewise makes frequent reference to the eternal will in terms of the kingdom community.

Stripped of its meticulous arrangement, Dionysius' schematization

---

[12] Scotus Erigena's translation is in MPL 122. See the entire corpus of Latin translations collated in *Dionysiaca*. A fundamental study is that of Théry, *Études Dionysiennes: I. Hilduin, traducteur de Denys*, and *II. Édition de sa traduction* (Paris, 1932, 1937). Consult V. Lossky, "La notion des 'analogies' chez Denys le Pseudo-Aréopagite," *Archives d'hist. doctrinale et littéraire du moyen âge*, V (1930), 279-309. Cf. H. Weisweiler, "Die Ps:-Dionysiuskommentare 'In Coelestem Hierarchiam' des Skotus Eriugena und Hugos von St. Viktor," *Récherches de théol. anc. et méd.*, XIX (Jan.—Juin, 1952), 26-47, and H. F. Dondaine, "Les 'Expositiones super Ierarchiam Caelestem' de Jean Scot Érigène: texte inédit, d'après *Douai 202*," *Archives*, XVIII (1950-51), 245-302; Th. Aquinas, *Contra Gentiles*, IV, 76; *S. Theol.*, I, Q.108 a. 3, etc.; NUS, 44: 228-29; Bonaventura, *In Hexam. Collatio XXI*, 17-37, *Op. Om.*, V, 434-37.

[13] Note the above references to Thomas. Consult the comprehensive tables and ascriptions in the *Dionysiaca*. Cf. Hugh of St. Victor, *Commentari in Hierarchiam Coelestem S. Dionysii Areopagitae*, MPL 175: 923-1154. See Gandillac, *op. cit.*, pp. 54 ff. Consult P. Lombardi, *Libri IV Sent.* (Quaracchi, 1916), II, 1047 ff.; "Index auctorum." Cf. *Sent*, Lib. II., Dist. X, cap. 1, for reference to *Coel. Hier.*, caps. 7, 9, 13, Quaracchi ed., I, 351, nn. 1-4; *Coel. Hier.* 6, *Ibid.*, I, 345, and n. 3.

reduces itself to the following: Every good gift comes down from the area of the triune Divine which is the fullness of all light, truth, power, glory, love, mercy, and grace. These supracelestial endowments are made available to the heavenly hierarchy in descending order from the highest to the lowest. Those at the lowest rank of the heavenly then transmit to the churchly hierarchy the divine gifts from above. The ecclesiastical ordering, with the bishop at its head, and with presbyters, deacons, and other officials following, then proceeds to mediate the divine benefactions to the people through oracles, symbols, and the Holy Communion in particular. The Church of earth, in the very heart of its liturgy, becomes the agent of the eternal through the hierarchies above it. Those called to reign in proper order within the ecclesiastical hierarchy respond to the eliciting, demanding call from the heavenly hierarchy. The communion which takes place in the liturgy is both symbol and reality. It betokens, and responds to, the fuller companionship with the angels in an abiding association with the divine life itself. The ecclesiastical hierarchs, the bishop and his subordinates, in celebrating the Eucharist reach up to the hierarchs and the Trinity on high. They help to weld their fellow men into a community of worship and action anticipating the eternal beatitude.[14]

Gregory the Great (d. 604) had little to offer the Church by way of profound scholarship. His interests and most profitable services proclaim him the Christian administrator par excellence, the vigilant pastor of the Christian flock, and the tireless preacher of the Lord's word. Nothing delights him more than eulogizing universal harmony and good order. Appearing first in the celestial world in graduated hierarchy, such concord communicates itself to a like hierarchy in the earthly church. Gregory returns to this theme in his many letters, and his remarkable commentary on the Book of Job, and, with special pertinence to the angelic gradations, in his *Thirty-fourth Homily on the Gospels*. This last is his classic utterance on the manner in which the angelic servants of the Trinity communicate the will and the blessings of the Godhead to all humanity. There the perfect harmony and unselfishness of the heavenly messengers proclaim the eliciting pattern for the earthly church's fruitful order.[15]

---

[14] *Hier. Coel.*; Gandillac, *op. cit.*, 185 ff.; *Hier. Eccl.*; Gandillac, *op. cit.*, 245 ff. Cf. *The Mystical Theology*, ed. C. E. Rolt, *Dionysius the Areopagite* (New York, 1920), pp. 191 ff.; also, Gandillac, *op. cit.*, pp. 177 ff.

[15] *Registr. Epist.*, MPL 77:411 ff.; *Moralia in Job*, MPL 75:511–76:785; *Hom. in Evang. XXXIV*, secs. 7-15, in MPL 76:1249-56.

In one of his letters to a contemporary churchman, Gregory recalls that the divine goodness has seen fit to order distinct ranks among the angelic beings with reverence shown the greater by the lesser and with loving mutuality exhibited by the superior to the inferior. Within this diversity of connections, however, one concord prevails. Indeed, no rational provision of the universe would be possible unless such a hierarchy did maintain. Equality of creatures could not exist in a feasible universe. The harmonious subordination of one to the other is best exemplified to the earthly in terms of the heavenly. As on high there are angels and archangels with their graded duties and opportunities, so among men, in the temporal church, there must be a distinction of ranks and functions. This is all the more true if the dictates of the eternal kingdom are to be served by the Church during its earthly pilgrimage in a human world. If such ordering is indispensable among heaven's citizens, how much more so among men! Truly, in this fashion only can peace and the mutualizing bonds of charity be manifested.[16]

In Book IV, Section 55, of his *Morals on Job,* Gregory discusses the same theme when he interprets the meaning of "kings and counsellors of the earth." There is, he says, an ascending order from the insensible to the sensible. The earth is rendered fruitful by the air, which in turn is governed by the quality of the heaven. Over beasts, man is placed. Over man, angels rise. Above the angels are the archangels, and so on to the very pinnacle of the Trinity itself. What would become of the ministrations of the Holy Spirit if the powers above did not direct those beneath? "One Angel would never have learnt from another what he should say to a man." The very Creator, himself, who holds all things in his supreme rule, guarantees a universe of beauty by inaugurating a defined order. Thus, "he rules one part by the governance of another." "Kings," therefore, may here be thought of as the angelic spirits who have things subjected to their rule the more devotedly they serve their common creator. These spirits are likewise called "counsellors" because "they 'consult' for the spiritual commonwealth while they invite us to the kingdom as fellow-heirs with themselves." [17]

Gregory believes that out of this orderly hierarchy, constituted by the divine will, there proceed all the ministering angels who bless man with God's salvation. Human beings are never wholly deprived

---

[16] Ep. LIV; MPL 77:785-86.
[17] In the Marrott translation of the Parker edition (Oxford, 1841), pp. 221-22 (cf. 220, 223).

of the impelling motivations and propulsive affections transmitted by such angelic ones. As the ecclesiastical hierarchy responds in its own gradations of service to the pattern of this celestial one, it too is permitted to pass on to the faithful, and indeed the whole earth, the beneficent plan of the eternal for the temporal.

Gregory apparently knows nothing of Dionysius at firsthand, though he does render him the homage of intermediate appreciation. He rearranges the particular ordering and functions of the angelic beings as the Areopagite had conceived them. But the idea of the impinging heavenly world of ordered services giving its form and pattern to the terrestrial hierarchy remains. The Church on earth with its destiny in heaven must thus perform its service to the temporal life of humanity.[18]

Within his larger work on the sacraments, Hugh of St. Victor (d. 1141) concerns himself with the problem of church orders.[19] He first classifies the parts of the Church according to the simple categories of clerical and lay. Lay Christians are those who of necessity deal with the problems of terrestrial life. As such, they are the left side of Christ's body. The clergy, on the other hand, dispense spiritual life, and have their place on Christ's right side. Neither of these categories is to be thought of as less a part of the whole body of Christ—his universal Church—than is the other. Hugh is not derogating the laity. But they deal with earthly life, whereas the clergy emphasizes the spiritual.

Both in the lay and in the clerical categories there are to be found certain orders of power and responsibility; even though they operate under common headship. Thus the terrestrial power has as its head the king. The spiritual power has the supreme pontiff. To the kingly power there pertain those things which are of earth. To the power of the supreme pontiff belong the things which are spiritual. To the precise extent that spiritual matters take precedence over things terrestrial, and to the exact degree that the spiritual outranks the bodily, the spiritual power precedes the earthly in its dignity.[20]

Hugh is here propounding no irritating doctrine. He is, rather, following an accepted line of reasoning which, in his day, regularly accorded to the spiritual power a certain priority over the temporal.

---

[18] *Loc. cit.* For references ascribable to *Coel. Hier.*, 7, 9, 13, see *Hom.* XXXIV, 12, MPL 76:1254; cf. P. Lombard, *Sent.* II, x, 1; Quaracchi, I, 341, and nn.

[19] Cf. *De Sacramentis*, Lib. II, Pars II, caps. III, ff.; MPL 176:417 ff. Consult the excellent translation of R. J. Deferrari, *Hugo of Saint Victor on the Sacraments of the Christian Faith* [*De Sacramentis*] (Cambridge, Mass., 1951).

[20] Cap. IV; MPL 176:418.

In both instances a definite order of progression in the regulating of life is called for. One may assume that such order as the Church requires is destined to even higher ends than that which temporal rulers find necessary. The treatment of ecclesiastical rankings recalls the conventional views of the Church in the centuries preceding.

Bernard of Clairvaux (d. 1153) was fully aware in his book *On Consideration* of the manner in which the life of the earthly priesthood derives its pattern and draws its substance from the heavenly realm.[21] As in his entire pastoral ministry, Bernard gives an eloquent dissertation upon the harmonious ordering of God's servants throughout the universe. His interpretation of the angels and their celestial country takes on qualities of intimacy and social motivation that have their transference value within the ecclesiastical community on earth. Perhaps his most signal contribution is the warm imagery by which he seeks to make real to the human mind the services performed, in God's grace, by the angelic hosts. Throughout his discussion there is an appeal to draw upon the divine communication of life for Christian contemplation and action in the present world. Pope Eugenius III, to whom he writes, is under constant reminder that he must tear his eyes from the purely human and fix them upon heavenly things if he would serve with the Church as a servant of the eternal kingdom in the temporal community.

Peter Lombard (d. 1160) adds nothing new in his *Sentences* to the discussion of the angelic hierarchy. His function, as always, is to collect and categorize the views prevailing to his time. He utilizes Dionysius as he came to the Middle Ages through John Scotus Erigena. He also includes materials from Gregory, Hugh of St. Victor, and Peter Abelard (d. 1142). Following the usual interpretation of Scripture, he discerns nine orders of angels. At the summit of the angelic hierarchy, and in the first group of three, he finds Seraphim, Cherubim, and Thrones. In a middle triad come Dominations, Principalities, and Powers. In the lowest ranking are the Virtues, the Archangels, and the Angels. This triple series, each with three parts, recalls for him the image of the Holy Trinity. He has his own ideas about the specific missions of the celestial beings, even as do other Fathers. He does not attribute an equal directness of contact with the earth to each body of the celestial servants. Among them, however, there rule a close concord and a creative harmony which, in their own good time and fashion, are communicated to the world

[21] *De Consideratione*, IV, iv, 9-10.

of men beneath. Here, among the uncorrupted angels, the fullness of all good things is enjoyed by all. An equality does not maintain among them. They are arranged in hierarchical series. But some simply have more than others of the things that are common to all. And none is dissatisfied with his station or his part in the divine economy.[22]

Hildegarde of Bingen (d. 1179) has a somewhat extended delineation "Of the Nine Orders of Angels." Her work, too, shows the influence of the Dionysian hierarchies—however intermediately that influence may have been derived. Thus the celestial order is shown, as in the Areopagite, to exercise a direct and motivating beneficence upon the temporal order.

Hildegarde reports, with her usual imagery and baffling mathematics, what seems to be her own enumeration of angelic ranks and battalions. From these battalions there come wonderful voices celebrating God's marvelous works among the blessed and praising him for having made every creature in an incomparable way to serve his established will. God has deputized certain creatures to remain on earth and others to dwell in heaven. He has, likewise, appointed blessed angelic spirits "as much for the salvation of man, as for the honour of His name." [23]

All of these supernal beings sing their sweetest music with its most mellifluous modulations when the good works of men below proclaim their heavenly aspirations. And humanity performs such acts, best, when it flouts all self-exaltation and comes in deepest humility to serve its fellows with sincere affection for the society above. Thus, too, the faithful Christian will love "while he dwells still in the body, the society of those who, running in the way of truth, have avoided the error of a lie." [24]

It is the supremely happy function of the celestial citizens in the angelic orders to call forth and empower, with God's own grace, the righteous actions of men. Beings in the human orders beneath have it as their peculiarly blessed privilege to live together in a way befitting the celestial company to which they are called.[25]

---

[22] Lib. II, Dist. IX-XI, Quaracchi ed., I, 345-59; MPL 192:669 ff. See references to Ps. Dionysius, *Coel. Hier.*, 6, via Scotus Erigena, MPL 122:1049; also Abelard, *Sic et non*, 49, MPL 178:1430 ff.; Lombard, *Sent.* II, IX, 1, Quaracchi, I, 345 and n. 3.

[23] *Scivias*, Lib. I, Visio, VI; MPL 197:437-42; Steele, *op. cit.*, pp. 138-52.

[24] MPL 197:442; Steele, *op. cit.*, p. 152.

[25] Steele, *op. cit.*, pp. 149-52. Compare with the foregoing *The Revelations of Mechthild of Magdeburg 1210-1297*, ed. L. Menzies (New York, 1953), III, 1, pp. 62-64 and n. 2.

Thomas Aquinas (d. 1274), like his contemporaries in the Church, discusses at great length the manner in which the hierarchy is required for the purposes of militant unity. Here, he wishes to show the supreme value of Christian unity in diversity. As in his commentaries on the Pauline Letters, he clarifies the manner in which a division of function may be secured within a unity of purpose.[26] Wherever one seeks the advantages of shared objectives and united growth, one looks for a proper consolidation of varied gifts and services for common ends of life.

Discussing the prime arguments for a hierarchy, Thomas regularly stresses two points. He frequently treats of the manner in which civil governments find greatest efficiency under a united kingship. The state at large is a continuing demonstration of the manner in which diversified services, if administered under one head, may best serve the common body politic. Thomas feels that this is a telling argument in favor of ordering the Church on earth to a similar efficiency among men. But he realizes, and always calls upon others to recognize also, the more basic reason for a hierarchical order within the Church militant. The need for such a division of power and responsibility is best suggested by the Church in its heavenly, or triumphant, character. It is well to remember that the militant Church is derived by similitude from the Church triumphant. John, in the Apocalypse, for instance, sees Jerusalem descending from heaven, and Moses strives to do all things according to the example given on the holy mountain. Now, in accordance with such divine leading, we cannot forget that in the Church triumphant one only may be said to preside. It is God himself who rules throughout the universe. That company of whom the Revelator speaks looks forward to being his people indeed and to having the Most High as their God. Thus, after such a pattern ought the Church on earth to follow its one leader and pastor. John's Gospel reminds us, in 10:16, that they shall be one flock under one shepherd.[27]

It is not enough to insist that the one pastor is Christ, the spouse of the whole Church. He it was who gave to the Church its sacraments and its temporal headship, likewise. But Peter received the Lord's commission to feed his sheep. To Peter, also, Christ said, in Matthew 16:19, "I will give unto thee the keys of the kingdom of heaven." This he did for the conservation of ecclesiastical unity in terms of the

[26] *Contr. Gent.,* IV, 76; *S. Theol.,* I, Q. 108, a.2.
[27] *Contr. Gent.,* IV, 76, secs. 1-4.

heavenly community. Peter, therefore, becomes on earth the symbol and expression of that unity which is first and foremost in heaven. But, according to Thomas, the powers given to Peter were likewise transmitted through him to others. Roman pontiffs following in his proper succession would likewise continue to be his representatives on earth until the end of time. Subordinate to them would be other loyal members of the hierarchy.[28]

In the *Summa Theologica,* as in the *Contra Gentiles,* Thomas is fond of drawing examples from the secular world that may serve as analogies to the spiritual. In a city there are several orders which may be thought of as its beginning, middle, and end. At the top are the nobles; in the middle are the honorable people or the middle class; at the bottom are the common folk. So in the angelic hierarchy there may be distinguished those orders of angels who follow the gradations according to summit, middle, and base. This is probably borrowed, however indirectly, from Dionysius' three orders.[29]

Thomas is deeply impressed by the instructive pattern of the heavenly world. As in the case of Dionysius himself, such angelic hierarchy gives the real outline for the one that is to be sought by the Church on earth. Thomas is sure that although "all things are possessed in common by the angelic society," some things may be more excellently held by some than by others. Analogically it becomes clear that such rankings are to be regarded as highly desirable, also, in the Church of earth.[30]

Whether or not the hierarchy is medievally derived through Dionysius, the necessity of preserving an order in the Church on earth as it is maintained in heaven is a continuing one. Bonaventura, for instance, like his great Dominican contemporary, Thomas, treats at some length the integrity of order. Without having recourse to the meticulous nuances of the Areopagite, the Franciscan shows the relation that should exist between the temporal and the eternal hierarchies. Thus he notes that, according to the Apostle Paul, heavenly things should be matters of example for things earthly. The Church militant, for its part, ought to imitate the Church triumphant. Since order of a fixed kind is apparent in the Church triumphant, as among the angels, it follows that order ought likewise to be found among Christians in this world. It is appropriate that those officials who

---

[28] *Ibid.,* sec. 4.
[29] *S. Theol.,* I. Q. 108, a.2; *Coel. Hier.,* 6; Gandillac, *op. cit.,* pp. 205-6.
[30] *Ibid.,* translation of the Dominican Fathers, pp. 69-70; *Op. Om.,* pp. 205-6.

have the responsibility of dispensing the sacraments ought likewise to enjoy an eminence befitting their corporate obligation.[31]

The unified rule of life observed in all God's universe, Bonaventura finds to be a development from the one to many; and a return from the many to one. Thus, as one goes in an ascending order of power and reality from the bottom to the top, one observes a reduction of the many to the few. In God's universe as a whole this represents a return by diversified life to association with the triune Godhead. On the earthly scene, within the functional responsibility of the Church's system of order, this represents an ascension from many priests to fewer bishops, to still fewer archbishops, to very few patriarchs, and to the one father of all bishops in the person of the pope himself. Bonaventura regards this as being altogther proper; there should be one special hierarch who stands as a representative on earth of the undivided headship of Christ himself. The supreme pontiff is the vicar of Christ. He represents in the world of men the spiritual fountain of all power and good. From this one, who holds the chief dignity in the ecclesiastical hierarchy, all powers down to the least member of the Church are derived.[32]

Placed in such a setting, it becomes ever more clear why the medieval world should derive a sense of satisfaction and comfort from an orderly procedure within the Church's officialdom. However little he may mention Dionysius directly, Bonaventura is, like Thomas and Peter Lombard before him, making the earthly hierarchy respond to the heavenly. This hierarchy becomes the responsive instrumentality, within the Church at large, for the heavenly kingdom's work in temporal society.

Having set up the primary basis of derivation as being that coming from above, Bonaventura is content to supply further incentive from the realm of earthly society itself. It is in this area that he turns to laity and clergy as having, alike, the requirements of diversified, efficient response to leadership. Within the laity, order derives from the emperor through kings, dukes, counts, tribunes, centurions, and decurions. The obvious significance for a churchly hierarchy need not be labored. Wherever there is a multitude, confusion is avoided solely on the basis of regimen. The avoidance of such divisiveness in

---

[31] *Sent.* Lib. IV, Dist. 24, Pt. 1, Art. 2, Q. 1 and concl.; *Op. Om.*, IV, 614-15; Dist. 24, Pt. 1, Art. 2, Q. 3, *Op. Om.*, IV, 617; Dist. 18, Pt. 1, cap. 2, *Op. Om.*, IV, 465; Dist. 13, Art. 1, Q. 2, *Op. Om.*, IV, 304-5; *Breviloquium*, Pars VI, Cap. XII, *Op. Om.*, V, 278.

[32] *Breviloquium*, VI, xii, 4-6; Nemmers, *op. cit.*, pp. 208-10.

the ecclesiastical, as well as in the secular, world is won at the price of orderly rule.[33]

The learned Nicholas of Cusa (d. 1464) —pastor, teacher, preacher, and bishop of his flock—records indelibly the impress of other great theorists of churchly hierarchy. In a rarefied atmosphere suggestive of the Areopagite, he nevertheless manages to regenerate the forthright thought native to Cyprian, Augustine, and the first Gregory.[34]

Upon reading his work on the *Catholic Concordance* as well as his sermonic tributes to universal order, one observes several basic emphases. There is, first of all, the manner in which he derives, in fully Dionysian fashion, the ecclesiastical hierarchy from the celestial. The unity and communicating powers transmitted by the threefold Godhead, with its perfect oneness, to the choirs and ranks of heavenly spirits are maintained in the earthly church through its hierarchical responsiveness. The socializing qualities of the eternal realm thus cast their spell upon the ecclesiastical community—that servant of the eternal kingdom in the temporal world. The sweet concordant harmony that prevails in the heavenly hierarchy thus distills within the ecclesiastical hierarchy a mutuality that shall save the world. The commonwealth of love and life as it is in God the Father, Son, and Holy Spirit is transmitted from the *patria* to the peregrinators of earth. In that concord with Christ that characterizes the Church triumphant, dormant, and militant, the saving powers of the universe are fully manifested. The impending close of human history simply heightens the vigilance required on the part of the Church militant as it prepares itself and all those souls recoverable by its care for the final association of the fatherland.[35]

As Vansteenberghe has lucidly pointed out, the total church is, in Cusa's eyes, a living, communicating oneness. It is the veritable union of souls with Christ in sweet fraternal harmony. In it hierarchical

---

[33] *Sent.* Lib. IV, Dist. 24, Pt. 1, Art. 2, Q. 1, *Op. Om.*, IV, 614-15.

[34] R. C. Petry, "Emphasis on the Gospel and Christian Reform in Late Medieval Preaching," *Church History*, XVI, 2 (1947) , 75-91. A useful introduction to, and cutting of, Cusa's works is M. de Gandillac, *Oeuvres choisies de Nicolas de Cues* (Paris, 1942) . See, especially, p. 45 for texts, translations, etc.; notably, pp. 46-47 for the critical *Opera* of Henri Petrus, 3 vols. in 1 (Bale, 1565) , the 3-Vol. edition of Lefèvre d'Étaples (Paris, 1514) , and the Heidelberg Academy edition of Hoffmann-Klibansky-Kallen (Leipzig, 1934) ; with the Kallen edition of the *De concordantia catholica* (CC) being vol. XIV, 1 (1939) . See F. N. Scharpff, *Wichtigste Schriften in deutscher Uebersetzung* (Freiburg 1/B, 1862) ; also two translated sermons and further literature in NUS, pp. 288 ff. and 313-14. Cf. E. Vansteenberghe, *Le cardinal Nicolas de Cues (1401-1464)* . . . (Paris, 1920) .

[35] CC. Lib. I., caps. 1-10, especially; Paris, *Opera* III, Fol. V-XI.

ordering is indispensable; but there is in all of this an intimate connection and an admirable continuity between all the portions of the hierarchy. So do the beneficent powers emanating from Christ interpenetrate and endow all the diversified actions of the united body. Thus the continuity between the Church militant, suffering, and triumphant leads the one ecclesiastical community in its diversity of experiences to the common association with God.[36]

In heaven are the Trinity, the angels, and the blessed ones, even as on earth there are the sacraments, the priests, and the faithful. A perfect harmony reigns between the sacraments as between the divine persons. A hierarchy provides the necessary division of function and rank among the priesthood which is to the faithful as soul and body. The whole ecclesiastical hierarchy recalls its celestial archetype. In each diocese unity is served by the bishop who represents his church; in the universal church this is assured by the pope, to whom, by necessity, all Catholics must adhere if they would remain in the body of the faithful.[37]

The foregoing résumé may be given yet further directness in terms of selected emphases from the *Concordance* and a sermon on the angelic rankings.[38] In the sixth chapter of Book I, Nicholas considers the entire ecclesiastical concordance.[39] He finds in it the pattern of the Trinity and three great orders—all in one marvelous connection with Christ at the head. The first of these, the divinest concordance of the Trinity in unity, has subordinated to it the ecclesiastical sacraments. Second, to the divine concordance of the angels, who are the ministers of the divine Trinity, there is subordinated the holy priesthood; because the priests are the ministers of the sacrament. Third, to the blessed spirits in the fatherland, there are subordinated the faithful on pilgrimage. In terms of the sacramental hierarchy, Christ the Head communicates himself in this life under the guise of symbol and the enigma of a glass seen through darkly. This befits human mortality. But in the triumphant church, Christ will be seen face to face.

In Chapter 7, tracing the heavenly orders with full Dionysian

---

[36] Vansteenberghe, *op. cit.*, pp. 36 ff.; CC, I, 1-10, especially cap. 4, *Opera* III, Fol. VIII ff.

[37] CC. Lib. I, caps. 1-11, 6-10, 14-17; cf. selections from books II and III of the CC. in Gandillac, *op. cit.*, pp. 51 ff.

[38] See the H. Petrus (Bale) ed., Lib. I, cap. 6, pp. 700 ff.; see the Kallen ed., CC. Lib. I, cap. VI, 54 ff. Cf. *Excitationum ex sermonibus* in the Bale edition, Liber VIII, 603-5; also Scharpff, *op. cit.*, pp. 417-20.

[39] Petrus (Bale) ed., pp. 700-702; Kallen (Leipzig), pp. 54-60.

complexity, Cusa stresses the fashion in which the various choirs transmit from higher to lower the impulses communicated to them. Both the powers and the delimitations characteristic of each rank are analyzed. That there is communication, not only between the various grades of angels, but also from the angelic hierarchy to the ordering of the human church, is insisted upon.

Proceeding to the ecclesiastical hierarchy, whose function it is to reproduce the harmonious contours of the heavenly, Cusa finds a like system of ordered choirs. Thus there is in the first order of the churchly hierarchy a descending gradation of bishops, priests, and deacons. The middle group contains subdeacons, acolytes, and exorcists. The lowest threefold grouping has readers, doorkeepers, and tonsurers. The monachal grouping is integrated with the tonsured choir because it stands midway between the lay and the clerical body of Christians.

In the eighth chapter of Book I, and following, Nicholas delineates more fully the subdivisions of hierarchical ordering in the earthly church. Emphasis is put upon that supreme sacrament, the Eucharist, which leads the faithful to the triumphant association with Christ, their head. The priestly order, whose function it is to celebrate the sacraments, ascends in its ecclesiastical hierarchy to the celestial one. This sacerdotal hierarchy, as Dionysius shows, is graded from the pontiff at its head to the lowest ranks of the minor orders at the bottom. From them there is communicated to the laity the divine graces that have been received from the Trinity through the angelic ranks.

Just as man is constituted of spirit, soul, and body, so the sacraments of the ecclesiastical community constitute the one spirit, with the *sacerdotium* as the soul and faithful Christians as the body proper. As the soul belongs in part to the body and in part to the spirit— being between, as it were, and thus providing the means of the spirit's contact with the body—so the priesthood fulfills its functions among the Christian body of the faithful. Where the whole priesthood is as one soul in the body of the faithful, there the priests constitute a ruling, vivifying, and illuminating power. They are, as Cyprian reminds us, the light of the world and the salt of the earth.

In the earthly hierarchy there is a presidency that rightfully belongs to Peter. Cusa quotes Cyprian, Jerome, Augustine, Optatus of Mileve, and other Fathers to this end. Such a primacy placed at the apex of Christian community is necessary so that things involving the common good may have their proper direction and outlet. Cusa dilates on the pastoral service thus made possible in the strength of the celestial powers and through the mediatorship of the earthly church to the world at large. By means of this presidency in ecclesiastical power, there is added to the temporal society that which is as soul to body.

As in Chapter 10, so throughout the rest of Book I, Nicholas depicts the priesthood enabling the earthly to be joined to the heavenly. With Gregory Nazianzen he celebrates the incorporation in the celestial society thus made possible by the participating unity of the whole church with its hierarchy. Thus, with the animating services of the priesthood in the body of the faithful, Christians souls come at last to the community of the triune God, the angels, and all blessed ones.[40]

In the eighth book of sermon excerpts drawn from Cusa, a like theme is stressed.[41] All multiplicity derives and maintains its existence only through its attachment to godly unity. Unattached diversity dies by reason of its separation from oneness. Being is possible only insofar as it inheres in unity. Therefore, multiplicity must return to the unity from which it has its rise. Proportion and harmony are to be found only where order rules. Likewise, the administration of the ecclesiastical community with all the multiple activities that spring from it depend on the godly hierarchy and from that whole concordance of celestial unity to which it returns.[42]

[40] Kallen, *op. cit.*, pp. 60-89. Lib. I, caps. 7-17, in Paris ed., *Opera* III, Fol. X-XV.
[41] *Excit.*, VIII, 603-5.
[42] Scharpff, *op. cit.*, pp. 417-20. A stimulating discussion of Cusa's organismic philosophy is found in J. Bohatec, *Calvins Lehre von Staat und Kirche mit besonderer Berücksichtigung des Organismusgedankens* (Breslau, 1937), pp. 581 ff.; particularly, pp. 594 ff—with key texts from the CC. via Schard.

CHAPTER IX

The Ecclesiastical Community
as Servant of the Eternal Kingdom
in the Temporal World
3. Nature and Supernature; Sacraments and Liturgy

THE HIERARCHICAL CHURCH ON EARTH ANSWERED TO THE CELESTIAL ordering that was invigorated by the Trinity and exemplified among the angels. The ecclesiastical community, therefore, became the servant of the eternal kingdom in its ministry to temporal necessities. In the structure of an ecclesiastical hierarchy responding to a heavenly one there was represented a communal experience that transcended the limits of earth with the joys of the eternal. The implicit suggestion increasingly developed during the Middle Ages is that man with all of his natural propensities subscribes to more than a purely natural end. The Church assisted individuals and groups to rise above their natural surroundings into the supernatural society that God had planned to share with them.

The concept of man as a natural being was current in the thought-world to which the Christian came. The Stoic, particularly, had developed the idea of natural fraternity so that it embraced a universal brotherhood.[1] This had its decided limitations, especially as regarded its power to supply more than a virtuous life and disciplined resignation. Among such early Christians as Paul, Clement of Rome, Ignatius, Clement of Alexandria, Tertullian, Cyprian, Ambrose, and Augustine, the thought of man's natural brotherhood was extensively developed. Ambrose, for instance, extended the

[1] On the relations of early Christianity with Stoicism see J. Weiss, R. Knopf, and F. C. Grant, *The History of Primitive Christianity* (New York, 1937), I, 234-35; II, 511-12, 579-80, 585. Cf. P. G. Chappuis, *La destinée de l'homme, de l'influence du Stoïcisme sur la pensée chrétienne primitive* (Paris, 1926); S. J. Case, *The Social Triumph of the Ancient Church* (New York, 1933), pp. 7-13.

Ciceronian pattern for a responsible citizenship in a good society to cover the behavior of Christians in a still nobler association.[2] Augustine derived his arguments for sociality from metaphorically represented conceptions of natural unity.

But none of these social incentives that derived their meaning from the natural life of man as a political animal was satisfactory to the confirmed Christian. Whereas the citizen of the Roman state might be content to eulogize the ever-widening circles of the *Pax Romana,* the Christian raised his eyes to a society that was infinitely more expansive and enduring. Augustine declaimed upon the superior merits of God's city compared with those of the so-called *urbs aeterna.* He knew, if his pagan contemporaries did not, that no lasting city was to be found in the purely natural associations of men. Like the Revelator long before him, the Bishop of Hippo directed the Christian's scrutiny to the configurations of a celestial homeland.[3]

A favorite theme in the early church concerned the manner in which the Christian's supernatural end transcended the intermediate objectives of his non-Christian fellow men. This in turn prompted the logical contrast between the ineffective attempts at brotherliness found in the Roman world and the more rigorous standards of mutuality called forth within Christian communities. As the Gospel of John, and the Letters also, had so ably declared, a new law of love and fellow regard had entered the world with the advent of the Christ. For John and for Paul all social experience within the temporal world must be a similitude of the mutuality found in the eternal kingdom. Paul had often appealed to his Christian brethren to make themselves ready, not for an experience comparable to anything previously known, but for a communal life that wholly transcended man's earthly approximations. Flesh and blood could not inherit the kingdom of God. Neither could the limited range of human friendship and solidarity match the infinite society of the future. It was therefore all the more incumbent upon Christian men to expose their natural potentialities to the gracious solicitations of the supernatural world. With their homeland in heaven, they must, as Chrysostom said, make the land of their pilgrimage something like the *patria.*[4]

---

[2] *De officiis ministrorum libri 3:* MPL 16; R. Thamin, *St. Ambrose et la morale chrétienne au IV* siècle (Paris, 1895).

[3] For example, *De Civ. Dei,* XV, 1, 2, XVIII, 54; *Retractationes,* XLIII (LXX), 2; G. Bardy, *Les révisions: oeuvres de Saint Augustin,* XII (Paris, 1950), 524-27.

[4] For a sermon attributed to Augustine see NUS 14:90-94; also 8:69-71, for Chrysostom.

In the late Middle Ages, Thomas Aquinas described this pilgrimage of man from the natural to the supernatural society as few other Christians have. Consequently, a number of treatises based upon his ideas soon gained currency in his name. One of these, *On the Education of Princes,* recapitulates the patristic and medieval positions just outlined. It derives its materials ostensibly from the Gospels, Ambrose, and Augustine, with occasional access to Stoic authors. Here the progression is from the irrational society to be found among the lower animals, through the natural fraternity that men exhibit among themselves when at their best, to the apex of supernatural community that is mediated to the world through the Church.[5]

Throughout the argument, one idea is propounded with discerning fullness. This is the contention that if fraternity is called for among animals and men in their purely natural relationships, how much more is solidarity in keeping with the Christian life! For the Christian's mutuality is but partly required because of his natural experience. It is demanded primarily by virtue of his supernatural heritage. Thus Adam as the progenitor of the race must give way to the fatherhood of the universal God who is in Christ. And Eve, as the natural mother of men, must surrender her primacy to the yearnings of mother Church for her children of earth that are destined to association in heaven. Seneca might be thoroughly sensitive to the natural demands of brotherhood. He could ill compete, however, with the Christian conception of supernatural inheritance and communal beatitude.[6]

In such diverse works as the *Summas* of Thomas and the multifarious treatises of Wyclif, the Middle Ages placed the culminating stamp upon the relationship of natural existence and supernatural destiny. Thomas expanded the treatment of the laws to cover the various phases of man's natural life unfolded in Eden and thereafter. Drawing widely upon the non-Christian as well as the Christian heritage of philosophy and theology, Aquinas explored the resources and the limitations of man's natural community. With regularity he returned to one prime conviction: namely, that the most fully natural association still possible to man under relative natural law was that which followed the dictates of a law more than natural. Man could participate in God's eternal law by means of the natural, though only in proportion to the capacities of his human nature. Something more was required if he was to gain supernatural ends. Not only must a

[5] *De eruditione principum,* Opusc. XXXVII, *Op. Om.,* XXVII, 583-85.
[6] *Loc. cit.*

human law be added to the natural; but a divine law must extend to humanity the graces necessary for his salvation.[7]

In Thomas' thought the wholeness of man was a perpetual concern. Man was a natural animal with natural propensities and objectives—yes. But he was more than such a truncated being. He was a whole person designed to participate in the supernatural association of Trinity, angels, and saints. His natural community must, therefore, be redeemed by, and directed toward, his supernatural beatitude. Only in proceeding to the goal of eternal felicity within such ultimate companionship could the human animal fittingly live his life on earth. If he would be fully natural within the limitations of the race of Adam, he must be answerable to, and redeemable by, the supernatural commonwealth of God.[8]

Delineating the manner by which natural beings attain a supernatural end required that Thomas clarify the service rendered by Christ's Church. The only means whereby man in his sinful state could be redeemed was through the Church instituted by Christ. And this Church, as Thomas saw it, had been made the servant of the eternal kingdom in the temporal world insofar as it dispensed eternal life through the sacraments. Each of these contributed its own specific portion to the saving qualities of ecclesiastical community. They were, as a whole, the means whereby men were raised in this life to a glimpse of the divine vision and to a foretaste of beatitude. Participating in Christ's body and blood, especially, humanity partook of the very bread by which men must be nurtured during their pilgrimage from the natural to the supernatural homeland.[9]

Wyclif concurred heartily in this conviction of the medieval church that the ecclesiastical community, its sacraments, and its priesthood must perform the service of the eternal kingdom in the temporal world. Thomas could never have stated more vigorously than he the insistence upon supernatural ends as the focus of natural association. Man was placed on earth for the purpose of aspiring toward heaven. Every similitude found within the natural heavens and supernatural universe proclaimed this God-ordained destiny of humanity. Man's great difficulty came with his refusal to look upward. His major sin consisted in his declination from celestial affairs to the

---

[7] *S. Theol.*, Ia IIae Q. 91 a.4., Reply obj. 1 and concl.; also a. 5.

[8] Consult R. C. Petry, "The Social Character of Heavenly Beatitude according to the Thought of St. Thomas Aquinas," *The Thomist*, VII (Jan., 1944) , 65-79, together with the primary and secondary literature there cited.

[9] *S. Theol.*, Ia IIae Q. 90. a.2; Q. 91, a.4; Q. 106, a.3; Q. 107, a.1-4; Q. 108, a.1-4; Q. 109; but, especially Q.108, a.2; Troeltsch, *Soc. Teaching*, I, 262-69.

In Anselm, Hugh of St. Victor, and Innocent III there is the undeviating and joyous certainty that in the moment of sacramental celebration the very angels are in attendance and that men come into companionship with the whole court of heaven. True it is that man cannot, as yet, be granted enduring association with the heavenly world. That must wait upon his admission, following the general Judgment, into the blessed realm. But here on earth, within the confines of his mortality and lured by the temptations of his natural state, he may already be assured of his supernatural inheritance; he may participate in the life that is to be realized later.[15]

With such a sentiment Gregory the Great heartily agreed. For him, as for a variety of early and medieval churchmen, the way was thus thrown open to the fatherland. Through the hierarchy on earth, following the hierarchy of heaven, the worshiping church communicated to its faithful the celestial nutriment.[16] Bede the Venerable, in his *Ecclesiastical History of England,* gives a moving account of the death of the poet Caedmon. Being about to pass from this mortal scene, that gentle soul insisted on the Eucharist and so "made ready for his entrance into the other life by partaking of the heavenly journey-bread." [17] Bede notes particularly how this experience conduced, as always, to the reconciling ministry of God among men. In the Eastern Church, John of Damascus (d. 780) had referred to this sacrament as a communion, because by means of it men communicated with Christ and so became joined with one another in mutualizing reconciliation. In such solemn moments man gives himself to Christ; and is, in turn, given the fullness of God in Christ.[18] Haymo of Halberstat, in his book *The Body and Blood of the Lord,* had marked how this feeding on the sacred body and blood and this incorporation with Him through the temporal church conduced to the eternal vision, the perfect refection, and the everlasting society of the future.[19] Hugh of St. Victor gathered up references from

---

[15] MPL 219:867 ff. Cf. Anselm, *Orationes,* XXVII-XXIX, MPL 158:917-925, especially 918, 922; H. St. Victor, *De Sacram.,* Lib. II, Pars VIII, cap. 1 ff.; MPL 176:461 ff.

[16] Cf. *Hom. in Evang.,* Lib. II—Hom. XXXVIII, 7; MPL 76:1279; cf. *Dialog.,* Lib. IV, cap. 55, MPL 77:416 ff.

[17] *Hist. Eccl.,* IV, 23; J. E. King, ed. and tr., *Baedae Opera Historica* (New York, 1930), II, 140-51; especially, pp. 148, 149. Cf. A. S. Cook and C. B. Tinker, *Select Translations from Old English Prose* (Boston, 1908), p. 57.

[18] Via P. Hughes, *Meditations for Lent* (London, 1937), pp. 136-37.

[19] MPL 118:817.

Augustine and other Fathers in support of a similar eucharistic interpretation.[20]

Peter Lombard's work, *The Sentences,* represented comprehensively the accepted Christian thought to his time. His interpretation of the sacraments, for instance, was not characterized by any revolutionary ideas. Thus, in dealing with the sacramental significance of baptism and the Eucharist, he found at hand the usual patterns for their prefiguration in the Old and the New Testament. His commentary on Psalm 77:25, by way of John 6, was striking only in that it focused a significant point of view with regard to the heavenly food. Mankind had indeed eaten the heavenly manna in the wilderness, but the result had been death. But partaking, in the Christian Era, of the true living bread which descended from heaven, the faithful had taken unto themselves everlasting life. The bread given to the people of old was to lead them out of the desert into the promised land. The eucharistic bread would more than suffice to conduct the faithful from the wilderness of this world into the heavenly order. To such nourishment of the spirit the term *viaticum* might rightfully be applied. For it was truly in this way that the faithful were led to the heavenly fatherland. As the ancient crossing of the Red Sea might be held to prefigure Christian baptism, so the manna of old looked forward to the supper of the Lord.

Over and beyond the mere matter of terms and figures, Lombard does convey a moving lesson. Just as manna in the desert fed those on pilgrimage through the physical wilderness, so the eucharistic manna nourishes those on pilgrimage from the present world to the heavenly. The body of Christ is literally and figuratively angels' food and bread of heaven.[21]

From the time of Lombard through the thirteenth century, perhaps no one expressed more directly the saving function of the Eucharist than did Thomas Aquinas. In his work *On the Humanity of Christ* he finds the sacrament of the altar to be, with regard to the past, a commemoration of the Lord's passion. Regarding contemporary life and the unity of the Church, the sacrament becomes a gathering together of all mankind. For this reason it is, truly, called the *communion.* For this he quotes John the Damascene as authority. "In regard to the future, the sacrament foreshadows that enjoyment of God which shall be ours in our fatherland. On this account the sacrament is called viaticum, since it provides us with the means of

[20] *Summa Sent.,* Tract. VI, caps. 2, 3, 8; MPL 176:139, 140, 144-45.
[21] Lib. IV, Dist. 8, cap. 2; Quaracchi ed., II, 788.

In all of these liturgical expressions there is preserved the sense of two societies, earthly and heavenly, with their constituent elements. Brought to mind and heart are the faithful on earth and in purgatory, as well as the inhabitants of heaven. These two societies are dramatically related in the Church's worship around the world. The definite sense of companionship between these groups is expressed through the invocation of the saints; by way of prayers for the defunct in purgatory; and, in fact, in relation to the whole Church: militant, triumphant, and suffering.

The liturgies, one and all, give priority to the conception and reality of the kingdom of heaven. This may come to attention by means of the peculiar fraction of the bread, or in some other distinctive way. However lacking in obvious symbols, the suggestion persists that pilgrims pursue their way from terrestrial exile to heavenly citizenship. The twofold character of the Church is specifically stressed in terms of the eternal fellowship operating in the temporal. Thus the duality in unity of Christ's ecclesiastical institution is thought of in terms of a series of matching characteristics. That is to say, in the liturgy one is reminded that the Church is at once eternal and temporal; visible and invisible; transcendent and empirical.[29]

Anyone who thus participates in the sacred mysteries of the altar or who assists in the celebration of the divine offices must be aware of the primacy of Christ as heavenly king and high priest. He it is who will return from God's right hand in glory to judge all mankind at the Last Day. He it is, also, who comes down on the altar in the hands of the priest to become, at one and the same time, both priest and sacrifice. He is sacrifice in that he gives his life anew for the world. He is priest in that he officiates in thus making himself a sacrifice. In both instances he is making possible to humankind the participation in a kingdom that shall know no end. The kingdom of heaven, even as Jesus said, is already partially in existence. Christ is the great high priest in the celebration of the eucharistic graces; he makes available the heavenly bread on which the faithful are nourished while on pilgrimage to the kingdom. The humble priest of the Church is simply, yet profoundly, the one who exercises authority on the Lord's behalf to swing wide the gates of the everlasting so-

The Holy Sacrifice of the Mass: Dogmatically, Liturgically and Ascetically Explained (St. Louis, 1941) ; A. Aigrain, *Liturgia* (Paris, 1931) ; M. Brillant, *Eucharistia* (Paris, 1934) ; R. Stapper and D. Baier, *Catholic Liturgics* (Paterson, New Jersey, 1938) , etc. Cf. Petry, *Francis*, Chapter VI, pp. 103-17, for the liturgy historically considered in its medieval setting.

[29] Cf. Anger, *Mystical Body*, pp. 321 ff.

ciety. One cannot read or witness any of the prevailing liturgies, with their obvious affinity to the Christian past, without becoming keenly aware of the reality which the medieval church felt in its worship. What Christ does as high priest—and what the priest implements if he has been properly ordained to his office—is to inaugurate on this earth, in some degree at least, the eternal kingdom in which man shall one day participate more fully.[30]

It is clearly observable, in each of the Catholic liturgies, that Peter is thoroughly central, after Christ himself. This is quite logical inasmuch as it was the prince of the Apostles to whom Jesus is purported to have committed his Church. He is the head of the hierarchy in accordance with Matthew 16:19; to him were given the keys opening and closing the kingdom of heaven. In the whole liturgical cycle the Eucharist is at the heart of worship. Here, in this supreme thanksgiving, the faithful discover the quintessence of social experience. What could be more collective in its mutualizing aspects than the bringing together of all the faithful, at Christ's table, who have as their predestined gift the bestowal of eternal life? Thus, in feeding as one upon the manna of heaven, they assume the nature of the fullest brotherhood possible on earth. Herein is their best preparation for the consummate society of eternity. Furthermore, the Church is the unchallenged instrumentality of this social experience which bridges the chasm between the eternal kingdom and the temporal society.

All of this amounts to the full communication of the faithful in the eternal world. One communicates, first of all, in the food of the kingdom. One communicates, also, to his fellows, the deepest impulses of human life under the direction of the Divine. What this communion becomes, at its best, is a participation in the life of God's elect in terms of bread and wine, of prayers and hymns, of flesh and spirit. No careful perusal of liturgical materials can overlook these significant implications.[31]

If one turns to medieval discussions of the missal, and its different parts, he is at once impressed with the versatility of expression regarding the eschatological power of the eucharistic service. Whether one studies Isidore of Seville, John Beleth, or Innocent III, he senses in the eucharistic sacrament and sacrifice the kingdom's claim on the

---

[30] Petry, *Francis*, Chaps. V and VI; also the references in note 26, above.

[31] The socializing qualities of the mass are stressed by Gihr, *Holy Sacrifice of the Mass*, pp. 192-228, especially; cf. Petry, *Francis*, pp. 114-17.

faithful.[32] For instance, in his discussion of the Kyrie, John Beleth repeats a frequently encountered explanation for the nine repetitions of the "Lord have Mercy." This is, he says, because we desire to become associated with the nine orders of angels. Again, in his interpretation of the Collect and its meaning, he reminds us of the ancient association that it carried in terms of the welfare of the whole people whose eternal salvation was thus sought. In fact, as Gihr says, this Oratio or Collecta

frequently designated in former times the religious assembly or congregation of the faithful for the exercises of divine service, and principally for the Sacrifice of the Mass. . . . Like the Mass prayers in general, this prayer before the Epistle is not merely a private prayer of the priest, but a liturgical one, that is, a public prayer which the celebrant recites in the name and by the commission as well as according to the ordinance of the Church, and with a special intention for the welfare of the whole Christian people. The priest stands at the altar as the mediator between God and man, he there presents the desires and interests of all before the throne of God.[33]

It is in such fashion that the Church serves in the mass generally, and in these parts particularly, as the servant of the eternal kingdom in the present society of faithful Christians.

Coming to the Gospel, Beleth, like his later brethren commenting upon the mass, sees in the good news a story which has far more than symbolic significance for the Last Days. One is forcibly reminded of the first advent, with all its benignant reality, and of the last coming, which is to be preceded by preaching on the part of Christ's followers. The signs of Christ's coming to the world will be evident to all. The Lord's word is to be made short on the earth in anticipation of it. Later interpreters stress at some length the crucial significance of the gospel readings in the mass and the manner in which they focus on the present corporate life of the faithful the eternal character of that final community to which their lives are even now being conformed. In that Gospel, Christ no longer spoke by anticipation through his prophets, but out of his very mouth the eternal word of

[32] For representative "Orders" see M. Andrieu, *Les "Ordines Romani" du haut moyen âge* (Louvain, 1948), 2 Vols. Cf. "Index de eucharistiae sacramento," MPL 219:849 ff.; "Index de Missae Sacrificio," 863 ff. John Beleth's *Rationale divinorum officiorum* is in MPL 202:13-166. Cf. Cabrol et Leclerq, *Dict. d'archéol.*, "Messe," XI, 1, cols. 513-774, and "Missel," XII, 2, cols. 1431 ff. Note P. Batiffol, *Leçons sur la Messe* (Paris, 1937).

[33] N. Gihr, *The Holy Sacrifice of the Mass*, pp. 390, 408-9. Used by permission of the publishers, B. Herder Book Co. Cf. *Rationale*, caps. 36-37; MPL 211:44 ff.

salvation. Following upon the more preparatory function of the Epistle, the Gospel reveals the entire plan of divine salvation. It is surely fitting that in the gospel passages of the mass there should come to fullest expression the divine purposes, revealed in Christ, for the salvation of the faithful to the heavenly world. It is understandable, also, that they should lay down the bases of life by which true Christians must proceed, singly and together, if they would pass from this temporal world through the portals that lead into the beloved community of the eternal.[34]

In that area of the mass which preserves the most deeply poetic chants of her history, the Preface is unfolded, essentially as it was in the Middle Ages. In such prayers the Church proclaims herself to be "the divinely enlightened proclaimer of the eternal." The ordinary Preface calls upon the Lord to bless his people. The cry is raised: "The Lord be with you." The response follows: "And with thy spirit." Again the word comes: "Lift up your hearts." Whereupon the response: "We lift them up unto the Lord." Here, when the celebration of the mysteries draws near, the priest and his people feel, as never before, the need of the Lord's heavenly assistance. Nothing less than the upward inclination of the heart can associate the faithful with those powers which will eventually lead to inclusion in the eternal beatitude.[35]

Whether the commentator be John Beleth or a modern author like Gihr, the mood is the same.[36] Man is called upon to remember that he is meant for a heavenly destiny; that his abiding place is truly in heaven; and that only by regarding the things that are above, can he truly discharge the obligations of life, here, in such fashion as to merit a communal experience, there, after the last ages of this world. Now, if ever, the Christian must purge his heart of purely earthly concerns, and transcend things temporal with those eternal. This leads to the fully associational life both now and hereafter. The

[34] *Rationale,* caps. 38-39, MPL 202:46, and 47-49, on Epistle and Gospel; Gihr, *op. cit.,* pp. 438-42.

[35] Gihr, *op. cit.,* pp. 552-54. See the "Order of Low Mass," "The Preface to the Canon," *The Missal in Latin and English* (London, 1949), pp. 722-23. Cf. "Preface," in R. Lesage, *Dictionnaire pratique de Liturgie Romaine* (Paris, 1952). Consult Cabrol et Leclercq, *Dictionnaire.*

[36] Note that Gihr in his specifically liturgical section is really a running commentary on the "Ordines." Cf. Beleth, *Rationale,* caps. 44-45, for the "Secreta" and "Praefatione," MPL 202:52-53. Cf. Batiffol, *Leçons,* pp. 191 ff. Invaluable studies linking the Church's past and present worship via the "Ordines" are *Miscellanea Liturgica in honorem L. Cuniberti Mohlberg,* 2 Vols. (Rome, 1948-49) and J. A. Jungmann, *Missarum Sollemnia: Explication génétique de la Messe Romaine,* 2 Vols. (Paris, 1951-52).

faithful must know that only in such ways, by this sacrifice of things terrestrial, can they hope to be joined to the joys of things celestial.

The very term "Advent" signalizes the coming of Christ. Medieval thinkers were wont to run the gamut of interpretation with regard to Christ's several comings. Of these, the two most often treated were the first coming of Christ to the world and the second Parousia, which would be his return to judge all mankind. In all of these, however, there was a common dedication to the last and most significant return.[37]

The modern service books of the Roman Church preserve virtually intact the liturgical emphases of the high Middle Ages.[38] The missal, in the "Proper for the Season," introduces at the outset Christ's various comings. It prepares in festival joyousness to celebrate those that have already taken place, as well as that one which will mark the end of the present world order. In the first Sunday of Advent,

we are reminded of Christ as the Judge of mankind. At the scene of the judgment we should be seized not only with dread and fear on account of our sins, but more especially with a longing for the manifestation of "the Glory of the Lord," with a desire to have Him rule over our hearts and sanctify them by his grace.[39]

It is to this end, and at this time, especially, that Christians are admonished to draw together with him in the liturgy.

With a particular sense of urgency, the faithful Christian participates in the mass of the first Advent Sunday. Here is the prayer for protection from impending dangers. After all, none but the Lord himself can protect against the evil machinations of one's enemies and bring him at last to eternal salvation. The Epistle, too, reminds us that now is the time to rise from sleep; that now salvation is nearer than might have been believed. Night has given way to daytime. This is the hour to escape from darkness into light. Now, if ever, is the time to put on Jesus Christ. The Gospel, likewise, calls attention to the signs of Christ's imminent return. These are no mere reminders

[37] Recall the treatment of Jacobus de Voragine in the *Golden Legend*.

[38] For a brief introduction to the medieval liturgists such as Odo of Tournae, Ivo of Chartres, John Beleth, etc., see Ghellinck, *L'essor*, I, 155 ff. Jungmann, especially vol. I, is indispensable for tracing the historical evolution of the liturgy. See Stapper-Baier, Gihr, etc., as well as the articles and literature in *Ephemerides Liturgicae*.

[39] Stapper-Baier, *Catholic Liturgics*, pp. 101-2. Peter of Blois differentiates the redemptive comings of Christ according to the mystery of the Incarnation, his entrance into men's hearts by grace, his final, awful coming as judge. Serm. III, *De Adventu*, MPL 207:669; Gihr, *Holy Sacrifice of the Mass*, pp. 384 ff.

of Christ's coming; rather do they proclaim the last Advent and the judgment that shall follow upon it. Everywhere, throughout the service, there is emphasized the preparation for "the coming festival of our redemption." [40]

Thus in the season of Advent the Christian recalls that Christ came in the flesh almost two thousand years ago. But Christians must be ready for another coming when we, too, shall be summoned before him for judgment. Standing there before him at the end of recorded history, mankind will learn its eternal destiny; whether to companionship with the saints, or to deprivation of God's fellowship in the realm of those who are irredeemably evil.

The second Sunday of the Advent season focuses the Christian's attention upon preparation for the great event. The faithful are reminded that the Lord has come to save the nations. Every effort of Christian charity should accompany the proclamation of his having come to *save* men in the first instance, and of his coming again to *judge* them at the last. Fortified by the gracious mercies of the Divine, the followers of Jesus make ready for the joy that is to come.

The third Sunday places upon the individual the joyous burden of making ready the soul within. Christ is "now nigh and close at hand." The season is one of joyous expectation. "May the sacrifice of our devotion, we beseech Thee, O Lord, be continually offered to Thee, both to perform the appointed holy mysteries and to work in us the wonders of Thy salvation." So reads the prayer known as the Secret. And, further on, the Communion intones the words: "Stay, ye faint-hearted, take courage, and fear not, behold our God will come and will save us."

The fourth Sunday is a call to action proceeding from the fullest catholicity that the Church knows. Every follower of the Master is admonished to make ready in his heart, and in relation to the whole world, for the Last Days. "Brethren, let a man so account of us as of the ministers of Christ, and the dispensers of the mysteries of God." The way in which each of the faithful may so prove himself is at once the production of fruit for which he shall not be ashamed at the Judgment, and the joyous cry of gladness that now, at last, the new day of the dawning kingdom has come. [41]

---

[40] *The Missal in Latin and English* (London: Burns Oates and Washbourne, 1949), pp. 1-4; Father Lasance's *The New Missal for Every Day* (New York: Benziger Brothers, 1937), hereafter, Lasance, NM, pp. 147-49; *Missale Romanum* (New York: Benziger Brothers, 1944), hereafter *Missale Rom.*, pp. 1-4.

[41] Following the translation of Lasance, NM, p. 153, for the "Secret" and "Com-

Hence, during Advent, the Church calls upon her children to face the problem of life in a Christian manner. The first Sunday contains an appeal to faith; the second to hope; on the third she insists on the need of charity, giving the example of John the Baptist; and on the fourth, the need of good works: Christ the Saviour of the world must find a fitting abode in every Christian heart.[42]

It is in the mass, particularly, that one perceives how intimately the Church serves as a relating agency between the eternal and the temporal. Thus the commemoration of the saints, as a body, is the liturgical means by which the investment of the temporal in the eternal is inspiringly recorded. From the early centuries the Feast of All Saints continued to be kept as such a reminder. Moving ever toward the eternal kingdom, the faithful of this life seek incorporation in the family of God. They do this through the Church, their mother, which bears children for the eternal commonwealth. Once having been admitted into the arcanum of the blessed, the saints themselves become the continuing inspiration and a further means of help to those who are still in pilgrimage.

It is right, therefore, that the Church should direct attention to those of her number who have gained membership in the realm triumphant. With good reason the Introit reads: "Let us all rejoice in the Lord, celebrating a feast in honor of all the saints, in whose solemnity, the angels rejoice and join in praising the Son of God." [43] These saints are rightfully praised and glorified; and they are likewise looked to for help via the channels of God's mercy operating through his Church in heaven and on earth. That Church in its two-fold capacity—at once transcendent and empirical—serves to transmit the blessings of the eternal to the passing world.

Quite appropriately, the lesson is drawn from the seventh chapter of the Apocalypse. Here, there are celebrated in dramatic fashion the anticipated triumphs of God's saints. Of these it may be said, now as always, that there is no lack to them that fear him. The gospel reading draws the attention of the faithful to Christ's sermon on the mountain. His beatitudes—the joys of those who will enter the king-

---

munion" of the Third Sunday; NM, p. 165, for the rendering of the Fourth Sunday Epistle; Gihr, *op. cit.*, pp. 385-86; *Missale Rom.*, pp. 4-14.

[42] P. S. Henry, *The Liturgical Year* (Milwaukee, 1940), p. 21. See R. Knox, *The Epistles and Gospels for Sundays and Holydays: Translation and Commentary* (New York, 1946), pp. 1-29, for modern interpretation.

[43] "Proprium Missarum: Die Sanctis—Die 1 novembris in Festo Omnium Sanctorum," *Missale Rom.*, 778-80; Lasance, NM, p. 888.

dom finally—are bestowed upon the poor in spirit, the needy, those striving after justice, the merciful, the peacemakers, and those suffering every kind of evil for the sake of the heavenly realm. As the Offertory proclaims, "The souls of the just are in the hand of God, and the torment of malice shall not touch them." [44]

It is appropriate that in honor of those who have met such tests of fortitude and have been received into the heavenly kingdom the living followers of Christ on earth shall be blessed of the Lord. The words of the Communion do well to point out that the kingdom of heaven is truly theirs who thus meet the requirements of the Lord's blessing. And the post-Communion bears the parting invocation: "Grant to Thy faithful people, we beseech Thee, O Lord, ever to rejoice in the veneration of all Thy saints, and to be fortified by their unceasing prayers. Through Our Lord . . . ." Thus does the missal proclaim once more the Church's function as a depository and transmitter of all those goods on earth which proceed from the heavenly kingdom. In emulation also of that heavenly communion which is already in existence, the faithful are called upon to give an account of their lives together on earth. [45]

In the liturgical offices of the breviary, as in the services of the mass, the careers of the saints, whether commemorated individually or in common, become the inspiration and delight of the faithful. The breviary, therefore, correlates the fullest resources of homily, prayer, hymn, response, and scriptural reading for the purpose of honoring those who are now within the portals of the redeemed. [46]

Thus the homilies for the "Feast of a Confessor not a Bishop" draw upon the great preachers of the past for prayerful guidance. Chrysostom and others lend their eloquence to the memorialization of the saint whose feast is being kept. The homilist reminds the reader that the blessed confessor has gone where no sickness, strivings, untimely deaths, lies, jealousies, lustings, and worrisome cares are to be found. This one, even as St. Paul said, has been raised above mundane matters, as befits one whose life was ordered aright on earth. Others, too, may hope to follow after him. Even as the Christian has

[44] "Offertorium," Sap. 3:1-2 and 3; *Missale Rom.*, p. 780; Lasance, NM, p. 890.

[45] "Communio" and "Post Communio," Lasance, NM, p. 890.

[46] On the character of the Breviary and its indisseverability from the Mass, see P. Parsch, *The Breviary Explained* (St. Louis, 1952), p. 9. For the medieval view of Mass and Breviary see Petry, *Francis*, Chap. VI. A convenient modern instrument is the *Breviarium Romanum* (London: Burns Oates & Washbourne, 1946), 4 Vols., abbreviated *Brev. Rom.* Translations follow John, Marquess of Bute, *The Roman Breviary* (Edinburgh, 1879), II, Summer.

recounted for him the manifold happiness of the blessed confessor in his heavenly home, he is made to yearn after that abiding city that has no equal here on earth. The happy one has

become a citizen of that other city, which is the city of the living God; from the Church here he is gone, but is come unto the Church of the first born, which are written in heaven; . . . he keepeth holiday with us no more, but he is passed to where he holdeth high festival with Angels.[47]

So the Church, which has its vantage ground in heaven and yet nourishes men on earth, becomes the means of bringing souls from the present world into the assembly of the redeemed. The breviary reminds us: "This is he which loved not his life in this world, and is come unto an everlasting kingdom." The Antiphons bear out this suggestion in praises for him who has thus become a member of the blessed company. The gospel lesson and homilies celebrate the attainments of this one who has truly followed the injunction of Jesus "to let your loins be girded about and your lights burning." Pope Gregory, in commenting upon this very saying of Jesus, declares that "our lights burn when, by good works, we give bright example to our neighbour; concerning which works the Lord saith: 'Let your light so shine before men, that they may see your good works, and glorify your Father Which is in heaven.' " [48]

The seventh Responsory follows: "This is he which wrought great wonders before God, and praised the Lord with all his heart. May he pray for all people, that their sins may be forgiven unto them." It is understandable that the Church and its membership on earth should seek advocacy with God through the one whose Feast-day is being kept. The homilist continues to recall how the confessor in question disciplined himself within and without, exercising himself through good works unto the winning of the heavenly fatherland. If others will but follow him in their vigilant waiting for the Lord, with lights burning, they, too, will be ready to give edifying example in the way that leads to salvation. Those who are prepared by a good life need not fear death in the Judgment. They will have

---

[47] "Commune Confessoris non Pontificis, in II Nocturno, Lectio IV, etc., Sermo s. Joannis Chrys.," etc., *Brev. Rom.* (Aestiva), 93 *; *The Roman Breviary* (Summer), 857 ff.—Sixth lesson 858.

[48] "In III Nocturno, Lectio VII-IX, Hom. S. Greg. Papae, Hom. 13 in Evan."; *Brev. Rom.*, 96 *. Tr. in *Roman Breviary* (Summer), pp. 859-60. See the entire eschatological setting in *Hom. in Evang.*, Lib. I, Hom. XIII, MPL 76:1123-27.

discharged their full stewardship and been made ready for an invitation to a higher place in the Lord's mansions.[49]

The hymn which follows places Christ in the center of the celestial brightness and stresses the joyous citizenship of the saint who shares with him the blessedness of the heavenly feast. The prayer enjoined is:

O God, Who, year by year, dost gladden us by the solemn Feast-day of Thy blessed Confessor *(here insert his name)* mercifully grant unto all who keep his birthday, grace to follow after the pattern of his godly conversation. Through our Lord Jesus Christ Thy Son, Who liveth and reigneth with Thee, in the unity of the Holy Ghost, one God, world without end. Amen.[50]

Liturgical prayers regularly employed in medieval and later periods were placed in closest juxtaposition with lessons drawn from sacred literature and the writings of the Fathers. Consequently, in honoring those who have attained the rank of Doctor of the Church, the ecclesiastical community pays highest tribute for their service rendered to all the faithful while on this earth. It is with a deeply appreciative sense of the manner in which they gave themselves as preachers of the divine Word that the Church pays them homage.

As is customary, the breviary expresses this affection for the Church's leaders by drawing upon patristic homilies as well as prayers, praises, and sacred Scripture. In the fourth and fifth lessons of the "Office for Doctors of the Church," Gregory's ever popular *Moralia* provides the commentary on the brightness of the crowns deservedly worn by these great souls. They helped make possible a brighter and more shining light in the hearts of the faithful. After the period of persecution was over, they arose, shining "in the firmament of the universal Church," making "the rain of holy preaching to fall upon the parched ground of man's heart." Their function included the day-by-day inculcation of knowledge regarding heavenly things. Through them the faithful have learned to know Christ better. And Gregory is convinced that "as the end of the world groweth nearer, the knowledge of things heavenly will grow greater, and continue to develop with time." [51]

---

[49] *Roman Breviary*, pp. 860-61.
[50] *Ibid.*, pp. 861-62.
[51] "Commune Doctorum, In II Nocturno, Lectio IV-VII"; *Brev. Rom.*, pp. 81 * ff.; *Roman Breviary*, 869-70. For the *Moralia in Job*, Lib. IX, cap. (VI) XI, see MPL 75: 865-69.

The seventh lesson for the Office continues on the same general theme. It is now St. Augustine who is gratefully appropriated to show how valuable is the service that is rendered by true teachers of the gospel. Taking as his text Jesus' statement to his disciples that they must be the salt of the earth, Augustine tries to show how foolish it is for men to lose things eternal through absorption in matters temporal. But if this is to be avoided, those commissioned by Christ must keep their saltiness.

This is as much as to say: Ye are they by whom the stale mass of mankind is to be sweetened; if ye, therefore, through shrinking from the trials of persecutions, which endure but for a moment, do yourselves cast away that kingdom which is everlasting, who will there be to correct your backsliding, seeing that ye be they, and none other, whom God hath chosen to correct the backsliding of all others?

The implications are here trenchantly set forth, not only as to the doctors' responsibility for the salvation of souls to the kingdom, but also as to the proper merit acquired by these same teachers in performing the Lord's service in the name of his Church.[52]

St. Hilary of Poitiers discourses in the same mood. The Apostles who first received this injunction to a salty life

are themselves the preachers of the kingdom of heaven, and in a certain sense the sowers of the seed of life everlasting, since that Word of God which they scatter hath power to make this mortal put on immortality. Meetly then are they called salt, the savour of whose teaching doth keep sweet the receiver thereof even unto life everlasting.

Only by preserving this savoring strength in themselves, whatever the vicissitudes of their earthly life, could the Doctors of the Church impart their seasoning qualities to others. Otherwise, corruption would grow and the Church would "cast them out of her buttery, and they and those that they should have salted, be together trodden under foot of such as enter in." How, possibly, could the homilist stress more graphically the common responsibility of all ecclesiastical leaders for the care of souls committed unto them?[53]

Chrysostom also stresses from within the breviary the highly social

[52] "In III Nocturno, Lectio VII, Hom. s. Aug. Episcop.," *Brev. Rom.*, p. 83 *; *Roman Breviary*, pp. 870-71. Serm. Mont. 6.

[53] "In III Nocturno, Alia Homilia (II), Lectio VII," *Brev. Rom.*, pp. 84*-85*; *Roman Breviary*, p. 872.

reponsibility of those who would transmit their saving saltiness to the society of their time. These disciples of the Master

have an account to render, not of their own life only, but for the whole world. Not unto two cities, saith the Lord, nor unto ten, nor unto twenty, nor unto one people, as I sent the Prophets, send I you. But I send you unto every land and sea, even unto the whole world, lying groaning, as it is, under the burden of divers sins.

Just as man, by his very nature, is "savourless and stinking with the strong corruption of sin," so must Christ's apostles possess in largest degree

such qualities as are most needful and useful to the furthering the salvation of many. He that is gentle and lowly, tender and just, shutteth not up all these good things in his own heart, but openeth these bright fountains that they may gush forth for the use of his neighbour. He whose heart is pure, and who seeketh peace, suffering persecution for the truth's sake, doth still lead a life for the good of the commonwealth.[54]

What such a series of admonitions to the social life, conceived of in terms of a beckoning kingdom of eternal bliss, must have meant to those who habitually followed the prayers of the Church in its breviary is beyond all quantitative calculation. It is the genius of the liturgy that it has surrounded the noblest motivations of man, conceived in terms of the divine commandments, with prayers, hymns, and praises—all unto the protective and inspiring benignity of mother Church.

In that part of the missal devoted to the "Common of one or more Supreme Pontiffs," a peculiarly poignant association is established between the original commission to Peter and the sacrificial service rendered by every true bishop of Rome to the faithful Christians placed under his care. The Introit, John 21:15-17, repeats the Master's words, "If thou lovest me, Simon Peter, feed my lambs; feed my sheep." The prayer then unites the lives and functions of the eternal shepherd and that one chosen to serve under him as the chief pastor of the whole Church: "O Eternal Shepherd, do Thou look favorably upon Thy flock, which we beseech Thee to guard and keep forevermore through the Blessed N. (Thy Martyr and) Supreme Pontiff, whom Thou didst choose to be the chief shepherd of the

[54] "In III Nocturno, Alia Homilia (III), Lectio VII-VIII"; *Brev. Rom.* p. 85 *; *Roman Breviary*, pp. 872-73; Chrys., *Hom. 15 in Matt.*

whole church. Through Our Lord." God, who established his Church on the apostolic rock, is further petitioned through the intercession of the given martyr and Supreme Pontiff that his Church "may adhere always to Thy Truth so as to enjoy at all times a sure defence." [55]

The Epistle is drawn from I Peter 5:1-4, 10-11. It places in sober outline the glorious responsibility of feeding the flock of God; living not from the motivation of self-seeking and domination, but as giving service in Christ to all for the glory of God. Such a pastor of the Church on earth shall receive a never-fading crown of glory when the Prince of pastors shall appear. Thinking of one who has already proved his right to the crown of life, the Church is happy in its prayers to praise him, even as the Epistle instructs:

Let them exalt him in the Church of the people; and praise him in the chair of the ancients. Let the mercies of the Lord give glory to him, and the wonderful works to the children of men.

It is upon such that the Church has been built as upon a rock. This one is, indeed, Peter. The Gospel from Matthew 16:13-19 recounts the moving story of Jesus' asking Peter as to the Son of Man's identity and Peter's reply: "Thou art Christ, the Son of the living God." And the lesson continues in the age-old fashion:

I say to Thee, that thou art Peter, and upon this rock I will build my Church, and the gates of hell shall not prevail against it; and to thee I will give the keys of the kingdom of heaven; and whatsoever thou shalt bind upon earth, it shall be bound also in heaven; and whatsoever thou shalt loose on earth, it shall be loosed also in heaven.[56]

Here, in the "Common of her Pontiffs," the Roman Church preserves the ancient tradition on which her whole earthly institution rests. Never more dramatically than here is the lesson brought home to the faithful: It was to Peter and his successors that the Church of God was committed; and through them it should serve till the end of time as the agency of the eternal kingdom in its temporal ministry among men. Quite literally, as the Church continues to conceive of it, the tradition here embodied makes the Supreme Pontiff on earth the chief of pastors in whose keeping the keys of the heavenly kingdom rest. What they and their subordinates within the hierarchy de-

---

[55] Lasance, *The New Missal for Every Day*, pp. (3a) ff. Used by permission of the publishers, Benziger Brothers, Inc.

[56] *Ibid.*, pp. (3a) - (3c). Used by permission of the publishers.

cree is a predisposition, to some degree at least, of eternal kingdom membership. Whatever they bind and loose on earth shall be bound and loosed in heaven. In this august solemnization of the Supreme Pontiff's powers and responsibilities, the minds of the faithful are turned to their eternal disposition. They rededicate their lives to the Great Pastor in heaven and his vicars on earth.

In the secret prayers of the liturgical offering, the Lord is invoked to aid his Church through its chief pastors, present and past. The Preface of the Apostles, at the conclusion of this service, reads:

> It is truly meet and just, right and profitable, humbly to beseech Thee, O Lord, to forsake not the flock of which Thou art the eternal shepherd, but through Thy holy apostles ever to guard and keep it, so that it be governed by those rulers whom Thou didst set over it to be its pastors under Thee. And therefore with the angels and archangels, with the thrones and dominations, and with all the array of the heavenly host we sing a hymn to Thy glory and unceasingly repeat: Holy, Holy, Holy.[57]

As the Church of Christ, given originally to Peter and sustained in his successors, continues to transmit the heavenly blessings to its members militant on earth, that Church continues also as the servant of an eternal kingdom in a temporal community. The memorialization of great pontiffs brings strikingly to bear in the hearts of the faithful the necessity of their following after the edifying service of their leaders. It is the Church's teaching that only in love and submission to Peter and his successors—the heads of his Church—may the faithful hope to reign forever in the heavenly company of the elect. As already said, these liturgical materials drawn from present-day missals and breviaries are not unrepresentative of their earlier prototypes. They continue the major emphasis of medieval worship.[58]

---

[57] *Ibid.*, pp. (3c)-(3d). Used by permission of the publishers.

[58] The fullest treatments of liturgical history and continuity with contemporary worship are found in Gihr, *Holy Sacrifice of the Mass;* Andrieu, *Les "Ordines Romani";* Jungmann, *Missarium;* Cabrol et Leclercq, *Dictionnaire d'archéol.*, and others already cited. Jungmann, like Cabrol and Leclercq, has constant reference to early and medieval data.

CHAPTER X

The Ecclesiastical Community
as Servant of the Eternal Kingdom
in the Temporal World

4. The Priesthood, the Kingdom, and the Church

INCREASINGLY IN THE EARLY CHURCH, AND WITH MOUNTING URGENCY during the Middle Ages, the responsible ministry of the priesthood was insisted upon. It was these ministers who held the keys to the eternal kingdom. In the center of the hierarchy, and with full responsiveness to their superiors, they shared in Christ's committal to Peter of the kingdom's powers. The hierarchy on earth must respond to its celestial prototype; the natural associations of men must follow their supernatural archetypes; the sacraments instituted by Christ must provide heavenly food and sustenance for those on pilgrimage to the eternal city. This could be effected only if there were given to the Church by the Master himself the means of answering eternal claims on the world's program of action. The priesthood, in the person of Peter and his successors, hierarchically ordered, had the power of binding and loosing. Priests were the functioning ministers of the servant-church—that Church which Christ had given to the world for the purpose of salvaging the race to lasting beatitude.

These and allied conceptions of the priesthood were reflected throughout the literature of the ancient and the medieval church. Handbooks were legion in which the duties and the opportunities of priests were commented upon. Quite naturally, some of these treatises were ascribed to men who had not composed them. Leaders of distinction in plenty, however, did emphasize the pastoral care required by the Lord of his episcopal and priestly ministers.[1] Of

---

[1] Consult MPL 219:710 ff.: "Index de Sacerdotio." J. T. McNeill, *A History of the Cure of Souls* (New York, 1951)), has pertinent analyses and bibliographies. Note F. van der Meer's massive *Augustinus der Seelsorger* (Cologne, 1951).

these, the famous treatise *On the Priesthood* by Chrysostom comes immediately to mind. His initial unwillingness to assume the heavy burden of responsibility is reflected in it. Likewise mirrored are his high ideals for the one who dares to stand in the Lord's place and communicate life eternal to the world's sinful population. For it is the priests, indeed, who beget to the life to come. They guard the entrance to heaven's realm. No one enters the kingdom without the birth of water and spirit and the communication in the Lord's body which it is the prerogative of consecrated priests to provide. How, then, can anyone escape hell fire or secure the crown of life without them? [2]

The universally admired work of Gregory the Great *On Pastoral Rule* is virtually a single emphasis on the episcopal and priestly function. Conceived, it is true, in terms of the bishop, it is equally applicable to all those entrusted with the cure of souls. The entire Middle Ages accepted gratefully its admonitions to the priest who would lead people of every category and disposition to the eternal society. Practically every whim of the spiritual climate is discussed. The manifold temptations of the spiritual minister to evade his duty are treated at length. But whether preaching or serving the altar, the priest is called to make himself available at heaven's behest for the needs of all men. So, likewise, in his commentary on Job, Gregory digresses in terms of priests and preachers who ought to be vigilant chanticleers in the face of all evil. Many of the later medieval instructions on priestly power and duty derived from these and other works of Pope Gregory. [3]

Phillip of Harveng produced one of the less known treatises on clerical dignity. Its major significance lies in the symbolism by which the author relates the priest at the altar to the people and the gospel word. The priests are the householders of the Church and the proclaimers of divine Scriptures. They dare not be confusers of heavenly and earthly things. Phillip's continuing play on the symbolism of the priestly garments is designed to promote the clerical significance

---

[2] *De Sacerdotio*, MPG 48:623 ff. Translated as *On the Priesthood,* by W. R. W. Stephens, NPNF, 1st Ser., IX, 33-83. See *Priesthood*, III, 5-6; NPNF, 1st Ser., IX, 47.

[3] *Liber regulae pastoralis* (MPL 77:9-128). Translated as *The Book of Pastoral Care* by J. Barmby in NPNF, 2nd Ser., XII (2nd Pt), 2 ff. Cf. Serm. 15:96 of NUS as tr. from Hom. XI, Bk. 1 (Ezech. 3:18, MPL 76:905-15). See Lib. XXX of the *Moralia in Job*, MPL 76:521 ff. and cf. The Marrott edition (Oxford, 1844), III, 2, pp. 361 ff. Cf. Bk. IV, 56, MPL 75:666; Marrott, I, 222; Altaner, *Patrologie*, pp. 417 ff.

in the priest's own eyes and so insure his careful servantship among the people, in the Lord's sight.[4]

In the later Middle Ages almost every writer of eminence tried his hand at a priest's manual. One attributed to Ambrose is probably that of Gerbert. Damian is credited with a work on the sacerdotal dignity. Whether or not Bernard of Clairvaux wrote the treatise of similar character listed under his name is immaterial. His authentic sermons and letters, not to mention the basic work, *On Considera-tion,* are full of this theme. An anthology of Bernard's works serves to clarify even further his sense of responsibility as the Lord's priest. Deferring until later an extended discussion of his views, one may note some distinctive aspects of related medieval thought.[5]

At an early date Jerome had emphasized the priestly right to the keys unlocking heaven's kingdom. Priests hold these until the very days of Judgment; serving, in the meantime, as the Lord's own representatives. Augustine had regarded the priesthood as the compatriots of the angelic citizens and those who led others to such association.[6] Julianus Pomerius (d. 498), in his praises of the holy priesthood, emphasized, not only the responsibility of those to whom the cure of souls had been committed, but also the dignity which thereby accrued to them. It was their function to serve, with God's permission, as judges according to the divine will. They were, after Christ's own Apostles, the founders of the churches, the leaders of faithful people, the asseverators of all truth, and the enemies of false doctrine. They were, likewise, preachers of heaven, battlers in the vanguard of invisible contests, exemplifiers of all good works, and provers of all virtues. In short, Pomerius conceived of them as being ornaments of the Church, the very doors of the eternal city, and the means by which all those believing in Christ might be admitted to his presence. They were janitors to whom the keys of heaven's kingdom had been given—dispensers of heaven's goods from the celestial household, by whose will the rank and station of each in the royal court were determined.[7]

---

[4] *De institutione laicale*, Lib. II, cap. 20, MPL 106:208-11; Isidore's *De ecclesiasticis officiis* is MPL 83:737-826; cf. Cayré, *Patrologie*, II, 258.

[5] See MPL 219:710 ff., where ascriptions are given to such works by Ambrose, Damian, etc. For Bernard's *Sermo de dignitate sacerdotium*, see MPL 184:981 ff. Cf. *De moribus et officio episcoporum*, translated in M. Davy, *Saint Bernard: Oeuvres* (Paris, 1945), I, 315 ff.

[6] MPL references 219:711 to 22:352 and 40:1299.

[7] *De vita contemplativa* (Long ascribed to Prosper of Aquitaine, d. after 455), MPL 59:415-520. See, especially, Lib. II, cap. 2; "De laude sanctorum sacerdotium,"

Jonas, Bishop of Orleans (d. 844), drew upon the writings of Jerome, Eusebius, and Isidore to emphasize the priestly power. The Bishop of Seville (d. 636) had written several works, including one on clerical offices, in which the priestly significance had been sufficiently dwelt upon. But Jonas stressed the manner in which priests, employing their heavenly keys, have the power of judging, even before the Day of Judgment itself. Thus with recourse to Eusebius he insists that they may judge men, but not be judged by men; for God wills it so.[8]

Much more famous was the work of Theodulf, Bishop of Orleans (d. 821). His admonitions to the priests of his diocese are distinguished for their incitement to heavenly ministry among men, their liturgical qualities, and their call to preaching and instruction. Few in his time were so moved to serve the needs of ordinary people. He rightly divined the necessity of raising up an educated priesthood if the people were to be taught the Catholic faith and have preached to them gospel doctrines. Only then could the populace be made ready through good temporal life for a share in the convocation of heaven.[9]

It would be possible to continue at great length the analysis of priestly manuals. A few more have particular significance. One of Bernard's sermons is especially adapted to the inculcation of the priestly virtues.[10] He is dealing with the mystical theme of the Church as the Bride of Christ, who is her Bridegroom. He examines the manner in which the Church is served in Christ's name by faithful counselors, teachers, preachers, and pastors. The Church requires the services of many humble-souled individuals who help to prepare the Bride for her nuptials with the heavenly Bridegroom. Those who are set as watchmen for the heavenly city are already responsible, on earth, to make ready for the coming of their people to the promised land. Like watchful sentinels, their business is to guard carefully and wisely against all the wiles of evil.

These are lovers of the brethren and of the people of Christ who pray

---

59:444-45. A modern English translation is that of Sister Mary Josephine Suelzer (Westminster, Md., 1947), Bk. I, cap. 2, pp. 58-60.

[8] *De institutione clericorum:* Bk. I: "De dignitate clericorum," caps. XI-XIV, MPL 203:682-83, 690-92; Ghellinck, *L'essor,* I, 202; H. Hurter, *Nomenclator* (Oeniponte, 1903-6), 2 Vols., Index.

[9] *Capitula ad presbyteros parochiae suae;* MPL 105:191 ff.; Manitius, *Geschichte,* I, 537 ff.

[10] *Serm. LXXVI in Cantica,* MPL 183:1153-55; tr. in NUS 29:158 ff., via Eales, *Works,* IV, 471-74.

much for the people and for all the Holy City. These are they, who, being careful and anxious for the sheep entrusted to them by the Lord, bear them on their heart at their waking, when the day breaks, to the Lord who made them, and offer intercession for them in the presence of the Most High.[11]

Predominant in the whole sermon is an awareness of the Last Days. Watching and praying are the best means to forestall disaster in the Last Times. The beloved Bride, the cherished flock of the Master, the new city coming down out of heaven—all require the patient, well-informed service of good pastors. To the first pastor, St. Peter himself, Christ committed his flock with loving tenderness. Following the representatives of Peter from time immemorial, all the clergy must exemplify a sacrificial contribution to the needs of the blessed. They can do no less than this for those in whose behalf Christ shed his own blood.

Those called to the office of the pastor have a responsibility which cannot be exaggerated. They have a city committed to their keeping. In it safety and concord will be preserved only through their alertness. A bride is presented to them "decked with the precious jewels of abundant virtues." They must study diligently to give needful pasture to their flock. Bernard mixes metaphors in an attempt to clarify the obligations that rest upon a good shepherd of souls. It is the edification of his people and not his own convenience that should be uppermost in his mind. Their proper service will require his having the gospel salt if he is to season them properly. Zealousness and learning are required of one who has the keeping of immortal spirits in his charge. How can a pastor be ignorant if he is to "conduct the Lord's flock to the sweet pastures of the Divine Oracles"? Learning must be joined to a praiseworthy life if he is to discharge the functions of his high calling.[12]

More important still is Bernard's illustrious work *On Considera-tion*.[13] Ostensibly diffident in the face of his former student's request for advice, he soon warms to the task of reminding Pope Eugenius III just what his sacred duties are. Coursing through the work is an undercurrent of suggestion that if the Pope, or any other priest, would be true to his people, he must fix his eyes on the eternal

[11] NUS 29:159 (*Serm. LXXVI in Cantica,* Sec. 7).

[12] NUS 29:160-62 (*Ibid.,* Secs. 9-10).

[13] *De Consideratione,* MPL 182:727-808; Cayré, *Patrologie,* II, 421, 423; portions translated in Davy, *Oeuvres,* I, 345-57. The translation followed here is that of George Lewis (Oxford, 1908).

world. To be too immediately concerned with temporal affairs, however pressing, is to lose the heavenly focus and to prove unworthy of the priestly obligation. Here, as in all his writings, Bernard derives his leverage for temporal ministry from his preoccupation with the celestial community. In the light of things above, the Pope may profitably look about him to see what things have been subordinated to his rule below.

For the Abbot of Clairvaux believes wholeheartedly in the dignity and power of ecclesiastical rulers. This, however, is not to be confused with the overweening ambitions of dominating princes and ecclesiasts. Set over other men, the Pope with his churchly subordinates is intended to exercise not lordship but ministry. In the prophetic example there is sufficient indication of the hard tasks that lie before the true bishop of the universal Church. The dignity and the power of the Pope belong together. Dignified with the Master's own bequest to feed his sheep and to prepare the faithful for entrance into his kingdom, the successors of St. Peter have likewise been endowed with appropriate powers. Other bishops share in the commission of Peter. But the Bishop of Rome captains the ship of salvation which is "the Universal Church throughout the world, the sum of all the other churches put together." Bernard's continuing refrain stresses the ministry of service, not of domination, that should be exemplified by the father of all the faithful.

The unseemly exhibition of ecclesiastical avarice in Eugenius' own day should be enough to spur him on. His is the power of redressing such wrongs and of guaranteeing the Church's role in time as the saving agency of the eternal kingdom. In a manner reminiscent of his correspondence with the Pope on other occasions, Bernard calls upon his old pupil to reincarnate the watchfulness of the Church's shepherds in ancient days. The tenderest admonitions as well as the most exacting requirements are here registered. Always mindful of his own mortality and the defectiveness of his own humanity, the Pope should fulfill his sacred functions as the vicar of the Lord. Bernard's peroration on the ideal pope extols the qualities that should be those of every good priest. Let the Pope, however, remember "that the holy Roman Church of which God has made you head, is the mother of churches, not their mistress; but that you are not sovereign lord of the bishops, but one of them, the brother, too, of those who love God, and a partaker with them that fear Him." Sadly needed is a model of righteousness, truth, and honor for the entire priesthood and all the faithful. Bernard makes specific, in terms of his own age, the social virtues by which the head of the Church on earth may respond as priest and servant to the high priest of heaven.

Concluding with a discussion of heavenly beings, Bernard returns to the focal point of his admonition. It is by observing the concord and harmonious life of those on high that the joyous responsibility of the Church's servants on earth may best be discharged. The heavenly hierarchy makes its demands upon the earthly one. The worshiping church below, with its sacraments administered by a faithful priesthood, leads the faithful to the promised land.[14]

Compared with the eloquence of Bernard, the *Sentences* of Peter Lombard seem pedestrian indeed. He gathers up the sayings of the Fathers and organizes them into an acceptable whole. He, too, believes that all priests have a share in the binding and loosing that goes with the keys. But they have it only if they follow the apostolic life and doctrines. To Peter is attributed the usual primacy. But in and through him there is bestowed a judiciary power and a spiritual beneficence that emphasizes the responsibility to heaven of all ministering priests. As noted elsewhere, the sacraments are the veritable bread of heaven. And it has pleased the Lord himself to make the *sacerdotium* the dispensers, within hierarchical ordering, of this heavenly manna—this viaticum.[15]

Peter of Blois, a specialist in the diseases that infect both sheep and shepherd of the Christian flock, has a sermon on good and wicked priests. He says, "Certainly a devout and prudent priest, while he stands at the divine table, will think of nothing else but *Jesus Christ and Him Crucified.*" He will certainly be filled with humility as he contemplates the sacrifice which Christ made on the cross. Furthermore, he can hardly fail to sense the importance of his own priestly function as he brings once more into the life of the faithful the saving death of the Master. "O how awful, how perilous a thing, my brethren, is the administration of your office! because ye shall have to answer not only for your own souls, but for the souls committed to your charge, when the Day of tremendous Judgment shall come!"

Since each priest has it within his power to speak as a watchman of the Lord, he cannot fail in this privileged obligation without encouraging the Lord's anger. For one who forgets his duty there is

[14] According to the edition of Lewis, *On Consid.,* II, viii, 15-16 (pp. 54-56) ; IV, vii, 23 (pp. 122-23) ; V, i, 1-2 (pp. 129-31) ; V, iv, 710 (pp. 136-41) .

[15] *Sent.,* Lib. IV, Dist., XXVIII, Secs. 1-6; also Dist. XIX, Sec. 1. See the translation of E. F. Rogers, *Peter Lombard and the Sacramental System* (New York, 1917) , 189-95, 198-200.

prepared a fitting place in the all-consuming fire—"From which may that Fire deliver us Who consumes not, but consummates—which devours not, but enlightens every man that cometh into the world. May He illuminate us to give the knowledge of salvation unto His people." [16]

Jacques de Vitry had a conception of the priesthood befitting his cosmopolitan station in the Church. His sermon to prelates and priests is marked by sensitivity to the divine ministry that is committed to the clergy. Let priests hear their call and discharge their functions as impartial shepherds of the whole flock, not as servants of special privilege. They must be especially careful lest they honor the rich on account of their wealth and condemn the poor on account of their indigence. Jacques had his usual fund of stories concerning bad priests and prelates who despoil humble people under the guise of dispensing ecclesiastical ministrations. Anyone denominated a rector ought surely to be right himself. This sermon registers indignation at the manner in which the priesthood is so often degraded in his own age; there is a stirring plea to all his fellow priests to venerate their high calling.[17]

Robert Grosseteste, Bishop of Lincoln from 1235 to 1253, was one of the most conscientious priests and bishops of the Middle Ages. His *Constitutions,* delivered to the clergy of his diocese, are full of biblical incentives to pastoral service. So, likewise, are the many letters with which he regales his own diocesan officials, and popes themselves. Such sermons as are preserved to us in the collection of Edward Brown bear out this same regard for a dignified yet humble ministration to fellow men. Here, as in his famous *Memorial* to the pope and his cardinals, Grosseteste places first the evangelizing of humanity with God's own word as well as the dispensing of liturgical offices. Good pastors and gospel preachers are likened to the keepers of cities. In living here, below, the life required of the ultimate community, worthy shepherds of the flock help prepare their followers for eternal fellowship.[18]

[16] Latin text in MPL 207:51 ff., 62-63 ff., for Ep. XV, XVII, etc. Cf. *Patres Eccl. Anglicanae, Op. Om.,* I, 53; Neale, *Med. Preachers,* pp. 208-9; NUS 33:174.

[17] *Sermones, Selecta ex sermonibus vulgaribus,* ed. J. Baptista Cardinalis Pitra, in *Analecta novissima spicilegii solesmensis altera continuatio,* Tome II (Paris, 1888), *Sermones,* pp. 344-442. Cf. NUS 36:186 ff.; Petry, *Preaching in the Great Tradition,* pp. 74-78.

[18] See H. A. Luard, *Roberti Grosseteste Episcopi . . . Epistolae* (RS 25, London, 1861), especially pp. 72-76, 154-66. E. Brown, *Fasciculus Rerum Expetendarum et Fugiendarum* (London, 1690), pp. 250 ff., and other literature cited in R. C. Petry,

In his little book *On Conscience,* Robert de Sorbon (d. 1274) chose to compare the examinations of Paris students with the grand accounting of all souls at the Last Day.[19] The seeming humor of such a comparison is quickly forgotten when one joins the author in grave assessment of pastoral and instructional qualities which involve heaven or hell for those whom priests lead. The idea of clerical responsibility in the present for the ultimate disposition of the faithful is clearly maintained.

Durand, the Bishop of Mende (d. 1296), emphasizes similarly the report that must be tendered by priests, bishops, and other church leaders at the Day of Judgment. He knows men in plenty who will certainly encounter the divine wrath at the Last Day because they have been derelict as servants of the Church on earth. Woe to such men who understand not the sacred mysteries of the altar any better than brute beasts that may be taught to carry bread to their masters! The whole presbyterial function, including the service of the altar and the preaching of the Word, consists in leading their people from the exile of this world to the paradise of the fatherland. Bishops, with their properly co-operative priesthood, become, indeed, mediators between God and man. Durand the Younger's (d. 1328) recommendations for reform incorporate practical suggestions for improving clerical life, augmenting priestly learning in the Scriptures, and enhancing true worship in the parish churches.[20]

Like his contemporaries, Durand the Elder and the Younger, Bishop William le Maire (d. 1317) was deeply disturbed by the sad state of the Church in his day. His recommendations to the Council of Vienne in 1311 give an analysis of conditions quite similar to that of Durand the Younger. He finds that the clearest obligations of the clergy are flagrantly ignored or stupidly perverted. Ignorance plays its part. But the priest and the people who follow him seem not so much lacking in knowledge as defective in the will to follow the Christian life. As one who kept a very careful account of his episco-

---

"Emphasis on the Gospel," *Church History,* XXI, 2 (June, 1947), 79 ff. Consult by index the numerous references to Grosseteste in J. R. H. Moorman, *Church Life in England in the XIIIth Century* (Cambridge, 1946).

[19] *De Consciencia* (Paris, 1902), ed. F. Chambon.

[20] *Rationale Divinorum Officiorum:* Lib. I, cap. 1; Secs. 1, 3 etc.; Neale-Webb, *Symbolism,* pp. 3-6. See the *Rationale,* Lib. II, cap. 1, Sec. 30; cap. IX, Secs. 6-19; cap. X, Sec. 6; Cap. XI, Secs. 13, 14, etc. Cf. G. G. Coulton, *Life in the Middle Ages* (New York, 1930), I, 201.

pal stewardship and recorded it in the so-called *Book of William Major,* this conscientious churchman knew where to place specific blame and how to propose definite cures. The preciseness of his recommendations cannot be demonstrated here in full. They are but one more documentation of clerical inadequacy and priestly failure. William holds it to be a never-ending disgrace that the churches of France should be empty on the days of worship; or, worse still, that the places and provinces of worship should be displaced by the willful secularism of priests and people. Vigorous sacerdotal leadership is the key to effective Christian living.[21]

Birgitta of Sweden (d. 1373) had a high sense of social consciousness involving the servants of the Church. She insisted that the highest calling of the priesthood was to fortify souls through the resourcefulness of God's Church; and thus to make them acceptable in the life of the eternal kingdom.

In one of her *Revelations,* granted by the Lord Jesus Christ, Birgitta explains the categories into which the Master fits various people. The first of these is the governor of holy Church and her clerks. The second regards wicked lay people. In the third classification come the Jews. The fourth constitutes the pagans. In the fifth are counted Christ's own friends.[22]

Speaking of the first group, Christ complains against—yes, even indicts—the head of his Church, to his face. The pontiff sits in a chair which the Lord had previously given to Peter and his successors for the exercise of a threefold dignity and authority. They were, first of all, to have the power of binding and loosing souls. Second, it was their function to open heaven itself to those who would do penance. In the third place, they were to bar the gates of heaven to the wicked, the cursed, and all despisers. But the pope has come far short of fulfilling his obligations. Jesus bluntly reprimands the governor of his Church. The pontiff, instead of loosing souls and presenting them to the Lord, actually slays them. Peter was ordained as the shepherd of Christ's sheep. The pope has become their despoiler. He is worse than Lucifer. That one, envying the Master, fled from Him, hoping to be Lord in His stead. The pope not only flees his Lord, opposing to Him his own will and works, but he also slays souls by his very example. Christ bought souls with His blood and entrusted them

[21] *Liber Guillelmi Majoris,* ed. M. Célestin Port, in *Mélanges historiques: Choix de documents,* II, 189-569 (Paris, 1877), especially, pp. 476-88; cf. Coulton, *Life,* I, 220 ff.

[22] Book I, Chap. 41, pp. 4-10 (Folios 3a-5f), W. P. Cumming, ed., *The Revelations of Saint Birgitta* (London, 1929).

to the pope's care. The pope promptly turns them back to the enemy from whom Jesus bought them at such a great price.[23]

The earthly head of Christ's Church is less righteous than Pilate; since Pilate doomed none to death but Christ, whereas the pope destroys innocent souls while he lets the guilty go unpunished. Judas, likewise, sold none but his Lord, whereas the pope sells his Christ together with the chosen of the Lord. The incumbent of Peter's seat has proved himself more abominable than the Jews who were content with the crucifixion of the Lord's body while his vicar crucifies the souls of the Lord's chosen. Seldom in literature has such an indictment been equaled in its directness and far-reaching implications. The severity of the judgments that Birgitta pronounces in the Lord's name is the measure of pontifical negligence in not making available to lost souls the saving ministry of Christ's kingdom-dedicated Church. Speaking of all unrighteous clergy and unfaithful Christians, the Master registers a fateful decision. These are not to enter his kingdom so long as he rules; unless, of course, they mend their ways. Heaven is open only to those who, humbling themselves, do penance. But the Lord's true friends, armed with Christ's own might, shall prove unconquerable.[24]

In a representative letter to Gregory XI, Catherine of Siena (d. 1380) states her conception of the pastoral function. This missive probably comes late in Catherine's correspondence with the Pope; probably after his return from Avignon to Italy. Disappointment, but not any slackening of her own definite convictions, is everywhere apparent. As in all of her letters, she summons the great ones of the Church to assume courageously their burdens of responsibility for the souls of men. Here, as throughout her life, she remains a loyal daughter of the Church which she loves with such unfaltering affection. She believes that this Church of Christ lays demands upon its priesthood for service to all society. She feels, furthermore, that such a mandate is placed upon the rulers of the Church in the light of their obligation to serve the ultimate community of God's heavenly kingdom.

The papal power is given to Christ's vicar that he may establish peace and justice in the earth. He is held all the more accountable inasmuch as he has been given the keys of heaven itself. Catherine reminds him that if he does not properly open and shut the way to heaven, he will be rebuked by God. She is sure that if she were in his

[23] Fol. 3a, Cumming, p. 5.
[24] Fol. 3b, Cumming, pp. 5-6; fol. 5b, Cumming, pp. 9-10.

place, she would be terrified of failure lest divine judgment come upon her. She is meek and lowly in thus appealing to the vicegerent of Christ for concerted and aggressive action befitting his eternal calling. Vested in the shepherd of the Catholic faithful is the power to shape Christian society into greater conformity with the heavenly dictates.[25]

Dr. J. M. Neale, that gifted and prolific, if sometimes overfree, translator of medieval lore, admitted a special fondness for an anonymous poem that he dated in the late fourteenth century. Taking its title from the opening lines, "Many Are the Presbyters," this little writing combines deep piety and Christian jocularity with a popular appeal for dedication on the part of simple men. Its spirit is that of sober admonition to priests, directly, and through them to their people, indirectly. The work is especially valuable, showing as it does how homespun thought on basic Christian issues could be elicited by an alert pastorate. The theme distinctly treats the manner in which the Church, represented by its ministers, becomes the agent of the eternal kingdom in temporal society.

The immediate appeal of the poem lodges in its teaching by analogy. The cock, yet to be found on some of our church towers, was in the Middle Ages emblematic of the vigilance which the pastor owed his flock. The poem begins:

> MANY are the Presbyters
>   Lacking information
> Why the Cock on each church tow'r
>   Meetly finds his station;
> Therefore I will now hereof
>   Tell the cause and reason,
> If ye lend me patient ears
>   For a little season.
>
> Cock, he is a marvellous
>   Bird of GOD'S creating,
> Faithfully the Priestly life
>   In his ways relating:
>
> Such a life as he must lead
>   Who a parish tendeth.

---

[25] V. Scudder, *Saint Catherine of Siena as Seen in her Letters* (London, 1905), pp. 233-35.

And his flock from jeopardy
Evermore defendeth.[26]

The chanticleer's facing in the direction of the wind shows his willing belligerence to those forces, especially Satanic, that threaten his flock. From his high vantage point he is privileged, as the priest whom he represents always is, to hear the singing of the angelic choirs. Knowing thus the harmony of the eternal world, he is prepared to quell the evil disturbances of the life about him. More significantly still, he can and must set the people's heart while yet below upon thoughts and joys above.

Little better than doggerel at its best, the work almost loses itself at times in a confusion of the symbol and the thing symbolized. But the difficulty is never too hard to rectify. The priesthood and the people for which it is responsible are always being reminded that in the analogy of the cock lies the significance of the priest.

The cock, then, even as the priest, is crested like a king and spurred like a knight. Tonsured is the priest and crowned is the cock for the purpose of vigilant defense in the face of all foes. The cock is physically prepared to strengthen every virtue and protect against every fault discovered among his hens; so the priest is obligated to raise the level of moral and spiritual life by discerning and punishing transgression through the offices of the confessional. Again, the cock who finds choice grains of wheat and distributes them to his cherished hens is a whimsical reminder of the clerk who shares with his people the choice morsels of scriptural nurture even as he busies himself in caring for the sick, the poor, and the maimed. The cock loses little time in disciplining the hens who are unduly receptive to the blandishments of his rivals. The priest is obligated, likewise, to correct all who have turned away from the Lord to evil ways. The priest, reminiscent of the cock that permits evil to flourish, may find Satanic issue hatched in his very midst. Satan's cause will grow apace where the priest does not teach men to fear infernal punishment or to anticipate supernal joys.

The cock never fails to retire in good time so that he may reappear promptly for his midnight crowing. Surely God's priests should always be prepared to rise punctually and sing their proper Matin service. Like the cock, also, who smites his sides with his wings before he

---

[26] "Multi sunt Presbyterii," tr. J. M. Neale, *Collected Hymns, Sequences and Carols* . . . (London, 1914), pp. 69-72. Used by permission of the publishers, Hodder & Stoughton, Ltd.

crows, should be the pastor, who properly imposes penitence upon himself before he gives praise to the Lord.

The poet is sure that this homespun analogy will, if properly meditated upon, bring edification both to priests and to people. The vigilance of chanticleer recalls the endless necessity of the priest's proclaiming the Lord's will. The people, too, are summoned to hear the priest as the representative of the Church, even as the hens find their only protection in the watch-care of the rooster. These conclusions, implied and expressed throughout the poem, have a deeply eschatological and therefore positively social implication. Social ministry and popular responsiveness are enjoined so:

> That at last it may said,
> "Come to joys supernal:—"
> Yea, bestow on all of us,
> FATHER, LIFE ETERNAL! [27]

It may be noted that priestly responsibility as conceived by leading medieval churchmen definitely involved the preaching function. Mention of a few representative positions must suffice in lieu of a fuller discussion to be found elsewhere.

Humbert of Romans (d. 1277) was well known in the later Middle Ages for his manuals on the art of preaching.[28] In his interpretation of the religious life, according to the Dominican Constitution and in his guidebooks to preaching effectiveness, he stressed the relationship of true priest and honest proclaimer of the gospel. For him as a good follower of St. Dominic, preaching is not in competition with learning, the pastoral virtues, or the care of souls. Predication is the peculiarly Dominican function whereby all of these may be given their proper meed in the Church at large. For the Friar Preacher the truth is best served and genuine learning is best demonstrated when put at the service of the saving gospel. Jesus himself sent his disciples to preach the kingdom of God. Paul felt himself called upon, not to baptize, but to preach. The Apostles in Acts 6 did not feel it in keeping with their vocation to wait on tables at the expense of God's word.

---

[27] Neale, *Collected Hymns, Sequences and Carols.* Used by permission of the publishers, Hodder & Stoughton, Ltd.

[28] See *De eruditione praedicatorum*, ed. J. J. Berthier, in *Opera de vita regulari* (Rome, 1889), Vol. II. Cf. W. M. Conlon, ed., *A Treatise on Preaching* (Westminster, Md., 1951); J. T. Welter, *L'exemplum dans la littérature religieuse et didactique au moyen âge* (Paris, 1927), pp. 70-73. Cf. Petry, *Preaching in the Great Tradition*, p. 78.

So far as his order is concerned, Humbert thinks of its supreme function and its most excellent work as being such gospel preaching. Others may point to callings which serve temporal goods. But this is a virtue ordained to man's ultimate good and his abiding salvation. Seen thus, preaching outweighs all other means by which men are led to Christ. Through it the whole world is made subject to the Lord. Preachers have it as their joyous duty to sing the songs of the celestial country.

At regular intervals throughout his work, De Romans adverts to the superior ends served by preaching. Thus other sciences may minister to temporal life; as, for instance, the knowledge of the law. They may advance the best interests of the body as in the province of medicine. But none except preaching has for its major objective the procuration of eternal life for all the faithful. Without such preaching the fullness of celestial glory cannot be consummated. With it, alone, the overflow of infernal designs can be effectively checked. When preaching ceases, the world becomes sterile and undergoes the dominance of demonic forces. No longer does the human heart swell with hopes of a celestial fatherland. Where preaching is in abeyance, Christian nations fall off, and the Church itself declines. Humbert goes on to show how indispensable, therefore, must be the office of preaching when its absence throws the whole world into shadow, brings about evil and pestilence, depopulates cities, and estops the waters of civilization at their very source. It is Humbert's contention in all of his writings that God sent his preachers into the vineyard of the world to serve the faithful and to make men ready for their heavenly home.[29]

Such sentiments drawn in large part from the first book of his *De Eruditione* are continued in the second.[30] Here the problems and the opportunities of preaching are discussed in terms of all kinds of people and every type of situation. His chapter which is intended to direct preachers in addressing the clergy is one of his best. It shows that he, like Jacques de Vitry and a multitude of other medieval

---

[29] *De vita regulari*, II, 31-36, 356-73, 380-89; Petry, *Preaching*, pp. 105-6. On the Dominican constitution and the priority of preaching see, further, G. R. Galbraith, *The Constitution of the Dominican Order 1216-1360* (Manchester, 1925), pp. 246 ff. and H. Denifle-F. Ehrle, *Archiv für literatur-und Kirchengeschichte des Mittelalters* (Berlin, 1885-1900), I, 193-227; V, 560 ff.; cf. P. Mandonnet, *Saint Dominique* (Paris, 1937), 2 Vols. Note P. A. Walz, *Compendium historiae ordines Praedicatorum* (Rome, 1948), pp. 18 ff., 250 ff.

[30] Liber II, "De modo prompte cudendi sermones," ed. in M. de La Bigne, *Maxima bibliotheca veterum patrum* (Lyons, 1677), XXV, 456 ff.

churchmen, was fully aware of the Church's shame and fully dedicated to its Christian reformation. In his materials designed to aid preaching to scholars, students, medical candidates, and, in fact, every kind of professional man, his emphases remain constant. Whether lawyers, doctors, masters of the liberal arts, or students in theology, they all need the same warning. However vital may be the disciplines of their own vocations, these are less important than the prior claims of religious truth. Students in theology, especially, ought to remember this.[31]

Humbert was one of those who refused to conceive of the preaching function as limited solely to the regular orders. The proclamation of the gospel was designed to be furthered by many preachers in cooperation. The good news must be declared in all corners of the earth. Only thus could the ultimate demands of the eternal society be met by the Church of earth.

Thomas Waleys (d. 1340) agrees essentially with this conception of the Christian leader's task. Such, especially, ought the preacher of God's Word to be. It is fitting, indeed, that he see far ahead. He ought to see the things done in hell that he may proclaim them to the edifying terror of others. He should see the things which are in heaven that he may teach others to yearn after them. He may well be expected to see things of the present and future. Not only must he preview the near future but the most remote as well, in order that he may know how to teach what will be in the Final Judgment, and what will follow it. Doubtless, for such purposes, the life of natural ingenuity is far from sufficient to him. For such ends he lacks, and must have most indispensably, the heavenly light. Thus Paul, the preacher to the Gentiles, before there was committed to him the office of holy preaching, received in the middle of the day an all-encompassing light.[32]

Jean Gerson (d. 1429) was primarily a preacher. But within the limits of his major service he also conceived of his ministry as embodying the pastoral life. His responsiveness to the needs of people in every walk of life demonstrates this fact. Scattered throughout his Latin sermons, as well as the more recently edited examples of his vernacular preaching, are appeals to pastoral service of a high order. One such sermon on the office of pastor contains his typical admonition to all clergy to feed the flock with spiritual, scriptural

---

[31] Cf. 456-91, especially 490-91.
[32] *De modo componendi sermones*, ed. in Th.-M. Charland, *Artes praedicandi* (Ottawa, 1936), pp. 351 ff.

food. He attacks those prelates who disparage preaching as being fit for Mendicants and undistinguished theologians, only. The character of his own work in the pulpit will be referred to elsewhere. It is enough to remember at this time that his whole conception of liturgical responsibility was inextricably joined to his convictions regarding the indispensability of gospel preaching.[33]

Extended researches that need not be reproduced here support a like contention ranging throughout the whole province of pre-Reformation preaching.[34]

[33] *Sermo Factus in Concilio Remensi, A.D. 1408,* ed. E. Du Pin, *Joannis Gersonii Opera Omnia* (2nd ed., Hagae Comitum, 1728), II, 542 ff. Consult the magnificent works on Gerson's French preaching by Louis Mourin, *Six Sermons français inédits de Jean Gerson* (Paris, 1946), and *Jean Gerson: prédicateur français* (Paris, 1952). See the old but distinguishing work of J. B. Schwab, *Johannes Gerson* (Wurzburg, 1858) and the informing study by P. Glorieux, *"La vie et les oeuvres de Gerson: Essai chronologique," Archives d'histoire doctrinale et littéraire du moyen âge,* XVIII (1950-51), 149-92. Cf. Petry, "Emphasis on the Gospel," *Church History,* XVI, 2 (June, 1947), 86 ff.

[34] See R. C. Petry, *No Uncertain Sound: Sermons That Shaped the Pulpit Tradition* (Philadelphia, 1948), and *Preaching in the Great Tradition* (Philadelphia, 1950), together with literature there cited. Note the pertinence of C. A. Robson, *Maurice of Sully and the Medieval Vernacular Homily with the Text of Maurice's French Homilies From a Sens Cathedral Chapter MS* (Oxford, 1952), pp. 82, 171 ff. Observe Nicholas de Clemanges's rebuke to the Mendicants on their overweening pride and their failure, actually, to make good their boast in predication, *La traité de la ruine de l'église (De ruina et reparacione Ecclesie),* ed. A. Coville (Paris, 1936), cap. 33, pp. 138, 182.

CHAPTER XI

The Ecclesiastical Community as Servant of the Eternal Kingdom in the Temporal World

5. The Spiritual Church, the Mystical Body of Christ, and the Communion of Saints

THE CONCEPTION OF THE MYSTICAL BODY, LIKE THAT OF THE COM-munion of Saints, is found throughout virtually the entire history of the Christian Church. As may easily be shown, the idea of a com-munity as analogous to a physical organism is not at all uncommon in the pre-Christian eras. The Stoics developed it at some length. But it remained for Paul, especially, and a long line of successors to develop the idea of the Christian brotherhood under the headship of Christ. This gave rise to an increasingly meticulous interpretation of the body spiritual with sometimes ludicrous parallels to a physical structure. Nonetheless, in spite of frequent distortions, especially in modern times, the very real values implicit in such a suggestive figure have outweighed many of the damages so often associated with meta-phorical expression. Consequently, the Church has made an ex-panding place for its doctrine of the Mystical Body. In the Middle Ages, particularly, almost every ranking scholar and unlearned ex-horter, as well, made his own commentary on the Pauline adapta-tions.[1]

The theological problems incident to the suggestive terminology of the *Corpus Mysticum* frequently found expression in almost iden-tical fashion under the caption *Communio Sanctorum*. In the litera-ture of the medieval church, it is well-nigh impossible to maintain entirely separate connotations for each of the two terms. Roman

---

[1] On St. Paul and the Communion of Saints see H. Leclercq in the *Dictionnaire d'archéologie . . . et de liturgie*, III, 2nd Pt., cols. 2447-54. For medieval references consult MPL 219:767 ff. Cf. Th. Aquinas, *In Ep. ad Ephesios*, cap. IV, Lectio II, *Op. Om.*, XXI, 307-8; *Ep. I ad Cor.*, cap. XII, Lectio III, *Op. Om.*, XX, 746-48.

theologians at the present day continue to use a rather confusing variety of interpretations which permit, on occasion, a virtually synonymous usage, but at other times require a specific differentiation. The *Patrologia,* for instance, gives indices for both, though in such fashion as to confuse, at times, their major relationships.[2] As already observed, the great Scholastics utilize both conceptions under an embracing unity which sometimes involves differentiation and sometimes not.

Practically all of the spiritual implications attributable to the *Communio Sanctorum* may be associated with the *Corpus Mysticum.* One observes this when he studies such voluminous interpretations as those of the Catholic scholars Mersch and Anger.[3] Almost no variation of thought which is relatable to the concept of community and to the members of the threefold Church is here ignored. More recently, in the *American Ecclesiastical Review,* Rev. J. C. Fenton has revived the whole aggravated issue by treating both conceptions together, with particular adherence to the view that makes the Church tantamount to both of the concepts involved.[4]

It is not possible, therefore, to discuss the Church as the functioning agency of the eternal in the temporal without considering both the Mystical Body and the Communion of Saints. Each of these terms has its own connotations in relation to the other. In his most useful work, Anger treats at great length the doctrine of the *Corpus Mysticum.*[5]

The concept of the Mystical Body puts the emphasis on that unity within diversity which inheres under Christ the head and in the multiplicity of functions represented by the different members. The Communion of Saints emphasizes the relating activities of the different members in terms of the threefold Church: militant, suffering, and triumphant. Anger says:

Viewed externally, the hierarchy, the Church, appears to us as a copy of the society within the Godhead Itself. The similitude appears everywhere. Christ Jesus said, "O Father, all My things are Thine; and Thine are Mine" (John 17:10). "All things which Thou hast given Me are from Thee. The words which Thou gavest Me, I have given to them" (*Ib.* 17:7, 8). This Church is a picture of the most Holy Trinity in com-

---

[2] Cf. MPL 219:674 ff., 767 ff., 973 ff., 220:213 ff., 249 ff.
[3] E. Mersch, *Le corps mystique du Christ* (Paris, 1936), 2 Vols.; Abbé Anger, *The Doctrine of the Mystical Body of Christ* (New York, 1931).
[4] "The Communion of Saints and the Mystical Body," CX, 5 (May, 1944), 378-89.
[5] *Op. cit.,* xi, 212-13, 227-28, 349, for example; also 277-79; 349-59.

munity of goods and of attributes. What her members possess, they possess in common. If the common sharing in temporal goods characteristic of the first Christian communities no longer prevails, the common sharing of spiritual possessions endures always. The Communion of Saints, like the Church herself, has both for its model and its type the society of the Three Divine Persons. This is the resplendent dogma which enraptures souls converted to the Catholic Faith, and the mystery of which can be entered into only through the teaching of the Mystical Body.[6]

In this connection Anger is evidently making no marked distinction between the two conceptions other than to emphasize the unity in diversity which comes with a mutualizing participation on the part of the various mystical members. When the Mystical Body exists, the Communion of Saints is a reality likewise.

The *Catholic Encyclopedia* gives a modern interpretation which is in all major particulars true to the medieval concept:

The communion of saints is the spiritual solidarity which binds together the faithful on earth, the souls in purgatory, and the saints in heaven in the organic unity of the same mystical body under Christ its head, and in a constant interchange of supernatural offices. The participants in that solidarity are called saints by reason of their destination and of their partaking of the fruits of the Redemption.[7]

The foregoing interpretations focus several crucial emphases. There is, first of all, the clear implication that the communion among the saints is a relationship of love and benevolent activity which springs out of the integrity of the *Corpus Mysticum*. The second indicates that the vitality of this communion which is drawn from the Mystical Body proceeds from an ultimate source; that it exists in terms of the society of the blessed which is to be consummated when the work of redemption has reached its fulfillment. Both medieval and modern writers of the Roman Catholic Church stress the very close connection between those of holy destiny who are on earth, those who are in the period of purgatorial preparation for bliss, and those who are already in heaven.

M. Valentin-Breton, in his revealing discussion, defines the Communion of Saints as the "society of the just, the community of all those who in Jesus Christ partake of the life of God. This community joins the faithful on earth to the saints in heaven by the secret bond

---

[6] *Op. cit.*, p. 252. Used by permission of the publishers, Benziger Brothers, Inc.
[7] (New York, 1913), IV, 171.

of the divine life." [8] The Protestant Robert Will analyzes the vitality and mutuality of the Christian group, now under the concept of the *Corpus Mysticum*, again by reference to the *Communio Sanctorum*. The supernatural end and point of origin are consistently stressed. The Christian life in its sociality and individuality reflects the characteristics of an ultimate community which gives life and distinctive atmosphere to the temporal association. [9]

Will insists that, however one thinks of the invisible Church, the Body of Christ is of supernatural essence. Employing the image of Christ's body, Paul imparts meaning to the bonds of love which unify Christians on earth. It is this collectivity which the Holy Spirit engendered at Pentecost. The supernatural power there received dedicates Christ's followers to purposes and activities transcending their own feeble capacities. The Holy Spirit not only communicates to them the living heart of the gospel; it also goes surety for Christ's mystical presence in their midst. This quality of life from above makes them more than masters in an antagonistic world environment. The power which moves among them is generated from an eternal community; such true mutuality as they know is sprung directly from the perfect society beyond. [10]

Having thus treated the Mystical Body, Will turns to the Communion of Saints. True, the New Testament did not recognize this term. Perhaps the expression *koinonia* applies not so much to the community itself as to the spirit of fraternal solidarity which animates it. This difference, however, is more technical than practical. The repercussions of this Christian solidarity are distinctly social and metaphysical. [11]

With respect to the Church, which is characterized by Holy Communication, one with the other, Valentin-Breton views three inescapable aspects: There is first the Church triumphant, embracing the Holy Virgin, the Angels, the Apostles, and the Saints that have come to companionship with the Trinity; next, there is the Church militant, embracing the just, the faithful, and the unfaithful; last, there is the Church suffering, which embraces the souls of the defunct who are

[8] *The Communion of Saints: History—Dogma—Devotion* (St. Louis, 1934), pp. 34-35. Used by permission of the publishers, B. Herder Book Co.
[9] *Le culte*, III, 39-47.
[10] *Ibid.*, pp. 39-44.
[11] *Ibid.*, pp. 44 ff.

in purgatorial preparation for the heavenly world. It is to this three-fold Church that the medieval Christian, like his modern Catholic brother, turns his face and his heart.[12]

Professor G. J. Slosser's guide to the Communion of Saints was prepared as a report for the "Commission on the Church's Unity in Life and Worship" of the 1937 Edinburgh Conference.[13] He has given in the first pages of his work a detailed analysis of the term "communion" (*koinonia*), as developed in the New Testament and later Christian literature. His conclusions are not radically different from those of Valentin-Breton, elsewhere referred to. He further examines the term "saints" and the idea of "holiness" in both the Old and New Testaments. The major concepts that emerge from a variety of New Testament references emphasize the thought of spiritual unity and solidarity resident in the Christian Church. The Communion of Saints involves "mutual sharing of temporal or material blessing." Involved also is "the mutual participation in one another's gifts and graces." He observes that with most of the Evangelicals this is limited to the earthly life. "Beyond that, they are hopeful without dogmatic certainty. The Catholics, with definite assurances in well-formulated dogmas, believe and practice this participation as between Saints in glory and Saints on earth." Slosser implies that for Paul the terms "Communion of Saints" and "Church" were virtually synonymous.[14]

A useful feature of Slosser's work is the consideration of varying interpretations given the expression *Communio Sanctorum* during the course of the first four centuries. A well-placed caution reminds us that not all the present connotations associated with the term may be ibid at the inception of the Church. This may or may not mean that inaccurate interpretations are read into the early documents. Certainly, however, the distinctive characteristics attaching to this concept of solidarity are found, not only in Testamental literature, but also in the apostolic and later Fathers. Dr. Slosser gives a well-integrated set of documentary references dealing with Ignatius, Polycarp, Hermas, Clement of Alexandria, Origen, Tertullian, the Synod of Laodicea, Jerome, and Augustine. He notes that the latter, like many others in the period under discussion,

urged honour, imitation, hymns of praise, adoration, prayers, worship

---

[12] *Communion of Saints*, pp. 103-21.
[13] G. J. Slosser, *The Communion of Saints* (New York, 1937).
[14] *Ibid.*, pp. 1-5.

[*dulia*] to the martyrs and others as saints, and forbade the invocation of angels. It was St. Augustine who specifically forbade worship [*latria*] of the saints, for such worship is offered to God only.

A further discussion regards Jerome's defense of fitting honors paid to martyrs, as over against the attacks made by Vigilantius, priest of Gaul. Protest against this priest was apparently the occasion, also, for the insertion of the phrase "communion of saints" in the baptismal creed of Bishop Faustus of Riez in Gaul.[15]

Slosser's investigation of the varied meanings associated with the term through the fifth century is valuable but not so immediately pertinent at this point. His treatment of the origin and meanings of the phrase as it appeared in articles of the creeds is pertinent. Seemingly, the term was first utilized by Jerome via an Armenian creed which had itself been derived from Bishop Firmilian of Caesarea around 250. By the beginning of the fifth century, it was in use in a formal creed by Bishop Niceta of Remesiana in Dacia. It was about this time that Bishop Faustus asserted his belief in the Communion of Saints in protest against Vigilantius. Out of a correspondence and formal set of homilies concerning the matter, Bishop Niceta finally provided a clear statement of his own interpretation, at least:

What is the Church but the congregation of all saints? From the beginning of the world patriarchs, prophets, apostles, martyrs, and all other righteous men who have lived or are now alive or shall live in time to come, are one Church, since they have been sanctified by one faith and manner of life and sealed by one Spirit and so are made one Body, of which Christ is the Head, as the Scripture teaches. . . . In this one Church you believe that you will attain to the Communion of Saints. Know that this one Catholic Church is planted throughout the whole world, and that it is your duty to hold fast to its communion. There are false churches, but you have nothing in common with them; they have ceased to be holy churches, since they believe and act otherwise than Christ our Lord commanded and the Apostles delivered.[16]

Slosser observes that from an early period the terms *"agion"* and *"sanctorum"* seem to have carried, for some at least, a neuter rather than a masculine meaning. This would make the pharse mean " 'participation in holy things,' i.e., in the elements of the Eucharist."

[15] *Ibid.*, pp. 5-7. Quotation used by permission of the publishers, Harper & Bros.
[16] *Ibid.*, pp. 10-11. Used by permission of the publishers, Harper & Bros. For another translation of the *Explanatio symboli*, MPL 52:871, see Breton, *op. cit.*, pp. 27-28.

Taken with its context, we then have the teaching that only those who are members of the Holy Catholic Church have participation in the Holy Eucharist. As over against the puritanic or other rigorist sects of those centuries, it was an assertion that the Catholic Church (contrary to the jibes of these sects) did possess the true Eucharist.[17]

As will be noted later, the controverted matter of Thomas Aquinas' attitude is not easily clarified. He undoubtedly utilizes the neuter meaning in some connections. Beyond his terminology, however, is the fuller treatment which he accords to the phenomenon of spiritual communion among the saints themselves. Whatever one may say about the term itself, the larger significance clearly remains: the Communion of Saints is much more than a participation in holy things; it is an interrelationship fostered among living beings in the one unified Church.[18]

The Catholic scholar J. C. Fenton, in a recent article on "The Communion of Saints and the Mystical Body," says:

Very few theologians, however, attempted to explain the *Communio Sanctorum* entirely as the common possession of instruments for salvation. Usually the proponents of Catholic teaching interpret this phrase to mean the fellowship or association with our Lord and with the blessed in heaven and the souls in purgatory enjoyed within the Catholic Church. Those in the state of grace in this world receive the full benefits accruing from this association. However, Catholics in the state of mortal sin are not wholly cut off from this communication. They receive some share from their fellowship with the Saints of God inasmuch as the blessings consequent upon the Communion of Saints tend to bring them to repentance and thus to eternal life.

No man can enjoy this fellowship apart from the Catholic Church. Those who enjoy the Communion of Saints either are actually members of the Catholic Church or really intend to become members. Thus those in the state of grace, the persons who derive the full benefit from their association with the Church triumphant and the Church suffering, possess that charity which demands the love of the brotherhood. Every person in the state of grace intends to live and to die within the unity of the Catholic Church, even though, for want of proper instruction, his intention should be merely implicit.

Some theologians have used the term *Communio Sanctorum* as a definition of the Catholic Church itself. In so far as the Catholic Church extends into heaven and purgatory, it may well be defined in the formula

---

[17] *Ibid.*, p. 11. Used by permission of the publishers.
[18] *Ibid.*, p. 11, n. 19; Breton, *op. cit.*, p. 59.

"the society of the saints who serve God under Christ." Naturally, those who use such a definition are at pains to insist that the term *sanctorum* in the definition is not equivalent to *iustorum*. It is heretical to teach that the membership in the Church of Jesus Christ is restricted to those in the state of grace. It is theologically correct to state that the Church is the congregation of the saints, in the sense that all of those who are gathered within it either possess or profess holiness. Those in the Church triumphant and in the Church suffering actually possess holiness in the sense that they all possess the life of habitual grace. The members of the Church militant do not all possess charity, but they at least profess the holy faith of Jesus Christ, communicate in His holy sacraments and live under the holy rule He has placed within His Church.[19]

Similar to Fenton's analysis is that of Pohle:

1. THE COMMUNION OF SAINTS.—The Council of Trent says that the poor souls in Purgatory "are aided by the suffrages of the faithful, and principally by the acceptable sacrifice of the altar." The efficacy of this intercession is based on the Communion of Saints.

   a) By the Communion of Saints we understand the spiritual union of the faithful with one another, with the blessed Angels, the Elect in Heaven, and the poor souls in Purgatory, under the supernatural headship of Christ, who is the font and well-spring of all grace; or, to put it somewhat differently, the mystic union of the militant, the triumphant, and the suffering Church of Christ.

   b) The ninth article of the Apostles' Creed teaches that there is a visible communion on earth, as well as an invisible interchange of blessings between the militant and the triumphant Church, of which latter Purgatory is a preparatory stage. This has always been Catholic teaching. Whereas an impassible gulf separates the Blessed in Heaven from the demons, the members of Christ's mystic body in Heaven and on earth are closely bound together by a supernatural communion of blessings, of which the innermost essence and principle is sanctifying grace, or theological love, and, to some extent, theological faith. For this reason even those Catholics who are guilty of mortal sin belong to the militant Church and consequently, in a restricted sense, also to the Communion of Saints. As for the angels, they form part of the *ecclesia triumphans*, and as such participate in the *communio sanctorum*.

   Through the Communion of Saints the faithful on earth, especially those who are in the state of sanctifying grace, share in all the Masses, prayers, and good works offered up by the militant Church. They are moreover benefitted by the intercession of the angels and the just in Heaven, and they can aid the poor souls in Purgatory by prayers, in-

[19] *American Ecclesiastical Review*, CX, 5 (May, 1944), 378-79. Used by permission of the publishers, The Catholic University of America Press.

dulgences, alms, and other good works, especially by having the Sacrifice of the Mass offered for them.[20]

If one consults the vast patristic collection of Migne, he is promptly reminded of the three great categories of the Church militant, suffering, and triumphant; none of which may be thought of wholly apart from the others. To be sure, for index purposes, we may be referred to citations which treat only the mutualizing relationships that should exist among the faithful of the Church militant. Or, our attention may be directed yet elsewhere, in the appropriate indices treating purgatory and the heavenly world, for the relating activities of other parts within the one indivisible Church. But this is for convenience only. The Church is not separated, one part from another. Actually, the life in all of its socializing qualities made available to the Church on earth and in purgatory is that which is given fullness and power from within the heavenly world. Those on earth pray for aid to the saints in the celestial realm; they also invoke blessings upon those in purgatory; those having reached the heavenly world are happy, for their part, to lend the support of their intercession and their merits to whatever areas the Lord may bless. One is impressed with the regard of early and medieval Christians for the Church's vitalizing function, as it proceeded from the realm of the saints in heaven to the needs of those in the Church militant and dormant.[21]

When one resumes with Breton, Will, Swete, Mersch, and numerous others the testimony for the Communion of Saints, he is at once confronted with two facts: There is, first, the indisputable evidence that the term itself is encountered for the first time about the fifth century. There is, second, the equally impressive evidence that what the term involves has been present in essence from the very beginnings of Christianity. There is no particular value in recapitulating at this point the many fascinating ramifications of related thought in the first century. The literature, both documentary and derived, is analyzed in a number of learned dissertations including those of Breton, Mersch, and Cabrol-Leclercq's liturgical dictionary.[22]

---

[20] *Eschatology or the Catholic Doctrine of the Last Things,* pp. 92-93. Used by permission of the publishers, B. Herder Book Co.

[21] "Index de relationibus membrorum omnium ecclesiae militantis ad invicem . . . sive communione sanctorum sensu, strictiori sumpta," MPL 219:767-70; "Index de Cultu sanctorum." MPL 219:974-86; "Index de Purgatorio," 220:250-55; "Index de Ecclesia," 219:666-86, etc.

[22] Cf. H. B. Swete, *The Holy Catholic Church, the Communion of Saints* (London, 1915), and the *Dictionnaire d'archéologie,* for example.

Clement's letter to the Corinthians voices a stern demand for unity. The circumstances of his writing to the Corinthian brethren were not wholly unlike those that motivated Paul in his own Epistle to the Christians at this city. Like Paul, he admonished them to submerge all differences of purpose in a common loyalty to the unifying headship of Christ. He found an edifying "mixture in all things"; this conduced to utility, as was observable in the body, itself.

The head without the feet is nothing; so likewise the feet without the head are nothing: even the smallest limbs of our body are necessary and useful for the whole body: but all the members conspire and unite in subjection, that the whole body may be saved.[23]

Clement insists that it is Christ and the communicating graces of incorporation with him that give strength and versatility to the social consideration of Christians, one for another:

So in our case let the whole body be saved in Christ Jesus, and let each man be subject unto his neighbour, according as also he was appointed with his special grace. Let not the strong neglect the weak; and let the weak respect the strong. Let the rich minister aid to the poor; and let the poor give thanks to God, because He hath given him one through whom his wants may be supplied.[24]

A wise man is to show his wisdom in good works. Edifying humility is to have its fruitage in neighborly services. Purity of the flesh is not to be made an occasion of boasting, inasmuch as it is given by the Lord. Ever present in the Christian's thought should be a recognition of the noble ends to which God dedicated his children from out of darkness and chaos. Perhaps Clement's most appealing quality is his dependence upon this common strength that is in God, Christ, and the Mystical Body for the socializing of Christian life in a troubled world scene. The writer is not dealing with hypothetical cases of disunity. Division has actually entered into the body of Christ; "it hath brought many to despair, many to doubting, and all of us to sorrow. And your sedition still continueth." As against this, the brethren at Corinth are admonished to find a real sanctification of life in cleaving to the Saints: "Let us therefore cleave to the guiltless and righteous; and these are the elect of God. Wherefore are there

---

[23] Ep. Clem., 37; ed. Lightfoot, *Apostolic Fathers*, Pt. I, Vol. II, pp. 290-91; Richardson, *Early Christian Fathers*, pp. 60-61.
[24] Ep. Clem., 38; *ibid.*, p. 291; Richardson, *op. cit.*, p. 61.

strifes and wraths and factions and divisions and war among you?" Those who have one God, one Christ, and one calling in Christ— those who are called to membership in the one Mystical Body— should remember how awful are the consequences of rending the fellowship of the Lord.[25]

Tertullian emphasizes the love and care of mother church for her children and the spiritual goods common to all the faithful. In his *Apology* he eulogizes the communalizing life of the brethren in their disciplined corporation of peace, hospitality, and charity. He knows that "the whole community must commiserate and collaborate in the healing of its members." Consequently he implores: "Let us pray then for all the faithful who are but *ONE* with Christ, and also for all whom divine grace awaits and seeks." [26]

Cyprian, likewise, in his letters and treatises, such as the *Unity of the Church,* scans the lineaments of reciprocating love that make the body of Christ truly one. Christians are admonished to pray for one another—"to supply by prayer the needs of each one and of all. The sharing in the merits of the just is founded on charity, the power of heaven." Prayer has the power to reconcile man with God.[27]

Origen, with all of his highly divergent interpretations of the Christian tradition, has a unified texture of thought on the mutuality of those in the Mystical Body and the Christian community. Valentin-Breton has arranged these with reasonable lack of bias. Checking the sources involved shows no essential misrepresentation of the Alexandrian's position. The homily on Leviticus 4:4 ff. shows the close connection existing between the society of the saints on earth and those in heaven. Through participation in the life of the Trinity and of the saints associated with them, the faithful on earth find an increment to their own community life. The saints are concerned, in the midst of their present glory, that their brethren of earth be safely reunited with them in the heavenly joy. Among angels, prophets, apostles, martyrs, there resides the same grace and there circulates the same life. By them there is deified the same body which will be resuscitated in glory. We are, insists Origen, the companions of the saints; and it is well that we should be so, for we are in society with the Holy Trinity. And, if with the Father, the Son, and the Spirit we have fellowship, why not with the saints; not only with those on earth,

---

[25] Ep. Clem., 46; *ibid.,* pp. 295-96; Richardson, *op. cit.,* p. 65.

[26] I Apol. 39; CSEL, LXIX, 91 ff.; Breton, *op. cit.,* p. 40.

[27] Cf. Breton, *op. cit.,* pp. 40-41, for references to Ep. LX, 5; LXXVI, 7, XXX, 6; *De Lapsis,* XVII, etc.

but with those in heaven as well? After all, Christ, with his own blood, reconciled things heavenly and earthly in order that the earthly might be brought into association with the heavenly. It is seemly, therefore, that we should take part, already, in an eternal communion. Acting upon such persuasion, the society on earth is, even now, knit in its life to that which is above.[28]

It is Origen's view that the Church of heaven promotes and sustains the Church of earth. More accurately stated, the Church of heaven is the mother of us all. Actually, there is but one Church which comprises all the just, from the origin of humanity to the consummation of heaven. Angels, prophets, apostles, and all the saints constitute but a single body, where a single life circulates, where there manifests and develops itself the same consortium of sympathies and interests. Stated in other terms, the Church in heaven is the type or model of the Church on earth. That aspect of the Church which finds itself consummated in triumph gives its full power and support to the aid of the Church militant. Origen believes that "the whole church in heaven devotes itself to advancing and supporting the church on earth." How, more eloquently, could he state his belief in the fructifying power of the eternal in the temporal? That, according to this view, the one Church thus becomes the servant of the eternal in the temporal cannot be denied.[29]

Origen is obviously under the impress of a deeply social experience. He repeatedly uses the stock word indicating fellowship or community. He observes within the Church of Christ a diversity of life which strengthens rather than destroys the community of spirit and action. "The souls of the saints really assist at liturgical gatherings of the faithful." None of the early Fathers felt more keenly than he the necessity of strengthening the bonds between what was and what was to be. None of them went beyond him in their realization that the communion of life on earth must proceed from the antecedent society yet to be realized in the future.[30]

Valentin-Breton notes that the post-Communion prayer for the third Saturday in Lent represents Hilary of Poitiers's position upon the Communion of Saints: " 'Grant, we beseech thee, Almighty God,

---

[28] Altaner, *Patrologie*, pp. 165 ff.; Breton, *op. cit.*, pp. 41 ff. See *In Leviticum*, Hom. IV, 4 ff., in *Origenes Werke, Die griechischen christlichen Schriftsteller* (Leipzig, 1920), Bd. VI, 319 ff.

[29] Breton, *op. cit.*, pp. 41-44; *In Jesu Nave*, V, 6, MPG 12:850-52; XVI, 5, MPG 12:909; *In Lev. Hom.* VII, 2, *Schriftsteller*, VI, 374-80; *In Num. Hom.* XXXVI, 7, *Schriftsteller*, VII, 254-55. *In Ep. Rom.*, VII, 6, MPG 14:1118.

[30] Breton, *op. cit.*, p. 45.

that we be numbered among his members in whose body and blood we communicate.' " [31]

In this way the Eucharist serves as the heart of communication for the enduring fellowship of the saints.

By it Christ dwells in us, we are one flesh, together we form the abode of the Holy Ghost, the Holy City, built of living stones, on the foundation of the prophets and the Apostles through the care of the angels.

The Church in heaven is the body of God's glory; it is the type of the Church on earth, we must conform ourselves to it in all things. [32]

Basil of Caesarea refers to the life that all Christians have from their communion with the Spirit. He thrills to the union of the Church that is in heaven with that of earth. [33]

A ringing plea for unity and spiritual reciprocity is not out of character in a work signalizing the opportunities and responsibilities of the Christian ministry. Nor is it strange that one so much interested as Ambrose in Roman conceptions of civic virtue should place a large emphasis upon the harmonious ways of nature. His discussion of clerical duties at one point gives way to a long treatment of the Corpus Mysticum. Primarily from the Pauline correspondence, and significantly also from the Roman-Stoic backgrounds available to his Ciceronian acquaintance, he develops the concept of organic unity native to the followers of Christ. There is nothing novel or peculiarly inspiring about his commentary on the Mystical Body. He does bring to it a measuredness and calm reasonableness derived from his Roman training. One is occasionally at a loss to discover whether his argument proceeds primarily from the law of nature or the law of Christ. No real antinomy exists at this point, however. As elsewhere in this work, modeled only superficially on the Ciceronian prototype, he gives main allegiance to the motivating power of Christ and the gospel. [34]

Ambrose is no less clear than Origen on the close link which unites the faithful on earth with other portions of the Church. He believes that the whole Church assumes something of the sinner's defects and applies to each of those who need it the superabundant merits of the entire ecclesia. Thus the sinner's faults are expiated by absorb-

[31] *Ibid.*, p. 50. Used by permission of the publishers, B. Herder Book Co.
[32] *Ibid.*, p. 51. Used by permission of the publishers. *In Ps.* 51:3, CSEL 22:98; *In Ps.* 64:14, CSEL 22:245; *In Ps.* 147:2, CSEL 22:854-55; *In Ps.* 124:4, CSEL 22:599-600.
[33] Breton, *op. cit.*, pp. 45-47.
[34] *Duties of the Clergy*, III, 3, NPNF, X, 69 ff.; Breton, *op. cit.*, pp. 51 ff.

ing them within the collectivity of mercy and virile compassion that the Church alone can provide. It is definitely not God's will that the common salvation be a solitary work. Thus the merits of each are available for the needs of others.[35]

In his work *On the Duties of the Clergy*, Ambrose declares that the Church is, in effect, a form of justice which renders to each his proper due. All rights are of the community. The prayer of the Church is in terms of all. It works for that common fellowship. It assumes the temptations and the griefs of all. Such is the solidarity of Christ's members, that nothing which pertains to them has a purely individual reference. Everything is undivided, collective, common.

This unity of the faith and of charity comes from Christ and the Holy Spirit. It remains unbroken across the chasm of death. The saints are not really departed. They still groan with, and for, the members of the Church militant. They rejoice over the prayers, fasts, and alms of the faithful. The very angels themselves are happy to witness the intercession of the saints for the men of earth and the prayers of those on earth that go up to the heavenly realm.[36]

Jerome's contribution to the doctrine of the Communion of Saints is not massive. It is, nonetheless, direct and useful. He reminds us that " 'if the Apostles and the martyrs, when they were living in the flesh . . . could pray for others . . . how much more can they do so after their victory, their coronation, and their triumph!' " [37]

St. Augustine is of primary importance in the whole doctrinal framework of the early church. His thought on the Mystical Body and the Communion of Saints contributes materially to the development of medieval thinking in these areas. Here again Valentin-Breton has culled from a plethora of materials the more pertinent data. There can be no doubt that for Augustine the Church comprises those within the heavenly as well as the earthly frames of reference. As seen elsewhere, his interpretation of the Church clearly bears out the contention that the ecclesiastical community has its motivating power from the celestial society; and that the temporal world derives its vitality from the eternal.[38]

The typical references which Valentin-Breton makes to the representative sources are scattered over an understandably wide area.

[35] Breton, *op. cit.*, pp. 51 ff.
[36] *Ibid.*, p. 52; *De Offic.*, I, 29.
[37] *Ibid.*, p. 53, and references. Used by permission of the publishers.
[38] *Ibid.*, pp. 53-56; Mersch, *Le corps mystique*, II, 35 ff.

The construction that he puts upon various works may well be challenged at certain points. There is value, nonetheless, in his selection of materials that cover mainly the concept of the Communion of Saints but that involve the Mystical Body also. A running sketch of related passages may be useful at this juncture.

The Church as the Mystical Body has Christ at its head. The unity which inheres in it is, naturally, that of charity. Unity cannot be preserved if love no longer operates among the faithful. No true fellowship can characterize the body of the saints when individuals put themselves above the common good. Apostates, heretics, and schismatics have torn themselves from the Christian body. Sinners, generally, are regarded as members still attached to the body, however much they may fail of deserving its benefits. They definitely have a share in the prayers of the just.[39]

A query may be entered as to the constituency of the Church. Augustine's answer is that all who have, or have had, Christ as their head belong to it; the larger Church is from the beginning of the world to its very end, and includes angels as well as men. He is as much concerned as Origen for the unsevered membership of the saints in Christ. Between the Church in heaven and that of earth there reigns an intimate union which is destined to become perfect. The universal Church in heaven and on earth constitutes one single temple of God. Obviously, Augustine is thinking in terms of a mystical attachment best described in terms of bodily structure. He takes every opportunity to laud the fellowship which exists among participating members of the Christian body. The comprising structure of this whole membership is the Church itself, viewed in both its celestial and its terrestrial aspects.[40]

For Augustine, the inspiring principle of life within the body of Christ is the Holy Spirit. It is to the Church what the soul is to the body. Thus it becomes the agency of individualizing fruitfulness proceeding from the common unity. Valentin-Breton notes that the idea of the Holy Ghost as the soul of the Church is properly attributable to Augustine. "The action of the Holy Ghost is exercised upon the *entire* Christ, who comprises head and members, not the head without the members, nor the members apart from the head." [41]

A place of eminence is reserved for John 17:22-23. A close bond

---

[39] *Ibid.*, pp. 53-54; cf. Serm. 137, MPL 38:754 ff.
[40] Breton, *loc. cit.*
[41] Breton, *op. cit.*, p. 54. Used by permission of the publishers. Serm. 267, 4, MPL 38:1231; Serm. 137, 1, MPL 38:754; Serm. 71, 20, MPL 38:463-64.

unites Father, Son, and Spirit. Jesus, in his moving prayer of consecration, pleads that all of those given him by the Father may be
joined with him in a unity such as he enjoys with the heavenly parent.
This not only reinforces the concept of an intimate mutuality bridging the barriers of space and time; but it also re-emphasizes the
manner in which the heavenly community becomes the model and
pre-existent unity out of which the temporal community must be
developed. In consequence of such unity, a total and universal
solidarity becomes effective. "The services are different, the life is
common." Members alike of the one Church, those of heaven and
those of earth find themselves vaulting over intervening space and
time to reinforce a cosmic oneness of life. With all of the natural
limitations apparent in a terrestrial existence, the faithful here below
may, nonetheless, reach upward to receive the overflow of merits
which are available to them from the celestial company. Such is
Augustine's conviction.[42]

Augustine is especially rich in those concepts of participation and
fellowship which belong to the Communion of Saints. Thus, as he
thinks of the Mystical Body, he meditates also on the concrete expression in human life of the charity that proclaims a division of labor
within a fruitful community. With Christ at its head and love at
its center, the Mystical Body exemplifies the spiritual sanity that true
communion alone can impart. Because that unity seeks to bring to
itself all potential members of the common association, the Church
continues to pray for those who are, for the time being, detached
from this wholeness of truth and life. Because sinners share the
prayers of the righteous, they have a continuing possibility of reclamation. The Church of earth is destined to become one with that of
heaven. Hence, the ecclesiastical community on this ephemeral stage
seeks to serve all potential members whom God may see fit to incorporate into his everlasting society of the blessed. Since the Holy
Spirit is at work knitting the bonds of unity in the one true Church,
the Community of Saints is truly an "answer to Jesus' prayer" of
consecration. Those who inhere in such unity do, indeed, become
one, as the Godhead is one. Such total and universal solidarity rightly characterizes the cosmic community, first; and the intermediate,
earthly community which proceeds from it, in addition.[43]

It can hardly be denied that Augustine puts into this concept of

[42] *Ibid.*, pp. 54-55; Serm. 267, MPL 38:1231; Serm. 280, MPL 38:1279-84.
[43] John 17:22-23; Breton, *op. cit.*, pp. 54-56; *De Civ. Dei*, X, 6.

Sanctorum Communio a new social power and pervasiveness. Perhaps none of the Latin Fathers makes more use than he of a terminology involving the root meanings of communion, community, and communication. He thinks invariably of the saints of earth as being governed by the happy prospect of an eternal society with the Deity, the angels, and those already in bliss. There is a marked commitment to the view that the community in the heavenly realm, which is already actual but not fully consummated, now operates as the eliciting quality in the life of the earthly church. The merits already acquired by the saints of heaven are placed at the disposal of their brethren on earth. If, strictly speaking, the faithful, here, cannot be of service to the saints, above, those on earth can at least pay proper tribute of love and affection to their brethren who have already achieved the crown of life. It is because those of earth wish to have communion with the saints in life everlasting that they imitate in their present social groupings the living qualities of eternal love. To this end, every energy of the individual must be bent in everyday fellowship that he may be worthy to sustain a living connection with the one Mystical Body.[44]

Augustine's capacity for distinctive phrasing and literary coloring stands him in good stead. He keeps before his people's eyes the thought of those who, before the time of Christ, pressed forward by faith to claim a share in the blessed society. He exhorts his fellows to be worthy likewise—by disciplines of mind, body, and spirit—to share a portion in that supernal city. No sacrifice is too great on the part of individuals, and of the fraternity at large, to help win their share of the eternal heritage in the glorious chorus of the Apostles. The citizens of the heavenly world await them eagerly. Desiring that his brethren be incorporated in that final blessedness, he calls for an imitation of its social structure within the earthly church.[45]

St. Augustine's discussion on the way in which the feasts of the martyrs should be celebrated clarifies the major relationships between the saints of earth and those of heaven. He calls upon his brethren, once more, to celebrate the solemnities of the holy martyrs with sentiments of the liveliest piety, moderate joy, chaste reunions, thoughts of faith, and predications full of hope. It is not at all unbecoming to applaud their virtues. They are great and we are small. One must not forget, however, that God has blessed the small with the great. They

[44] *Sermo de Symbolo*, XIII, MPL 40:1197.
[45] *Loc. cit.*

have preceded their earthly brethren and have attained an eminent degree of virtue.[46]

If, perhaps, we are not able to follow them and their works, we may at least follow them by our desires; even though we may not be able to attain their glory, we may be associated with them in their joy; regardless of our inability to imitate them literally in their sufferings and attainments, we may at least hope to remain forever united with them. Is it a slight thing that we should be members of the same body to which these glorious ones belong? Did not Paul say that if one member suffers, all the others suffer with him, and that if any one receives honor, all the others rejoice with him? The glory which is given to the head of the body pertains to inferior as well as to superior members of it. Christ, our head, has given his life for us. The martyrs have imitated him. They have also given their lives for their brethren, pouring out their blood to make available the richest resources to Christians everywhere. We are ourselves the fruits of their labor. We offer them the tribute of our admiration while they, in turn, have compassion on our ills. We applaud their triumph and they pray for us. Together we obey the same Lord, follow the same Master, accompany the same Prince, are united to the same Charity, and embrace the same Unity. Thus Augustine gives his measure of adoration to the life of the holy ones, who in their very attainment of the celestial glory, draw the faithful of earth to them and their beatitude.[47]

Peter Chrysologus declares that all are one, and one, all, when the one Spirit of God lives in the whole. Gregory the Great emphasizes the solidarity of Christian charity and unity. The members of Christ sorrow and rejoice with each other; they participate as a whole in the fortunes of all their fellows. However diversified their functions, the members of the Body Mystical conduce to a common end; even as a foot sees by means of the eye and the eye walks by virtue of the foot. Haymo of Halberstat rejoices that, as in a physical organism many members make one body, likewise a multitude of the faithful conjoined by faith and love to their head, who is Christ, may be one body with him. Hincmar of Rheims extols the communion of the Church signified by Christ's seamless tunic.[48]

Such sentiments were expressed with only slight variation through-

---

[46] Serm. 280, 6, MPL 38:1283-84.

[47] *Loc. cit.*; Mersch, *op. cit.*, II, 120-38. *Enarr. in Ps.* 54, 3, MPL 36:629; *Ep.* 185, 9, CSEL 51:36-37; *In Joh. Evang. Tract.* 21, 8, MPL 35:1568; *Tract.* 21, 15, MPL 35:1613-14.

[48] See the references in MPL 219:767 ff.

out the entire Middle Ages. Mersch, who gives extended treatment to the vital ramifications of Christian thought on the Mystical Body, collates with these the more outstanding references to the Communion of Saints. Following his lead and that of similar authorities, one may cite in brief a few of the more celebrated among such doctrines, while reserving larger treatment for a selected group of medieval authors.[49]

Lanfranc, in his commentaries on Pauline writings, has an easily recognizable, if somewhat stereotyped, awareness of the Mystical Body.[50] Anselm, in his more formal treatises, as also in his *Meditations* and *Prayers,* has a vibrating eloquence when dealing with the concepts of spiritual community.[51] Whether extensively allegorized as in his homilies, or emotionally surcharged as in his devotional works, his pleas for Christian communion are unusually effective. They gain momentum from his portrayal of impending world judgment and the final incorporation of the blessed in heaven.[52] Abelard, in his poetical works, particularly, rises to a moving appreciation of Christian mutuality.[53]

Hugh of St. Victor expands the analogy whereby the human spirit that vivifies physical head and members represents Christ the head and his Christian members. The one head with its many members constitutes the single body in which the one Spirit dwells. In the fullness of the head, the members participate. None who lacks the Spirit of Christ can belong in his membership. Within this body no death exists; beyond it no life is found. Through faith and love a living unity is maintained. As in the sacrament of baptism one comes to this incorporating unity, so by the Lord's Body and Blood the follower of Christ attains the life-giving participation.

Holy Church is the body of Christ, vivified by the one Spirit, united and sanctified by one faith. Diversified as are the functions of individual members within this body of the faithful, none discharges his office with insularity. As in the human corpus, so in the body of Holy Church, the endowments of each member are bestowed and held answerable to the common good of all the participants. Seeing,

---

[49] *Le corps mystique,* II, 294 ff.

[50] *In D. P. Epist. Ep. I ad Cor.,* MPL 150:189, 197-98, etc.

[51] *Hom. et Exhor.* VI, MPL 158:621-27. Cf. F. S. Schmitt, *S. Anselmi Opera Omnia,* III; 10—Orat. III, etc. Consult "Les méditationes réunies sous le nom de saint Anselme," in Dom A. Wilmart, *Auteurs spirituels et textes dévots du moyen âge Latin* (Paris, 1932) , pp. 173-201.

[52] *Medit.* I, Schmitt, III, 76 ff.; Prosolog., 25, Schmitt, I, 118-20.

[53] Ghellinck, *L'essor,* p. 289, n. 55, and pp. 293 ff. for sources and literature.

hearing, walking, are functions performed not selfishly but for the community welfare by eyes, ears, and feet. Here every member employs his gifts so that each may be for all and all for each. Such solidarity dispels all undue singularity and gives rise to the universal body of Christians living in the spirit of their Christ. What, therefore, is the Church if not the multitude of the faithful, the whole commonwealth of Christians? The very incarnation of Christ, their head, was effected so that sinful men might be reconciled with God and reassociated with the Trinity in everlasting participation of heavenly joys.[54]

Bernard of Clairvaux has a remarkable appreciation of the spiritual fraternity which exists among the saints on earth and in heaven. It is in his treatment of the heavenly world that he comes closest to an amplification of his views. Thus his sermons on the Song of Songs are replete with references and interpretations involving the holy community. He admonishes all true confessors to look forward to peace with God in a blessedness which is not possible in this world. But the day of the new redemption dawns. The time when the faithful are kept in captivity to the flesh and to the devil is about ended.

During the period of pilgrimage toward the celestial country the faithful ought especially to remember that their struggles are being watched with sympathetic interest by the angelic host and the saints who are already within the Church triumphant. Thus it is that we are made a spectacle, not only to the eyes of this world, but also in the gaze of angels and martyrs. The latter anticipate the Day of Judgment, not because they are desirous of revenge, but because they long for their fellows to be joined with them in final beatitude. They, therefore, await the coming of other saved ones without whom their joys cannot be fulfilled. In a high pitch of eloquence, Bernard exclaims:

O if we could comprehend with what earnest and eager desire they expect and await our coming! how anxiously they enquire about, and how willingly listen to, any good actions that we do! Yet why do I speak of these, who have learned compassion by the sufferings they have themselves endured, when our coming is desired by the holy Angels themselves? [55]

[54] *De Sacram.*, Lib. II, Pars II, cap. 1, II ff., MPL 176:415-17 ff., cf. Lib. II, Pars I, cap. XII, MPL 176:412-13.

[55] For the *Sermones in Cantica Canticorum*, see MPL 183:585 ff. This particular sermon is No. II, for the Eve of the Nativity, especially, secs. 1-8, MPL 183:90-94; Eales, *Works*, III, 359 ff. On the biblical interpretation of Bernard see J. Leclercq, *Saint*

Bernard further extols the citizens of the heavenly Jerusalem as they wait for the consummation of their heavenly city.

> With what solicitude do they await the coming of the living stones, who are to be built in together with them? How they pass to and fro between us and God, bearing to Him most faithfully our groans and complaints, and bringing back to us His grace with admirable zeal! Unquestionably they will not disdain to have us for companions, whose helpers they have already become. . . . Let us hasten then, beloved, I entreat you, let us hasten, since the whole multitude of the heavenly host awaits us.[56]

In this beautiful passage Bernard does not discriminate rigidly between the parts of the heavenly company. Angels and saints are both involved in the services of ministration placed at the disposal of earth's faithful by those of heaven. But enough is said to indicate a definite relationship on the part of the saints in glory sustained to those of the Church militant. The eliciting regard of the celestial citizenry for their brethren on earth carries with it an ultimacy of motivation for the men of Christ's Church on pilgrimage. There are evident convictions as to the necessity of a reciprocating fraternity on earth if Christians would make ready for the final mutuality of God's kingdom in heaven.

Bernard's works are full of impassioned tributes to the Mystical Body. Linhardt has gathered a mass of such correlating emphases. Clearly emerging is the stress laid upon the mystical nuptials of the earthly with the heavenly Church—of the Bride with the Bridegroom—and the mystical bread by which the ecclesiastical community is maintained in its service to the temporal world. Upon that Church, responding on earth to the dictates of heaven, the whole divine plan rests in fructifying blessing for humankind. Outside it there is hope for none; within it, the deficiencies of each are assuaged and surmounted with the fullness of the eternal.[57]

Bernard Mystique (Paris, 1948), pp. 132 ff., 480 ff., and C. Spicq, *Esquisse d'une histoire de l'exégèse latine au moyen âge* (Paris, 1944), p. 119.

[56] Serm. II, "For the Eve of the Nativity," 6; Eales, *Works*, III, 359; MPL 183:93; NUS 27:148.

[57] See R. Linhardt, *Die Mystik des Hl. Bernhard von Clairvaux* (Munich, 1923), especially Chap. II, pp. 118-19. Cf. W. Williams, *The Mysticism of S. Bernard of Clairvaux* (London, 1931); also Leclercq, *op. cit.*; likewise, E. Gilson, *The Mystical Theology of Saint Bernard* (New York, 1940). Cf. *Serm. in Cant.* 61, MPL 183:1072, Eales, *Works*, IV, 367; *Serm. in Cant.* 12, MPL 183:833, Eales, *Works*, IV, 66-67; *Serm. in Cant.*, 49, Eales, *Works*, IV, 300; *Serm. in Cant.* 71, MPL 183:1123-28; Ep. 243 (1146), Eales, II, 7—Letter 319 in B. G. James, *The Letters of St. Bernard of Clairvaux* (London, 1952), pp. 391-94.

Peter Lombard follows St. Augustine in declaring "that from the Holy Ghost comes the social bond which makes of all the faithful one body, that of the only Son of God." This union groups together faithful souls and angels; between the saints and the faithful exists the communication of prayers and merits. By the "Communion of Saints" Lombard understands the society which associates all the faithful with Jesus Christ their head in the membership of the united threefold Church.[58]

Such ideas are fully in keeping with other passages from the great Parisian. Elsewhere, he recounts how the saints and angels hear prayers supplicating the Lord's aid and intercede for those invoking assistance. Peter is clearly a believer in the services which those in the heavenly realm may perform for the men of earth, if those in the Church militant seek heavenly aid. With Ambrose, Jerome, Augustine, and later Fathers of the Church, he finds in sacramental life —especially that of the Eucharist—the mutualizing efficacy of the Mystical Body. The Church, itself, is referred to under the figure of the one bread and body, since, as one piece of bread is composed of many grains and one body of many members, so the Church is drawn together in procreative charity from a diversity of the faithful.[59]

William of Auxerre in referring to the Communion of Saints noted how "this article affirms our unity with all others in Christ and in the Church." [60] Alexander of Hales asserted: "I believe that the unity of the Church is so perfect, that each of its members has a share in the goods of all. Such is the force of this unity, that whoever is a member of Christ, is also a member of the servitors of Christ." [61] Earlier and later scholars of the Middle Period agree that in sharing thus, one with the other, none can lose anything; for in a state of unity everything still belongs to each.[62]

Thomas Aquinas, like his master Albertus, consistently granted to the concept of the Mystical Body an exalted place. In the commentaries, yet to be noted, he treats at length the analogy existing

[58] Lib. IV, Sent. III, Dist. 28, cap. II, Quaracchi ed., II, 680; III, Dist. 28-29; IV, Dist. 38 and 41, Quaracchi ed., II, 678 ff., 967 ff., 982 ff.; Breton, *op. cit.*, 59.

[59] Lib. IV, Dist. 45, cap. 6, Quaracchi ed., II, 1009-11. On the Eucharist cf. Lib. IV, Dist. 8, caps. VI-VII, Quaracchi ed., II, 791-92; Dist. 12, cap. 4, Quaracchi, II, 811-12. See J. De Ghellinck, *Le Mouvement théologique du XII° siècle* (Paris, 1948), index; especially pp. 211-29 on the *Sentences*.

[60] Mersch, *Le corps mystique*, II, 294, n. 2.

[61] *Ibid.*, II, 204, n. 2, and 295.

[62] *Ibid.*, II, 295 and n. 2; see H. de St. Victor, *De Sacram.*, Lib. II, Pars 2, cap. 2, MPL 176:416-17.

between spiritual and physical bodies.[63] In his *Summa Theologica* he is concerned to show that the different states and duties in the Church have a relation to the mystical unity of Christ's Body. He points out that the very perfection of the Church is represented in any apportioning of functions and significance in terms of multiplicity and unity:

> For even as in the order of natural things, perfection, which in God is simple and uniform, is not to be found in the created universe except in a multiform and manifold manner, so too, the fulness of grace, which is centred in Christ as head, flows forth to His members in various ways, for the perfecting of the body of the Church.[64]

Furthermore, the Church has need of a diversity of actions, which, in turn, necessitate a diversity of men, each one in his own place. Likewise, this distribution of people and functions to the advantage of the one Church represents the kind of order that the body, itself, possesses. However great or small may be the portion of a given member, it receives its full honor in terms of a participating, organic unity. As, in nature, duplication of function is not desirable; so, in the Church, the community of the faithful is directed in a co-operative manner to ultimate, and therefore temporal, concord.

Just as in the natural body the various members are held together in unity by the power of the quickening spirit, and are dissociated from one another as soon as that spirit departs, so too in the Church's body the peace of the various members is preserved by the power of the Holy Spirit, Who quickens the body of the Church.

Self-seeking in the spiritual as in the earthly kingdom dissipates all peace. Conversely, the unselfish contribution of each citizen to the activities of the commonwealth is the best guarantee against schism and the surest preservation of mutuality. The Church itself in its earthly pilgrimage may hope to know this peaceful prosecution of corporate life if the analogy of the *Corpus Mysticum* is intelligently applied.[65]

[63] Mersch, *op. cit.*, II, 294, n. 2, and 295, nn. 4 and 5; cf. Albertus Magnus, In IV Sent., Dist. XLV, Art. 1; Dist. XIV, Art. 2; In III Sent., Dist. XXIV, b, Art. 6; Dist. XXII, A, Arts. 2-4; Th. Aquinas, *Super symb. apost.*, Art. 10.

[64] IIa IIae Q. 183, Art. 2, conclusion. Translation by the Dominican Fathers, p. 146; *Op. Om.*, IV, 483-84. Used by permission of the publishers, Burns Oates & Washbourne, Ltd.

[65] IIa IIae Q. 183, Art. 2, Reply obj. 3. Dominican Fathers' translation, p. 147. Used by permission of the publishers.

In the third part of his theological *Summa,* Thomas states even more flatly his convictions on the Mystical Body of Christ. In a physical organism, where there is one body there must be one head. The various members are designed for a common task; the whole body has the happy obligation of making each part conform to that solidarity of purpose. In the case of the Mystical Body, the end to which it moves is that of divine fruition and blessedness. To this ultimate end, with its full sociality, both angels and men are destined. For the *Corpus Mysticum* of the Church consists not only of men but likewise of angels. And of this whole multitude Christ is head. He is closest to God the Father and participates more fully in his life and gifts than men or angels. In his participating fullness, both men and angels find their completion. God has placed Christ at his right hand, supreme over all principalities, powers, virtues, and dominions, with a name above all others in this world and the next. To him all are to be subject. And it must not be forgotten that, as the head of this Mystical Body, Christ gives, not only to its final existence but also to its wayfaring life on earth, the consummate sociality of his Church.

Thomas is always aware of certain radical differences between the earthly body and its spiritual counterpart. He exploits suggestive parallels without being reduced to the necessity of stressing likenesses where they do not exist. Thus there is, in the Mystical Body, a differentiating sense of relationship among the three phases of the Church; which differentiation finds no parallel in the purely physical organism. There is in this spiritual body a time-and-space-transcending power that comes from its having been destined from before the beginning of the world to an end that shall outlast history, itself.

Human beings are found in a threefold ranking as regards their final end. Thus there are those who, in a period of exile, move solely by faith. Others in purgatorial cleansing are united to Christ through the offices of supplicating charity. A third group is joined with the Lord in the heavenly fruition. If one keeps in mind the different stages through which men have passed and are passing, he must see that Christ is the head of all men, regardless of their gradations. With the persistence so characteristic of him, Thomas goes on to show the relationship of human life to Christ in a variety of actual and potential experiences.[66]

Thomas' running commentary on the Letter to the Ephesians is here apropos. He brings into a varied frame of reference the integrat-

[66] Q. 8., Art. 4; *Op. Om.,* IV, 634.

ing characteristic of the *Corpus Mysticum*. Christ is head of the whole Church. This involves those militant, who are in the present life, as well as those triumphant, who are made up of men and angels in the heavenly fatherland. At this point Thomas goes on to establish the multiplicity of services which inhere in Christ's common headship. Diversification of function is the proof that the whole body is brought under the comprising and mutualizing unity of Christ, himself. This, again, bridges the gap which only superficially separates the eternal company from those on earth whom it draws to itself in ultimate blessedness. The entire context is one in which Thomas thinks of the unified body of Christ in all its variegated parts as working toward the fulfillment of his true Church. He draws from Dionysian sources a clear pattern of Christ's illuminating influence on both lower and higher angels. A mellifluous passage shows how the Church, which is instituted by and for Christ, has the richness of his power and distributes to all his members those spiritual gifts which are his.[67]

As noted elsewhere, Thomas makes some use of the doctrine concerning the Communion of Saints—even though in his discussion on the Symbol he interprets the *Communio* as the participation in holy things. His further thought, particularly with regard to the invocation of the saints, leaves no doubt as to his view. He is sure that we should supplicate their aid. Since the divine order was established so that all might ultimately be brought back to God; and since the saints in heaven are the nearest to God,

the order of Divine law requires, that we who are in the body, journeying to the Lord, be brought to Him through the intercession of the Saints; which happens in very truth, when through them God pours out upon us the effect of His Divine goodness. And because our return to God should correspond to the progress of His goodness in us, just as through the prayers of the saints, blessings and favours come to us; so should we return to God, that we might again and again receive God's favours through the medium of His saints. Hence it is that we call upon them to be our intercessors with God, to be our mediators; while we ask them to pray for us.[68]

Thomas believes, also, that although the major saints have a greater acceptability to God than those of lesser dignity, it is none-

---

[67] *Ep. ad Ephesios,* cap. 1, Lectio 8; *Op. Om.,* XXI, 277-78.

[68] IV, Dist. 45, Q. 3, a. 1 and 2, as translated by E. C. McEniry, *Thomas Aquinas Meditations for Everyday* (Somerset, Ohio: The Rosary Press, 1938), p. 433. Later editions published by Long's College Book Co. Used by permission of the author.

theless useful for us to pray to the minor ones as well. Sometimes one may have greater devotion to a minor than to a greater saint; if the effects of prayer which depend upon devotion are not to be lost, recourse to the one to whom greater devotion is given is clearly in order. It may also be better that some diversity be brought into our devotion, here. Again, certain saints have committed to them the work of defending special cases. This will doubtless necessitate regard for minor as well as major saints. Furthermore, proper honor is due all of the saints, not just a few. And it must not be forgotten that favor sought without success "through the intercession or prayer of one saint, is sometimes obtained through the prayers and intercession of many saints." [69]

"The saints know when we pray." They are conscious of our prayers. "Moreover it pertains to the glory of the saints, that they obtain help for those on earth, who need it for salvation. Consequently, 'the saints are co-workers with God, and nothing is so Divine,'" writes Dionysius. "Therefore, it is clear that the saints have a knowledge of those things which are required for this Divine work. And so it is evident that they know in the Word, the promises, and prayers and devotions of mankind; imploring their help and intercession with God." [70]

Valentin-Breton clarifies further the position of Thomas regarding this formulary when he quotes the Rev. P. Bernard:

"It is useless," says this learned author, "to take from S. Thomas the elements of a doctrine fixed before and apart from him." Because he took the word "saints" to have a neuter meaning, his teaching manages only indirectly to establish the communion of the faithful among themselves; moreover, it would logically exclude the angels from this communion, if he had not associated the angelic spirits with the saints on account of the unity of supernatural life and of the last end, common to them both. But, we repeat, these differences in the constitution of the doctrine affect only the method; the practical synthesis remains the same. [71]

M. Valentin-Breton ascribes to Bonaventura the crystallization, among the Scholastics, of those doctrines derived from the Communion of Saints. With a minimum of overgeneralization, he groups

---

[69] McEniry, *Meditations*, p. 434. Used by permission of the author.

[70] *Loc. cit.* Used by permission of the author.

[71] *Communion of Saints*, p. 59; cf. Mersch, *Le corps mystique* II, 456, and index, for Aquinas.

in seven articles the great Franciscan's contribution to this all-important theme. Briefly summarized, these seven areas of thought are as follows:

1. The faithful are united in one body in Christ. The Holy Spirit constitutes the living principle of this union. It is one and the same throughout the whole body.

2. The union of wills operating in reciprocal and mutual charity finds its prior example in the unity of the divine persons. The whole discussion of the manner in which the unity and community of the faithful on earth proceed from the Trinity through the heavenly realm to the faithful below is a cardinal principle; the part, however indirect, that Dionysius plays in it is probably large; though, of course, it can be immediately derived from the Scriptures themselves.

3. This communication of spirits is brought about and made supremely effective by the eucharistic participation. It is signified by the sacramental union of the real body of Christ with the species. And the breaking of bread in three parts symbolizes the three states of the Mystical Body: militant, suffering, triumphant. It should be noted that Valentin-Breton, like many others, frequently lists these three portions of the Church as being at once parts of the Mystical Body and areas of the Communion of Saints.

4. Among the three states of the one universal Church, subsisting across time and eternity, there exists a close bond such as that which maintains among the organs of a natural body. This assertion, which may be amply documented to Bonaventura, stresses the transcendence of the Communion of Saints beyond things merely natural and time-bound. It brings into correct focus Bonaventura's own thought concerning the fashion in which the eternal society operates in the lives of men on earth and souls in purgatory.

5. A common solidarity brings together all of these members. The good of each is literally the good of all. However, each participates according to his own measure. This protects the well-established doctrine that each one may have the fullness of that which pertains to him without duplicating the degree and extensiveness of that which makes up another's portion.

6. Not only by its prayers does the Church come to our aid, many times preserving us from sin; but through the superabundant merits of the saints it makes satisfaction for its culpable children. There is here a strong reference, not only to the preventive quality, but also to the remedial powers, of the saints.

7. The saints have a right to veneration and invocation by the faithful. They, for their part, intercede for all who require their aid. Thus the unity, the charity, and the hierarchy of services are maintained. The faithful owe prayers for the dead and honor to those in heaven. The structural efficacy of the mass is here put in proper perspective.[72]

A survey of Bonaventura's writings impresses one with the fundamental accuracy of Valentin-Breton's summary. Bonaventura does have a remarkable sensitivity to the mutualizing experience which belongs to the Mystical Body and to the saints in communion with each other. Furthermore, his basically eschatological framework permits him to put in proper focus the socializing qualities within the Church militant and suffering as they proceed from the ultimate kingdom and the Church triumphant.[73]

The beautiful prayer of Peter Canisius, the ardent sixteenth-century missionary, recapitulates the Roman Church's teaching through the ages:

I petition Thy aid, O Lord, and I pray Thee to sustain me, not only by the merits of Christ who is our head and the Holy of Holies, but furthermore by the merits of his most august members and of his whole body, which is the Church. Grant that I may be a participant, not only in general, but also in particular, with all those who, in heaven and on earth, fear Thee and keep Thy commandments. May those who serve Thee, Father of all majesty, serve Thee at the same time for me, I pray Thee, so that, for me, they may intercede, adore, love, and glorify Thy holy name which is properly honored in Thy humblest creatures. Let this name be exalted in the elect, whom Thou hast predestined and loved

---

[72] Pp. 60-66; significant documentation for each numbered position is as follows:

1. *Com. in 1 Librum Sententiarum* Dist. 14, especially Art. 11, Q. 1; *Op. Om.* I, 249.
2. In I Lib., Dist. 10, Art. 1, Q. 3; *Op. Om.* I. 199.
3. In IV Lib., Dist. 8, Pt. 2, Art. 2, Q. 1; *Op. Om.*, IV, 196; Dist. 12, Pt. 1, Art. 3, Q. 3 and concl; *Op. Om.* IV, 285-86; cf. *Breviloquium* VI. 9.
4. In IV Lib., Dist. 8. Pt. 1-2: Dist. 20. Pt. 2: *Op. Om.* IV, 530.
5. In IV Lib., Dist. 45, Art. 2, Q. 1-2; *Op. Om.* IV, 943 ff.
6. In IV Lib., Dist. 17, Pt. 2; *Op. Om.*, IV, 415 ff.; Dist. 15. Pt. 2; *Op. Om.*, IV, 361 ff.
7. In III Lib., Dist. 9, Art. 2; *Op. Om.*, III, 213 ff.; cf. In IV, Dist. 45-46; *Brev.*, V, 10, VII, 3.

[73] As may be seen from note 72, the *Com. in Lib. Sent.* is central (*Op. Om.* I-IV), together with the *Breviloquium*, especially Pars 7 (*Op. Om.* V, 281 ff.). A convenient selection of his writings is *Saint Bonaventure, Oeuvres* présentées par le R. P. Valentin-M. Breton (Paris, 1943).

from all eternity, in order that they may become conformable to the likeness of Thy Son, who is, and will always be, the first born of his brethren. Grant that these may celebrate in me your exalted and adorable name, and that for me they may pray this glory.[74]

[74] Adapted from Mersch, *Le corps mystique,* II, 796; Mersch translates into the French, from the Latin of Canisius' *Confessiones,* I, 6, ed. O. Braunsberger (Friburg, 1896), I. 28. See an English translation in J. R. Kelly's version, *The Whole Christ* (Milwaukee, 1938), p. 528.

CHAPTER XII

The Ecclesiastical Community as Servant of the Eternal Kingdom in the Temporal World

6. Temporal Church, United Christendom, and the Christian Body Politic

THE EARLY CHURCH INTERPRETED ITS LIFE IN TERMS OF THE BODY OF Christ, the *Corpus Christi*. Originally there was no such separation between doctrine and life as our modern world habitually considers. Being in Christ was an experience which carried with it the necessity of being the light of the world. Thus what God did for, and with, his children in Christ required a response on their part. No reactions to the society of their day could result apart from their own incorporation in the Mystical Body of their Saviour. The love which was to manifest itself among them had to reflect the love which God exemplified in his saving them by means of his Son. The Christian had to live his life in the midst of earthly society on the terms laid down by God through Christ.

Not only is the kingdom primary in such a view; it also gives to the Church a communal and socializing function which rules the relations of Christians to each other and to the whole world as well. The Church must look to its own final reincorporation in the kingdom after the Last Days. In the meantime, it is held to be the business of the Body of Christ on earth—his true Church among men— to be a community worthy of the ultimate kingdom. The Church receives its power and its guiding principles from God himself by means of his Word. These principles work themselves out in the brotherhood so as to preserve best the individual character of each member when he, as a part, grows out of the Christlike whole.[1]

---

[1] A statement inspired by a Memorandum of June, 1940, issued via W. A. Visser 't Hooft, Geneva (Mimeographed), especially pp. 3-7. Quoted by author's permission. Cf.

In those portions of the Gospels where the faithful are considered most directly as constituting the Church, their qualities of life most completely take on the contours of a community inspired by the ultimate society. Being thus the very Body of Christ himself, Christians do stand, in a sense, separated from the world, in that they are an elect race, a holy nation, and God's own Church.[2]

But such a body of Christians can exemplify no isolated qualities of purely individual experience. "For to be 'in Christ' does not mean an individual experience; it means to be part of his Body." The socializing consequences of such a concept may best be documented in connection with the historic life of the pioneer Christian communities. They could not think of themselves as being a Church except as they were in Christ; they could not be in Christ unless they made themselves, together, a responsive ministry to the whole group by sharing in his life to the full.[3]

The early Christian realized that he was free, not to violate the best interests of the group in terms of his own desires, but to discover his own welfare in subordination of his selfish will to the common good in Christ Jesus. Within the natural limits of human fallibility, a given member of the Church of Christ might feel called upon to speak to the ecclesia and to the outside world in the name of the community; as befitted a conscience given direction by the Lord's Spirit. This had immediate repercussions for the development of the Christian common life, and through that mutualizing experience, the redemption of the world at large.

The Church, then, was not limited in its witness to the elect. In a real sense the Church was true to its leader and to itself when it testified its convictions to the whole world. Such passages as Acts 9:31, I Peter 2:11-12, Philippians 2:15, and Matthew 5:16 interpret the Church as the enlightener and redeemer, in Christ, of all mankind. This is not to make of the Christian community an indistinguishable segment of humanity. Christians maintain a separateness which is theirs by reason of their being associated with Christ. This differentiates them from any group that does not accept Christ's life as the final determiner for all social action. Christians are in the world but not of it, even as the Master himself is. But, just as the world needs Christ, so it needs the Church.

The Church and Its Function in Society by J. H. Oldham and W. A. Visser 't Hooft (London, 1937), pp. 24 ff.

[2] *Memorandum*, pp. 7-8; *The Church*, pp. 24-25.

[3] *Ibid.*, p. 6; *The Church*, p. 25.

This signifies but one thing: the enlivening quality of the Church's own life, as the community in Christ, gives to the *koinonia* and to the world as a whole the benefits of a distinctly missionary experience. Nonetheless, this can hardly be interpreted as involving an identification of the Church and its aims with the destiny of the world at large. Professors Case, Troeltsch, and others insist that the ancient church never conceived of its function as being the rehabilitation of society, generally. The Church certainly had no such conscious conception of its task in the beginning.[4] On the other hand, the Body of Christ could not be an organic unity, with the driving power of the eternal community within it, without imparting certain blessings to society as a whole. Thus Dr. Visser 't Hooft can say that

the world which is outside the Church, and which does not accept the Gospel, is not abandoned to its fate. Even before it recognizes Jesus Christ as its true Lord, as it will have to do on the Day of the Lord, it is already in a provisional way subjected to His reign. The life of the State, of society, of nations, is already under His reign, though at the moment that reign is "hidden" rather than "public." God has a will for the world, but the Church has only partial knowledge of the content of that Will.

Again he says:

If, therefore, the ecclesia speaks to its own members of their life in the world, it does so on the basis of its insight into the provisional plan which God has for the "world" outside the ecclesia. The conception of the provisional status of the world contains implicitly a duty for the Church to remind the world of that status whenever the opportunity to do so is given to it.[5]

The Church, then, as the Body of Christ, is the instrumentality of God's kingdom working out its will on earth as in heaven. As such, it must reflect the divine *agape* in its communal relations within itself here below, if it would be true to the ultimate kingdom. However this may be brought about, it must speak to the world in the name of Christ and his reign. The Church is, veritably, the servant of the eternal kingdom in the temporal world. Until the Middle

---

[4] *Ibid.*, pp. 7-8; S. J. Case, *The Social Triumph of the Ancient Church* (New York, 1933), pp. 97 ff., 203 ff.; E. Troeltsch, *The Social Teaching of the Christian Churches* (New York, 1931), I, 39 ff.
[5] *Memorandum*, p. 8.

Ages, however, the Church continues to stress its called-out quality much more than its primacy in a Christianized order.

The consideration of the *Corpus Christianum,* like that of the *Corpus Christi,* raises many possibilities of overgeneralization and distortion. It also directs our attention to certain inescapable characteristics of medieval Christianity; particularly as these diverge from ancient Christian thought. Dr. Visser 't Hooft's statement is a useful one:

> The expression Corpus Christianum needs definition. In this study we will use it to indicate the overlapping of Church and world, so that either Church and State, or Church and Nation, are considered as co-terminous realities which have distinct tasks, but which cannot be separated from each other. The relation between the elements within the Corpus may be conceived very differently (Ecclesiocracy, Caesaropapism, Symphony or Collaboration), but in every case that relation is one between a Church which considers the State or Society as a Christian State or Society, and a State or Society which recognizes that Church as the true Church. The Church is publicly acknowledged by the authorized representatives of the secular world, and the world is looked upon by the Church as a baptized and christianized world. That situation is not the one of the New Testament Church. Nor is it our own situation. But since it has lasted for many centuries and has left an indelible impression on the whole of Church history, it is of the highest importance that we should consider its meaning and its relevance for our own situation today.[6]

Truly enough, this transition "from the Corpus Christi, the ecclesia called out from the world, to the Corpus Christianum, the intermingling of Church and world, is a long, complicated, and in many ways mysterious story." The use of the term *Corpus Christianum* is, perhaps, a modern one. That which it connotes, however, was integral with medieval thought and life. The way in which the spiritual and the temporal became associated in an almost inextricable unity in duality is represented in various utterances of the medieval period. Such diverse authorities as Stephen of Tournai and William of Ockham stress alike the oneness and the twofold expression of Christian society. Here, says Visser 't Hooft, is

a unity which comprises both the church and the world, but which is in reality the church in its wholeness. As a matter of fact, this is precisely

[6] *Loc. cit.*

the characteristic of medieval theory (and practice) :—Church and world, *Corpus Christi* and *genus humanum* are at one moment considered as two distinct entities, and in the next moment as completely identical. Even Thomas Aquinas makes this identification:—*Genus humanum consideratur quasi unum corpus, quod vocatur mysticum, cujus caput est ipse Christus et quantum ad animas et quantum ad corpora.*[7]

Can the *Corpus Christianum* be thought of as the Church itself— an all-embracing totalitarian society, requiring the subjection of all other societies and powers? However indirect the power which the Church wields over temporal affairs, it is, nevertheless, a very real one. Thomas Aquinas was by no means the only medieval man who saw in it the "only unifying power in the world." A provocative statement asserts:

In the *Corpus Christianum* the Church appears as it were twice, first, as the eternal and spiritual reality, secondly, as the empirical institution which is to guide the whole life of the world; but the world only appears once, and that in a place of dependence.[8]

The papal-imperial struggles were certainly not waged over the integrity of the *Corpus Christianum* as a satisfactory conception but about the place of each power, spiritual and temporal, *"within* the Corpus as a whole." The anti-papalists accepted the doctrine of unity no less than the curialists. What the anti-papalists objected to was the acquisition of unity on the grounds of complete dependence by the temporal upon the spiritual.[9] Dr. Barker here reconstructs the basic medieval pattern of thought. This holds that

the Church should, *formally,* permeate and Christianize the existing world of the community-state, and make it a single integrated community-state-and-Church. In other words, the universal empire could, and did, become also, and at the same time, a universal or catholic Church. One body of men had henceforth two aspects: in one aspect it was a community-state, and in the other it was a Church.[10]

---

[7] *Ibid.,* p. 9; Bohatec, *Calvins Lehre,* pp. 585 ff.; Th. Aquinas, *S. Theol.,* III, Q. 8, a. 1 and 2.

[8] *Memorandum,* pp. 9-10.

[9] *Ibid.,* p. 10.

[10] *Loc. cit.;* cf. E. Barker, *Church and Community,* being Vol. V in the *Church, Community and State* (London, 1938) , p. 45.

Seen in this perspective, the Church's problem involves a conscious regard for society in the large as it constitutes Christendom. Perhaps it may be thought of as seeing in its population, not a group to be Christianized, but a Christian *corpus* to be made ever more responsive to the social instincts and mandates of the kingdom of God. Certainly, too, the life of the individual is here caught up in significant "holism." No one who reads the Thomistic synthesis can fail, for a moment, of the realization that the individual is a part created and sustained by the whole. One may readily concede that in the medieval concept of Christendom and of *Respublica Christiana* there exists a definite social empowerment for the remaking of life:

The Church conception underlying the Corpus Christianum is in fact a radical anticipation of the eschatological promises of the New Testament. The heavenly city which, according to the Bible, is "to come," that is to be expected, is here taken to be a present and given reality. The original distinction between *Ekklesia* and *Basileia tou theou* is forgotten and replaced by St. Augustine's view that *Ecclesia et nunc est regnum Christi, regnumque coelorum.* Similarly the hope that "every tongue should confess that Jesus Christ is Lord" is transformed in the theory that already, though in *potentia* and not *de facto,* all men belong to the Church, and the Church thus becomes an all-embracing institution based on divine prerogatives rather than the community of those who live in Christ. It is by ascribing to the Church the characteristics of the Kingdom of God and by even identifying the ordinance of God with the ordinance of the Church (as does Bonifacius VIII in his Bull *Unam Sanctam*) that it becomes possible to see Church and world as already united in one great comprehensive and unified system.[11]

Gierke's analysis of medieval postulates is deservedly famous:

Political Thought when it is genuinely medieval starts from the Whole, but ascribes an intrinsic value to every Partial Whole down to and including the Individual. If it holds out one hand to Antique Thought when it sets the Whole before the Parts, and the other hand to the Modern Theories of Natural Law when it proclaims the intrinsic and aboriginal rights of the Individual, its peculiar characteristic is that it sees the Universe as one articulated Whole and every Being—whether a Joint-Being (Community) or a Single-Being—as both a Part and a Whole: a Part determined by the final cause of the Universe, and a Whole with a final cause of its own.

This is the origin of those theocratic and spiritualistic traits which

[11] *Memorandum,* p. 11.

are manifested by the Medieval Doctrine of Society. On the one side, every ordering of a human community must appear as a component part of that ordering of the world which exists because God exists, and every earthly group must appear as an organic member of that *Civitas Dei,* that God-State, which comprehends the heavens and the earth. Then, on the other hand, the eternal and other-worldly aim and object of every individual man must, in a directer or an indirecter fashion, determine the aim and object of every group into which he enters.

But as there must of necessity be connexion between the various groups, and as all of them must be connected with the divinely ordered Universe, we come by the further notion of a divinely instituted Harmony which pervades the Universal Whole and every part thereof. To every Being is assigned its place in that Whole, and to every link between Beings corresponds a divine decree. But since the World is One Organism, animated by One Spirit, fashioned by One Ordinance, the self-same principles that appear in the structure of the World will appear once more in the structure of its every Part. Therefore every particular Being, in so far as it is a Whole, is a diminished copy of the World; it is a *Microcosmus* or *Minor Mundus* in which the *Macrocosmus* is mirrored. In the fullest measure this is true of every human individual; but it holds good also of every human community and of human society in general. Thus the Theory of Human Society must accept the divinely created organization of the Universe as a prototype of the first principles which govern the construction of human communities.[12]

The essential thesis here advanced is borne out by Kraus, Jacob, and other more recent researchers in medieval political theory.[13] It brings into sharp focus the relationship existing between the supernatural ends of man and the realization of his best life in the natural realm. Viewing this nexus, one observes how the Church, acting as the immediate agent of the eternal, and the temporal power, serving less directly but nonetheless actively in the same course, are subordi-

[12] O. Gierke, *Political Theories of the Middle Age,* tr. F. W. Maitland (Cambridge, 1900), pp. 7-8. Used by permission of the publishers, Cambridge University Press. See Gierke's notes, *op. cit.,* pp. 101 ff., for references to Dante's *De Monarchia,* I, 7, also 6, as derived from Th. Aquinas, *Summa Contra Gentiles* III, 76-83; also *De Regimine Principum* Lib. I, cap. XII (Parma Edition, New York, 1950), XVI, 235. Cf. Nicholas de Cusa, *De Concordantia Catholica* I, 1-4.

[13] J. B. Kraus, *Scholastik, Puritanismus und Kapitalismus* (Munich, 1930), particularly pp. 66-69; F. Gavin, *Seven Centuries of the Problem of Church and State* (Princeton, 1938); C. H. McIlwain, *The Growth of Political Thought in the West* (New York, 1932); J. Bohatec, *Calvins Lehre von Staat und Kirche,* especially Buch III, "Staat und Kirche: Staat und Kirche im Lichte des organischen Gedankens im Mittelalter," pp. 581-96; Troeltsch, *Social Teaching* I, 201 ff.; B. Jarrett, *Social Theories of the Middle Ages* (London, 1926), and the various writings of E. F. Jacob.

nated to the one great authority of the divine will in the universe. This is to raise again the fundamental issue with which Thomas dealt so comprehensively; namely, the way in which man might live so acceptably in the natural sphere as to be called up higher to a supernatural experience with God, his angels, and his saints.[14]

Gierke, showing how political thought starts from the whole, emphasizes anew the role of eschatology in its relation to social existence. From the beginning, all life springs from the oneness of God; and the goal of life is to be interpreted in terms of a return to that same oneness. Consequently, as human society discovers its pattern in the creating unity of the Godhead, so it finds its sustaining and driving motivation in the preparation for an ultimate, societal reunion with Deity.

This necessitates a highly theocratic and spiritualistic element in all the affairs of medieval government. It also requires a description of political and social life on the part of all human beings in terms of loyalty to the divine community. Precisely because all earthly groups have their being and their meaning as organic members of God's own city—"which comprehends the heavens and the earth"—all political organization must keep this supraterrestrial community in mind. The Middle Ages could not conceive of groups without those individual parts which were, in themselves, integers. Gierke's further contention therefore has weight: that is, the "eternal and other-worldly aim and object of every individual man must, in a directer or an indirecter fashion, determine the aim and object of every group into which he enters." In other words, both men as parts of groups and groups as they comprise multitudes of men must answer to the communal-individual patterns established by the divine commonwealth. Thus, politics takes on a distinctly teleological coloring.[15]

Naturally, any consideration of the political state must lead to a reconsideration of the spiritual powers and agencies which serve the eternal world in the present one. The Church is once more seen as the agent of the eternal in the temporal. However distinct and specially privileged the functions of a king may be in their own right—or however much they may be thought by some individuals to derive solely from the Church—they must be answerable, always, to the unity and the organic wholeness which God has placed in the center of his universe.

Powers both temporal and spiritual must, therefore, assume a rela-

[14] *S. Theol.*, Ia. IIae Q. 90, Art. 2; *Contr. Gent.*, III, 151, 129.
[15] Gierke, *op. cit.*, pp. 7-8.

tion of serviceability to the destiny of mankind. However divergent may be the opinions as to their mutual relationship, political and ecclesiastical institutions must serve on earth as closely related agencies of the ultimate society in the construction of the temporal one.[16]

We may profitably continue the summation of Gierke in terms of that unity which medieval men ascribed to Church and temporal society. The basic principle of the universe is found in unity. God, who is one without division, comes before all that which is many. He himself constitutes the beginning and the end of all being. Whatever finite individuals may think, God's will is always working in his world, "and is directing all that is manifold to one only end." [17]

Deducible from this position is the medieval contention for the unity of all mankind. Unity must always precede multiplicity.

All Manyness has its origin in Oneness (*omnis multitudo derivatur ab uno*) and to Oneness it returns (*ad unum reducitur*). Therefore all Order consists in the subordination of Plurality to Unity (*ordinatio ad unum*), and never and nowhere can a purpose that is common to Many be effectual unless the One rules over the Many and directs the Many to the goal.[18]

This experience of unity that precedes multiplicity has reference to the heavenly bodies and every living organism. Soul, Reason, and Heart declare a primal and all-pervading unity. In the human social order, as in the whole of animate and inanimate nature, plurality must answer to ruling unity.

In the thought of the Middle Ages, mankind as a partial whole following its own final cause is embodied within the universal whole. Christendom, with a destiny identical to that of mankind,

is set before us as a single, universal Community, founded and governed by God Himself. Mankind is one "mystical body"; it is one single and internally connected "people" or "folk"; it is an all embracing corporation (*universitas*), which constitutes that Universal Realm, spiritual and temporal, which may be called the Universal Church (*ecclesia universalis*), or, with equal propriety, the Commonwealth of the Human Race (*respublica generis humani*). Therefore that it may attain its one

---

[16] *Ibid.*, Sec. III: "Unity in Church and State," pp. 9-21.
[17] *Ibid.*, p. 9.
[18] *Loc. cit.* Used by permission of the publishers.

purpose, it needs One Law (*lex*) and One Government (*unicus prin-cipatus.*) [19]

Medieval society sought oneness on the basis of eternal unity. That is, the eternal community, quite often thought of as God's kingdom, set the pattern for human society on earth. How this sovereign one-ness, exemplified by the Godhead, led to social co-operation in medieval life is not always clear. Gierke stresses the necessity for recognizing different spheres of operation within a single earthly com-munity. The medieval man accepted it as an eternal counsel of God, that there should be two organized orders of life, the spiritual and the temporal. Temporal and eternal qualities within man himself doubt-less suggested subdivisions of the one society that ministered to these two aspects of his life.[20] We should remember with Professor Mc-Ilwain that medieval terminology involves the "temporal and spirit-ual" rather than "church and state." [21]

Thinkers of the Middle Ages see these two orders coming under one comprising unity, rather than constituting mutually opposed and antagonistic entities. As Gierke concludes, the very suggestion of this duality of function reminds the medieval man that there is a unity which rises above all duality. The major question—and one for which no easy solution was ever found—pondered how the recon-ciling oneness of power and service could be instituted and made operable. To use Gierke's own words: "The Medieval Spirit steadily refuses to accept the Dualism as final. In some higher Unity reconcil-iation must be found. This was indubitable; but over the nature of the reconciling process the great parties of the Middle Age fell a-fighting." [22]

It is evident that the Middle Ages could entertain an embarrassing tension at this point and still maintain a passionate belief in a larger unity of society. What resulted was a series of explanations and proximate policies for making duality work within unity. One group, which Gierke denominates the Ecclesiastical party, sought to resolve the tension through elevation of the spiritual power. This was a ready, though by no means uncontested, device for making the Church the one comprising agency of the eternal in the temporal.

In its most expansive form such an approach asserted that every-

[19] *Ibid.*, pp. 9-10. Used by permission of the publishers. See Gierke's notes, 3-7, pp. 101-3, emphasizing further the doctrines of Th. Aquinas, *De reg. prin.*, I, 2, 3, 12, and *S. Theol.*, III, Q. 81; Dante, *De Mon.*, I, 15-16, III, 16, etc.

[20] *Ibid.*, pp. 10 ff.

[21] McIlwain, *Growth*, p. 226.

[22] Gierke, *op. cit.*, p. 11. Used by permission of the publishers.

thing of order and power to be encountered in this world might be subsumed under the pope's rights as Christ's earthly vicar. When, as it often did, this interpretation pointed out the necessity of a subdivision of functions, it was quick to place the princely under the direction and power of the priestly. The temporal power might be given grudging place as a necessity in a world of sin; or it might be accorded a certain cognizance within God's own voluntary plan. But in any case it must secure its validity through the Church and not from God himself, directly. Put in these terms:

It is from the Church that the Temporal Power receives its true being, and it is from the Church that Kaiser and Kings receive their right to rule. And all along the Temporal Government when it has been constituted remains a subservient part of the Ecclesiastical Order. It is a mean or instrument of the single and eternal purpose of the Church. In the last resort it is an Ecclesiastical Institution.[23]

Out of this orientation, also, stemmed the idea that the two swords, by whomever employed, belong finally to the pope. Both of these had been given by God to Peter; the spiritual for his own use and that of his papal successors; the temporal to be delegated to others who would use it in his name. The far-reaching effects of this theory could only be interpreted as casting a grave shadow upon the particular functions and dignities accorded the temporal power. Naturally, this theory was opposed with increasing vigor throughout the medieval period.[24]

The appeal of such a position to the imagination of churchly theorists cannot, however, be overlooked. Since the demands of God's kingdom are committed to the keeping of individuals in this life, how can these dictates be more effectively mediated to his people than through his Church? Can it not be maintained that all temporal powers and privileges are quite ancillary to the more eternal ends of life for which the Church must always stand surety? Surely, such a clear and radical solution to the whole problem left little confusion over the possibilities of one embracing community of mankind. It was not difficult for advocates of this position to show how humanity might be united in all of its social activities under the direct headship of Christ's ministers. Had he not, himself, commissioned these for the prosecution of ultimate ends? [25]

[23] *Ibid.*, pp. 12-13. Used by permission of the publishers.
[24] *Ibid.*, pp. 13-15; cf. Gierke's notes, 22 ff., pp. 113 ff.
[25] *Ibid.*, pp. 15-18.

What seems a more reasonable approach than the foregoing was instituted by advocates of the temporal power. Rarely, if ever, did they push their claims to the extent of demanding theoretical subservience by the spiritual to the temporal. Even William of Ockham would not have gone this far. Marsilius of Padua, likewise, maintained a spiritual primacy for the servants of God that is much more truly medieval than some authorities have recognized. A favorite counterproposition to the proponents of exaggerated ecclesiasticism was that advocating two co-ordinate authorities. According to this view, God himself had given graded portions of responsibility to the spiritual and the temporal powers, respectively. Here the battle was fought on the basis of temporal *imperium* from God and nontemporal *imperium* as granted by the Church. This interpretation sought to guarantee a reasonable division between the prerogatives of each authority. Actually, it went so far as to admit of the Church's "having the sublimer aim"; hence "a higher intrinsic value . . . [and] a loftier external rank." [26]

Nevertheless, the important point to remember is that the protagonists of co-ordinate powers were no less interested in unity than the representatives of sovereignty. They "could see in the spiritual and temporal orders but two sides of the Christian commonwealth." They also sought for a reconciling oneness which should rise above competing powers. Insisting that the social experience of mankind constituted one universal realm, they sometimes pointed to the heavenly head of all mankind as its only necessary sovereign. On occasion, they stressed the desirable effects of priestly and imperial powers operating in mutualizing concord. They were willing to concede that each of these powers might intervene upon occasion in the other's field. Thus, under circumstances of a vacancy within the imperial authority, the pope might have to be called upon for judgment; in cases of necessity the emperor might have to play the guardian and director of the Church's best interest.[27]

Gierke accents a salient fact: whatever viewpoint is taken, its representatives see their plan conducing to a working unity within the whole of society. His own words have a provocative inclination:

Then when each of these two Orders is taken by itself we once more see the medieval Principle of Unity at work and constituting that Order as a single whole.

[26] *Ibid.*, pp. 16-17.
[27] *Ibid.*, pp. 17-18.

From it there arises within the Church the idea of the divinely instituted, visible and external Unity of the Spiritual Realm. Throughout
the whole Middle Age there reigned, almost without condition or qualification, the notion that the Oneness and Universality of the Church
must manifest itself in a unity of law, constitution and supreme government, and also the notion that by rights the whole of Mankind belongs
to the Ecclesiastical Society that is thus constituted. Therefore it is quite
common to see the Church conceived as a "State." That the Principle
of Oneness demands of necessity an external Unity was but very rarely
doubted. Very slowly was ground won by a reaction which protested, not
merely against the increasing worldliness of the Church, but also against
the whole idea of a "Spiritual State." It was reserved for Wyclif and Hus
decisively to demand that the Church should be conceived in a more
inward, less external, fashion, as the Community of the Predestinated,
and so to prepare the way for that German Reformation which at this
very point broke thoroughly away from the medieval Idea of Unity.[28]

Whatever the comprising forms governmentally employed, medieval society as a whole was ecclesiastically conceived. The ends of life,
to which temporal and spiritual powers on earth were alike directed,
demanded the Church as an agency of the eternal in the temporal.
Representatives of the co-ordinate theory, no less than those of ecclesiastical sovereignty, would surely grant to the Church the special
prestige involved in its unique service to men. This service to men
would be interpreted, in turn, as conveying powers and destinies more
than natural. It could never be forgotten that if men were to live a
natural life and be made ready for a supernatural destiny, they must
inhere in God's Church. No arguments that any representatives of
temporal primacy might advance could touch this spiritual saliency
of the Church.[29]

In the discussion of these materials, more questions have been
raised than can easily be answered. Some of them must wait a long
time, still, for any definitive answers. Carlyle and Carlyle feel that the
normal doctrine of the Canon law is that "the two authorities, the
ecclesiastical and the civil, were equally and separately derived from
Christ, and that strictly each was supreme in its own sphere." This
was certainly the contention of Dante and others like him. The
Middle Ages as a whole held to the doctrine of unity within society,

---

[28] *Ibid.,* pp. 18-19. Used by permission of the publishers.
[29] *Ibid.,* pp. 19-21, *et passim;* consult Gierke's valuable notes, especially pp. 101-28.

however much of overlapping and friction this might entail—theoretically and practically.[30]

Lodged within this problem is the pertinent contention for the *Corpus Christianum*. Bohatec, Visser 't Hooft, and others inquire anew how the two contending powers ever hoped to bring about a comprising and reconciling unity in duality. Bohatec reminds us that the term *Corpus Christianum* was not current in medieval parlance. He insists, however, that the idea was.[31] He, like Carlyle, Troeltsch, and numerous others, goes back to the famous statement of Stephen of Tournai. This summation from Stephen may be sufficiently gauged in free translation.

> In the one commonwealth and under the one king there are two peoples, two modes of life, two authorities, and a twofold organisation of jurisdiction. The commonwealth is the Church, the king is Christ, the two peoples are the two orders in the Church, that is, the clergy and the laity, the two modes of life are the spiritual and the carnal; the two authorities are the priesthood and the kingship, the twofold organisation is the divine law and the human. Give to each its due and all things will be brought into agreement.[32]

Carlyle has reason to point out how little this high-sounding Gelasian theory solved the real problems that turmoiled the twelfth and thirteenth centuries. Just the same, this must not blind us to the fact that Stephen speaks a sentiment that is stubbornly held, however frequent may be the infractions of its practice. In a real sense, the terrestrial church does become a binding link between the heavenly and earthly world. Clergy and laity play their respective and respected parts. The spiritual and the temporal are thought of as functioning separately, yet within a comprising whole. Two powers, the sacerdotal and the regal, have their own responsible opportunities. A double jurisdiction of order is divided into the divine and human. All in all, Stephen is not merely euphemistic in saying that when each gets its due, real harmony will reign.[33]

That such a view is by no means peculiar to Stephen, the excellent

---

[30] R. W. and A. J. Carlyle, *A History of Medieval Political Theory in the West* (London, 1903), II, 254.

[31] Bohatec, *op. cit.*, p. 583.

[32] *Summa des Stephanus Tornacensis über des Decretum Gratiani*, ed. J. F. von Schulte (Giessen, 1891), "Introduction," pp. 1-2; translation of Carlyle and Carlyle, *A History of Medieval Political Theory in the West*, II, 198. Used by permission of the publishers, W. Blackwood & Sons, Ltd.

[33] *Loc. cit.*

notes of Gierke and Bohatec testify. On such a wide front as that represented by Thomas Aquinas, Augustus Triumphus, Alvarius Pelagius, and Jean Gerson, the integrity of the Christian common-wealth is maintained. The Church regularly appears as a *regnum*, a *communitas*, a *respublica*. Whether in Hincmar of Rheims, John of Salisbury, or Nicholas of Cusa, the unity of Christendom is explored and praised.[34]

Selected references will show how thoroughly medieval churchmen subscribed to a theory of ultimate Christian responsibility for temporal as well as spiritual rulers in the *Corpus Christianum*. Hincmar of Rheims (d. 882) gathers up much of the Gelasian and Augustinian idealism as well as the later thought of Christian political theorists.[35] Approached at the end of a varied career to recapitulate the political wisdom with which a young king might be guided, he reviewed the maxims of good government. Looking to the restoration of peace and honor for Church and realm, the youthful king might by such government gain the eternal kingdom.[36]

Administrators have their own responsibility before God's bar of final judgment for the governing of their realms. The Gelasian theory of powers properly divided among temporal and spiritual authorities is developed in the light of the immediate situation to which Hincmar addresses himself. Kings and princes are to be careful lest they violate the divine laws. Contravention of ecclesiastical rules offends the King of kings. Rather is it the province of a good ruler to defend the Church's integrity and to assist her in serving the faithful. In governing those committed to his care the effective king or prince elicits from them in turn the responses of fear, obedience, and love. For him who fails in such responsible rulership of his people, there is laid up implacable judgment in the other world.[37]

John of Salisbury in his *Policraticus* (1159) gives an expanded treatment to the commonwealth as a body "endowed with life by

---

[34] For the exhaustive notes of Gierke, see pp. 122 ff.; cf. Bohatec, *op. cit.*, pp. 581-96.

[35] Related to the work of Hincmar is that of Agobard (760-840), on whom see Mgr. Bressolles, *Saint Agobard de Lyon* (Paris, 1949). Note, also, J. Reviron's *Les idées politico-religieuses d'un évêque du IXᵉ siècle: Jonas d'Orléans et son "De institutione regia,"* *étude et texte critique* (Paris, 1930). See, by index, the references, in the latter, to the influences of St. Augustine of Hippo and Pope Gelasius, particularly *De inst. regia*, cap. 1, Reviron, *Les Idées*, p. 135. Jonas was born *ca.* 780 and died *ca.* 842 or 843. For Hincmar's *De Regis personae et regio ministerio*, see MPL 125:833. Consult Hincmar's *De ordine Palatii, Texte Lat.*, translated and annotated by M. Prou (Paris, 1884), also in MPL 125:993-1008.

[36] *De ord. Pal.*, I, ed., Prou, Lat. p. 4, Fr. p. 5.

[37] *Ibid.*, IX, X; Prou, *op. cit.*, pp. 24-25 ff., 28-29 ff.

the benefit of divine favor." [38] At its head is the prince; the priesthood functions as its soul. Senate, judges, governors, officials, soldiers, financial assistants, and farmers serve for their part as heart, eyes, ears, and tongue, hands, sides, viscera, and feet. With an ingenuity and fulsomeness gratefully levied upon by the medieval world, John of Salisbury pressed the organic analogy to limits almost unsurpassed to the time of Cusa. His conception of social solidarity and Christian mutuality makes of the commonwealth a proving ground for all the consolidating virtues of a healthful body politic. With all of its static gradations and governmental rigidities, his society is, nonetheless, characterized by a marked fellow feeling.[39]

The priesthood, serving the Church which is the agent of the eternal in the temporal, has a priority that reaches its apogee in the papal primacy. Important as his function is, and religious as his office becomes in helping to further the divine laws, the prince must, nevertheless, admit the superiority of the priestly power. This primacy of the spiritual, however, does not justify arbitrary expressions of its prerogatives any more than it derogates the highly esteemed service that the king may render in supporting the righteous ministry of the priesthood. The premium placed upon the vitalizing functions of the commonwealth's soul does not obscure John's censures of unworthy servants in the ecclesiastical community. The priestly functionaries cannot be judged by temporal authorities, who are clearly inferior in dignity. But Salisbury, like Bernard of Clairvaux, abominates a corrupt hierarchy, however temporizing he may be in stigmatizing it openly.[40]

The temporal ruler, moreover, though inferior to the spiritual power, has a definitely religious character and accountability. The higher law of the commonwealth is that of God, and "every office existing under and concerned with the execution of the sacred laws is really a religious office." Ministering in a sense to "the priestly power for the purpose of enforcing the divine law by physical sanctions" and receiving "his sword from the Church," the prince is not humiliated but rather ennobled thereby. He, too, is a trusted

---

[38] For the critical text see C. C. J. Webb (2 Vols., Oxford, 1909), on which is based J. Dickinson's *The Statesman's Book of John of Salisbury, being the Fourth, Fifth and Sixth Books, and selections from the Seventh and Eighth Books, of the Policraticus* (New York, 1927). Cf. C. C. J. Webb, *John of Salisbury* (London, 1932); Carlyle and Carlyle, *Mediaeval Political Theory*, III, 136-46; McNeill, *Christian Hope*, pp. 51-53; McIlwain, *Growth*, pp. 228-30; Dickinson, *op. cit.*, pp. xxi, 64; Pol. V, 2.

[39] Pol. V, 2; IV, 1; VII, 20.

[40] Pol. VII, 21, VIII, 17, etc.

servant of that commonwealth which fosters the divine rules and precepts.[41]

Furthermore, in exercising concentrated power of a directional and temporal sort the prince answers to God for his efficiency in evoking the best qualities of his people.

Though he is "the minister of the common interest" and, to some degree at least, "the servant of the people," the prince is, characteristically, something far more. He is the "image of God on earth." Empowered by God, however much he may be subordinated to the priesthood, he "is placed at the apex of the commonwealth by the divine governance." [42]

Kings, therefore, are subject only to God and to the priesthood by whom God is represented on earth. To God they must render an account for their ministry. As one responsible *for* the commonwealth but not *to* it, the prince rules as "the Lord's servant, but he performs his service by faithfully serving his fellow-servants, namely his subjects." With his title derived from God, and his office a religious one, the king must exalt the Church, extend religious worship, protect ecclesiastical prerogatives and, generally, bring happiness to the society committed unto him.

"Patriarchal-ecclesiastical" as this conception of monarchy was, and devoid of the larger vitality of a free society though it might be, it did confer upon sacerdotal and princely rule, co-ordinated within the same commonwealth, the dignity of a like, eternal accounting. The Church as servant of the eternal kingdom in temporal society utilized both priests and princes as its loyal ministers. In serving the Christian commonwealth they acknowledged the indispensable graces of the ecclesiastical community that lived among men.

As already stated, one of the most vexing problems of the medieval period was the exact relationship sustained by the spiritual to the temporal. The lengthy discussion joined by Gierke, Troeltsch, Carlyle, and other modern scholars hinges upon this aggravating issue. There is general agreement upon one point at least: The medieval world stubbornly refused to admit of any real break between the temporal and the spiritual authorities. These were frequently regarded, theoretically at least, as having co-ordinate association, the one with the other. Under given circumstances and in terms of specific personalities, a more controversial position was often taken. Thus a representative of an extremely temporalized conception of

[41] Pol. IV, 3; Dickinson, *op. cit.*, pp. lviii-lix.
[42] Pol. V, 4, IV, 1, 2, V, 6; Dickinson, *op. cit.*, pp. xxiii, xliii-xliv, 7, 83.

the spiritual power might insist that God gave all power, material and spiritual, to the latter, and permitted the more secular employments to be deputized to other than spiritual rulers. Rarely, indeed, did an emperor insist that his function was definitive in the sense that the sacerdotal powers were final. In general, both spiritual and temporal rulers admitted some degree of immediacy involved in the responsibility of each major power to God himself.[43]

As the Middle Ages continued this discussion in relation to prevailing practice, a fairly acceptable theory was possible to all alike. This held that king and prince were answerable to God for the way in which they ruled their subjects on earth; and that popes, bishops, and the clergy, generally, dispensed far more ultimate benefits in terms of the eternal destiny of mankind. An emperor ought to direct his people in a material fashion that would be most conducive to their preparation for an eternal world. The clergy would have little or no responsibility for temporal rule as such; but they would shoulder the heroic burden of leading men in the present to an eternal homeland in the future. Ideally speaking, priests ought to anticipate no circumstance calling for their intervention in temporal rulership. In all cases where some spiritual-temporal conflict was involved, their interference must be solely in terms of defending spiritual prerogatives.

What this meant in practice was simply this: The priest claimed a higher dignity as well as a more awful responsibility in his leadership of human souls than did the secular ruler in his prosecution of effective kingship within the commonwealth. After all, a king could only be expected, principally, to dispose the affairs of men for the good of those living in earthly society. No conflict need be expected here. In reality conflicts often did occur; but even in the midst of these, both sides continued to present the prior claims of the commonly accepted theory.

In spite of the foregoing, it is not quite accurate to leave the impression that the king had any lesser responsibility than that of a priest. His obligations were less and clerical prerogatives were greater only in terms of the peculiar dignity and specialized character of their respective offices. Within the limits of his office, the secular ruler

---

[43] Pol. V, 2, IV, 10-12; VI, 1, IV, 7; Dickinson, *op. cit.*, pp. xliii-xliv, li; Gierke, *op. cit.*, pp. 9-21; Troeltsch, *Social Teaching*, I, 201-7, 223-37, 280-328; McIlwain, *Growth*, pp. 205 ff.; C. E. Osborne, *Christian Ideas in Political History* (London, 1929), p. 54.

was as responsible to God to lead men in the direction of their ultimate good as was the bishop-priest.[44]

By the thirteenth century an increasingly welcome tenet of political theory was being presented. Thomas Aquinas, in his work *The
Governance of Princes,* gives it clarity and cogency.[45] The significant
fact emerging here is that a king had far more answerability to the
Lord for the manner in which he ruled his subjects on earth than
might be expected from a cursory investigation. What we often forget, though the medieval world seldom did, is that the life in the material world here below is only an interlude in the pilgrimage to the
beatitude of the everlasting society in heaven. Since men have as their
supreme good this heavenly association, they must respond through
their political life on earth to that which reaches beyond the polity
of the present. Because happiness, as Thomas conceives of it within
the framework of Aristotelian thought, has reference to this eternal
beatitude, all human existence must have regard to an ultimate,
theological end. Thomas says:

> Since the end of the life which we live well at present is heavenly hap-
> piness, it pertains to the duty of the king to make the life of the multitude
> good, in accordance with what is suitable for that heavenly happiness.
> . . . The way to true happiness and the obstructions on the way are re-
> vealed in the divine law, the teaching of which is the duty of priests. . . .
> The king, having learned the divine law, ought to study especially how the
> multitude subject to him may live well.[46]

Nothing could describe more precisely than this the theological
import borne within the politics of the Middle Ages. Hard as it is for
the modern man to conceive, the medieval Christian felt that the
king himself must rule under the tutelage of the Lord. This meant a
necessarily close relationship between the functions of spiritual and
temporal rulers. It meant, further, that the king should cheerfully
grant a precedence of dignity to the princes of the Church. Still
further, this necessitated a willingness on the king's part to rule

[44] Carlyle and Carlyle, *op. cit.,* V, 348; cf. Th. Aquinas, *De reg. prin.,* I, 15; N. Cusa,
De Concord. Cath., III, 7; Gandillac, *Oeuvres,* pp. 61-62.

[45] *De regimine principum ad regem Cypri* (Opusculum XVI) is XVI, 225 ff. in the
Parma ed. (reimpressed, New York, 1950). A usable translation is that of G. B. Phelan,
On the Governance of Rulers (London, 1935), revised by I. Th. Eschmann as *On Kingship, To the King of Cyprus* (Toronto, 1949). There is a translation of Bk. I, Chap. 15,
in F. W. Coker, *Readings in Political Philosophy* (New York, 1938), pp. 219-21.

[46] *De reg. prin.,* I, 15; Coker, *Readings in Political Philosophy,* p. 220. Rev. ed.,
copyright 1938. Used by permission of the publishers, The Macmillan Co. Cf. Phelan-
Eschmann, *On Kingship,* pp. 63 ff.

his temporal sphere in a manner that would be thoroughly consonant with the Church's ministry to mankind. It was felt, on general principles at least, that no secular prince need resent the greater honor accorded those servants of God within the hierarchy who dealt at firsthand with the ultimate destiny of faithful Christians. No more could the clergy fail to appreciate a good king's serving the dictates of heaven by way of willing obedience to the Church on earth when he helped his people to live devotedly within the body politic.[47]

This whole conception throws further light upon the meaning of the *Corpus Christianum*. The Middle Ages held insufferable any suggestion that the life of the spiritual and the welfare of the temporal could for one moment be separated from each other. Those services performed by the temporal and those carried forward by the spiritual had, for the medieval man, a relationship so close as to be almost an identity. Far from subscribing to a separation of temporal and spiritual powers, the medieval Christian looked upon their operation in everyday life as being one undivided unity served by two mutually supporting dedications. Thus Christian society was one. Not only was there a belief in the *Corpus Christi;* there was also a passionate devotion to the *Corpus Christianum*. This was the actualization on earth, in terms of Christian ideals and governmentally fostered practices, of the one Christian life.

It may seem strange, today, to envisage a king studying theology in order to be better prepared for the rule of his subjects. Something closely akin to this was actually expected, in theory at least, of medieval sovereigns. Thomas believes that the king ought to learn and study the divine law if the multitude subject to him is to live well. The good life here portrayed certainly looks to the life eternal. If that eternal existence is to be made secure, the king must play his part. He must think, not only in terms of isolated individuals, but also of the whole group under his care. He must strive to bring about conditions of peace and justice that will serve the common welfare on earth by way of preparation for the common blessedness in heaven. His concern throughout must be to serve as an example, himself, of virtuous responsiveness to the laws of God as they operate among

---

[47] Cf. Carlyle and Carlyle, *op. cit.,* V, 348-54, in relation to *De reg. prin.,* I, 14, 15, and other Thomistic sources. Cf. McNeill, *Christian Hope,* pp. 65-68; J. J. Baumann, *Die Staatslehre des hl. Thomas von Aquino* (Leipzig, 1873) , and O. Schilling, *Die Staats -und Soziallehre des hl. Thomas von Aquin* (Munich, 1930) ; also, W. Muller, "*Der Staat in seinen Beziehungen* zur sittlichen Ordnung bei Thomas von Aquin," in *Beiträge zur Geschichte der Philosophie des Mittelalters* . . . ed., C. Baeumker, XIX, 1 (Münster, 1916) , 45 ff.

men. In so doing he will find indispensable a close relation to the priesthood and the hierarchy upon whom devolve the supreme responsibility for fostering, in this world, the eternal lives of the faithful. This constitutes, for Thomas, the introduction on a fuller scale to a crucial question: How may priest and king discharge, together, their separate and distinctive responsibilities to the eternal society?

"Just as the founding of a city or a kingdom may suitably be learned from the way the world was created, so too the way to govern may be learned from the governing of the world." With this direction of thought, Thomas reintroduces the whole matter of man's present life in a political order as deriving its objective from an eternal society.[48]

Aquinas is, of course, fully convinced of the dignity which belongs to kings and their functions. He believes that one who commendably discharges the duties of his office shall merit, not only appreciation by his people, but a due reward from God himself. He may justifiably expect to "receive a high degree of heavenly happiness." The argument swings about the contention that merit is to receive a recompense befitting the excellence involved. Since a king assumes responsibility for others in addition to himself, the apt fulfillment of this obligation brings him added consideration on the part of the divine rewarder. Ruling oneself is less difficult than ruling a household. Even more praiseworthy than this is the worthy administration of a state or a kingdom.

In things which involve the welfare of the multitude, good government on the part of a virtuous administrator becomes a primary concern. Certainly one who does good in terms of a whole group should receive a reward that surpasses recognition accorded a private person. It is no easy thing for a king to bring peace to those in discord, to see that justice is done, to restrain violence, and, in short, to make the whole state resemble on this earth the goodness of God's own administration in the universe. Thomas believes that "the greatness of kingly virtue also appears in this that he bears a special likeness to God, since he acts in his kingdom as God in the world." [49] The true quality of a king is manifested in the way in which he shows his authority. One who has the use of power is not always virtuous in the application of it. Kings have special temptations to the abuse of

---

[48] *De reg. prin.*, I, 15, 14; Phelan tr., p. 95. Used by permission of the publishers, Pontifical Institute of Mediaeval Studies.

[49] *Ibid.*, I, 9; Phelan tr., pp. 73-77, especially, 73, 75; cf. I, 14, Phelan tr., pp. 95-100; Phelan-Eschmann, pp. 41, 58 ff.

their rights. They have to struggle against almost insuperable difficulties. It is all the more necessary, therefore, that they be properly
rewarded for their good deeds. Thomas says that it is not only reasonable to accord appreciation to kingship but it is also in keeping with
divine authority. He quotes Zechariah 12:8 to the effect that

in that day of blessedness, wherein God will be the protector of the inhabitants of Jerusalem, that is in the vision of eternal peace, the houses
of others will be as the house of David, to wit, because all will then be
kings and reign with Christ as the members with their heads: but the
house of David will be as the house of God, because just as he carried out
the work of God among the people by ruling faithfully, so in his reward,
he will be closer to God and will cling to Him.[50]

This reinforces other sentiments of Thomas which give a special
place of prominence in the Lord's plan to the work entrusted to
kings. They definitely perform a service which follows the divine will
as it is to be done in heaven. The part played by kings and emperors
in this world has an ultimate as well as an immediate reference to the
leadership of men. And the reward conditioned upon good rulership
is an eternal one. This should be noted in relationhip to Thomas' insistence on the spiritual priority of priests. The conclusion is just
what one should expect: a prince who properly discharges his duties
to the civic commonwealth is also playing his part in the program advanced by God's Church. In and through that Church, and under
the direction of priestly dignitaries, the king also serves the eternal
kingdom by being true to the responsibilities of his earthly sovereignty.[51]

Thomas frankly accords priority of a spiritual kind to those whose
main business is spiritual overlordship. Without in any sense com-
promising the worth of temporal rulership, he demands primary appreciation for the priestly function. He is well aware that the priesthood, itself, has a kind of kingship inherent in it. Thomas' argument
is well worth noting. Here, too, Thomas is under the spell of final
ends. In ruling a kingdom as in all other things, finalities are to be
kept in mind. Whether a ship is to be brought to port, or a man's life
is to be preserved in health, certain activities are to be expected in
line with the ends to be served. In the case of all human beings—in
all cases with the exception of God—the major ends lie outside those

[50] *De reg. prin.*, I, 9; Phelan tr., 76-77. Used by permission of the publishers. Cf.
Phelan-Eschmann, pp. 42-43.
[51] *De reg. prin.*, I, 14, 9; Carlyle and Carlyle, *op. cit.*, V, 348-54; cf. Phelan, pp. 99-100.

who move toward them. So long as mortal life endures, every human being looks toward a good that is over and beyond himself. It is final beatitude, therefore, that man longs for. The blood of Christ was shed so that man might be brought with the aid of the spirit to the harbor of eternal salvation; "and this care is provided for the faithful by the ministers of the Church of Christ." This is simply to reiterate that the Church is most completely and effectively the agency of eternal destiny within the area of human life.

As regards the purpose of society as a whole, the chief considerations are similar to those concerning the goal of one man.

If, therefore, the end of man were some good that exists in himself, then the ultimate end of the multitude to be governed would likewise be for the multitude to acquire such good and persevere in its possession. If such an ultimate end either of an individual man or a multitude, were a corporeal one, namely, life and health of body, to govern would then be a physician's charge. If that ultimate end were an abundance of wealth, then some financier would be king of the multitude. If the good of the knowledge of the truth were of such a kind that the multitude might attain to it, the king would have the duty of teacher. But it is clear, that the end of any multitude gathered together, is to live virtuously. For, men form groups for the purpose of living well together, a thing which the individual man living alone could not attain. . . . Therefore a virtuous life is the end for which men form groups.[52]

The corporate end for which people as a body live is not virtue in itself but the attainment through virtue to that final beatitude, the acquisition of which requires a more than human aid. Not only each human being individually, but human society as a whole, needs that instrumentality of the divine power which will bring one and all to fraternity in the heavenly realm. But it is fitting that the power which is divine should have its own particular servants through whom it brings man to the kingdom. Those who have the task of leading individuals and society to the ultimate end have a place in divine government not merely human. "Consequently, government of this kind pertains to that king who is not only a man, but also God, namely, to our Lord Jesus Christ, Who by making men sons of God, brought them to the glory of Heaven." It is from Christ himself that a royal priesthood is derived. All the faithful, since they are his members,

---

[52] *De reg. prin.*, I, 14; Phelan tr., pp. 96-97. Used by permission of the publishers.

therefore become both kings and priests.[53] As Carlyle paraphrases it:

The ministry (ministerium) of this kingdom, in order that spiritual things may be distinguished from earthly, belongs not to the earthly kings, but to the priests, and above all to the chief priest, the successor of Peter, the vicar of Christ, the Roman pontiff, to whom all kings of the Christian people ought to be subject, as to the Lord Jesus Christ Himself, for those who have the charge of the lower ends must be subject to him who has the charge of the final end, and must be directed by his authority.[54]

Thomas' somewhat fuller statement reads:

Consequently, in order that spiritual things might be distinguished from earthly things, the ministry of this kingdom has been entrusted not to earthly kings, but to priests, and in the highest degree to the chief priest, the successor of St. Peter, the Vicar of Christ, the Roman Pontiff, to whom all the kings of Christian peoples are to be subject as to our Lord Jesus Christ Himself. For those to whom pertains the care of intermediate ends should be subject to him to whom pertains the care of the ultimate end, and be directed by his rule. Because the priesthood of the gentiles, and the whole worship of their Gods existed merely for the acquisition of temporal goods (which were all ordained to the common good of the multitude, whose care devolved upon a king), the priests of the gentiles were very properly subject to the kings. Similarly, because in the old law earthly goods were promised to a religious people (not indeed by demons but by the true God), the priests of the old law, we read, were also subject to the kings. But in the new law there is a higher priesthood by which men are guided to heavenly goods. Consequently in the law of Christ, kings must be subject to priests.[55]

Here as elsewhere, Thomas probably intends no invidious comparison between priesthood and kingship. He is merely saying, quite disarmingly, that there is a kingship above that of this world which inheres in the priestly office of the Church. Just as the main function of the temporal order is "to lead men to that heavenly blessedness which is the true end of life," so there is a realm of authority which conduces most directly and most completely to that end. This spiritual power, without mutilating the rights of the temporal, enjoys

[53] *Ibid.*, I, 14; Phelan tr., pp. 98-99.
[54] Carlyle and Carlyle, *A History of Medieval Political Theory in the West*, V, 348, on *De reg. prin.*, I, 14. Used by permission of the publishers, W. Blackwood & Sons, Ltd.
[55] Phelan tr., pp. 99 ff.; I, 14. Used by permission of the publishers.

certain privileges and is answerable for certain duties beyond those which any king may boast or be held accountable for.[56]

Carlyle reminds us that in the *Summa Theologica* the following attitude is characteristic:

> The secular power is subject to the spiritual, even as the body is subject to the soul. Consequently the judgment is not usurped if the spiritual authority interferes in those temporal matters that are subject to the spiritual authority or which have been committed to the spiritual by the temporal authority.[57]

Carlyle is also quick to declare that Thomas did not regard the pope as holding a strictly temporal power. Rather, the spiritual power which was headed in the pope directed the temporal authority to the consummate ends of life. In the last sections of his book on government, Thomas actually stated the limitations of the spiritual power and the bounds of the temporal authority. Of course, he left a place for the Hildebrandine principle involving the excommunication and deposition of princes. By this he probably did not mean to imply that "the spiritual authority, in principle, also holds all temporal authority." It is true that in a few isolated passages, which Carlyle discusses, some possible implications of this kind might be derived. Carlyle's deductions, however, are that normally

the Pope had an indirect rather than a direct authority in temporal matters. It was the spiritual authority of the Pope which should direct men to their final end—that is, the knowledge and enjoyment of God; the temporal power was subject to him in the sense that it should obey the Pope in all that concerned the ordering of human life to this end.[58]

Even in stating the higher authority and dignity of the spiritual power, as it resided in the priesthood, Thomas was permitting a very large element of significance to the temporal. Whatever his immediate function, the king was following the superior direction of the priest in facilitating humanity's pilgrimage to the eternal commonwealth.

[56] *De reg. prin.*, I, 14, 9; Phelan tr., pp. 95-100, 73-77; Carlyle and Carlyle, *op, cit.*, V, 348 ff., on the entire context.

[57] II a II ae. Q. 60 Art. 6, rep. obj. 3; tr. of the Dominican Fathers, p. 156; Carlyle and Carlyle, *op. cit.*, V, 349.

[58] Carlyle and Carlyle, *op. cit.*, V, 348-54, especially, 351-54, for quotation and discussion of the bearing of Thomas' Commentary on Peter Lombard, *In Lib. II, Sent.* Dist. 44, q. 2, Art. 3, etc. Used by permission of the publishers, W. Blackwood & Sons, Ltd.

A number of pertinent insights may be derived from Professor McNeill's analysis of Thomistic political thought.[59] He sees here a theory which regards the State, not as an end in itself, but as an instrument toward making the good man. Now man is a social animal. But he is much more; he is also an immortal being. And, in bringing to him eternal salvation, the Church has the primary place; with the Church, however, the State can co-operate.

Higher, even, than the indispensable State is the realm of the Church and its priesthood. In keeping with its more elevated duties and prerogatives the Church stands above the temporal powers. Thus the sphere of the temporal ruler is subordinate and instrumental to that of the priest. McNeill says: "Hence the ruler is in last analysis subjected to the priesthood, and his kingdom is the province of the universal monarchy of the pope." Again, "For [Thomas] the existing papacy, then so superior in fact to all rivals, stands as a universal *'societas perfecta,'* the dominant factor in the total Christian commonwealth." [60]

True as this may be, it is proper to observe that in such a perfect society the king, as well as the pope, helps the faithful on the way to an even more glorious commonwealth. For, according to Thomas, the whole human race may be considered under the similitude of a body that is called mystical; the head of which is Christ himself, both as regards the soul and as regards the body. "The Christian religion points the way, not only to the happiness of the soul, but also to that of the body." Universal in the scope of its interest and its surveillance, its rules govern the total life of man. With the power of the secular subordinated to the spiritual as body to soul, and with human rule derived from that of the divine which it ought to imitate, the civil power may yet serve ultimate ends in full dedication of present energies.[61]

Dante (d. 1321), with all of his dependence upon the theological postulates of Thomas Aquinas, stressed, as the great Dominican would hardly do, the immediate authority which the prince has from God. The author of the *De Monarchia* defends the necessity of two guides for human life with its twofold end. The Supreme Pontiff is needed "to lead mankind to eternal life, according to the things revealed to us; and the other is the Emperor, to guide mankind to hap-

[59] *Christian Hope for World Society*, pp. 65-68.
[60] *Ibid.*, pp. 68, 65.
[61] *S. Theol.*, III, Q. 8., Art. 1-2; IIa IIae Q. 60, Art. 6; IIa IIae Q. 10, Art. 11; cf. Troeltsch, *op. cit.*, I, 283-84 and notes, 128-29, on pp. 412-14.

piness in this world, in accordance with the teaching of philosophy."
The temporal ruler answers to the universal law of God as it is found
in Unity by proving Monarchy "necessary for the highest welfare of
the human race." [62]

Yet, the Emperor, in making possible a degree of happiness for men
in this life, is by no means divorced from either the immediate or the
ultimate plans of God. It is important that "in this little plot of earth
belonging to mortal men, life may pass in freedom and with peace."
Moreover, the ruler who conduces to this end is not simply fostering
an indifferent boon to mankind; he is, as surely as the pope, though in
different manner, serving the final purposes of God for his people.

And since the order of this world follows the order of the heavens, as
they run their course, it is necessary, to the end that the learning which
brings liberty and peace may be duly applied by this guardian of the
world in fitting season and place, that this power should be dispensed by
Him who is ever present to behold the whole order of the heavens. And
this is He who alone has preordained this, that by it in His providence
He might bind all things together, each in their own order.[63]

To this divinely disposing will for all men, all are answerable for
their share in the ordering of human life. "God alone elects, God
alone confirms," though there are those who forget this in arrogating
God's prerogatives to themselves. Actually, the authority given temporal monarchy for its support of the divine purpose is as immediately derived from God as is the spiritual. This "authority of temporal
Monarchy comes down, with no intermediate will, from the fountain
of universal authority; and this fountain, one in its unity, flows
through many channels out of the abundance of the goodness of
God." [64]

This, Dante hastens to remind his readers, is not to overlook a manifest uniqueness in the Pontiff's commission or "to deny that in certain matters the Roman Prince is subject to the Roman Pontiff."

[62] For a text of the *De Monarchia* see E. Moore, *Tutte le opere di Dante Alighieri*
(Oxford, 1904), pp. 341-76. See *De Mon*. III, 1, 3, 16, and I, 15, in the translations of
A. Henry, *The De Monarchia of Dante Alighieri* (New York, 1904), portions in Coker,
Readings, pp. 226-41, and H. W. Schneider, *On World-Government or De Monarchia by
Dante Alighieri* (New York, 1950). Passage quoted from *De Mon.*, III, 16, Coker, *Read-
ings*, p. 240.

[63] *De Mon.*, II, 16; Coker, *Readings in Political Philosophy* (rev. ed., copyright 1938),
pp. 240-41. Used by permission of the publishers, The Macmillan Co.

[64] *Ibid.*, III, 16; Coker, *Readings*, p. 241. Used by permission of the publishers.

True, such happiness as is subject to mortal limitations must be directed yet further to the bliss that is beyond death.

Let, therefore, Caesar be reverent to Peter, as the first-born son should be reverent to his father, that he may be illuminated with the light of his father's grace, and so may be stronger to lighten the world over which he has been placed by Him alone, who is the ruler of all things spiritual as well as temporal.[65]

The end of the kingdom, temporal as it may be, lends itself to that greater end which is "finally an ultimate one for which the Everlasting God, by His art which is nature, brings into being the whole human race." Serving to facilitate that peace by which men in pilgrimage move toward their eternal goal, the monarch or emperor demonstrates his indispensability to the welfare of human society and his usefulness, under God, to the unfolding plan of the Divine. Himself the human principle of social unity and the guardian of human mutuality, the earthly ruler does his part as he was specifically called of God to do it. The basis of his authority is divine because he has a share in the divine plan for the world. Dante proposes no conflict with the spiritual power, to whom he readily concedes an even more august privilege than that of the emperor. He asks only that the temporal governor be dignified with a recognition of his call to service by the dispenser of both civil and ecclesiastical powers.[66]

Marsilius of Padua, author with John of Jandun of the famed *Defensor Pacis*, is generally regarded as having disparaged almost to the point of annihilation the primacy of the spiritual in temporal society.[67] His reinterpretation of the State calls for the "People," or its "weightier part," to be the legislator. His definition of the Church is in terms of the whole "body of the faithful who call upon the name of Christ." All faithful followers of the Lord, whether priests or not, are properly called ecclesiastical men. They, rather than the hierarchy,

[65] *Loc. cit.* Used by permission of the publishers.

[66] *Ibid.*, I, 3, III, 16, I, 3, 4, 5; I, 3 quoted from Coker, *Readings*, p. 228.

[67] For the critical text consult O. W. Previté-Orton, ed., *The defensor pacis of Marsilius of Padua* (Cambridge, 1928). Cf. *Marsilius von Padua Defensor Pacis für übungszwecke bearbeitet von Richard Scholz* (Leipzig, 1914). An admirable, if now obsolete, collection of old texts is M. Goldast, *Monarchia sancti romani imperii: sive tractatus de iurisdictione imperiali seu regia, et pontificia*, 3 Vols. (Frankfurt u. Hanover, 1611-14) —including Marsilius, Ockham, and others. Useful studies are Gewirth, *Marsilius of Padua, the Defender of Peace* (New York, 1951), Vol. I; E. Emerton, *The Defensor Pacis of Marsiglio of Padua, a Critical Study* (Cambridge, Mass., 1920), and G. Lagarde, *La naissance de l'esprit laique au déclin du moyen âge: II Marsile de Padue* (Wien, 1934).

are the churchmen, properly speaking. This has seemed to many a clear example of Erastianism born out of due season. Marsilius' restriction of papal claims and priestly prerogatives, as well as his invoking the Bible on the one hand and conciliar representatives of the legislator on the other, to curtail ecclesiastical pretensions, has strengthened such impressions.[68]

Early in his work, he apparently disavows any primary interest in eternal life as a motivation for civil justice. But almost immediately thereafter he declares the need within the political world itself for something more than the immediately practical concerns of existence.

There is something else which those who live together civilly need: it relates to the affairs of the future life promised to mankind through supernatural revelation from God, though it is useful also for the affairs of the present life; we mean the worship and honor of God, and the giving of thanks to Him for the benefits received in this world, as well as for those to be received in the future world. For instructing and guiding men in these things the state must provide teachers.[69]

Like other medieval theorists, therefore, Marsilius finds in a properly ordered, harmonious state the subdivisions of function that will conduce both to good earthly life and to the happiness beyond. With the legislator as the "whole body of citizens or its weightier part," and the executive power "governing by virtue of the authority conferred upon it by the legislator," a signal alteration in the political scene is envisaged. Yet the common good of the citizens is placed in a paramount position, and the eternal needs of man still call for spiritual and temporal services in collaboration.[70]

William of Ockham (d. 1394), like Marsilius of Padua and John of Jandun, proclaimed "the sovereignty of the people as the source of all political power." [71] In his work *Imperial and Pontifical Power* he

[68] Cf. Emerton, *op, cit.,* pp. 72 ff.; Dictio I, cap. 12, Pars 3. See his famous conclusions in C. Mirbt, *Quellen zur Geschichte des Papsttums und des römischen Katholizismus* (4th ed., Tübingen, 1925), translated in O. J. Thatcher and E. H. McNeal, *A Source Book of Mediaeval History* (New York, 1905), pp. 317 ff.; cf. Coker, *Readings,* pp. 246 ff.

[69] *Def. Pacis,* I, 4; quoted from Coker, *Readings,* p. 248. Used by permission of the publishers.

[70] *Ibid.,* I, 12, 15; Coker, *Readings,* pp. 250, 253.

[71] *Ockham, Studies and Selections* by S. C. Tornay (Lasalle, Illinois, 1938), p. 196. The text used by Tornay is *De Imperatorum et Pontificum Potestate,* ed. K. C. Brampton (6th ed., Oxford, 1927). For the selected texts and translations, particularly of the *Dialogus,* see G. J. Jordan, *The Inner History of The Great Schism of the West: A Problem in Church Unity* (London, 1930), based largely on Goldast's *Monarchia.*

declared his trust in Holy Writ as over against the consensus of mankind so often in error. He did not accede to the steadily expanding claims of the spiritual lords for an unlimited pontifical power. Christ's appointment of Peter as "head and sovereign of all the faithful" involved "no plenitude of power in temporal matters." Even in spiritual matters the pope does not have complete fullness of power, "because, then, the law of the Gospel, which Saint James . . . calls a 'law of perfect liberty,' would impose a greater servitude than the law of Moses. Saint Peter did not receive such plenitude of power whether in temporal or spiritual matters." When, in cases of necessity, the pope meddles in temporal concerns, "he is thrusting his sickle in alien crops, unless he be entrusted with power to do so by the emperor or by some other person." [72] What right has Christ's vicar to deprive men of goods and rights when the Lord himself, infinitely greater than the pope, ministered rather than dominated?

Ockham counsels no interference with spiritual procuration of "the eternal salvation of men," or "the rule and government of the faithful" to that end. The community of the faithful is best subordinated to a single spiritual head. "The pope is the head and supreme judge of all the faithful under Christ. Not so the emperor, who must not concern himself with spiritual matters, not even occasionally."

This rigid exclusion of temporal powers from participation in spiritual things is hardly maintained with full consistency; especially in the light of the imperial relation to conciliar activities. But William is here striving to establish the principle of reasonable uses and reduced abuses on the part of both powers. The rights of the Roman Empire rather than those of the Roman Episcopacy are being violated. If papal powers are permitted to inflate themselves, as they purpose, until they equal the divine power itself, they will end by presuming to deprive kings, princes, and every human being; they will "destroy the perfect freedom of the law of the Gospel." [73]

No, for the sake of the papacy's true rights and responsibilities, as for the welfare of all Christians, the limits of papal power ought to be discussed freely and imposed fearlessly.

Consult L. Baudry, ed., *Guillelmi de Occam Breviloquium de Potestate Papae* (Paris, 1937), and, established on it, P. Hammann, *La doctrin de l'église et de l'état chez Occam* (Paris, 1942). Cf. J. G. Sikes *et al.*, eds. *G. de Ockham Opera Politica, I* (Manchester, 1940).

[72] Tornay, *Selections*, pp. 196-97, translated from *De Imp. et Pont. Pot.*, I, 3, 5, III. 1, II, 1, 3; cf. Baudry, *Breviloquium*.

[73] Tornay, *Selections*, pp. 197-99; translated from *De Imp. et Pont. Pot.*, VIII, 1, XII, 1, 2, etc.

The pope has no power to dominate emperor or kings as he seeks to do. In thus overstepping its very real powers, the Avignon Church damages not only the empire, but, "as regards ecclesiastical affairs . . . all Christians, too, in a very material way." Tyranny, extortion, and war are joined to the stultification of scientific progress, the enslavement of the intellect, the violation of the Scriptures, and the prostitution of the reason.

It is the whole Christian people, not just imperial pride, that is thus hurt. For peace cannot reign in a Christendom where powers, temporal and spiritual, are not carefully apportioned. "Until the clergy and laity settle irrefragably and sanction what powers the pope possesses by divine right," the papal see will wage war on Christians; "the stubborn strife between the pope and the people will not cease." [74]

In his assessment of the medieval concept later denominated as the *Corpus Christianum,* Bohatec gives a brief but highly informing account of Nicholas Cusanus' thought. This is drawn from the *Catholic Concordance.*[75] He observes that Cusa's picture of the human organism is even more carefully developed and meticulously articulated than that of Salisbury. Nicholas concerns himself, as does John, with both orders of life, the temporal and the spiritual, in relation to the whole and its parts. Cusa sees in all of this a pre-established, God-willed, sweet harmony. When speaking of the whole—this all-embracing society, this all-comprising unity—he designates it as the Catholic Church. In it the holy priesthood, which is added to the empire, carries the likeness of the soul, which vitalizes the body. Through this soul, the spirit of God, by way of the sacraments, per-

---

[74] Tornay, *op. cit.,* pp. 200-1; translated from *De Imp. et Pont. Pot.,* XXIV, 1, XXVI, 1.

[75] *Calvins Lehre,* pp. 594 ff., with references to the *De Concordantia Catholica* in the edition of Schard, *De iurisdictione auctoritate et praeeminentia imperiali ac potestate ecclesiastica* (Basel, 1566), pp. 465 ff. For the critical editions of Cusa's *Opera* and, particularly, of the *De Concordantia,* as well as translations, see the literature in M. de Gandillac, *Oeuvres choisies de Nicolas de Cues* (Paris, 1942), pp. 45-48—especially the older texts of Lefèvre d'Étaples, 3 Vols., 1514 (*De Con.* is Vol. III), the Bale edition of Henri Petrus, 1565, and the modern edition of Hoffman-Klibansky-Kallen (Leipzig, 1934), *De Con.,* being XIV, I, 1939; cf. F. N. Scharpff, *Wichtigste Schriften in deutscher Uebersetzung* (Freiburg 1/B, 1862); also, a translated sermon and literature in NUS, 57:289, 313 ff.; Coker, *Readings,* pp. 257 ff. Consult E. F. Jacob, *Essays in the Conciliar Epoch* (2nd ed., Manchester, 1953), Chap. IX.; also in F. J. C. Hearnshaw, *Social and Political Ideas* (London, 1925); H. Bett, *Nicholas of Cusa* (London, 1932), and E. Vansteenberghe, *Le cardinal Nicolas de Cues (1401-1464)* (Paris, 1920) with valuable commentary on the *De Con.* Cf. E. Hoffmann, *Das Universum des Nik. von Cues* (Heidelberg, 1929-1930), pp. 5, 19-24, 27.

vades the whole body of the Christian people—the faithful living together in one holy empire. In such manner the priestly soul and the body of the faithful live as constituent parts in one comprising Church of Christ.[76]

Cusa, therefore, thinks of the Church as a unity involving both soul and body. When speaking of the primary element in this concordant life, he specifies the *totum compositum*—that is, the Church itself. He next treats the soul, which is the sacerdotal power; and finally, consideration is given to the body, which symbolizes the Holy Empire. The clergy may be given a place of special importance without disrupting the unity which they share with the imperial powers. Under the one Church, both *sacerdotium* and *imperium* stand in closest union and co-operation. They are as close to each other as the soul is to the body. God is the spirit who, by the means of the sacraments, the ministers of which are the Lord's clergy, is joined to his faithful people. Thus the whole, which is the Church itself, is made up of body and soul. Into this spiritual-temporal integrity the divine spirit brings happy concord; and as a result of this intimate conjunction, a working community is set up.[77]

As Bohatec notes, a striking feature of Cusa's thought is his conception of the Church as the all-embracing Mystical Body under the headship of Christ, that brings together members called from the beginning of the world to a predestined solidarity. They are members of the invisible Church insofar as their ultimate destiny is known only to the highest Lord of all. So far as the present world is concerned, faith and charity alone suffice to weld into their proper totality those who are elected to a final unity. Cusa's social thought is strongly eschatological. This governs his concept of both the ultimate society and the interim community which leads the faithful to their destined fellowship. The Church, which is made up of those called to a final association—a lasting heredity which the Lord has reserved for them —has been drawn from the very foundation of the world to the endless fellowship of God's children. Within human society the sacraments are as the spirit, the priesthood as the soul, and other faithful ones as the body.[78]

[76] Bohatec, *op. cit.*, pp. 594 ff.; Schard, *op. cit.*, 466 ff.; Vansteenberghe, *op. cit.*, pp. 34-51; *De Con.*, I, 1, 5, 6, 7; Excit. VIII, 603-5; Scharpff, *op. cit.*, 417-20.

[77] Bohatec, *op. cit.*, pp. 594-95; Schard, op. cit., pp. 673, 478, 480, 484, 467; *De Con.*, II, 19; *Oeuvres*, pp. 51-52.

[78] Bohatec, *op. cit.*, pp. 595-96; Schard, *op cit.*, 467, 461, 484; *De Con.*, I, 1-10; Vansteenberghe, *op. cit.*, pp. 50, 164-65.

The relationship existing between the *sacerdotium* and the *imperium* is one of powerful creativeness. Developing according to the ways of nature and its laws, it is an association of God-given harmony. This proceeds out of the one King of Peace, who reaches in his grace to all members of the whole. When this harmony is destroyed, the soul takes leave of the body.

One ought not anticipate in Cusa any radical departures from the accepted medieval position. The Church of the predestinate about which he concerns himself is the visible Catholic Church set forth as the *totum compositum*. There is for him no hiatus between the Church militant and the Church triumphant. The visible Church, as such, is already being conducted to its heavenly habitat. But Cusa thinks of the Holy Catholic Church as embracing the faithful only. One must be careful not to equate the *totum compositum* with all mankind.[79]

It is natural to conclude that in Cusa we have, at most points, a typically medieval thinker who represents the best elements of the organismic concept applied to the *Corpus Christianum*. He reminds us forcibly of John's *Policraticus* as well as of Stephen of Tournai.[80] However far he may be from them in some particulars, he, like his earlier prototypes, represents in the later Middle Ages an attempt to find a comprising unity in which the Church will have a prior, universalizing role. This unity will, of course, embody noncompeting and ideally co-operating constituents as it accomplishes its destined work.

[79] Bohatec, *op. cit.*, pp. 594-96; Schard, especially pp. 466, 673, 478, 484, 467; *De Con.* I, 8, III, 7; *Oeuvres*, pp. 61-62.

[80] Cf. Bohatec, *op. cit.*, 594; *De Con.*, I, 1-4; Vansteenberghe, *op. cit.*, 50-51, 164-65; Gierke, *Political Theories*, pp. 101 ff. and note 10, pp. 105-6 ff.

CHAPTER XIII

Last Things, the Resurrection, the Last Judgment, and the End of History

1. Preview of Basic Principles

IT IS NATURAL THAT THE MEDIEVAL MAN, LIKE THE EARLY CHRISTIAN, should think of his temporal existence in terms of ends as well as beginnings. Both Jewish and Christian traditions had emphasized the significance of ultimate destiny as being even more important than human genesis. The Christian was frequently reminded that his main concern was the preparation for the end of time. Thus the faithful Christian looked to the end of history, not as marking the completion of his life, but as fixing the transition to a new order. He was taught to believe that his whole personal and social destiny was at stake in his preparation during temporal existence for an eternal order of experience. The Last Times, therefore, were thought of as completing one life cycle and making ready for a new one.

Last Things as the Christian conceived of them were, however, final only in the sense that they represented the conclusion of history and its temporal institutions. They signified the truly ultimate world only in the sense that they were thought of as being the gateway to the heavenly kingdom. Man had been created for a destiny which lay beyond the terrestrial orbit. In order to reach a more completely unified existence in heaven, he must run out his course until he as an individual reached an end to his physical life and until the race as a whole was summoned to the bar of judgment. The end of history for humankind would mark the point where preparation for a new world was no longer possible. Individuals and temporal society as well would have come to the end of time.

The whole purpose of man's being given a span of years to live in was that he might have a period in which to make ready for his eternal destiny. The significance of the Last Days, therefore, lay in the suggestion which they carried as to man's responsibility, individual and social, for the preparatory stages of his career. Men might well fear the end of time if it connoted for them the period beyond which no opportunity remained for multiplying the fruits of their efforts. The constant refrain of early Christians, and of medieval ones as well, was this: Life on earth has been given to man that he may work for himself and others in love. This is the final test of his readiness for citizenship in the society of everlasting blessedness. If he refuses to utilize his fleeting time on earth for the service of neighbors, he really does greatest injury to himself. For nothing that man does, unless it be in the name of Christ, is really fruitful for his own salvation. And what Christ clearly demands, in his name, is that friends and enemies alike be served for the Master's sake. When time has run out and eternity is set to begin, Jesus the Great Judge will decide whether or not his would-be children have passed this final test.

The whole period, therefore, from the beginning until the end of earthly history is one of pilgrimage to heaven. It is the stuff of life for those who use it in ministry to fellows. It is living death to those who take no opportunity for unselfish service. Christian teachers throughout the range of ancient and medieval history realize the difficulty of getting their followers to live as if tomorrow were to be the end of all further opportunity. Only when they are made to feel that their life span has terminated do they fully realize the purposes for which it was designed. There is nothing, however, which prevents one from anticipating the dreadful significance of the last chance while there is still time to give evidence of socially redemptive service. Christian thinkers through the ages have sought to focus the minds of the faithful upon the Last Days as a means of redeeming all intervening moments for the service of God and fellow men.[1]

It is, therefore, most unfair to think of the medieval concern with the Last Days as constituting nothing but craven fears about a single, awful event in history. That event was dreaded, in part, because of the terrifying circumstances which would be associated with it. But it was anticipated with foreboding by the best of men because it was feared that the time preceding it would not have been sufficiently employed in the doing of God's will among men on earth.

Theologians of the medieval period were not at all vague in their concepts of final happenings which should precede Resurrection and Judgment. An accumulation of theories and traditions clustered

[1] A convenient summary of basic elements in medieval eschatology and their application to particular situations may be found in the text and notes of Petry, *Francis of Assisi,* pp. 86 ff. Cf. "Index de duratione mundi et eius fine," MPL 219:49-52.

about the role to be enacted by the Antichrist. Jesus himself had predicted a great battle that would take place between his followers and those of Satan at the close of the age. Medieval versions of this highlighted the wiles and seductive powers of the one who would simulate Christ and attempt the ruin of Jesus' true followers.[2]

As medieval Christians conceived of the oncoming battle, they thought in terms that were at least reminiscent of Jesus' declaration that two orders of life are in deadly conflict in the universe. Christ, representing all of the redemptive forces of God, seeks to recruit the citizenry of heaven even while time endures. He who is against Christ strives to make good his control over the world as it now is. There can be but one outcome to this deadly conflict. Jesus, and those who truly follow him, will defeat the order of life arrayed against them. No failure on the part of any would-be disciple can compromise the ultimate victory of the Lord. But it is easily possible for individuals and groups to fight on the wrong side and so lose their share in the fruits of victory. Once lost, the rewards of faithfully supporting the Christ can never be regained. Nor can anyone hope to be neutral at the great Armageddon. Jesus himself had said that men, individually and collectively, must be either for or against him. Satan would not countenance any division in his own ranks. Neither would Christ permit his followers to be divided in their loyalty.[3]

Most medieval thinkers assume that the Last Days of the temporal order will see the decisive struggle. What men do then will determine in no small degree their right to be registered in the kingdom of God. But their activities will not be judged on any purely individual basis. Rather will they be assessed in terms of their having come to the support of Christ's hosts in spite of all the wiles of antichrist. Since he will have had the advantage of confusing the issue under the appearance of being the real Christ, fighting him will not be a simple matter. The faithful will be tested by ruthless power. This will be brought against them in terrible persecution hitherto unimagined.[4]

---

[2] For a brief discussion of the primary literature see R. C. Petry, "Medieval Eschatology and St. Francis of Assisi," *Church History,* IX, 1 (March, 1940), 55 ff. and notes. Note, especially, Wadstein, *Die eschatologische Ideengruppe* (Leipzig, 1896); also, MacCulloch, *Medieval Faith and Fable,* pp. 287-99. Cf. Roger Bacon's *Compend. Studii,* Rolls Series 15:399-402, translated in Coulton, *Life,* II, 55-62.

[3] Luke 11:14-23; Matt. 12:22-30; Mark 3:23-27.

[4] Otto of Freising, *The Two Cities: A Chronicle of Universal History to the Year 1146 A.D.,* tr. C. C. Mierow (New York, 1928), Book VIII; Anselm, *Médit. et orat.* II, MPL 158:722-25; Honorius of Autun, *Elucidarium,* Lib. III, MPL 172:1161-75; Petry, "Medieval Eschatology," *Church History,* IX, 1 (1940), 56-57.

The pattern of anticipation laid down by the Revelator here comes sharply into play. Christ's true people will draw together as a body and stand firm against every onslaught. Having been long prepared for the signs of antichrist's coming, they will not easily be caught unaware. They know quite well the futility of trying to stand as individuals against the collective minions of Satan. They will, therefore, be ever more closely drawn together as a body of those responding to the ideals and practices of their Master. When he comes, finally, to judge the earth, he will find them worthy of his leadership in this last victorious counterassault on the pseudo-Christ. The best assurance possible that individuals and groups shall have a part in the Lord's plan of liberation is their own increasing fruitage of social life lived under his direction. This pattern is true to the Middle Ages, in the main, whether one thinks of Lombard the theologian, Otto the chronicler, Hildegarde the prophetess, or Thomas the great synthesizer of medieval thought. The expectation of horrible persecution will no more dissuade true Christians from following their leader in the Last Days than impending tragedy in the time of John the Revelator kept the Christians of his day from supporting the Master's cause. They were then committed to an order of life that should be triumphant on earth as it was already in heaven; Christians more than a millennium later were also encouraged to believe that they were standing for an eternal order that should surmount even the last days of history. The manner in which they acquitted themselves as a community of faithful believers would go far in determining their place in the society of everlasting joys.[5]

There was, of course, no uniform thought concerning the Resurrection in all periods of ancient and medieval history. Nonetheless, the thinking represented by such men as Peter Lombard and Thomas Aquinas is reasonably indicative of typical Christian viewpoints on this all-important matter. The position of Thomas, therefore, may be taken as a kind of framework for the development of Christian views. Other thinkers will be introduced as occasion demands.

Thomas points out that the last end of man is happiness. By this he means that the ultimate experience which the medieval world conceives of is one to be lived in eternity, not in time. Final beatitude is obviously impossible in a temporal world which has its individual

---

[5] Rev. 12:20, etc.; Otto of Freising, *Two Cities*, VIII, 17: Hildegarde of Bingen, *Scivias*, Lib. III, Visio XI-XII, MPL 197:700-30; Mechthild of Magdeburg, *Revelations*, tr. L. Menzies (New York, 1953), Pt. 6, Sec. 15, pp. 179 ff., 6 (35), 198, 7 (1), 206-10; *De Civ. Dei*, XX, 1-30, especially 7.

endings for each person at death. Anything assuming final characteristics must go beyond history and physical demise. In order that the individual, as well as the human group as a whole, may get beyond a world that is partial and temporary to one that is complete and eternal, the resurrection of man as a person and of men as a society must take place.

It is necessary, not merely for one person to be resurrected, but for all men to rise again, as well. The Resurrection by its very nature must be denominated as a social experience. Man must conform to his part in the human species. His being resurrected as human is in keeping with his being remade a recognizable part of the relationship that he sustains to humanity as a whole.[6]

From the very dawn of Christian history—at least as the early Christian Church records it—the Resurrection has been thought of as constituting the most significant convocation of all rational creatures since the world began. Suggestions to this effect found in the Pauline Letters are rephrased with some distinctive variations, to be sure, in the whole literature of the Middle Ages.[7]

Furthermore, the Resurrection is habitually thought of as being a conformation on the part of man to the resurgence of Christ himself. In Christian thought, this is, of course, no mere figure of speech; though it does have its symbolic aspects. The Christian did feel, literally, that the resurrection of Christ made possible his own, individual renaissance. In a sense, Christ's rising again was, at the same time, an indication of man's being brought beyond the boundaries of history into the realm of the eternal.

One cannot ignore at this point the insistent reminder that various groups frequently made: namely, that a period on earth might intervene between the end of history proper, and the beginning of a new, eternal world order. Such millennial reminders were recurrent throughout the ancient and medieval period. But they were rightly criticized as putting all too much emphasis on special times and seasons; whereas Christ and Paul had repeatedly warned that the prime

[6] P. Lombard, *Sent.* Lib. IV, Dist. 43 ff., Quaracchi ed., 994 ff. For Thomas Aquinas' Commentary on Lombard's Lib. IV, particularly Quest. I, Art. Iff., see *Op. Om.*, XI, 276-83. Note the bearing of Anger, *Mystical Body*, pp. 41, 53, 55, 313-26. Cf. *S. Theol.*. III, Supplem. Qq. 88-91, as arranged from Thomas Aquinas by Reginald of Piperno. Consult the *Compendium Theologiae ad Fratrem Reginaldum*, II, 9 (*Op. Om.*, XXVII. 126); C. Vollert, *Compendium of Theology by St. Thomas Aquinas* (St. Louis, 1952), pp. 329-43. See R. C. Petry, "The Social Character of Heavenly Beatitude According to the Thought of St. Thomas Aquinas," *The Thomist*, VII, 1 (Jan., 1944), 65-79.

[7] I Thess. 1 and 2; Pohle, *Eschatology*, pp. 149-54; H. von Hügel, *Essays and Addresses*, 1st Ser., Pt. II, pp. 136-48; F. Cavallera, *Thesaurus*, Nos. 436 ff., pp. 708 ff.

necessity was in preparing for the ultimate world with a vigilance that was not limited in terms of human predictions. Thomas and hundreds of other medieval Christians like him exhorted the typical Christian to be ever on the watch for Christ, without calculation as to the likely date of his reappearance. It was in this connection that Joachim of Flora had, however unwittingly, led many people astray. His main emphasis had appeared to fall too unguardedly upon seasons or eras too much subject to chronological computation. It may be remarked parenthetically that this is, perhaps, an unfair judgment upon the major objectives of the Calabrian seer. Quite possibly, he, too, was merely directing Christian followers to a date in history which would serve a yet more fundamental purpose. This would remind them of still other events that were to be assessed socially, as well as individually, against a background transcending all history.[8]

Germane to any conspectus of Christian thought is the medieval conviction that the Resurrection is necessarily social as well as individual. No man can be brought to stand again in his physical body unless he constitutes a part of that whole genus called humanity. In fact, the Resurrection symbolizes a starkly realistic fact: this is, that one cannot be an individual without being part of a group; and that groups are in turn made up of individuals. It will be instructive to observe, shortly, how the last great Judgment that is to follow upon the Resurrection necessarily constitutes a social-individual phenomenon.

The general Judgment, which is sharply distinguished from—yet in immediate continuity with—the particular, is, for the early and medieval Christian, a supremely corporate affair. This Judgment is passed upon man as a part of the human race. As such, it will differentiate between people good and bad. Of course, each individual will be cognizant of his own judgment immediately after death. But this will not obviate the necessity of each individual's assessment being announced publicly in relationship to the judgment of all other persons. Thus, all those who have died will have had a particular Judgment revealed to them at that time. But they will stand again in the last public assize to hear together the verdicts passed upon themselves and all others. It is a fact of signal importance that medieval faith

[8] I Cor. 15; Revelation, *passim; De Civ. Dei,* XX, 7. Pertinent passages from Joachim are found in Aegerter, *L'évangile éternel,* II, 32, 86, 93-95, 103-6, 112 ff., 132, 142, 163, 168. On Joachim, also, see A. Dempf, *Sacrum Imperium* (Munich, 1929), E. Benz, *Ecclesia spiritualis* (Stüttgart, 1934), and Petry, *Francis of Assisi,* p. 89, n. 9.

stresses the publicity given this final pronouncement as it affects both individuals and groups.⁹

Throughout the Christian centuries much speculation has been advanced as to the manner in which each person will be made aware of the judgment of others as well as of himself. It has been quite popular to use the scriptural phrase concerning the public opening of the books. Whether or not one thinks with Lombard and De Sorbon of those books as preserving the writings of conscience, he is called upon to anticipate some kind of public pronouncement in which the affairs of each are revealed to the consciousness of the others. Out of this the basic emphasis emerges quite clearly: What one does in the field of history not only affects his fate in the society of the future; it also becomes known, generally, at the Last Judgment.

As a result, the general Judgment becomes a highly socializing factor in the temporal lives of the faithful. None but a thoroughly foolish man—or perhaps one criminally neglected by his pastor—can fail to realize his incorporation, finally, in the congregation of endless life, or the assembly of unending death. Each soul is admonished to remember that if he would stand at the Judgment within the society of the righteous, he must identify himself on earth with the community of the just. If he would do this, he must be in preparation, always, to serve others—whether they be those of his own household, city, kingdom, or of the whole Church. It is at such junctures that a work like *The Pricke of Conscience* attains maximum pertinence. Here assuredly, though not here alone, there is expressed with unforgettable directness the responsibility of each life for the other.¹⁰

Such a view pictures the corporateness of those being judged. It also stresses the solidarity of those who assist in judging. In the Church's early documents and in the later adaptations of them, there is a belief, now implied, now expressed, that certain individuals will be associated with Christ in passing judgment on the rest. Peter

---

⁹ P. Lombard, *Sent.*, Lib. IV, Dist. 43, Quaracchi ed., II, 994 ff.; Otto of Freising, *Two Cities*, VIII, 17; Honorius of Autun, *Elucidarium*, MPL 172:1162-75; Hugh of St. Victor, *De Sacramentis*, II, 17 (de fine saeculi), MPL 176:597-610; Thomas Aquinas, *S. Theol.*, III, Supplem., Qq. 88, 89, Art. 5.; Diekamp, *Manuale*, IV, 470 ff.; Pohle, *Eschatology*, pp. 18 ff., 103 ff.

¹⁰ R. Morris, ed., *The Pricke of Conscience (Stimulus conscientiae)* . . . (Berlin, 1863). Book V, pp. 108 ff., Ll. 3966 ff., concerns eschatology. See, especially, Ll. 4960, pp. 135 ff., Ll. 5424, pp. 147 ff., Ll. 5544, pp. 150 ff., Ll. 5556, pp. 151 ff., Ll. 5908, pp. 160 ff. Consult Wells, *Manual*, pp. 447 ff., 838, Index and Supplements. Cf. *Cursor Mundi*, V, Ll. 21139 ff. (EETS, 68, 1878), Appendix, pp. 1608 ff.; Wells, *Manual*, pp. 339, 816 ff.

Lombard, Otto Freising, and other medieval writers assume a four-fold division among those judging and those being judged. Varying conditions control the nature and degree of each classification. One hears frequent mention of a corporate Son of man. Thus the disciples are thought of as sitting on twelve thrones judging the twelve tribes of Israel. However this may be, it is clearly apparent that Christ, in a unique sense, judges all human beings. In this capacity, he judges as man, not as a divine being. This judicial power and right is bestowed upon him as a reward for his humility during his passion. He shed his blood for all; though it was not effective in all. It is fitting, therefore, that all men should assemble in judgment, together, to see his exaltation in his human nature.[11]

In the acts of judging, Christ is thought of as pronouncing sentence of the most social kind. Representative medieval authors depict him as handing down, according to Matthew 25, verdicts favorably or unfavorably conditioned by responsiveness or callousness to the needs of his humble followers. Some of the most eloquent sermons and treatises of pre-Reformation Christians have dwelt on this theme. The individual ought certainly to be concerned with his own inner life as well as his overt personal actions. But Christ enthroned in judgment will make his accounting on the basis of service rendered fellow men, and not in terms of any isolated perfection. Thus, human beings brought together in an awe-inspiring totality at the Judgment Day will receive certification to a destiny corporately good or evil; insofar as they have assumed the obligations, or failed in the responsibilities, of neighborliness on earth. Since Jesus clearly taught an expanding conception of neighbor and neighborhood, his demand that others be neighborly entailed far-reaching social repercussions. Those who would hear Christ's voice in benediction upon their lives at the Last Judgment must give such evidences in advance, as they lived in temporal society. Thus, and thus only, might they hope for an abiding citizenship established for them from the very foundation of the world.[12]

Dr. Bonhoeffer, a theologian referred to earlier, has epitomized much of the classic Christian position at this point. The whole problem of Christian eschatology is one which involves the relationship of the temporal to the eternal. For we walk by faith and not by sight,

---

[11] See T. W. Manson, *Teaching of Jesus*, pp. 305 ff., on the corporate "Son of Man" theme; Otto of Freising, *Two Cities*, VIII, 17, Mierow ed., pp. 476-77; Pohle, *Eschatology*, pp. 151, 153, and n. 22; Matt. 19:28.

[12] Matt. 25:31-46; Pohle, *Eschatology*, pp. 149-54.

so long as history lasts. And history itself cannot bring the final solution to life; though it may possibly point to that from which there will come a conclusion to one era and a preparation for another. Naturally, the limitations of church history are quite apparent when one is dealing with problems of Christian eschatology. Presumably, however, church history can record the Church's thought about history, and the beyond as well. Significantly enough, as Bonhoeffer makes clear, the Communion of Saints, while in part involved by the temporal order, has regard to an experience that can be consummated only in an eternal society. While making ready for an ultimate association within eternal life, all Christians must live to the full in an earthly existence that is made responsive to the heavenly. They must continue to be aware of faults, not only within the world at large, but also within the empirical church. That is, they must continue to oppose antichrist, and all that menaces the ultimate kingdom of God, while they live in history; so that they may be a partial means of helping to prepare the Church, and individuals within it, for a life beyond history.[13]

Rightly enough, Christian eschatology has been denominated as community eschatology. It never deals with individuals as if isolated from groups; nor can it think of any ultimate grouping that does not give fulfillment to the meaning of individual life. And since the kingdom of God lies beyond all the kingdoms of this world, the consideration of that divine realm is a challenge to preparation in the present order for a community life that shall be truly ultimate.

Here the problem of judgment leading to eternal life forces the consideration of God's community in the hereafter. For, according to orthodox Christian thought, whether presented in the medieval period or outlined by a modern Lutheran commentator, the Judgment, with all of its highly social implications, is the only means of ingress to the kingdom possible for individual or group. Once more we must insist, as Bonhoeffer does, that Judgment so conceived involves persons to be sure, but not only individual persons; it has to do with collective persons as well. Individuals are to be judged, not by themselves alone, but as members of a collectivity, likewise. Inasmuch as human communities have come from a creative unity grounded in the very life and will of God, they must stand as such before God in the Last Judgment. That which God established from the very beginning on a social basis, must come to its historical end in terms of a social accounting. It must also make way for that which is transcendingly social beyond anything limited to history.

Bonhoeffer, like medieval Christians whom he unwittingly recapitulates, insists that the judged ones, standing before God in the Last Days, will be separated into a company of grace and a federation of wrath. That fellowship which will have its only unity in terms of its having been cut off from God and his chosen assembly will cease to have anything of real life about it. Conversely, those admitted to the society of God will have all of life that can ever be— life that comes to the full in companionship with others associated with God.

To be sure, God recognizes a certain freedom of human will; even when that will is used to revolt against him. But wills so utilized band themselves together in a separation from God and his saved ones. In so doing they find their appropriate end to be a spiritual death. They demonstrate the old contention that only in society with those joined to God do men continue living at all. Individuality can never be spoken of as an isolated factor. Individual personality exists only when it is given actuality in relation to the community. It is because men are being fitted for a collective beatitude or a community of despair that they must come before a board reviewing their mutuality during the reign of history. Only thus can it be determined to what collective destiny they shall be committed.[14]

If one goes to modern works of Catholic dogma, such as that of Pohle, he is at once reminded of the scriptural basis for the Church's continuing beliefs.[15] Matthew 24:37 draws upon the more apocalyptic statements attributed to Jesus. Whether or not they are his own is a problem secondary to the Church's rigidifying conviction that they are. In such passages he is said to have warned his followers against those later arising in his name to mislead the faithful. A falling away owing to persecution, the rise of false prophets, and the intensified cultivation of wickedness are among the unhappy experiences which Jesus presumably foretold.

Regardless of the many sorrows of such a time, those believing in Christ are to continue looking for the true Master, the Son of Man, who, when he comes, "shall [by means of his angels] gather together his elect from the four winds, from one end of heaven to the other." At the same time, Jesus says flatly that none may be sure of the exact hour of his appearance; this is all the more reason that

[14] *Ibid.*, pp. 175-77.
[15] *Eschatology*, pp. 103 ff., 149 ff.

the faithful be always prepared for his coming. A slave is blessed who is found by his returning master to be doing the will of the household; so also will Christ's followers rejoice who are ready to greet him in fullest loyalty when he returns to judge the earth.

The author of Second Peter (3:3 ff.) likewise warns the faithful that there will be those in the latter days who will mock all believers in the Lord's promised coming. But, of course, the real believer knows that, whatever the time, there is a day approaching when "Godless men are to be judged and destroyed." Time as men reckon it is not known to the Lord. With him one day is like a thousand years, and a thousand years like one day. If he seems tardy in his reappearance, it is not that he is recreant to his promise; but, rather, that he graciously extends man's opportunity to repent and be saved. It is because the day of the Lord will come like a thief that all those who believe on him are to make the interim one of "holy and pious lives." In the light of this sobering fact, the writer calls upon his friends, during their period of waiting, to make themselves irreproachable in conduct and at peace with each other. Especial precaution is to be taken against seduction "by the errors of unprincipled men." While awaiting the Lord's return, his true followers are to "grow in the blessing and knowledge of our Lord and Saviour Jesus Christ."

Paul in his First Letter to the Thessalonians (5:1 ff.) reminded them that times and dates are beyond the Christian's power to know. But the suddenness and awfulness of the occasion should not catch any of Christ's loyal supporters unaware. Those who are of the nature of light have no occasion to be found in darkness. Unlike men in general, the Lord's followers must be particularly vigilant and composed. Such readiness will characterize those alone whom God has destined for salvation through Jesus Christ. It was for this purpose that he died for them. Because of his sacrificial love, they will once more live with him. Thus, out of the context of expectancy with regard to the Last Day, Paul calls upon his brethren, while yet on this earth, to live at peace with one another; to be busy with constructive and mutual services; and to live happily in the Spirit as Christ's children ought.

In his Second Letter to the Thessalonians (2:1 ff.) Paul further exhorts his brethren not to be led astray by false rumors or by attempts to prove that the Parousia has already occurred. More important still is his admonition that they stand firm in a community of preparedness that shall be ready to resist the evil one and to join the Lord in company with all others who have served him. Once again, Paul reminds them that such preparation includes the prosaic tasks of daily labor, peacefulness, and Christ-mindedness.

As Pohle remarks, such signs as the Scriptures discuss apropos of the Last Days are to be thought of in terms of concurrence, rather than in the light of any particular happening. One should not have the temerity to say that this or that date can be accurately predicted. The faithful have consistently held within Catholic dogma that a certain grouping of phenomena may become the basis of edifying generalization; so that in meditation upon them Christ's loyal servants may better prepare, now, for the future judgment. In this outline of signs most frequently referred to, Pohle follows the lead of St. Augustine. A series of chapters in the *City of God* discuss the widely separated events which are to precede the Last Judgment.[16]

An acceptable, though not an inflexible, delineation of six major events frequently thought of as preceding the last accounting is given in the following order: (1) The preaching of the Christian religion all over the earth; (2) the conversion of the Jews; (3) the reappearance of Enoch and Elias; (4) the great Apostasy and the reign of antichrist; (5) unusual disturbances of nature; (6) a universal conflagration.[17]

If one considers these divisions of thought, consistently recurrent in patristic and medieval authors, he is at once impressed with their basically social structure. Without the least expectation that all men will finally accept Christianity, they consider paramount the Lord's admonition to preach the gospel in the whole world for a testimony to all nations. This same gospel of Christ, which will finally be the basis of judgment, must become the ultimate stone of reconstruction or rock of demolition for all human beings. Regardless of apparent unconcern with this gospel, men will finally be confronted with its decisive implications for all humanity. The conversion of the Jews, partial though it may be, will receive its direction from this same gospel. The return of Enoch and Elias, so frequently treated by the writers of the Middle Ages, has an even more direct reference to the co-ordinating activities that shall affect the faithful in the Last Times. The medieval tradition of such a return underscores the Christian consciousness of need for those who will solidify the faithful in the hour of crisis. Medieval literature represents in somewhat elastic fashion and with multiform order the details of stiffen-

[16] *Ibid.*, pp. 102 ff., 153-54; *De Civ. Dei* XX, 30.
[17] *Ibid.*, p. 104.

ing resistance to antichrist and numerous false prophets. Otto of Freising, for example, says that while antichrist is himself preaching and leading the human race astray, Enoch and Elijah will come so that the world previously deceived by error may return to "the knowledge of the truth." [18]

In the case of antichrist, a more extended treatment is naturally given by ancient and medieval authors. Pohle rightly says that the great apostasy is "described partly as the cause and partly as an effect of the appearance of AntiChrist." [19] Certain it is that in the early and medieval period most Christians expected this enemy of the Lord to draw away many of the erstwhile faithful. Paul's own references in II Thessalonians 2 and 3 refer to some such apostasy at the hands of one proclaiming himself to be God. Though the name "antichrist" is not found in the Pauline writings, it is encountered in I John 2:18, 22; 4:3; and II John 7. In such contexts the more personal, as well as the more corporate, aspects of evil appear. However widely Christian authors diverge in their identifications of antichrist with this or that person, or groups of persons, their view of his major role seems fairly clear. He proposes to destroy the society of God's faithful. Consequently, it is necessary now, if ever, that the followers of God stand firm as a unit in their defense of Christ and his house against antichrist and his company. The need of corporate action by Christ's children in the Last Days is amply attested. Final events, insofar as they involve convulsions of nature and a reconstitution of the universe, have less pertinence than some other phenomena for the issues of social thought. They do betoken, however, the universality of the signs which herald the Last Judgment. In so doing, they reinforce the significant fact that all matters pertaining to the world as human beings have known it have now reached the end of an epoch; and that a new era, fateful alike for the society of good and the company of evil, is about to dawn. The Judgment itself is the dividing line between these two eras. [20]

A broad survey of the basic aspects associated with the general Judgment, such as is available in authoritative Catholic handbooks, is distinctly valuable. Pohle is especially helpful in that he preserves the main outlines discoverable in the literature of the early and medieval church. These may then be checked against the specific

[18] Petry, "Medieval Eschatology," *Church History*, IX, 1 (1940), 55 ff.; Pohle, *Eschatology*, pp. 105-9.

[19] Pohle, *Eschatology*, p. 109.

[20] *Ibid.*, pp. 110-14.

works of men like Chrysostom, Augustine, Peter Lombard, Hugh of St. Victor, Bonaventura, Thomas Aquinas, and others.[21]

It is at once apparent that special significance attaches to the Last Judgment because it does mark "the last important event in the history of the human race." This in itself accentuates the division between one order of life now drawing to a close and the coming of another, fateful for the life of every human being since the beginning of time. The Judgment is rightly called universal; both by reason of those decisive effects held to be definitive for the entire time-world, and because of its dramatic issue in eternal societies of good and evil. However sympathetic one may be in his understanding of chiliasm, one must appreciate the soundly Catholic instinct of Pohle. He considers the Judgment to be so intimately conjoined with the resurrection of the dead as to leave no logical occasion for an earthly millennium. To hold with Augustine, in his earlier view, that such an interim association will come to pass is to be confronted, as he was, by the necessity of looking beyond to the final society yet requiring inauguration.[22]

Again, the words of early Christian writings, whether creedal or otherwise, emphasize the belief that Christ will indeed come "to judge the living and the dead." Here again is a universality that reaches beyond physical life and death. It projects a loyalty to Christ and his Mystical Body that finally vaults all vicissitudes of time and all interim joys, however ecstatic, to celebrate the reunion of heaven itself. However chiliastic may have been the inclinations of many early Fathers, they did, with general unanimity, expect a judgment which would make men ready, not only for a millennial sojourn, but also for a final immutability of celestial citizenship.[23]

As regards the circumstances associated with the Resurrection, the features stressed by modern Catholic works are not significantly different from the basic medieval texts. Thus there is general agreement in the insistence that Jesus Christ will himself conduct the final test in person. He will be assisted by the angels, who will serve to gather his chosen ones from every corner of the earth and the whole universe. Doubtless, too, they will help to make ready the judgment of the wicked as well as the good. All men without exception whether living or summoned from the dead, whether bad or good, will come

[21] *Ibid.,* pp. 149 ff.; Diekamp, *Manuale,* IV, 501 ff.

[22] *Ibid.,* pp. 149, 155-60; *De Civ. Dei,* XX, 7, 30; Sermo 259, MPL 38:1197.

[23] Pohle, *Eschatology,* pp. 149-51; P. Althaus, *Die letzen Dinge* (Gütersloh, 1949), pp. 172 ff.; Bonhoeffer, *Sanctorum Communio,* pp. 175 ff.

before Christ's tribunal. People of all nations shall present themselves to him for separation to the realms of righteousness and wickedness. Even infants, whether baptized or unbaptized, will come forth
for examination. Baptized ones who have not done good or evil
and are, therefore, strictly speaking, not to be judged will be present
that they may behold the glory of the Judge. "The unbaptized will
probably appear in order to be convinced of the justice of God in
denying them the beatific vision." [24]

Angels and demons, though they are already judged, will also
participate in the Judgment to the extent that they will receive
accidental rewards or punishments in terms of their part in influenc-
ing human affairs. It is generally accepted that the twelve apostles
will sit in judgment over the twelve tribes of Israel. Some have held
that the Virgin Mary, the Old Testament prophets, and other saints
will assist the judge.[25]

The Judgment is general and all-embracing in that it will have
regard to every thought, word, and deed—both good and evil—
of all mankind. Even the "forgiven secret sins of the just will also
be revealed on the Last Day, in order that the judgment may be
made complete and the justice and mercy of God be glorified." [26]

Pohle, however, goes so far as to admit what few medieval authors
would have conceded: namely, that such expressions as those involving the separation of goats and sheep may be allegorical. Thomas,
it is true, decides that a completely literal interpretation of verbal
judgments is hardly likely in view of the time that would thus
seem to be required. But, regardless of apparent obstacles, each individual who has ever lived will become a part of the last accounting. What is more important, each will hear the Judge's decision
on every person's future. Peter Lombard's disquisition on "the opening of the books" and Robert de Sorbon's distinctive treatment of
social accountability at the Judgment bar are not atypic of many
other thinkers in the pre-Reformation period; as indeed in times
since.[27]

It is enlightening to follow the chain of official Catholic references

[24] Pohle, *Eschatology*, p. 152; P. Lombard, *Sent.*, Lib. IV, Dist. 43, caps. 1-7;
Quaracchi ed., II, 994-99; Bonaventura, *Breviloquium*, VII, Nemmers ed., pp. 215 ff.;
Thomas Aquinas, *S. Theol.*, III, Supplement, Q. 89, Art. 5, ad 3.

[25] Pohle, *Eschatology*, pp. 152-53; *S. Theol.*, III, Supplement, Q. 99, Art. 2.

[26] Pohle, *Eschatology*, p. 153; *S. Theol.*, III, Supplement, Q. 87, Art. 2.

[27] *Eschatology*, p. 153; P. Lombard, Sent., Lib. IV, Dist. 43, cap. 4, Quaracchi ed., II,
996-97; *De Consciencia*; Althaus, *Die letzen Dinge*, Chap. V; Bonhoeffer, *Sanctorum
Communio*, pp. 175-80.

regarding early and medieval beliefs on the Last Things. These consider, especially, the state of souls after death, the Resurrection, Christ's judgment of the living and the dead, heaven, purgatory, and hell. In the earliest creeds of the Church such as the Apostolic and the Nicene, the belief in the resurrection of the body, the coming of Jesus to judge living and dead, and the acceptance or rejection of men for Christ's eternal kingdom are clearly and cogently set forth.[28] Pope Damasus in his *Confession of Faith* (*ca.* 384) pronounces anathemas against anyone who doubts that Christ will return in his humanity from his place at the right hand of the Father to judge the living and the dead. This is the burden, also, of the first council of Toledo.[29]

Pope Pelagius I discusses in greater detail the manner in which all men from Adam until the consummation of the ages, both living and dead, shall stand before the tribunal of Christ to receive judgment for his deeds, whether good or evil, done in the body. At such time those who are brought through God's grace to eternal life are to receive the boon of inclusion in the society of the angels. The wicked, for their part, who through the use of their own will have been brought to a judgment of dishonor, shall be consigned to eternal punishment without.[30] Gregory I in his *Fides* (*ca.* 590) similarly conceives of Christ's coming to judge the living and the dead with full revelation to all of each one's sins; after which the saints shall be received into the unending kingdom of heaven and the wicked into the suffering of eternal fire.[31]

The eleventh council of Toledo is particularly noteworthy for its sense of the corporateness attending the Judgment and the reign of the just in the kingdom of God. Those drawing up its Confession pray that when the time shall come in which the Son shall deliver the kingdom to God his Father, they may become participants of his reign; reigning without end with him in whom by faith they now inhere. Nothing essentially new is added to the official statements in the centuries immediately following.[32]

Leo III (809) calls attention to the fact that the wicked shall see Christ the Judge in the form in which he was crucified; not, however, in that humility which he manifested when he was un-

---

[28] Cavallera, *Thesaurus*, nos. 1436 ff., pp. 707 ff.; H. Denzinger, *Enchiridion Symbolorum* (Editio 28, Freiburg, 1/B, 1952), Index Syst. XIV a&b., (54)-(55).

[29] Cavallera, *Thesaurus*, nos. 1437-38, p. 708.

[30] *Ibid.*, no. 1441, p. 708.

[31] *Ibid.*, no. 1443, p. 709.

[32] *Ibid.*, no. 1446, p. 709.

justly judged, but in the brightness of his eternal majesty which the just shall behold.[33] The fourth Lateran Council (1215) states as its faith the conviction of the Christian centuries that both living and dead shall be judged and that each shall be recompensed according to his own works, whether good or evil. Thus the wicked shall go with the Devil into perpetual punishment, and the righteous with Christ into everlasting glory.[34] Michael Palaeologus (1274) offers a like credo but adds a section on the effectiveness of prayers for those in purgatory. The suffrages of the living faithful, the sacrifice of the mass, and prayers, alms, and other offices of piety receive full emphasis.[35] Benedict XII (1336) brings Catholic tenets on Last Things to a thoroughly social culmination in his recapitulation of the Church's faith to his day.[36]

[33] *Ibid.*, no. 1449, pp. 709-10.
[34] *Ibid.*, no. 1454, p. 710.
[35] *Ibid.*, no. 1455, pp. 710-11.
[36] *Ibid.*, no. 1458, pp. 712-13; for later utterances see Denzinger, *Enchiridion*, etc., by index.

CHAPTER XIV

Last Things, the Resurrection, the Last Judgment, and the End of History

2. In the Thought of Representative Fathers

THE CLASSIC VIEWS OF A FEW REPRESENTATIVE FATHERS AND THE occasional utterances of several others will reinforce the general principles already analyzed in the last chapter.[1]

Chrysostom, in one of his homilies on Matthew, deals with circumstances of the Last Days.[2] His thought is characterized by a high sense of social responsibility—particularly as a preparation for the Judgment and the world that lies beyond. The sufferings of those in prisons, mines, and famine areas remind this public-minded preacher of the judgments which are to come. "For these persons would not suffer these things here, unless vengeance and punishments were to await all the others also that have committed such sins." It is not like God to punish some for the selfsame things from which he exonerates others. As a result, every human being ought to look forward in humility to the Judgment that is to come.

Let them who are obstinate unbelievers of the judgment, believe it henceforth, and become better men; that having lived here in a manner worthy of the kingdom, we may attain unto the good things to come, by the grace and love towards man of our Lord Jesus Christ.[3]

In the succeeding homily, Chrysostom continues to treat of the signs that precede the end of the world and of the proper vigilance that should attend the uncertainty connected with it.[4] Because we do not know either the day or the hour, it is all the more incumbent up-

[1] The present chapter is thus an intensification of principles already stated and derives from the same basic category of sources.

[2] *Hom.* 76—Matt. 24:16-18; NPNF, 1st. Ser., X, 456-69. With this compare Wyclif, *Opus Evang.*, Libs. III-IV, caps. 51 ff., Loserth ed., pp. 227 ff.

[3] *Ibid.*, X, 461-62. Used by permission of the publishers, Wm. B. Eerdmans Publishing Co.

[4] *Hom* 77—Matt. 24:32, 33; NPNF, 1st Ser., X, 462 ff.

on us to be watchful and profitably employed. Teachers and all others in authority ought especially to realize how important it is that they be serving as faithful and wise householders when their Master comes. The Lord does not lightly pass by any failure on the part of his stewards to serve the household committed to their care. An evil servant who has failed in his obligation will not be able to stand when the day of accounting comes. This has application to all Christians—whether they be learned or wealthy—who have the opportunity of serving their fellow men but do not properly discharge it.

In the concluding sections of this work, Chrysostom manifests once more his characteristic sensitivity to the requirements of neighborliness placed upon all Christian souls. Anyone who remembers his own pleasures and desires to the exclusion of his neighbor is provoking the anger of Christ. Those, on the contrary, who serve others in Christ's name will be evidencing the best preparation for the Judgment whenever it may come. "To this way then let us hold, for this is especially the way that leads up to Heaven, which renders men followers of Christ, which makes them, as far as possible, like God." For one who considers his own good without regard to his neighbor, there is nothing but condemnation. Christ pleased not himself but others. Chrysostom calls upon his hearers in whatever vocation or state of life to take every opportunity for their neighbors' edification. Those who are selfishly inclined to the rewards of martyrdom might well remember that, upon certain occasions, it is better to live and help others than to die with a martyr's gratification. "For this is in the highest sense to be with Christ, even to be doing His will, but nothing is so much His will, as that which is for one's neighbor's good." [5]

Christ has definitely called for a full discharge of all possible obligations ere the grand accounting comes. In worldly matters people are ever so careful to pay public dues and thus avoid any public disgrace. Chrysostom feels that this should be all the more true in things spiritual. Thus we may "render what is due to God, the King of all, first, that we may not come to that place, 'where is gnashing of teeth.' " [6]

The preacher enjoins virtues that will be not merely selfish aggrandizement but acts greatly profitable to neighbors. To this

---

[5] *Ibid.*, X, 468. Used by permission of the publishers.
[6] *Loc. cit.*

end, prayers and alms, among other things, are needful and effective. Again he pleads the analogy between the spiritual and the temporal:

> For, if in worldly matters no man lives for himself, but artisan, and soldier, and husbandman, and merchant, all of them contribute to the common good, and to their neighbor's advantage; much more ought we to do this in things spiritual. For this is most properly to live: since he at least who is living for himself only, and overlooking all others, is useless, and is not so much as a human being, nor of our race.[7]

The spiritual corollary of this calls for unselfish dedication to all those whom one can help. And none is so weak but that he may help one still weaker. Such is the proper regard for one's fellows in the light of impending judgment. If the Christian is ever to come into eternal life, he must do so with regard to the eternally valid principle of mutuality which Christ himself laid down:

> By all which things being persuaded that it is not possible for one to be saved, who hath not looked to the common good, and seeing this man that was cut asunder, and him that buried his talent, let us choose this way, that we may also attain unto eternal life, unto which God grant we may all attain, by the grace and love towards man of our Lord Jesus Christ, to whom be glory, world without end. Amen.[8]

In an earlier work, some of whose views he repudiates by implication in his *City of God,* Augustine accepts the chiliastic views often expressed in initial centuries. Significantly enough, he precedes his discussion of the "Thousand Years," as he follows it, with an admonition to consider the future life in all of its corporate felicities. Only by living a good life in the present community of Christians can one hope to join, not only the intermediate society of the millennium, but also the ultimate association of unending bliss which is heaven itself. He says explicitly:

> We exhort you and we conjure you, because you are Christians and carry the name of Jesus Christ on your foreheads and in your hearts, direct all your desires toward this life which we will have in common with the angels, toward this life where there will reign an unalterable repose, an eternal joy, a beatitude without end.[9]

[7] *Ibid.,* X, 469. Used by permission of the publishers.
[8] *Loc. cit.* Used by permission of the publishers.
[9] Serm. 259:1, MPL 38:1196; *De Civ. Dei,* XX, 7. See Thomas Aquinas' Commentary on P. Lombard's *Sentences,* Lib. 4, Dist., 43 in Thomas *Op. Om.,* XI, 270 ff., 282; note the convenient summation in *S. Theol.,* III, Supplement, Q. 77, Art. 1.

It is following this admonition that Augustine discusses his original view with regard to the "Thousand Years." [10] It is based, of course, upon the Apocalypse and the discussion found there concerning the reign of Jesus Christ with the saints on the earth. Augustine says that the eighth day is the emblem of the new life which awaits us at the end of history. Presumably, this is to follow upon the conclusion of the millennial reign. His concern with this final society to be consummated after the close of history is testimony once more to the fact that for chiliasts—Joachim, for instance—the thousand-year reign itself is not enough. This with all of its corporate joys is but a preview to the final beatitude in heaven.

After speaking of the eighth day, Augustine reverts to the seventh, which, he says, is the figure of the future repose which the saints will enjoy on the earth—in effect, the millennial Sabbath. Augustine goes on to say that in accordance with the Scriptures the Lord must thus reign with his saints on the earth and that his Church will not then number any wicked ones. This Church, he says, will appear at first on the earth in all its brightness, dignity, and justice. The Lord himself will come into its midst. There will be a separation of sinners from the good. Then the saints will appear. In a further section he proceeds to discuss the process whereby the saints will thus be established. He concludes that this then will be the seventh day; the preceding ones in their order will have been: first, from Adam to Noah; second, from Noah to Abraham; third, from Abraham to David; fourth, from David to the exile in Babylon; fifth, from the Babylonian exile to the coming of the Lord Jesus Christ; sixth, from the Advent of the Lord to the time in which Augustine and his friends dwell. Just as man was created on the sixth day in the image of God, so in the present time that sixth day is represented in our own regeneration through baptism, which registers in us the image of our creators. Now, upon the conclusion of this sixth day, there comes the repose and the mysterious Sabbath of God's righteous ones. After this seventh day, we shall enter into that repose of which Paul speaks when he says, "The eye of man has not seen, nor the ear heard. . . ." [11]

With the conclusion of the seven days, a spiritual week may be said to have come to a close; the eighth becomes the first of the week following. After the seven ages of this world have passed, we shall return to that blessed immortality from which man has come.

[10] Serm. 259:2, MPL 38:1197 ff.
[11] *Ibid.*, MPL 38:1198.

That is why it is the eighth day on which there terminate the feasts of the sacraments of infants.

It is at the conclusion of this rather lengthy discussion of the millennial period that Augustine stresses the preparation for the final beatitude. As he says at the beginning, if one hopes to enter this lasting repose, and if one would come from his pilgrimage into the celestial Jerusalem, he must practice works of mercy. Only by being merciful ourselves can we obtain graciousness from the Lord. The atmosphere is definitely one of mutuality. This is indispensable in the present life if one is to come, not only to the Sabbath repose, but also more significantly still to the eternal community of heaven. In his chiliastic period, Augustine is no more deprived than other chiliasts of a truly social concern for the ultimate hereafter; or for the present corporate preparation that must guarantee it.[12]

Coming next to the later position of the Bishop of Hippo, we find all the more interesting the reasons for his repudiation of his one-time millenarian views.[13] He recapitulates in the *City of God* the Revelator's mention of the two resurrections and of the thousand years in which the saints are to enjoy a kind of Sabbath-rest, "a holy leisure after the labors of the six thousand years since man was created, and was on account of his great sin dismissed from the blessedness of paradise into the woes of this mortal life." This position, Augustine thinks in retrospect, would not be amiss "if it were believed that the joys of the saints in that Sabbath shall be spiritual, and consequent on the presence of God; for I myself, too, once held this opinion." [14]

Augustine is here emphasizing the main tenet which the more balanced chiliasts stressed: namely, the assurance of a life with Christ on this earth in a community anticipating an even greater one. As he phrased his earlier opinions, the more objectionable aspects of chiliastic thought were not apparent. But Augustine had come to believe that many millenarians put an emphasis upon the period of Sabbath rest which permitted the expression of a shocking carnality. Speaking of these more exaggerated proponents of the Millennium, he says, "They who do believe them are called by the spiritual Chiliasts, which we may literally reproduce by the name Millenarians." [15]

[12] Actually, 259.3-6, MPL 38:1198-1201, bears in its entirety upon this problem.
[13] *De Civ. Dei*, XX, 7; NPNF, 1st. Ser., II, 426; cf. Serm. 259.
[14] *De Civ. Dei*, XX, 7; NPNF, 1st. Ser., II, 426.
[15] *Loc. cit.*

Disavowing any attempt at a satisfactorily detailed critique, he proposes a suitable interpretation of the scriptural Millennium. The Millennium may be understood in two ways: First, one may think in terms of a sixth period of one thousand years, the latter part of which is now current. During this sixth day, which is to be followed by a Sabbath unending, there is to come the endless rest of the saints. Thus under the partial symbol of the Thousand Years the whole portion might be denominated. Second, one may conceive of the Thousand Years as an equivalent to the whole duration of the existing world; in which case the number seven, indicative of perfection, would be held to mark the fullness of time. Whereupon Augustine employs mathematical calculations to show how this may be true.[16]

Pohle, for his part, interprets Augustine and Gregory the Great, who follows his viewpoint, as meaning that Christ's millennial reign with the saints on earth—that is, the first resurrection—represents the kingdom of heaven, "where the Blessed reign under the headship of our Lord before the 'second resurrection' (i.e., the Resurrection of the flesh)." This would make the term "first death" apply to the separation of the body from soul, and the "second death," to eternal damnation. Obviously, if this interpretation is accepted, the number One Thousand loses a literal significance and simply refers to "an indefinite period of considerable length." [17]

There is little virtue in expanding the suggestions of official documents or in multiplying references to early medieval teachings on Last Things and Final Judgment. Whether in the sermons of Bede, the utterances of Columban, the commentaries of Maurus, or the somewhat distorted reporting of Glaber, the emphasis upon eschatological expectations remains a commonplace. Anselm and Hugh the Victorine, as well as Honorius of Autun and Peter Lombard, do little more than rearrange the long-standing convictions of the Church. The writings of historians like Ordericus Vitalis and of crusading annalists like Guibert de Nogent and William of Tyre are full of references to the portents of evil and the anticipations of antichrist.[18]

---

[16] *Ibid.*, II, 427.

[17] *Eschatology*, p. 158.

[18] See the copious references to these and others in MPL 220:291 f., "Index de judicio universali et ultimo." A convenient summary of representative sources is MacCulloch, *Medieval Faith and Fable*, pp. 287-99; also, Petry, "Medieval Eschatology," *Church History*, IX, 1 (1940) , 54 ff., and notes. Consult, for example, Gregory I's *Hom. I in Evang.*, MPL 76:1077 ff., the Bede the Venerable's report of Pope Gregory's Letter to King Ethelbert,

It is not difficult to demonstrate the prevailing eschatological mood of leading popes as well as of great theologians and common people in the Middle Ages. Thus Urban II, at the Council of Clermont, is reported to have said, "as the times of anti-Christ [are] approaching and as the East, and especially Jerusalem [will] be the central point of attack, there must be Christians there to resist them." He was sure that the times of the Gentiles were about to be accomplished and that the end of the world was near. Apparently, this involved a certain measure of literary hyperbole; but it was not wholly limited to this. Urban and others like him do seem to have anticipated, seriously, the Final Days. It is significant that they, like Hildegarde, felt it necessary to call for a stiffening of the Christian community against the onslaught of Christ's enemies.[19] Innocent III, likewise, insisted that the resources of Christendom must be consolidated more effectively as the end of this beast—that is, antichrist—draws near. Of course Gregory VII often despaired of the world in his own day, even as Gregory I had in his.[20]

Hildegarde of Bingen (1179) comes in that group of remarkable medieval women who are not without right to the rank of prophetess. Her whole concern with the divine revelation is represented to us through the medium of numerous visions which she is supposed to have transmitted to others who then put them in written form. One of the most fearless souls of Christian history, she derived from her contact with the Divine a sense of obligation to speak, not only to given individuals, but also to the society of her era. Her direct analysis of existing conditions is preserved likewise in a large body of letters; some of which may not be genuine, but a large proportion of which accurately record her dealings with every type and condition of people in a variety of circumstances.[21]

As reputable historians have pointed out, she was ready, not only to criticize, but also to suggest the bases for social and individual improvement. Many of her castigations of the clergy are still referred

---

Hist., Eccl. Lib. I. cap. 32, Loeb edition, I, 172, 173 (Greg. Ep. 66, MPL 77:1203), R. Glaber's *Chronicon*, II, 5-7, III, 5, IV, 5, 7, 9, etc., in MPL 142:634 ff. (Coulton, *Life,* I, 1-8), Ordericus Vitalis' *Hist. Eccl.* Pars II, MPL 188:375, Hugh of St. Victor, *De Sacram.,* Lib. II, Pars 17, MPL 176:597-610, Wilmart, "La complainte de Jean de Fécamp sur les fins dernières," *Auteurs spirituels*, pp. 126-37, C. Clair, *Le Dies Irae* (Paris, 1881), K. Young, *The Drama of the Medieval Church* (2 Vols., Oxford, 1933), II, 360-96, 524; I, 544, 682, Appendices, and R. de Gourmont, *Le Latin Mystique* (Paris, 1930).

[19] MacCulloch, *Medieval Faith and Fable,* p. 290; Hildegarde, *Scivias,* Lib. III, Visiones XI-XIII, MPL 197:707-30.

[20] *Reg.* Lib. XVI, Ep. 28, MPL 216:818 A-B; cf. Wadstein, *op. cit.,* p. 125.

[21] MPL 197 for her *Scivias.*

to as examples of the nontemporizing quality so admired and yet so often feared in the true prophet. Like the prophet, also, she felt called upon to lay down the bases of constructive effort as a preventive against imminent doom. She apparently had no childish desire to incriminate. Like the Old Testament prophets, she preached doom in order to avoid it. If she found many faults, not only in the clergy, but also in kings, princes, and other men of power—not ignoring the many shortcomings of lesser individuals—she also felt called upon to proclaim the ultimate society of God's kingdom as the basis for an inspiriting program of social responsibility in her own day. Countless letters, as well as her *Visions,* clearly evidence this fact.

She was no more inclined than the average medieval person to suggest a revolution in the classes and total structure of society. What she did demand was a more Christian concept of the individual and of the existing social pattern, together with a revitalized response in terms of the Christian ethic.[22]

Beginning with the eleventh Vision of her third book, she lends new color to a well-worn theme. Having stated in the conclusion of the previous Vision how necessary it is for the faithful to exemplify good works, she now comes to a consideration of the Last Days which shall witness the coming of antichrist and the whole train of disasters that shall precede the Last Judgment. The symbols that she utilizes are freely adapted from the Revelation of John. After recapitulating the well-known series of phenomena that were generally attributed to the Last Days, she proceeds at last to treat the challenge and sufferings of the faithful in the heyday of antichrist. It is her wish that Christians everywhere be prepared to read the signs of the Last Days and to make preparation for the tragic circumstances attending them.[23]

She has much to say about the six days in which God completed his work of creation and the seventh on which he rested from his work. These six days are, she thinks, a sign of the six ages of the world. They look toward a seventh. In fact, in her own day the seventh age has already begun and leads directly toward the Last Things. She reminds her hearers that the gospel was to be preached in the whole world before the conclusion of history. This, it would appear, has now been done. What is most dolorous is the observable

[22] G. G. Coulton, *Five Centuries of Religion,* III, 327-28 (MPL 197:336).
[23] Cf. MPL 197:714-22, on the pertinent data of Visio XI, Lib. III.

fact that Catholic faith now vacillates; that the gospel finds itself defectively utilized among men. The burden of Hildegarde's admonition is that now if ever is the time for proponents of the gospel to speak to their age with a message of Christian word and life.

Hildegarde appeals to fruitful doctors and spiritual leaders to redeem their souls and strongly clamor this vital, scriptural word; let them not be incredulous. If they spurn this word, they will betray the Lord and condemn themselves. God's ministers have the continuing duty of nourishing his people on his law. Let them now prosecute this task while there is still time; before those days come in which there is no longer an opportunity to work. The Son of Perdition is even now on the way. The faithful ministers of the Lord, his own elect, need to arise and be prepared. Antichrist will not long postpone his attack upon the followers of the Lord. It has been foretold that in those Last Days some in the Church will fall into errors. Now, if ever, is the time for all to take precautions against being seduced. This is the time for Christian leaders to help make the faithful proof against error.[24]

The Church itself cannot be conceived of as existing apart from its head and true members. Nothing must be allowed to compromise its integrity. A head without viscera and other members is unthinkable. The head of the Church is the Son of God; the viscera and other members are the body of his Sonship. The Church is not as yet perfect in its constituency; but in the Last Days, when the number of the elect shall have been made up, the Church, also, will be complete.[25]

Those same days will be the time of final testing; of disastrous defection for some and of final reconciliation with the faithful for others. The time of the sixth age is now finished, and the time of the seventh is come. Those days are about over in which the faithful may do their work. Faithful Christians may not expect to know those secrets of the Last Days and their exact times, which are in the hands of God alone. But plentiful evidence will be available to them to indicate the mounting danger and the necessity for fulfilling their responsibilities.[26]

Hildegarde's passionate hope is that her hearers may not be swept into destruction through the wiles of the evil Son of Perdition. It is her opportune responsibility to transmit to them the Lord's own

[24] *Ibid.,* 714-18; Mechthild, *Revelations,* VI, 15 (179 ff.).
[25] *Ibid.,* 715-16.
[26] *Ibid.,* 716-18.

warning lest they be overcome. Let them be well prepared to make a valiant stand whatever the cost to themselves. The prophetess' voice is stern and clear in its depiction of the signs that precede the last awful days. She takes the imagery of the Biblical Apocalypse and fits it with awe-inspiring precision into the proximate circumstances of her own days. She stresses the scriptural warning that people of every social class and every kind of life will be drawn into tragic defeat by the hideous subterfuges of the antichrist. It will take every quality of Christian discipline and awareness to foil the incursions of this opponent of the Lord.

Not the least of his devilish ingenuities will be the manner in which he will simulate the qualities of the true king. The only ones who will be proof against him are those who hold fast the faith in continuous alertness against all evil. But in the Last Day, the evil one will move about with stupefying power to compel men's minds and hearts. It will be all too easy to follow him in place of the true Lord. The old gospel admonition to take one's proper side in behalf of Christ against Satan comes once more to mind.[27]

Because there is such great need to counteract the speciousness of antichrist's appeal, the Lord will send his two faithful witnesses, Enoch and Elias; it will be their task to repel the evil one and restore errant souls to the way of truth. These will have been recalled to the human scene in order to solidify the faithful. These two witnesses of the truth will then proclaim their mission. It is for this very time of testing that they have been held in reserve by God; to this end they have been sent to the faithful, that they may contradict the flagrant errors of untruth and rescue the men of faith. Enoch and his companion will prevail with the aid of right doctrine against the cohorts of the Lord's detractors; thus bringing stability and cohesiveness to the ranks of the just.

Those strengthened by the witness of the Lord's two great servants will seek to draw their brothers together in the hope of a glorious eternal life. But the monstrous one will continue in his attempt to support himself with those drawn from the ranks of the previously faithful. He will try to compromise the unity of Christians and to join unto himself all whom he may. He will have at his disposal innumerable arts of cunning for waging his subtle campaign. Only at the very last will he be conquered with God's righteous power. Then, only, will limits be fixed to his power. In the meantime he

[27] *Ibid.*, 718-19.

will wage war to the very death against the Lord and his faithful. Hildegarde reverts once more to her oft-repeated warning: The only possible way in which to live through this terrifying series of events to come is to be prepared well in advance. It is for the final Judgment, which shall surmount all of these happenings, that all must stand in readiness.[28]

Hildegarde's vision of the future is permeated with a sense of corporateness. She believes that the faithful must stand together as a body of Christ in anticipation of eternal society if they are to prevail as individuals. It is, of course, the peculiar opportunity and dangerous responsibility of all leaders to help make their fellows a more unified band in the testing-time just ahead. Her word pictures and her eloquent pleas are reminiscent of the Great Apocalypse. Only those will be worthy to join in the final beatitude with the Lamb who have proved themselves faithful against every suffering, including death itself, which the present life can impose. The only way of guaranteeing a place for the individual in the eternal society is the commitment of the individual to the common interest of the present Christian body. The social life of the present will thus be a preparation for the ineffable joys of everlasting community.

The twelfth Vision, much shorter than the one preceding, is a colorful summation of accepted teachings on the Resurrection and the Judgment. Following the calamitous events of the latter days, the Son will come with a commission direct from the Father himself to judge the whole world. This he will do under the form of his humanity. Hildegarde, like her medieval contemporaries, has no reservations as to the completely social character of this last great assize. None will be absent from it. Following the defeat of the evil one and his angels, the Lord will come to confront all men in their state of bodily resurgence. A great voice will cry out: "Oh, you sons of men who lie in the earth, arise all of you." The flesh and bones of all those who have passed away will come together in a moment, and every person will stand forth again in his proper bodily state. The Lord, appearing with his holy angels, will carry out his proper function of Judgment as he separates the evil, eternally, from the good. To the just he will speak with gentle voice, calling them to a blessed reign with him in heaven. With a terrible voice he will consign the evil ones to the pains of hell.[29]

No long-drawn-out inquiry or argument about one's judgment

[28] *Ibid.*, 720-24.
[29] *Scivias*, Lib. III, Visio XII, MPL 197:725 A ff.; Steele, *Visions*, pp. 169-72.

will be necessary or countenanced. After all, the works of each, whether good or evil, will be apparent to the eyes of all in an instant. Hildegarde, in a few moving words, directs the attention of the Christian to the splendor with which the happy ones shall be associated in the celestial joys. With the Son of God and with the holy angels, they shall have unceasing rejoicing; just as the wretches who are forever consigned to the infernal regions shall have unceasing woes. These things are beyond the power of any human being to describe.[30]

Similarly, Hildegarde looks forward to the destruction of the world and its renewal. Now looking far ahead to the conclusion of the whole process, now reverting to some items of special interest in the preceding judgment, the prophetess sees the whole vast panorama of Last Things and the end of history. She is under an inner compulsion to proclaim the indispensability of a good life, social and therefore individual, if Christians are to hear the joyous pronouncement of their salvation at the Last Judgment. Some will be signed with the marks of faith; others will not. Some will bear about them the unmistakable signs of their devotion and good works. Others will lack these signs of faith; for they will have had no desire to concern themselves either with the old law or with the new grace; nor will they have concerned themselves with a knowledge of the true and living God which these proclaim. The Son of God in the form of his humanity and his passion will now proceed to judge those unto whom he formerly offered the means of salvation. This will be most fitting inasmuch as the Son always retained his share of the divine life, but accepted humanity through his human birth. Thus, he who is at once God and man judges in that human capacity with which he first came to earth.[31]

It is only just that the good and evil men should be forever separated, since their works are fundamentally dissimilar. Those who rejoice in eternal life because of the lives which they previously lived will comprise every kind of human beings. The flowers of God's Son will include patriarchs and prophets who were before his incarnation, as well as those who came after it. Every age and condition since the world began will have been judged. Naturally, therefore, those admitted to the heavenly company will include martyrs, confessors, virgins, widows, and all who have imitated the Lord; whether in the regular or in the secular areas of the spiritual life. Not only anchorites

---

[30] *Ibid.*, 725 C-D; Steele, *Visions*, 172-73.
[31] *Ibid.*, 726-27; Steele, *Visions*, 174-79.

and monks who followed the way of fleshly mortification, but all others, likewise, who put eternal life before present consideration, seeking the Lord in humility and daily conversation, are to be called to high places in the heavenly country. When finally the whole transaction shall have been consummated, the elect shall be ushered into the splendors of the celestial company and the reprobate into that irrevocably damned condition which has companionship with the devil and his angels.[32]

Bernard of Cluny's judgment scene is replete with references to the social responsibility of those who come up before the man-God; he will appear, not as father, but as judge. His objective will be to restore justice. It behooves all mankind to "Arise, and walk the narrow path." This king, who will come at an unknown moment, knows all the facts of all men's lives. Bernard counsels his fellows to remove guilt and dross while there is yet time. This means giving to the needy. "Make ready a lowly place for him that aspires too high. The Judge stands over us, and will tell exactly what he means to give us and what he has given."[33]

Bernard has a thoroughly socialized conception of the great Judgment. Those sent to the left hand are an impious band. Those on the right hear the invitation: "Come into my kingdom, my flock." Their happy concourse enters heaven with Christ at their head.[34]

The earth and all its glories quake as they face an imminent Judgment Day. Volatile imaginations conjure up stories about bands of the dead rushing to the place of judgment. Too much of evil, both individual and social, is already on the Domesday Books to avert the reckoning much longer. The end is coming and the world's glory is vanishing in a flood of terrorizing injustice, murder, oppression, and war. Unless the Scriptures lie, the Last Days are at hand. Antichrist is ready. The Judge threatens. This is no time for bestiality and delay. The signs Paul spoke of as being irrefutable evidences of the end are multiplying everywhere.[35]

The last paragraph of the first book calls upon a reckless race to repudiate its impiety while it may. Now is the time for every man to hold to the right and repent of wickedness. The obvious trouble with humanity is that it has "refused to stand and has drifted into

[32] *Ibid.*, 728-30; Steele, *Visions,* 180-86; Mechthild, *Revelations,* VII, 1 (206-10). For a discussion of Mechthild on Judgment and Last Things see J. Ancelet-Hustache, *Mechtilde de Magdebourg (1207-1282)* (Paris, 1926), pp. 272 ff.
[33] See Chap. V, nn. 30, 31; SJG, I, 105; DCM, I, 1-11 (1).
[34] SJG, I, 105; DCM, I, 19-22 (1-2).
[35] DCM, I, 985-1048 (34-36).

evil; let it stand by the good." Since the hour of doom is near and the times are all awry, the old Pauline admonition deserves full sway: "Let us awake." [36]

Reginald of Piperno, who arranged Thomas Aquinas' writings on the Last Days, deals with the uncertain time of the Last Judgment. His readers are reminded that salutary effects result from this very inability of human beings to know the time of man's Final Judgment. This conduces to watchfulness in two ways:

> First, as regards the thing ignored, since its delay is equal to the length of man's life, so that on either side uncertainty provokes him to greater care. Secondly, for the reason that a man is careful not only of his own person, but also of his family, or of his city or kingdom, or of the whole Church, the length of whose duration is not dependent on the length of man's life. And yet it behoves each of these to be so ordered that the day of the Lord find us not unprepared.[37]

Further evidence as to the accepted thought about antichrist and the Last Judgment is readily available. Otto of Freising gave a detailed analysis of Last Things.[38] Adam Marsh, the learned Franciscan, was highly pessimistic as he surveyed his own age. Antichrist and the end of the world were surely not far off.[39] Roger Bacon demonstrated the impress of thoroughly medieval ideas when he speculated upon the manner of reforming the Church.[40] Many learned scholars had, from their studies of the Bible, become convinced that the days of antichrist were near. Bacon was not ready to commit himself completely on such speculative matters; but he did feel that the sobering possibilities called for the utmost in a social reordering of Christendom. There must be a reform of faith and morals together with a further missionization of the heathen. This could not be accomplished aside from the efforts of some good pope or emperor; or apart from the results of improved theological knowledge with all of its consequences for the world of science and the arts. Barring such creative efforts of a co-ordinated kind, some great disaster would have to bring about what Christian effort failed to do. In spite of some passages of ambiguous slant, the total thought of Bacon clearly involves

---

[36] SJG, I, 128-29; DCM, I, 1049-78 (36-37).

[37] *S. Theol.* III, (Supplement), Q. 88, Art. 3, Reply obj. 4. Dominican Fathers' translation, pp. 16-18, especially p. 18. Used by permission of the publishers, Burns Oates & Washbourne, Ltd.

[38] *Two Cities,* Bk. VIII.

[39] Ep. 244:407 ff.

[40] *Phil. Studii* (Coulton, *Life,* III, 55-60).

a belief in antichrist and the necessity of planned efforts on the part of the faithful to forestall him.[41]

The late medieval work *Pricke of Conscience* contains a graphic account of Last Days.[42] Men must answer at the Judgment for all gifts of grace and knowledge. All honors, power, and riches lead to a final reckoning. Some will stand condemned for failure to use their God-given gifts for the good of the whole. Just as each limb of a body is ready according to its powers to serve all the others, so every man that lives here on earth should, with all that God graciously gives him, serve others as they have need, on pain of the fiend. The mighty are obliged to defend them that are less so; and those of great riches, to give to them that here walk in poverty. Lawyers owe a service to those in need of counsel; leeches have a responsible ministry to the sick. Learned men have a service to perform to the unlettered. Preachers must proclaim "Goddes Worde" and teach the way of life to others. Thus each man is bound with good intent to help others with that which God has lent them. Freely, for God's love and for nought else, one is responsible for administering to others the graces and the goods that have so freely been given to him.

At the great Assize, sons and daughters formerly unchastened by their parents shall accuse these of their neglect. Such fathers and mothers have failed to teach them good manners; out of the father's negligence and discipline has come damnation to the child. And the father, too, goes to destruction, since he is the cause of his children's guilt.[43]

The medieval world sought least of all a social revolution in class and purse. Yet there was a sense of social obligation, however unlike that of our times. At Domesday those would stand accused and ultimately condemned who failed in their duties to the poor. In sight and sound of all assembled, the sovereign Judge would hear the poor accuse the irresponsible rich of having no mercy to the indigent. Refusing to feed or clothe the needy, the wealthy had preferred, rather, to let their gold rust. They had kept their stored-up treasure houses unopened to the alleviation of sore distress. Therefore, their rusted coins would, themselves, witness against them. The very worms and moths breeding in the unused garments of the superabundant rich would plead the poor man's case against his wealthy fellow man.[44]

---

[41] *Ibid.;* cf. R. Carton, *L'expérience physique . . . l'expérience mystique . . . la synthèse doctrinale de Roger Bacon* (3 Vols., Paris, 1924).

[42] Book V. See Chap. XIII, n. 10.

[43] Ll. 5908-6003, pp. 160-62; Ll. 5544 ff., pp. 150 ff.

[44] Ll. 5560-75, p. 151.

There is here no suggestion that rulers shall not be obeyed. But kings have a responsibility to God for the well-being of their subjects. At the Day of Doom, subjects will accuse their sovereigns who have grieved them through "maystie and myght" and otherwise "wald do tham na right." [45]

John Bromyard in his handbook of preaching analyzes Final Things.[46] Dr. G. R. Owst deduces from this Dominican's frenzied cries for justice in the Last Day a sincere, but mainly negative, social attitude. But Bromyard is positing in the awful Judgment scene a corporate dramatization of the necessity for greater social righteousness in the days that will have preceded it. The friar-preacher has not created his judgment setting for the sole purpose of wreaking anticipatory vengeance upon the powerful of the earth. As Professor Owst shows in his digests and translations from the original, the condemned ones represent a wide gamut of life: Included are wicked churchmen who have failed in their responsibility to the poor; also usurers, false merchants, and scoundrels from the lowest reaches of society, as well as the upper strata of both Church and State.[47]

Stating their case against those who oppressed them on earth, the aggrieved ones turn to Christ the Judge. They describe themselves in Jesus' own terms as the hungry from whom the unscrupulous took both labors and goods. A further accounting is sought by those who were beaten and afflicted in their infirmity. They fix accusing eyes on the men now under judgment who, in addition to exacting such a toll of misery, were also the cause of evicting the shelterless from home and country. Yet others depict the imprisonment to which they were brought by false charges. The bodies of some victims have even been denied consecrated ground. The righteous Judge is called upon to avenge the blood thus shed and the injustices thus perpetrated.

The just God and mighty Judge is reminded that the game played on earth was not fairly divided between the victims and their oppressors. When their lords were merry with joust and tournament, they profited at the expense of the poor. The scarcity of the impoverished was made to yield the plenty of their masters. The excesses of the rich were the mockery of the indigent.[48]

The time has now come for such injustices to be rectified. Let

[45] Ll. 5576-81, p. 151.

[46] *Summa praedicantium* (2 Vols., Venice, 1586), especially Pars I, Cols. 306-9, 410 ff.

[47] *Literature and Pulpit in Medieval England* (Cambridge, 1933), pp. 210 ff., 224 ff. 301-3; Coulton, *Five Centuries*, II, 576; *Summa praedicantium* I, Col. 308, Sec. 10.

[48] *Ibid.*, I, Col. 308, Secs. 11-12.

those who called themselves great and noble on earth now prepare for the dire sentence that is sure to be handed down against them. Owst is justified in apostrophizing the superb quality of this literary recapitulation. Inflammatory and revolutionary in its oratory, it need not rank second in anything to the *Vision of Piers Plowman*—a work properly described, though improperly appreciated in its motivation, by some critics as "the cry of an injured man who appeals to Heaven for vengeance." As Dr. Owst further observes, the discussion on the wealthy and their riches in Bromyard's great *Summa* involves a well-considered rebuke for the rich of earth. These holders of earthly stewardship departed far from their divinely charted course in using their substance for their sole benefit.[49]

One would certainly fall under censure of the facts if he were to deny the more selfishly embittered character of much pulpiteering like the above. Nonetheless, the corporate judgment there envisaged places, in admonitory relief, the collective responsibility of all who face its imminent coming. One should not construe this as a modern plea for social reconstruction applied on a grand scale within the established order. It is only fair to remind ourselves, however, that Bromyard, as well as Piers Plowman, Chaucer, and the rest, was prepared to counsel improved mutuality on the temporal scene as the best possible preparation for the judgment test and the consummately social joys that lay beyond.

One of the striking passages in Birgitta's *Revelations* concerns that time when the sovereign emperor of the universe makes ready to "hear doomes upon the princes of earth." "The kings that I saw were not bodily but spiritual," says Birgitta. First of all came King Abraham, with the saints that were of his generation. Patriarchs and prophets succeeded him; after which the four evangelists, whose shapes were similar to the four beasts, came upon the scene. The prophetess next had her attention called to twelve seats in which sat twelve apostles, waiting the grand consummation. Adam and Eve next appeared with martyrs and confessors and all other saints. As yet, however, Christ in his manhood was not visible, nor was the body of his blessed Mother. The very earth and the waters in it seemed to be lifted up to heaven, and all the things that were in the earth made obeisance and reverently waited the coming of "the Power." [50]

[49] Owst, *op. cit.*, pp. 302-3.
[50] *Revel.*, Bk. VIII, Chap. 58, fol. 59b, Cumming ed., p. 94.

After this an altar that was in the very seat of majesty became visible; and a chalice appeared with wine, water, and bread in the likeness of a host offered upon the altar. At this moment Birgitta saw, as it were, a priest beginning mass, properly arrayed in priest's clothing. When he had done all that belonged to the mass, and when he had come to the words with which he should bless the host, Birgitta seemed to see the sun, moon, and stars with all the other planets and all the heavens with their courses caught up in a heavenly melody. The sweetness of the sound was beyond all description. Those that were in the light beheld the priest and inclined to "the Power" with reverence and worship; and they that were in darkness had horror and dread.[51]

Birgitta explains that, as the words of God were said by the priest over the host, it seemed to her as if this same host were in the seat of majesty, yet abiding nonetheless in the hands of the priest. And this same holy host became a living Lamb, which took unto itself the face of a man. A bright light was seen all about him. To look on his face was to see the Lamb and to look upon the Lamb was to see that bright face. The Virgin herself sat, crowned by the Lamb; and all the angels served them. An innumerable multitude was all about. Some vacant places were observable. These were yet to be fulfilled in the worship of God.[52]

Just at this time a great voice comes out of the earth, proceeding from thousands who cry aloud. They demand a verdict of doom, from God the great judge, upon their kings and princes. These rulers are guilty of shedding the blood of their subjects and of bringing anguish to wives and children. The plaintiffs offer as further evidence their wounds and imprisonments, the burning of their homes, and the violation of women. They point to the mistreatment of clergy and to the general victimization of the people—all this being brought about to uphold the pride of the regnant classes.[53]

A great cry now wells up from hell—the voices of countless thousands who call upon the Lord to pronounce doom upon these lords whom they served while on earth. Because of their former masters they are drowned deeper in hell than they ought to be. Their earthly lords lacked true charity. They cared no more for human souls than for dogs. These callous leaders were unconcerned over the spiritual obligations of their subordinates to the common Maker of all. Such

[51] *Ibid.*, fol. 59b-60a, Cumming ed., pp. 94-95.
[52] *Ibid.*, fol. 60a, Cumming ed., p. 95.
[53] *Loc. cit.*

disregard by temporal leaders for the soul welfare of their subjects must incur rejection from heaven. This disservice to inferiors by superiors will entail the rewards of hell, which can be set aside only by the gracious intervention of God.[54] Thus does the indictment of the infernal city itself come up against those about to be judged.

In their turn, the inhabitants of purgatory break out in piteous cries for judgment against the lords that they knew on earth. Because of remissness on the part of their superiors they require a longer period of purgatorial suffering. Good government, together with exemplary life and counsel, was not forthcoming from the rulers to help save those ruled. Purgatorial sufferers remember how, on the contrary, they were actually condoned in evil and provoked to it, further, by their overlords. As a consequence, they now suffer longer and all the more pitifully.[55]

Abraham, the patriarchs, the prophets, and the evangelists next submit their indictments against the princes of earth—these who have failed in their responsibility, although they have clearly been given an opportunity to follow the Lord in his charity and saving life. The Apostles remind the Judge of their own judicial responsibilities. They, too, call down the divine wrath upon these despoilers of God's body and his precepts. When, however, the blessed Virgin who sits by the Lamb calls upon her "most sweet Lord" to have mercy upon the accursed, the Judge cannot deny her. He declares that those who turn from sin and do worthy penance shall find mercy. Doom shall be turned away from them.[56]

Obviously, the judgment here represented in process is an imaginative reconstruction of what may ensue if lives are not amended in accordance with social and individual responsibility. Birgitta does not mean to suggest that at the Last Judgment there will still be opportunity for a reassessment of accounts. The context indicates that we deal here with a combination of images conjured up by meditation on the Final Judgment. A salutary exercise of the imagination attempts to see the Judgment in process by anticipation—while there is yet time to make ready for it.[57]

The last part of the *Towneley Plays* deals with Judgment. Introduced into the dramatic narrative are some distinctive characteristics.

---

[54] Fol. 60b, Cumming ed., pp. 95-96.
[55] Fol. 60b, Cumming ed., p. 96.
[56] Fol. 61a, Cumming ed., pp. 96-97.
[57] See the entire section, Cumming ed., pp. 87-97. For a Latin text, see *Revelationes Selectae S. Birgittae* († 1373), ed. A. Heuser (Cologne, 1851).

The conversations between the demons and devils who take part in the Last Judgment are rather novel. One demon complains that if Doom's Day had been delayed much longer, hell would have had to be considerably enlarged. Another speaks of the extra labor involved in carrying increasing numbers of the depraved to their fitting abodes.[58]

The really significant portion of the work, however, is to be found in the latter part of the play. Here the patently social consequences of the Judgment are clearly delineated. The blessed in heaven are taken into Christ's kingdom because they had proper regard for the needs of other men. The wicked are summoned to hell because, in the words of Matthew 25, they did not minister to Christ in the name of his little ones.

There is a typical description of the personnel of heaven and the society of the damned. The sins of the wicked are held up to intimate scrutiny. Included are the seven deadly sins, the vices of usury and extortion, and an extended sweep of social enormities.[59]

The impact which prevailing theological views made upon the medieval mind is perhaps best adduced from the literature that was current in visual form among the ordinary people. Thus the pantomimes and dramatic representations of the mystery of redemption were widely encountered in medieval England, as elsewhere.[60]

In a representative play, appearing with variations in many eras, Christ appears surrounded by angels with Michael holding the scales. Other angels carry the cross, nails, spear, and other instruments of his suffering on the tree. Gabriel is ready with his trumpet. Entombed ones are represented by a great group which lies upon the stage in readiness for the last trump. The Father may be seen in heaven, seated in glory. In turn, the various members of the cast play their parts in what must have been a most sobering reminder of final events.[61]

Michael is the first to come forward. He calls upon all men to rise in preparation for the Final Judgment. The Judge is already in the skies making ready the Day of Doom. The archangel declares that great and small must now come forward. No one will be spared in

---

[58] Ed. George England and A. W. Pollard (EETS, ES, 71, London, 1897); Wells, *Manual*, pp. 555 ff., 860-61.

[59] XXX, "The Judgment," pp. 367 ff.; especially Ll. 233 ff., 282 ff., 296 ff., 359 ff., 434 ff., 568 ff.

[60] H. W. Wells and R. S. Loomis, *Representative Medieval and Tudor Plays* (New York, 1942).

[61] *Ibid.*, pp. 201-6; Scene IV: "The Last Judgment."

the final questioning or in the reward which shall follow upon the Lord's decision. The divine knowledge will cut through every subterfuge and bring the whole truth to light. In his preliminary address, Michael reminds his hearers that all mankind of every condition— whether pope, prince, priest, king, kaiser; whether poor, rich, famous, lout, lady, knight, or clown—will be brought into the limelight of this final assize. Each one may as well start searching his conscience; "for God's revenge admits no screen." [62]

Souls now come forward from the imprisonment of clay to see their "sins in heaven's glass." The devils set up a great hue and cry. The souls again call upon the Lord for help; though well they know that "it is too late to pray for grace." God calls to his blessed ones, his brethren all, his children dear, to advance toward him in his "high hall." All are admonished to come forward fearlessly who have held him in righteous fear:

> All foul worms from you shall fall;
> With my right hand I bless you here,
> Burnishing you bright as the sun's ball,
> Like a keen crystal cleansing you clear,
>   Your filth fades suddenly.
> Peter, my servant, go you straight
> To loose the locks of heaven's gate,
> Let not my blessed children wait,
>   But bring them glad to Me.[63]

Peter declares the gates of heaven open to these dear brethren. They are invited to come and sit on God's right hand, where mirth and melody never cease. And as the saved ones move forward, in utter humility and gladness, to claim their place in worshipful joyousness with the one who died to save them, God again proclaims them welcome to that felicity which shall be eternal.[64]

The damned cry to God for mercy; but the Lord replies: "What have you done that I should save your souls? What was your merciful deed that mercy here might win?" The first devil knows well enough that there is no mercy for such as these. Christ, being unwilling to pronounce a verdict without explanation, speaks further in language

[62] *Ibid.*, p. 201.

[63] From *Representative Medieval and Tudor Plays*, pp. 202-3. Translated and edited by Henry W. Wells and Roger S. Loomis, copyright 1942 by Sheed & Ward, Inc., New York. Used by permission.

[64] *Ibid.*, p. 203.

reminiscent of Matthew 25. He shows how truly social are the standards of judgment for those who would enter the final society of the kingdom. He says:

> To the hungry and thirsty who asked in My name
> For meat and drink, you would give none.
> You left poor naked folk in shame,
> You sought no prisoners nor men undone.
> You had no pity on sick or lame;
> You did no charity, no, not one.
> You treated the homeless man the same,
> You buried no poor man under the sun.
> These deeds condemn you still!
> For your love I was rent on the rood,
> And for your sake I shed my blood.
> When I was so merciful and so good
> Why have you worked against My will? [65]

A second devil promptly reminds the sinful that they were stern in their pride and had no regard for the poor man and his needs. Yet a third devil remarks in the faces of the damned the clear signs of hardheartedness: A thirsty man would stand no chance with such as these. Other devils in turn then add their abusive verdicts. Those whom the Lord now turns aside are those who were characterized in life by backbiting, anger, and spitefulness. Envy was their constant companion. Prisoners got no cheer from them. To neighbors they were unkind. The approach of death itself brought no helping response from them. Slothfulness obscured their vision. The regular services of the Church received no support from them. The dead were left "to rot in the wind." Not the least of their viciousness came as a result of gluttony and riotousness which "broke good people's rest." Sinful pleasures crowded out their response to the needs of helpless people:

> For the naked or men in poor array
> You would not spare a drop of dew,
> Or a single thread, the truth to say,
> When they asked in heaven's name.[66]

The damned in one last frenzy of despair call upon the Lord to

---

[65] *Ibid.*, pp. 203-4. Used by permission.
[66] *Ibid.*, p. 205. Used by permission.

render them mercy and not his rightful justice. But the Lord is now adamant. The unhappy ones are led off to eternal hell and its companionship of woes.[67] The saved, on the other hand, move upward in glad rejoicing:

> But we have risen above the skies,
> Where all our bliss and gladness lies.
> We greet the Lord with glad surprise:
> *Te deum laudamus!* [68]

Literary interpreters have noted how pervasively the thought of the Last Judgment imbedded itself in the consciousness of medieval people. This is not, of course, to place reliance in the old myth of the year One Thousand, or to assume that the common people were constantly racked with torturous fears of world's end. This article of Catholic belief was, however, never far below the level of popular awareness. A long series of writings, poetical and otherwise, shows the preponderance of eschatological thought—much of it all the more significant because it constituted a part of the subconscious scheme of life. Men did consistently think of the Last Judgment as a certainty; they regarded it, also, as a time and circumstance when human justice with all of its inequalities would be replaced by an eternal disposition that would be all-righteous. It has been said with reason that the doctrine of the Last Judgment was at once "the care and also the consolation of the Middle Ages." [69]

One cannot easily forget the role of the *Dies Irae* and other related works. This famous writing is available in numerous forms, partly owing, no doubt, to its having come down in a plethora of versions from an ancient, or at least early medieval, provenance.[70] *The Day of Wrath* adds nothing new to the early and medieval conceptions of the Last Judgment. It, too, represents the terrifying circumstances that are to attend the Last Days of disorder and the ushering in of systematic Judgment. What terror there will be when the divine King himself comes to judge us all! When, too, the Judge will have seated himself and his tribunal, nothing will remain unrewarded; everything and everybody, both good and evil, will be clearly known to all.

---

[67] *Ibid.*, p. 206.
[68] *Loc. cit.* Used by permission.
[69] R. de Gourmont, *La Latin mystique*, p. 289. Cf. Wadstein, *op. cit.*, p. 194; P. Sabatier, *Études inédits sur S. François d'Assise* (Paris, 1932), pp. 288-89.
[70] C. Clair, *Le Dies Irae: Histoire, traduction, commentaire* (Paris, 1881).

The poem emphasizes the corporateness which will be characteristic of that awful and most total accounting. Well may the Christian seek to be delivered from the unfavorable verdict of the Judge. It is the sinner's plea that the blood of Calvary may not have been shed all unavailingly in his case. Oh! that his sins may be effaced wholly before the Day of Judgment comes. Above all, he prays that he may be counted among the sheep at the Lord's right hand; far from the infamous goats who are to be led into everlasting torment. None may safely contend that this is but a literary expression; it is far more, for it places before us, after the fashion of art, the throbbing convictions which are a part of the innermost Catholicism of the Middle Ages.[71]

From authorities on medieval culture—in the areas of architecture and sculpture, particularly—there come indubitable proofs of the role played by eschatology in general, and the Last Judgment in particular. The works of Mâle and the much later researches of Morey —to mention only two representative studies—make this readily apparent.[72] What is at once clear from a perusal of cathedral iconography is the sociality portrayed in the final accounting. The Last Judgment as there depicted conveys quite strikingly the sense of universality. However restrictive the form of art, one falls under the spell of mighty events involving all men. Likewise apparent is the duality of human destinies. Nonetheless, these destinies, whether good or evil, are incontestably corporate. Thus the rejected souls form a society that proceeds to the hopelessnes of doom. Those, on the other hand, who have faced the Judge in the awful day and heard his words of commendation move forward in undeniable joyousness to the City of Heaven. Whether one consults the Cathedral of Bourges, the great monuments of Chartres, or, indeed, any other of the great architectural-sculptural forms, the answer is the same. The windows, too, tell the same story. Theirs is the message that Vincent de Beauvais so reverently conveys in the appendix of his *Historical Mirror*. It is this *Mirror* that Mâle so effectively uses in his interpreta-

---

[71] See the full text and notes in Clair, together with De Gourmont, *op. cit.*, pp. 321-41.

[72] Particularly *L'art religieux du XIII° siècle du France* (4th ed., Paris, 1919), Chap. VI; also his *L'art religieux du XII° siècle en France* (3rd ed., Paris, 1928), notably pp. 406 ff.; "Le jugement dernier." Cf. C. R. Morey, *Mediaeval Art* (New York, 1942), pp. 253 ff., "High Gothic, the Scholastic Synthesis"; cf. Index, "Last Judgment."

tion of medieval iconography. With him, as in Bréhier, the handwriting of the arts proclaims in vivid characters the dominant motifs: These are the Last Days, Resurrection, Judgment, and the passage from a temporal society to an eternal world.[73]

[73] L. Bréhier, *L'art chrétien* (Paris, 1928), pp. 286-98 ff. Cf. A. Chastel, "L'apocalypse du 1500: la fresque de l'antéchrist à la chapelle Saint-Brice d'Orvieto," *Bibliothèque d'humanisme et renaissance*, XIV (Mars, 1952), 124-40.

CHAPTER XV

Heavenly Beatitude and the Mutuality
of the Eternal Kingdom

SCATTERED THROUGHOUT THE VOLUMINOUS COLLECTION KNOWN AS the *Patrologia* are well-nigh innumerable references to the heavenly fatherland. Many of these have a somewhat extended treatment of the heavenly society. Others are passing allusions which are all the more significant because they have no full development or systematized thought. As a whole, however, they indicate both the persistence of the Christian hope for a new order of glory and a continuing interpretation of the future life in terms of fellowship experience.[1]

If one takes, almost at random, some typical expressions anent the celestial fatherland, he is at once struck with the recurrence of certain highly traditional, but frequently vital, concepts. Thus one encounters repeatedly the mention of the *Visio Dei*, that carries with it a thoroughly associative experience. The blessed look forward with perfect right to becoming members of a consociation with the angels.[2] Bernard of Clairvaux eloquently anticipates the heavenly conviviality and admission into the angelic choirs.[3] Still others think of attending heavenly banquets and of hearing the ever-celestial symphonies.[4] A frequent reference stresses the heredity of the blessed in the eternal society. These are heirs and coheirs with the Lord himself in his glory. The heavenly beatitude is veritably the empire of Christ. Throughout Christian tradition, heaven is thought of as country; not only a place—though it is that—but, more significantly, a

[1] MPL 220:217 ff., "Index de Coelo." Cf. studies previously referred to, such as H. R. Patch, *The Other World* (Harvard, 1950) and St. John D. Seymour, *Irish Visions of the Other World* (London, 1930).

[2] MPL 220:224 ff. Cf. Thomas Cisterciensis, *Comment. in Cantica Cantic.*, Lib. I, MPL 206:57.

[3] *Sermones in Cantica*, XXVI (179), MPL 183:906; *Tract. De charitate*, cap. XXXIV, MPL 184:634.

[4] Peter Chrysolog., MPL 52:214.

banding together of those who have a common purpose, loyalty, and destiny.[5]

A favorite term which carries with it a wide range of connotations is that of "Zion." This is the city of all the elect. It is, indeed, the one city of all the saints as well as of the elect. It is composed of both angels and men, and is founded upon the All-Highest himself. However mystical may be the references to the New Jerusalem, they carry with them a wide diversity of suggestions as to the blissful experiences reserved for heavenly citizens in perfect concord. Those of the future world are almost uniformly thought of as giving perfect obedience to the King of kings in a happy and enduring reign. Triumph, truth, dignity, felicity, and peace are regular attributes of such a society. In this eternal realm of the Father, the saints have a share in reigning. Being of one will with God and constituting the heirs of his promise from the beginning of time, they reign together. Having been called by God to this ineffably joyous destiny, they now have the fulfillment of all true knowledge in perfect mutuality.[6]

Here, according to the traditions of the Fathers, the saved shall rejoice as much as they shall know. With such a fulfillment of harmony and interparticipating community, peace is a natural consequence. Peace and joy go together with enlarged vistas of comradeship in the heavenly world. Hugh of St. Victor discusses at length the character of that good life in which God will be all in all. In this blessed city no jealousy can exist, for fullness of joy and unending beatitude are given unto all to the fullest measure of capacity.[7]

A modern Roman Catholic work affords an opportunity to test the relationship existing between medieval and later Christian thought.[8] The emphasis upon the solidarity of the heavenly community is essentially a reinforcement of views derivable from medieval works. Thus we are assured: "The inhabitants of Heaven do not lead a solitary life but are associated together in a mystic body called the Communion of Saints (communio sanctorum) ." These are members of the Church triumphant. As such, they have opportunity to look upon the angels in their various hierarchies, just as they are per-

[5] Godefridus Abbas Admontensis, *Homiliae Festivales*, VIII, MPL 174:657-58

[6] Rupertus Abbas Tuitiensis, *De glorificatione Trinitatis* . . . , Lib. I, cap. 3, MPL 169:16; Hilarii Pict., *Tract. in CXLIV Ps.*, MPL 9:855-56.

[7] Hugh of St. Victor, *De Sacram.*, cap. 20, MPL 176:616-18; also, *De Claustro Animae*, Lib. IV, caps. 20 ff., "De Coelesti Hierusalem," etc., MPL 176:1159 ff. Cf. Anselm, *Prosologion*, XXV, Schmitt ed., I, 118-20; Bonaventura, *Breviloquium*, XII, 7, Nemmers ed., pp. 237-44.

[8] Pohle, *Eschatology*, pp. 36 ff.

mitted to see the various degrees of dignity and happiness shining forth "in their glorified fellowmen." The author reinforces his belief with references to earlier writings such as Hebrews 2:23 and the later discussions of leaders such as Cardinal Bellarmine. The concept of mutuality within the heavenly house and of reciprocating love in the kingdom of God is repeatedly stressed.[9]

It has sometimes been charged against the medieval Fathers that their interpretations of the eternal beatitudes are too lacking in vitality and imaginative flexibility. They lend themselves too much, it is said, to an intellectualized concept of social felicity. This allegation cannot be fairly brought against Augustine. It is true that he emphasizes the superbly mental quality of association in the kingdom of heaven. But he is, likewise, convinced that real beings will not be deprived of spontaneous experiences. Enhancement rather than diminution of vitality will follow upon man's entrance into heaven.[10]

Frequently in the *City of God* Augustine insists upon the interrelating quality of life that the blessed shall know in heaven. They share with each other in God all of the resources which heaven knows.[11] Large words in the vocabulary of Augustine are participation, mutuality, joy, perfect union, and intimacy of heart. All of these are placed within a setting of universalizing peace and everlasting happiness.[12] Augustine knows no more than any other Christian Father the exact character of the eternal beatitude. But he is sure that it will be social beyond the most joyous approximations of companionship in this life. And he knows, furthermore, that the best preparation for social beatitude in the future is a corresponding neighborliness, in the present, with all of one's fellows.

Augustine depicts the joys that shall be perpetual when the City of God shall come completely into its own. He is hard pressed to evaluate that felicity where no evil will be; where no good things shall be wanting; where God shall be praised perpetually as all in all. No lack will there be experienced. Eternally joyous hymns shall be raised in praises by those who inhabit the Lord's house. Fullness of personality will not be hindered by any indigence of body or spirit. Peace will have its perfect fulfillment. In a famous phrase, Augustine celebrates this end of all ends, which will be fulfillment of all our desires, wherein God shall be seen and loved and praised without weary-

---

[9] *Ibid.*, pp. 36-37. Cf. Diekamp, *Manuale*, IV, "De Caelo," pp. 543-59.
[10] *De Civ. Dei*, XIX, 13.
[11] *Ibid.*, XXII, 30.
[12] *Ibid.*, CSEL 40, Pars 2, pp. 664-66, 670.

ing. And this will reach its finality in an eternal community that will spell the fullest of life for all.[13]

Augustine is confident that, regardless of variations in the ranks and orders of the blessed, no one will sever the bonds of concord through envy or jealousy. True mutuality will be everywhere. Each shall share in the joys of others. What each has, will measure up fully to his desires. The experiences of that eternal world will constitute the end which is without end. For what other end is there, unless it be to come to the kingdom to whose duration there is no limit? [14]

St. Augustine often remarks about the angelic society with which the saints shall have cocitizenship in the blessed realm of heaven. He never leaves any doubt as to the societal qualities of that eternal existence. He is convinced that the order of the angels is a "supremely happy society." When it comes to differentiating their various orders and their specific functions and powers, he is commendably reserved. He ventures to say that the bodies assumed by angels raise a very difficult and not very useful subject of discussion. He is much more loath than Dionysius to discuss the ramifications of such speculative hazards. He prefers to exult over the joyous concord which these angelic beings know and in which the faithful shall one day share, not as two sharply differentiated orders, but as one unity of those praising God.[15]

Augustine's eloquence varies little in his numerous descriptions of the celestial country. The flexibility of his language, however, does suggest something of the social experience that he associates with the heavenly world. He calls upon the faithful to pursue with diligence the way of righteousness which, alone, conduces to the *patria*. It is here that one has the angels for cocitizens. God is the temple of this commonwealth. The Son is the light and the Holy Spirit is the bond of love. This is the Holy City, the Blessed City, the city where one will not lose any friends or find an enemy; where no one dies because no one is ever born. Here no one undergoes suffering because joy knows a life incorruptible. Here fear and famine have no place. The lack of fatigue makes unnecessary any rest or repose. Nothing needs to be replaced because nothing is exhausted. In such a world and in such a society, the faithful will live and reign, and be forever in the midst of joy. If speaking of it brings joy, by way of anticipation

---

[13] *Ibid.*, p. 666.
[14] *Ibid.*, p. 670.
[15] *Enchiridion*, 57-60; NPNF, 1st Ser., III, 256-57.

only, what will the realization be like? To see God, to live with God, to live of God—that will be the destiny of those who praise and love him without end.[16]

A favorite theme of Augustine's in delineating the joys of the blessed hereafter is the full communion which all the saints shall have together. All shall have a part in the things given to each. The kingdom shall be possessed by one and all in harmony. As the number of those who enjoy it increases, the portion of that joy is not diminished in any. In a real sense each shall have the plenitude of that given to all. This oneness shall be had by many without any affront to the joyousness of individual members. The whole kingdom of God shall be possessed by each.[17]

In his well-known tract on St. John, Augustine tries to fathom Jesus' meaning of the many mansions in his Father's house.[18] Christ himself declares that he goes to prepare places for his followers; though in a way these are already in existence from the beginning of the world. Augustine here introduces his doctrine of foreordination. This helps to explain the fact that the Lord has prepared mansions from the beginning of the world, and is, nonetheless, preparing them, still. Again, Christ is not only preparing mansions for the faithful; he is also preparing dwellers for their places in the mansions. Nothing else can possibly be meant than that the faithful are being prepared for their portion in the house of God, which is truly his kingdom. One may, therefore, speak of the kingdom as being present in temporal life, but only in the sense that it is being gathered together, although not yet reigning. There will come a day when those who are not yet ruling completely will be gathered into a kingdom in which God will be unequivocally sovereign:

This house of God, therefore, this temple of God, this kingdom of God and kingdom of heaven, is as yet in the process of building, of construction, of preparation, of assembling. In it there will be mansions, even as the Lord is now preparing them; in it there are such already, even as the Lord has already ordained them.[19]

It is the business of the faithful to be acquiring merit, even now, as they walk by faith. The Lord meanwhile goes forward to prepare

---

[16] *De cantico novo*, X, 9-10; Péronne ed., XXII, 279-80.

[17] *Sermones ad populum*—1st Ser., Serm. 88, cap. 17, Péronne ed., p. 37.

[18] No. 68, NPNF, 1st Ser., VII, 322 ff.

[19] *Ibid.*, VII, 323. Used by permission of the publishers, Wm. B. Eerdmans Publishing Co.

the place. In the longing that belongs to faith and love, the Christian moves ahead to claim his share in the eternal household. Augustine prays that the Lord will establish what he is preparing: namely, the faithful for himself, and himself for the faithful; since he is preparing a place both for himself in us, and for us in himself.[20]

Augustine next proceeds to one of his favorite themes: that is, the treatment of diverse rewards in a unity of eternal life. Insofar as each one has partaken of the Lord, some less, some more, so also "will be the diversity of rewards in proportion to the diversity of merits; such will be the multitude of mansions to suit the inequalities among their inmates; but all of them, none the less, eternally living, and endlessly blessed."[21]

Pope Gregory I (590-604) lauds the joys of the heavenly society with its unlimited spiritual pasturage provided by the great Shepherd for the celestial flock.[22] There, too, are the angelic choirs. There is the society of supernal citizens safely gathered from the dangers of their temporal pilgrimage. Prophets, apostles, victorious martyrs, and noble confessors are all joyously associated in the presence of their glorious King.

Conjoined with these are faithful men who were sufficient in their virility against the temptations of the world, and holy women more than proof against the snares of life and their sex. Young and old rejoice together in their common victory over the world. Gregory calls upon all the faithful to seek the heavenly food in company with the flock of the joyful elect. May all diversions from the heavenly way be rejected and all desires for the heavenly fatherland be fostered by the viatores.

In contrast with such eternal life, temporal existence is more like dying than living. Mortal powers are helpless to express the joys of that celestial city with its choirs of angels and blessed spirits, glorious in the light of God's faith and free from all sin or taint.

Like Augustine, Gregory thinks at times of the Church as virtually identifiable with the heavenly Jerusalem—that city set upon a lofty mountain, that congregation of saints destined even during the buffeting of its earthly pilgrimage, and shaped thereby in its living

[20] *Ibid.*, VII, 323-24.
[21] *Ibid.*, VII, 324. Used by permission of the publishers.
[22] *Hom. in Evang.*, Lib. I, Hom. 14, MPL 76:1130 ff. Cf. S. A. Hurlbut, *The Picture of the Heavenly Jerusalem* (Washington, D. C., 1943), I, 15.

stones, for its reign in heaven. To that end does this city, holy Church, which shall reign in heaven, labor on earth.[23]

So, likewise, does a majestic hymn, dating possibly from the seventh century and reproduced in the ninth, celebrate the beauties of the heavenly Jerusalem. This is the vision of peace constructed of living stones, both men and angels, and built upon Christ, its angular, integrating rock. Here in joyous community the praises of the triune God swell upward.[24]

Several hymns at least have survived from the work of the versatile Bede. As already observed, his sermons have a highly poetic quality and lend themselves admirably to their present place in the liturgical prayers of the Church. In one of his most beautiful writings, we have hymns of praise to the martyrs and innocents. These lines celebrate the sufferings and heavenly joys of those who have been found worthy to join in the angelic rhapsodies. These have been called together into the glory and brightness of a reign that is perpetual. Here, each has prepared for him a spacious mansion in the house of the Father.

This little flock has no cause for fear. The teeth of the lion cannot touch them. The good pastor has given to them a celestial homeland and heavenly food. In spite of the destructive frenzies of the impious ones, these are forever preserved from final harm. All tears are to be wiped from their eyes. Are not those who sow in tears destined to reap in joy? Oh, what a beautiful city this is, in which the Redeemer is come among the thousands who are its citizens. Theirs will be eternal rejoicing and fellowship.[25]

Among the works attributed to Haymo of Halberstat is one dealing in its first portion with the problem of the future life. Whether or not it is Haymo's own work is of little immediate consequence. The views which it advances constitute a rather satisfactory summary of the early Fathers to at least the ninth century. Generally speaking, the materials are drawn, with proper deference, from Augustine, Chrysostom, Julianus Pomerius, Gregory, Prosper, and Bede. The Scriptures are, of course, plentifully utilized.[26] From the very beginning one is struck with the highly social coloring of the work. The author, or, more properly, the collector, of the Christian views

[23] *Hom. in Evang.,* Lib. II, Hom. 37, MPL 76:1275 ff.; Hurlbut, *op. cit.,* I, 15; VII, 18, 19; *Hom. in Ezech.,* II, 1, MPL 76:938; Hurlbut, *op. cit.,* I, 16.

[24] "Urbs Beata Hierusalem," in Hurlbut, *op. cit.,* 1, 16-18.

[25] *Manitius, Geschichte* I, 86; W. A. Merrill, *Latin Hymns* (Boston, 1904), pp. 23-24; Duckett, *Anglo-Saxon Saints and Scholars,* pp. 324 ff.; Ghellinck, *L'essor,* index, II, 325.

[26] "De Amore Coelestis Patriae," MPL 118:875 ff.; Cayré, *Patrologie,* II, 373.

here dealt with, clearly represents the prevailing conviction that heaven will be a place and condition of real companionship; by no means a dull and solitary existence.

In the beginning of his first book, Haymo treats in outline the quality of the future, perpetual life. It is important to note how completely he reserves this first section for a discussion of the more societal aspects of the ultimate community. He is aware that people believe much more fully in the future life than they are able to speak authoritatively about it. The mere thought of such a world is enough to make one temper his speculations with modesty. The author explains that Christians, generally, think of the future existence in terms of blessed eternity and eternal blessedness where there is certain security, secure tranquillity, tranquil happiness, happy eternity, and eternal felicity. Here are found perfect love, the absence of all fear, eternal day, ease of movement, and perfect community in the contemplation of God. This body of the faithful constitutes a city which is a blessed congregation of angels, saints, and men. In the midst of this saved body, truth reigns eternal. Here there is no absence of any good thing. From this society none of the blessed will ever be ejected; no unworthy ones will ever be admitted. Those who enter into the companionship of the blessed angels become a part of that society which will reign forevermore with God.[27]

Joining with each other in the mutuality of appreciation, they see God with a perfect joyousness that is unending. No fearsome experience or evil person may now destroy their blissful companionship. Each is now cleansed from the corruptions of sinful earthly existence. Here are no sins and no sinners; none will ever be. Native to each citizen is a joyous share in the angelic choruses. They are now a part of that society of supernal citizens among whom the sorrows and tribulations of earthly peregrinations are completely forgotten in the joys of their endless fraternity. On every hand are prophets, martyrs, apostles, and confessors. Holy men and women, and children as well, now live in a state that transcends the conditions of youth, age, and former bodily life. Among the saved is one common perfection, however different may be the merits of individuals. The rewards of each are sufficient to him. Here no one seeks to arrogate to himself more than is his, because arrogance is forever done away. There is likewise no sense of inferiority or superiority, because invidiousness is no longer possible.[28]

[27] Cap. 1, MPL 118:875-77.
[28] *Ibid.*, 877.

The author believes wholeheartedly in the ancient Christian tradition that there may be a difference of mansions in glory without destroying the equality of the common perfection shared by all. The Lord's parable of the penny, as it is recounted in Matthew 20, is capitalized for purposes of analogy. Thus equal pay was given to each of the laborers in the vineyard, regardless of the duration of his services. The recompense of each individual in the vineyard signifies eternal life itself. From this point of view, one is unable to have more than another, although many mansions signify a diversity of merit within the one eternal unity. To be sure, there is one glory of the sun, another of the moon, and still another of the stars; star even differs from star in glory. So, also, it will be after the Resurrection. However much these stars with their diversity of brilliance may signify the various saints with their differentiating mansions of light, no one is separated from the King and his kingdom.[29]

It is to be recalled that one common payment of eternal life was advanced to each laborer in the vineyard. In their midst, God will be all in all. And because God himself is charity, and operates according to charity, everything that each one has is common to all the others. No jealousy is possible where the unity of charity shall reign throughout. Dignities and stations will, of course, be different, but the joy of each in the common beatitude of all will be in keeping with the fullness which is appropriate to every one. John said: "In my Father's house are many mansions." But this was not to suggest the tempering of the one true reward of eternal life common to all; it signified, rather, the variety of dignities which should be distributed, appropriately, according to the various merits of each blessed citizen.[30]

The effect of this, Haymo insists, is to admit disparity of merits, but no diversity of joys. Although one may be exalted to a higher and another to a lesser position, all will rejoice with one common rapture. In the vision of their blessed Lord and Redeemer, each will know the supreme beatitude of participating in eternal life under the gaze of him who is the author of their happiness.

Among the blessed in the heavenly country, there will be knowledge without terror, memory without oblivion, cogitation without rambling, charity without simulation, sense without offensiveness, soundness without debility, health without sorrow, life without death,

---

[29] *Loc. cit.*
[30] *Ibid.,* 878.

facility without impediment, satisfaction without fastidiousness, and total health without any sickness. This apparent descent to the realm of the physical in describing the superabundant society of the spiritual is not at all unusual among contemporary thinkers. When associated, as it invariably is, with an attempt to describe the ineffable, it readily becomes a means to the further depiction of both communal and personal fulfillment.[31]

Haymo is assured that in the heavenly country all the saints shall know perfect love, a complete absence of fear, and everlasting joy. This society will be characterized by rightness of will and a total lack of cupidity. In a land where all good things will be available to all, there will no longer be a cause for jealousy, concupiscence, and the unruly passions that disturb peace and security. The reign of true peace and lasting good without fear or sorrow spells the full spiritual health and salvation of all the Catholic faithful. Stripped of all corruptibility, they are forever ensconced in a blessed immortality. Here is true perfection of prudence and wisdom, a total cognition of all things. None can perish in such an order of life where the soul, perfectly obedient to God, and the flesh, wholly subject to him, shall reign in eternal peace.[32]

Haymo is certain of one thing, at least: all language fails to describe, and no intellect is sufficient to understand, the joy that will be in such a supernal city where the blessed, in company with the angelic hosts, know the delights of companionship with God, face to face. No one mortal is able to say, or even think, how great the joys of the just will be in that everlasting society. Paul was surely right in saying that eye has not seen, and ear has not heard, nor the heart of man compassed, such delights. Obviously, every energy of the faithful should be bent toward making themselves worthy of a place in this holy society of angelic citizens, in this eternal Jerusalem. Here will be the abiding society of all the elect with sure solemnity, perfect rest, true peace, and life everlasting.[33]

The remaining chapters of Haymo's first section are given over to the consideration of such problems as the greatness of glory which is to be the elects' portion in seeing God; the clarity with which they shall see him; the resurrection and life of the saints resurgent; the perfection of unity among the beatified; and, finally, the inexpressible joys of the righteous in heaven. Each of the brief chapters is

[31] *Loc. cit.*
[32] *Loc. cit.*
[33] *Ibid.*, 878-79.

given over to a treatment of some one problem, and its related aspects, that has already been suggested in the introduction. Each category of problems and discussions is approached by way of the leading Christian thinkers whose views Haymo is attempting to co-ordinate and summarize. The total impact convinces one of the mounting communality in that life ascribed through the Christian centuries to the fellowship of heaven.[34]

Scholarly and extended studies of the Anglo-Saxon poets have done much to clarify our picture of medieval conceptions about the heavenly realm. Not one, but substantially the whole group of such poets produces a pattern that is essentially unified and informing. Their belief about heaven and the eternal reward is full of richly socializing connotations. Heaven, according to the Anglo-Saxon concept, emerges as a specific kingdom somewhere above the earth. It is a bright and beautiful city: "the hereditary stronghold, as it were, of the Eternal King, the happy home of his followers." The Prince of heaven is a mild, gracious one, who sits upon his throne in his spacious hall. His people have immediate and loving access to him as they live together under his paternal eye. "The good not only enjoy the presence and blessings of God, the fellowship of the angels, the light and glory and beauty of their heavenly home, but are also free from every torment of hell." [35]

In contrast with hell, heaven is broad, beautiful, radiantly alight, and sweetly perfumed with flowers. It is the happy home of the blessed ones who know the fellowship of God and the angels. Such conceptions are obviously Bible based, however much they may deviate from its literal characterization. As a matter of fact, the Bible outlines have been freely embellished with Germanic interpretations. Thus they "give us a glimpse at what they considered an ideal Germanic kingdom, while others are doubtless even relics of heathendom." Heaven is far from being a philosophic abstraction. The kingdom and its king reflect reality in terms of German qualities integral with the period:

As a city, the heaven of the poets is not so much like the "heavenly city" of the Bible as like an ideal Germanic stronghold, with its shining gates and glittering walls surrounded by trees. . . . Truly Germanic, too, as

[34] Lib. I, caps. 2-20, MPL 118:879-88.

[35] See recent literature, source analyses, and texts in G. K. Anderson, *Literature of the Anglo-Saxons* (Princeton, 1949), K. Jost, *Wulfstanstudien* (Berne, 1950), and M. Williams, *Word-Hoard* (1940), also *Gleewood* (1949). Quotations from W. Deering, *The Anglo-Saxon Poets on the Judgment Day* (Halle, 1890), p. 69.

we have seen, is the relation of the heavenly king to His people. He is not so much the Bible "king of heaven," not simply, "the Son of Man," but the strong, brave and manly hero, the people's king, the prince of victories, the heir on the throne of his inheritance, mild and gracious in the midst of his faithful thanes, dispensing to them all the rich gifts of heaven.[36]

However much this may be a projection of Germanic life into that of the beyond, the undoubted and undaunted companionableness of people and king, together, is one of its most refreshing adaptations of biblical thought. Far from Jesus' concept it may be; yet it has the same pithy, colorful realism that characterizes Jesus' pictures of the Father's house.[37]

In that portion of *The Christ* which celebrates the Advent hymns, Cynewulf's interpretation of the eternal beatitude comes to beautiful concreteness.[38] The concept of king and kingdom is more than a literary figure with him. His very thought of heaven is that of a kingdom—a king ruling his thanes—and a joyous commitment on the part of those thanes to the will of their sovereign:

O Thou Vision of peace! Holy Jerusalem! Choicest of kingly thrones, fortress of Christ! Homeland of angels—and in thee forever rest the souls of the righteous alone, joying in glory.[39]

Again Cynewulf stresses the community of life with Christ the King and his children:

None is so discerning or so wise of heart that he may fully tell Thy kingship unto the children of men. Come, Thou Victor-Lord, Shaper of man, graciously make known thy mercy upon us. Great is our craving to know the wonder of Thy mother-kinship; that Fatherhood we may not comprehend. Bless the earth mildly by Thine advent hither, O Saviour Christ; and bid Thou open, Thou High King of heaven, the golden gates that full long stood locked in days of old. . . . Wherefore, O Saviour, with yearning hearts we pray that Thou make haste to help us, weary wretches, that . . . Thy handiwork, Creator of mankind, may mount and

[36] Deering, *op. cit.*, pp. 70, 71.

[37] *Ibid.*, pp. 71-72.

[38] C. W. Kennedy, *The Poems of Cynewulf Translated into English Prose* (New York, 1910), pp. 27-34, 153 ff., with which compare Kennedy, *Early English Christian Poetry Translated into Alliterative Verse* (New York, 1952), 85 ff. 259 ff., 268 ff.; also Anderson, *Literature*, pp. 123-32, 148-49.

[39] Kennedy, *Cynewulf*, p. 154; *Early English Christian Poetry*, p. 86.

come to righteousness, unto that glorious and celestial kingdom, whence by lust of sin the dusky Spirit drew us down by guile.[40]

This vigorous, poetic conception places the social life of the ultimate beatitude in a strong, radiant light. These of the heavenly kingdom "shall know the blessedness of peaceful life with God, which shall be given unto all saints within the heavenly realm." In the realistic imagery of Anglo-Saxon kingship, God reigns supreme over a body of the blessed that is vibrantly social. Here, in a land of endless joy, is liberation from all sin, blissful in its never-ending praise of "the lord of hosts, dear Saviour of their life, all wreathed in light, enwrapped in peace, safe from sorrows, glorified with joy, loved of the Lord." As they share this unending bliss, they are to "know the fellowship of angels." Amidst the angels' songs the Lord's face shines with indescribable splendor "more radiant than the sun unto all happy souls." [41]

The poet, anticipating with forgivably human understatement the unspeakable joys of deathless fruition, depicts "a gladsome band of men; . . . love between friends forever without discord; peace without strife for blessed souls in heaven in the company of holy men." The writer continues: "But that blessed band, fairest of hosts, shall know the favour of their King forever and glory with the Lord." [42]

The man known as Peter Damian was as uncompromising in his devotion to Christian idealism as he was eloquent in his description of the good life that the faithful should follow. Committed as he was to a high conception of the clerical function, both regular and secular, he emphasized, particularly, the art of preaching as a means to the consistent edification of the people. Like most of his colleagues in the Middle Ages, he was concerned in his sermons to paint the joys of the heavenly world. Those who were truly blessed were the ones who should come at last to the societal experience of the kingdom of Christ. "Think, therefore, how blessed is he, who, when such a multitude of the reprobate are shut out, himself is counted worthy to enter the nuptial feast with the glorious company of the elect." [43]

---

[40] *Cynewulf*, pp. 160-61. Used by permission of the publishers, Routledge & Kegan Paul, Ltd. Cf. *Poetry*, pp. 88-89.

[41] *Cynewulf*, pp. 202-3.

[42] *Ibid.*, p. 203.

[43] Neale, *Mediaeval Preachers*, pp. 73-77, quotations, p. 73; Merrill, *Latin Hymns*, pp. 38-40; S. A. Hurlbut, "On the Joys and Glory of Paradise," in *Hortus Conclusus*, Pt. VI; Peter Damian and Hildebert of Tours (Washington, D. C., 1932). Cf., further, Manitius, *Geschichte*, III, 986-98, Ghellinck, *L'essor*, II, 254-59 ff.

The good Cardinal is most vocal in his description of the beauty and the joy of those who contemplate the Deity face to face. Over and beyond this, however, is the happiness which belongs to those who see God in the company of their beloved ones. No one can imagine from this side of the Great Divide the enchantment which shall be the share of men and women, as well as of children, who sit in the midst of the heavenly choir of angels. Here there will be no foreshadowing of some future misadventure. The light and the happiness which surround all of God's redeemed are the ineffable and unending reward of all their fellow citizens. Even the somewhat prolix Cardinal searches for words to describe the completeness and the unity of the celestial blessing.[44]

Thinking in terms of a city that is without parallel in all human existence, he draws upon the usual scriptural foundations in depicting the beauty of the heavenly realm. Suffice it to say that the streets of this heavenly commonwealth will know no slightest discord. Here, fullness of life and openness of all secrets are the prime characteristics of a mutuality in love that cannot otherwise be known. Adverting for the moment to the fleeting joys associated with human banquets and their inevitable aftermath, Peter recalls his biblical assurances that in heaven no joy will ever fail. Here all wills are common. Here, too, all of those who are remembered most in happiness and delight are forever gathered together. Ignorance is now done away. All possibilities that are known to their collective and individual minds are realized within their fraternity.

There, with open face, we shall behold how the Father ineffably begets the Son, how the Holy Ghost proceeds from both. There we shall see how He, Who is absent nowhere, can be everywhere, not partially, but wholly. . . . There, in those meadows which are ever decked in the beauty of spring, the snowy lily never dies off, the purple rose and the crocus never fade. And surely, O Heavenly Jerusalem, there is incomparably more of everlasting blessedness in thee, than the human heart can conceive: and the human heart can conceive more than can be expressed by any words.

Damian can go no further in limning the joys of the celestial citizenry. He knows that all is in obedience to their common will. All nature responds to their desires. God and those who are his are one together in their every living experience. In eloquent peroration the

Cardinal cries out: "God Almighty introduce thee . . . to these joys, and Himself be thy reward when He takes thee, Who became thy price when He redeemed thee." [45]

More effective still, in his poem "On the Joys and Glory of Paradise," the Cardinal eulogizes the celestial beatitude. In the translation of Hurlbut, the Latin flavor is not wholly lost:

> Knowing well the Source of all things, naught there
>   is they cannot know;
> Every secret penetrating, which was hid from them below;
> Unity of thought and purpose, perfect unity they show.
> Granted that the prize be varied, and with toil com-
>   mensurate,
> What in others love desireth, love doth this appro-
>   priate;
> Thus the common good combineth what in each was sep-
>   arate.
>
> . . . .
>
> Ever filled, yet ever eager, need and appetite agree;
> Hunger brings not torment with it, plenty not satiety;
> Ever eager for the feasting, ever feast they eagerly.[46]

The writings of Johannes Fiscamnensis, second Abbot of Fecamp (*ca.* 995-1078), underwent various recensions to appear as the *Meditationes S. Augustini* with English translation by Thomas Becon in 1558 and as *St. Augustine's Prayers* with English translation by Thomas Rogers in 1581. Carefully edited by Hurlbut in his *Picture of the Heavenly Jerusalem,* these editions and translations recapitulate much medieval thought concerning the beatitude.[47]

According to such sources, heaven is the land of peace where God is seen face to face. Here is the blessed realm full of light and uncharted by time whose captain and conqueror-king is accompanied by angelic choirs and joyous men. This is indeed the city of glory, happiness, and peace. Its uncounted mansions, noble citizens, and mighty king defy mortal description. In the midst of Mother Jerusalem is the King of kings, surrounded by a ministering citizenry. Righteous men and women, young men and maidens, and all the chorus of the

---

[45] *Ibid.,* pp. 76-77; cf. Hurlbut, *Hortus Conclusus,* VI, pp. 13 ff.; Merrill, *op. cit.,* pp. 38-40.

[46] Stanzas 13 and 14, p. 13, Pt. VI, *Hortus Conclusus;* stanza 16, p. 15., *ibid.* Copyright by S. Hurlbut. Used by permission of the publishers, St. Albans Press.

[47] Washington, D. C., 1943.

ages serve him in love and exultation. Different is the glory of each individual, "but common is the joy of them all." "They love, and they praise him; they praise and they love him; all their work is to praise God without ending, without fainting, without toiling." What more joyous destiny could any faithful Christian seek than to be incorporated in these singing bands of the heavenly country waiting on king, God, captain, and Father? [48]

Anselm is perhaps best known for his more scholastic contributions to Christian thought. It is in his prayers, meditations, and mystical effusions, however, that his spiritual character is best discerned.[49] It is true that, like most of his contemporaries, he brings a picture of horror and terrorized humanity into focus when he treats of the Last Judgment. But this should not blind one to the beautiful quality of his social eloquence when discussing the eternal beatitude.

The ultimate world that God will give to the righteous when they finally enter his kingdom will be one of complete fulfillment. Among the other delights that men now wish for, but know only approximately, is that friendship to be matured fully in the great society. This will be the comradeship of those who love God more than themselves and one another as themselves. Surrounded by the leaven of God's own affection, they will transmit perfectly this divine quality. Concord so long desired will now be spelled with a singleness of purpose and will that they shall derive from God.

The more usual qualities attributed to the fatherland are repeated by Anselm with little deviation. Power, honor, riches, security, and all that makes up the final happiness of man shall spring from its perfect source in the divine mutuality.

In striving to express the heavenly joys, however, Anselm both feels his limitations most keenly and expresses himself most movingly. What yearning soul having suddenly bestowed upon him all these blessings would know how to express his overflowing joy! But if that same person were to realize his own joy, doubly, through the happiness of a loved one, how much more would be the intensification of his ecstasy!

But, if two, or three, or many more, had the same joy, thou wouldst re-

---

[48] "S. Augustine's Praiers," Chap. 24 (25), tr. Thomas Rogers, 1581; Hurlbut, *Picture*, VII, 26-31.

[49] See, especially, his *Opera Omnia*, ed. T. S. Schmitt, Vol. III (Edinburgh, 1946); also, D. A. Castel, *Méditations et Prières de Saint Anselme* (Paris, 1923); cf. Ghellinck, *L'essor*, I, 36 ff. Note A. Wilmart, *Auteurs spirituels* (Paris, 1932), pp. 173-201, and the other articles in the same work.

joice as much for each one as for thyself, if thou didst love each as thyself. Hence, in that perfect love of innumerable blessed angels and sainted men, when none shall love another less than himself, every one shall rejoice for each of the others as for himself.

Such is Anselm's foregleam of the perfect felicity that shall come with the realized kingdom of heaven to filter into man's present prospects. The perfect mutuality of loving and rejoicing that is to be there cannot but provoke unto good works the social life that is man's portion now.[50]

Peter Abelard, with the vicissitudes of life always on the threshold of his consciousness, wrote a number of hymns—some of them depicting the joys of perfect friendship that had been denied him in his earthly pilgrimage. One of these extols the happiness of the celestial fatherland.[51] He here thinks of the abiding peace that shall come upon those who dwell with God and his angels throughout eternity. He cannot represent, fairly, the beauties of that celestial Sabbath. The peace and participation of each and all in the common joy is beyond expression. This will be the true Jerusalem, the veritable City of God. Here all desires will be achieved; where all heartaches and molestations will be done away, and the common happiness of a blessed people will be properly referred to the common Lord and Father. Ineffable joys shall be sung by the faithful in the company and with the assistance of the angels. That glory will be perpetual, out of which, by which, and in which are all things. Out of which, the Father is; by which, the Son; in which is the Spirit of Father and Son.[52]

In the eighth book of his *Chronicle*, Otto of Freising (d. 1158) comes at last to the summation of the heavenly bliss as it will be experienced in enduring kingdom fellowship. Following a discussion of the saints' memories which shall bring them delight but no unhappiness, he inquires concerning the arrangement of the heavenly hierarchy. The Lord, in insisting upon a variety of mansions within one house, not many houses, explained that "the blessedness would be one, but that there are differences in the enjoyment of that blessedness." Otto reminds his readers that in the present life and within

---

[50] *Meditatio* I, *Op. Om.*, ed. Schmitt, III, 76-80; cf. *Prosologion*, XXV, *Op. Om.*, ed. Schmitt, I, 118-20; S. N. Deane, *Prosologion*, pp. 30-32.

[51] Ghellinck, *L'essor*, II, 289, n. 55, 293 ff; *Le Nouv. Theol.*, pp. 126-50; Merrill, *Latin Hymns*, pp. 36-38; cf. MPL 178:1759-1824 for poems and hymns; Cayré, *Patrologie*, II, 413, n. 8.

[52] Merrill, *Latin Hymns*, p. 38.

the one Church of the faithful there are varying grades of honors and superiority. This, he says, follows after the likeness of the heavenly assembly.[53]

It is quite reasonable, therefore, to conclude that in the Father's house

various mansions [are] to be occupied by various saints as one is more glorious than another, and as one is holier than another, because so much the more closely and, as it were, more directly shall each saint be lighted by the splendor of the divine radiance as he is in this life the more ardently and earnestly inflamed by love for Him through the faith which worketh through love. And even as when many together flock to one fountain, and taste its waters together, he that is thirstier drinks the more, so they that hasten to God, the fount of life, are the more abundantly satisfied with the fatness of His house, with the river of His pleasure, as they wait for Him the more zealously and eagerly in the greater ardor of their thirst. Therefore, in accordance with the diversity and the capacity of individuals, the blessed glory of the saints will be varied and yet will be one.[54]

In his next section Otto deals with the relationship existing between angels and men in that city which is "compacted of two walls." He now embarks upon the most complicated portion of his whole treatise. Taking first the threefold hierarchy of angels, he discusses them with high appreciation for the work of Dionysius. This had infiltrated his age through the translations and commentaries of Hilduin, John Scotus Erigena, Hugh of St. Victor, and others. Although Otto feels it necessary to give some detailed exposition to the matter, he is by no means ready to deal with the more speculative aspects of the problem. He gives the kind of information which was probably derived by him from the Areopagite through the commentary of the learned Victorine.[55]

Otto notes that there are three hierarchies, each divided into three orders in turn; thus making up nine orders of angels. In the first of these, he follows Dionysius in placing Seraphim, Cherubim, and Thrones. The second grouping includes Dominions, Powers, and

[53] Sec. 29, *The Two Cities: A Chronicle of Universal History to the Year 1146 A.D.* Tr. C. C. Mierow (New York, 1928), pp. 498-99.
[54] *Ibid.*, p. 499. Used by permission of the publishers, Columbia University Press.
[55] VIII, 30, Mierow ed., pp. 499-500 and n. 237; cf. *Hier. Coel.*, caps. I-VI, in *Oeuvres du Pseudo-Denys L'Aréopagite*, M. de Gandillac, ed. (Paris, 1943), pp. 185 ff.; cf. *Dionysiaca*, II, 729 ff.; Greg., *Hom. XXIV, in Evang.*, MPL 76:1254; Hugh of St. Victor, *Summa Sent.*, II, 5-6, MPL 176:85-88; *Com. in Hier. Coel* . . . MPL 175:923 ff.; Scotus Erigena, MPL 122; *Dionysiaca*, I, LV-LVI; Théry, *Études Dion.* (1932), and tr. (1937) of Hilduin.

Virtues. In the third are Principalities, Archangels, and Angels. The first hierarchy has immediate access to, and illumination from, the Trinity. The second, which is "midway between the first and the last, is both illumined by the preceding hierarchy and in turn illumines the succeeding." Otto is convinced that Dionysius had his highly intricate system of names and attributes, as regards the nine orders of celestial beings, from St. Paul himself. Since he did not derive this information from Paul's canonical writings, he must have secured it from private conversation with the Apostle.

Freising describes the manner in which, according to Dionysius, the three hierarchies of angels are associated with God and men. Thus the first hierarchy is "united more immediately to God than the rest." The lowest triad of angels is made up of those who "are either sent to the outer world, as the angels and the archangels are, or by their invisible might arrange for their sending, as the Principalities do." The intermediate, threefold groupings of hierarchies administer, "according to their dignity and their functions, such commands as must be carried from the hierarchies above them to the hierarchies below them." In explaining the privileges and duties of each of these, Otto interprets according to Hugh's commentary on Dionysius. As in the case of Dionysius himself—and as with Hugh of St. Victor—the community that exists between the angelic hierarchies in their association with God is clearly instanced by Otto. Although some of the angels may be taught by their superiors, whereas others may be immediately enlightened by God, all have their place in the divine society.[56]

Passing from a consideration of the angelic hierarchy—which, he says, "has been derived not from our own opinions but from Holy Writ"—Otto discusses the fashion in which the elect "must be received into their [these celestial spirits'] orders to make one City with them." How will these members of the elect "be taken in varying degrees into fellowship with them [i.e., the angels]?" [57]

Otto's discussion is not wholly clear or precise. Following Dionysius, he declares that the faithful ascend by the steps of spiritual advance through varying degrees of enlightenment to this fellowship. "It has been said that, even as we are in this present life graded proportionately through gifts of graces and grades of honors—that is, by differing and ordered participation in such graces and honors—so

[56] *Two Cities*, VIII, 30; Mierow ed., pp. 501-5; Dion. *Hier. Coel.*, VI-XI.
[57] *Two Cities*, VIII, 30-31; Mierow ed., pp. 504-5.

355

we are to be promoted in varying degrees to fellowship in the heavenly company." The gist of the whole matter is this: Those that have been faithful in little will be set over many things; those serving well "will gain a high station, since faithful stewards of the Church are more splendidly crowned in the heavens in proportion as they have by word and example toiled upon earth, feeding the Lord's flock." The parable of the talents is here important:

The saints therefore shall ascend by differences of progress (that is, they shall go forward according as they have done well) and by increase of enlightenment (that is, in so far as they have well taught those placed under their care) through grades of spiritual advance. That is to say, [they shall go forward] from strength to strength, not of the feet but of the mind, to varying dignities or differences of gifts—the divine gifts of grace—through the various orders of the blessed spirits. Inasmuch as these qualities are in them and among them—according to the saying of the Psalmist, "Blessed is the man whose help is from thee; he hath set in his heart the ways of ascent"—that famous theologian well declares that "in proportion to our several achievements and varying degrees of enlightenment we ascend by the steps of spiritual advance in ourselves or by the difference of gifts that exist between us" into fellowship with the angels. Moreover, how separate individuals are taken out of the elect into the separate orders of the blessed spirits—so that they become like unto the angels, not only in purity of mind and of body but in rank of advancement, and equal to them in blessedness—the blessed Gregory has discussed in words flowing with honey, words based solely upon this text, "He set the bounds of the peoples according to the number of the angels of God," clearly showing that the number of the elect in that state would be as great as the number of the sacred angels that remained with God.[58]

Without making himself responsible for a judgment on things far too deep for him, Otto serves to reinforce the companionship that is to exist between angels and men. In a further section he launches into a fairly involved calculation of the manner in which a certain number of the elect shall replace a given number of lost angels. Eventually, he decides to leave these intricacies to wiser men.[59]

Still another portion of the *Chronicle* explores the blessedness of the heavenly country. This consists, essentially, in beholding the Creator according to the full promises of eternal life. Here, where

[58] VIII, 31; Mierow ed., pp. 505-6. Used by permission of the publishers, Columbia University Press.
[59] VIII, 32; Mierow ed., pp. 506-8.

all mirrors and riddles are replaced with full understanding, God is to be seen by the saints with perfect delight. This experience "does not grow common through familiarity, and familiarity with it does not produce distaste for it." The reasonable admiration and pleasure with which human beings look upon kings and emperors in all their transient glory is by no means to be compared with that ineffable exultation which rises in those who look upon the King of kings who is the Creator of the universe; as he shall there be attended in all of his matchless grace and glory by "his celestial hosts of angels and men." Their experience is not to be one of passive vision but of active love. They praise him as those who dwell in his very household. No sadness or weariness enters into the full consummation of their joyous society. Such blessedness is properly "reserved for that heavenly City." [60]

Peter Lombard's discussion of the heavenly society is less an original presentation than a compilation of patristic materials, Augustine's especially, and scriptural references. He inaugurates his discussion with a quotation from the *Enchiridion*. According to this view there will be two kingdoms after the Resurrection and the completion of the universal Judgment. One will be Christ's, and the other will be the Devil's. One will be made up of the good, and the other of the wicked. Both, however, will consist of angels and men. The angels will have no will to sin. Men will have no power to do so. On the part of neither will there be any power to choose death. In the kingdom of Christ, angels and men shall live in a perfect beatitude. The citizens of the Devil's community will, of course, drag out "a miserable existence of eternal death without the power of dying." In a section from Augustine which Lombard does not quote, but to which he later makes allusion, it is pointed out that there shall be different degrees of happiness among the blessed, "one being more pre-eminently happy than another"; even as there shall be degrees of misery among the damned.

Lombard deduces from his Augustinian context that as the good shall be differently glorified, some more, some less, so shall the evil be variously punished in hell. As in the Father's house—that is, in the celestial kingdom—there are many mansions—that is, differences of reward—so in Gehenna will there be diverse mansions—that is, a differentiation of sufferings. His ensuing discussion is, as usual, an

[60] VIII, 33; Mierow ed., pp. 508-11.

effective composite; in this case it clarifies no point not already treated.[61]

Bernard of Cluny's panegyric on the heavenly community has been referred to elsewhere.[62] A closer scrutiny of his thought on the beatitude is now called for.[63] The main outlines of his description of "Jerusalem the Golden" found in Book I of his *Scorn of the World* run fairly true to medieval form. The peace, comeliness, and unity of the celestial city are dwelt upon extensively. God is known as fully as is possible to human beings. To gaze upon him is to see what lies within. Once having crossed the barriers of temporal world and awful judgment, no one needs to feel a sense of shame on this side of the final reckoning. Each shall know his neighbor's wrongdoings on earth and still feel no shame. Transcending these temporary griefs is an everlasting joy that comes from God's free graciousness and forgiveness. This is the lasting Sabbath full of glory and total redemption. Here is a community of beings united in Christ without fear of any separation, however short or slight. Into this company those who have for a time been on the earthly pilgrimage shall be fully incorporated. "Thou, a stranger, shall be united with the citizens of heaven, thyself a citizen." [64]

Bernard's imagery fluctuates between a description of the heavenly country as it shall be fully realized and a portrayal of the celestial fatherland even now calling unto itself those wayfarers who are yet to join it. This consolidation about Jesus the Christ, true King of Nazareth and crucified Leader, is already reflected before the end of time as it calls out its goodly seekers after Jerusalem. For it is the very character of the heavenly society that it alters after its own pattern, however incompletely before the Judgment, the corporate activities of the earthly citizenship.[65]

Once having been attained, however, this citizenship of the blessed leaves nothing of mutuality to be desired. True, the Christian on earth is sustained by hope and fed on milk, but in the eternal realm he "shall eat the bread of life." [66] The quintessence of orderliness is to be found there; the order after which Bernard would have his people yearn, even in this shadowy realm. The new world is a

[61] Lib. IV, Dist. 49, cap. 1, Quaracchi ed., II, 1027-30; cf. Aug. *Enchiridion*, Lib. I, cap. 111, MPL 40:284; NPNF 1st Ser., III, 272.
[62] See Chaps. V and XIV of this book.
[63] DCM, I, 1-392 (1-14); SJG, I, 105-13.
[64] SJG, I, 108.
[65] DCM, I, 275-304 (9-11).
[66] SJG I, 110; DCM, I, 221 (8).

country fair beyond description. Its constituency is wrought into a heavenly congregation of which Christ is the ever-re-creating nucleus. Bernard exhausts his resourceful phraseology in seeking terms fit to denominate this one who is both Door and Doorkeeper; not only Ferryman, but Haven, also.[67]

This is the great metropolis of the spirit to which all Christian hearts should turn with glowing love during their earthly sojourn. It alone can redeem the ways of earthly, corporate life. Here is the City of Zion, all-surpassing in its harmony and light, which, with its joys, is "ever drawing the pious heart." It is the true home of the faithful, the arena of happy fellowship, the courtyard of martyrs, now forever alive. It boasts "a race glorious in its Leader, a company shining in white raiment," and living fraternally "in kindly halls." [68]

This is the city built on the foundation of a new people. It fraternizes within the ranks of the angels and luxuriates in the company of prophets, patriarchs, virgins, and all the true hearted. The Father is there. His only begotten Son, the only Son of Mary, is likewise there. The Trinity is in all and with all. Celestial festivals are held without ceasing. Out of this heavenly abode of unconquerable grace and mercy comes the only power that can save the world. Bernard prays that such grace may suffice to "relax the great punishment, unloose the tremendous chains of the wicked, overcoming the devil." [69] In the name of his fellow aspirants to this final citizenship, the monk of Cluny makes his most eloquent petition. Let them not be denied their portion in this glorious country of heaven. May his fellows now with him on earth not turn their backs upon it. With all possible vigilance let them prepare themselves for the Judgment if they would enter that happy land.[70] Social responsibility intelligently discharged in the present world is the best way to make ready for the rapturous solidarity of the celestial fatherland.

In his treatise on the Lord's Prayer, Thomas Aquinas analyzes the desirability of the heavenly kingdom:

First, because of the highest justice which abounds there. "Thy people shall be just, and they shall inherit the land for ever" (Isaiah 60, 21). Here on earth, the good and bad mingle together, but there in God's kingdom, there will be no evil and no sinner.

Secondly, the heavenly kingdom is most desirable, because of its most

[67] SJG, I, 110; DCM, I, 247-49 (9).
[68] SJG, I, 111; DCM, I, 265-80 (10).
[69] SJG, I, 113.
[70] DCM, I, 276-392 (10-14); III, 893-914 (100-101); SJG, I, 113; III, 170-71.

perfect liberty. Here in this world, there is no perfect liberty, although all naturally desire it; but there in God's kingdom there will be every liberty, which is contrary to every slavery. "The creature shall be delivered from the servitude of corruption, into the liberty of the glory of the children of God" (Ro. 8, 21). Not only will men be absolutely free there, but they will be kings. "Thou art worthy O Lord,—and hast redeemed us to God, in Thy blood, and hast made us to our God a kingdom" (Apoc. V, 10) ; because all in heaven will be of the same will with God, and God will wish whatever the saints will wish, and the saints, whatever God wills. Hence the will of God will be the will of those in heaven; and therefore all will rule, because the Lord will become the will of all, and the crown of all." In that day the Lord of hosts shall be a crown of glory, and a garland of joy to the residue of His people" (Isaias 28, 5).

Thirdly, the kingdom of heaven is most desirable, because of its wonderful riches. "The eye hath not seen, O God, besides Thee, what things thou hast prepared for them that wait for Thee" (Isaias 64, 4), "Who satisfieth thy desire with good things" (Ps. 102, 5).

Observe also that man will find in God alone, everything more excellent and more perfect than everything which he sought after in Him in this world. If you seek delight, you will find the greatest delight there in God. "You will see and your heart will rejoice. Everlasting joy shall be upon your heads" (Isaias 66, 14). If you seek duration of joy, it will be there eternally. "The just shall enter into eternal life." If you seek riches, there in God's kingdom you will find an abundance of riches, by reason of which riches exist, and so in regard to all other good things.

Wherefore Augustine says, "Whatever there is, that thou O holy soul can desire, there you will find it entirely in God." [71]

The theme of a homily attributed to Thomas is "The Heavenly House." [72] This house is eternal life and in it there are six mansions. Three of these are given over to the holy angels and three belong to the saints. Briefly summarized, the three angelic mansions contain, first, the upper hierarchy with its three chambers for Seraphim, Cherubim, and Thrones; second, the middle hierarchy with its provision for Principalities, Dominations, and Powers; third, the lower

---

[71] Translation of E. C. McEniry, *Saint Thomas Aquinas Meditations for Everyday* (Somerset, Ohio, 1938), pp. 430-31. Later editions published by Long's College Book Co. Used by permission of the author. Cf. Anselm, *Prosolog.* XXV; Petry, "Social Character of Heavenly Beatitude," *The Thomist*, VII, 1 (Jan., 1944), 65-79; *Op. Om.*, 27:187-89.

[72] *Hom. for St. Phillip and St. James Day*, in J. M. Ashley, *St. Augustine the Preacher: Being Fifty Short Sermon Notes Founded Upon Select Passages from His Writings* (London, 1877), pp. 26-28.

hierarchy in which there dwell the Virtues, the Archangels, and the Angels. It is the last of these, the Angels, "who declare the will of God to men."

After having outlined, according to the time-honored division, the hierarchies of heaven, the author indicates the inhabitants that have their places in the three mansions reserved for the saints. In the first mansion are those soldiers of the Church who defended it with their strength. They dwell in the first mansion in three appropriate chambers. In the first room are the martyrs for the faith. These, like St. Stephen and many others who died for the love of Christ, belong to the Seraphim. In the second room are those who were martyred for doctrine as, for example, the Prophets; they belong to the Cherubim. In the third room are the ones who, like John the Baptist, fought zealously for righteousness and became martyrs for it; "these belong to the Thrones."

In the second mansion reserved to the saints is another threefold division wherein there dwell "the confessors, by the counsels of whom the Church is governed." In the first of these rooms are the religious, who represent the Principalities. The second is given over to the prelates, who belong to the Dominations. The third room contains the married, who belong to the Powers.

The third and last mansion prepared for the saints has a three-chambered provision for "those virgins, the domestics, by whose beauty the Church is adorned." In the first of these rooms "dwell those virgins which are women; these belong to the Virtues. In the second live the men who are virgins; these belong to the Archangels. In the third dwell the child virgins; they belong to the Angels."

This fanciful treatment, whether or not an authentic work of Thomas, presents a schematization quite in keeping with the prevailing theology. It is a patent attempt to preserve the Augustinian pattern whereby both angels and men are finally to be wrought into a single order of celestial life. Thus the house of eternal life is here thought of as being twofold, with three mansions given over to angels and three to men. It is to be noted, however, that the hierarchical ordering found among the angels necessitates a conformity on the part of blessed humanity. The entire arrangement fits into the Dionysian frame work—at least into the popularization that was current in the thirteenth century.[73]

[73] Cf. Sermo 70, *Sermones Festivi, Op. Om.* (Paris, 1950 ed.), XV, 228, regarding the relationship of the Pauline Dionysius, the Ps. Dionysius, and *The Hierarchies;* cf. *Opera* VII: "Com. in Div. Nominibus," *Op. Om.* (Parma), XV, 259 ff.

Bonaventura's conception of the heavenly beatitude is not dissimilar to that of his Dominican contemporary. The greater eloquence of his description found in the *Breviloquium* must be attributed, however, not to him, but to Anselm, whom he quotes almost verbatim. Aside from this, Bonaventura's is a less satisfying interpretation than that of Thomas.[74]

Ludolph of Saxony (d. 1370 or 1378) was, perhaps, a Dominican who later became a Carthusian prior. His famous *Life of Christ,* based on the four Gospels, was, as a modern Catholic author says, a work more spiritual and ascetic than historical. But in his meditations, drawn not only from his own deeply spiritual life, but also from a wide acquaintance with the Fathers, he made an enduring contribution to Christian social thought. This last emphasis is often neglected by Catholics and Protestants alike; for he is frequently credited with a merely individualized reaction of pious character. Actually, nothing could be farther from the truth. Ludolph's is a very real ability to consider the pertinent experiences of Jesus' historic existence as the eliciting quality best suited to evoke true Christian deportment; this appeal to both individual and social dedication in the Master's name merits exposition of a more ample sort.[75]

Ludolph's section on the sufferings of hell and the joys of paradise is not new in its matter. It is largely drawn from Jerome, Chrysostom, Augustine, Gregory Nazianzen, Gregory the Great, Anselm, and Bernard. Real significance attaches to it, however, in that it emphasizes eloquently, if not originally, the way in which the greatest griefs of hell ensue upon lasting separation from heavenly companionship. This is but a balancing of the accent which Ludolph places upon the social joys of the saved. Drawing upon Chrysostom and Augustine for his heart-rending account of life excluded from the kingdom, he finds nothing worse than this alienation from the City of God.

As for the joys of those in paradise, not all the skills of arithmetic, geometry, grammar, dialectic, and rhetoric can set them forth. Free to the blessed are the vision of God, the visible beauties of all his creation, the glorification of souls and bodies, and the unimpeded association of angels and men within the celestial fellowship. With

[74] Pars VII, cap. 7, Quaracchi ed., *Op. Om.,* V, 288-91; Nemmers tr., pp. 241-44; cf. Anselm, *Prosolog.,* XXV.
[75] Hurter, *Nomenclator,* II, 566-67; *Vita Jesu Christi,* ed. L. M. Rigollot (4 Vols., Rome, 1870); Sister Mary Immaculate Bodenstedt, *The Vita Christi of Ludolphus the Carthusian* (Washington, D. C., 1944).

the joys and intentions of each open to the other, the just shall be seen in ecstasy and the reprobate in their agony.

Better still, each one of the heavenly company will now see God in himself, as well as God as he is shared among the blessed, to say nothing of the complete participation that the beloved shall have in the Trinity. Here God is all in all. From such union come all the glories involved in God's becoming man so that man might be brought to beatific communion with him. Augustine and Gregory here supply the major testimony utilized in Ludolph's almost sensuous description of the good that shall be all-powerful and the evil that, by its very absence, shall proclaim true beatitude.

Ludolph's discussion of the seven spiritual goods approximates his best in its portrayal of mutuality and concord. Friendship and spiritual intercommunion are here in perfect evidence within a company that has become, once and for all, the integral body of Christ— the body of which Christ himself is the single head. Such an interchange of love, in which each regards the other as himself, is an ineffable experience. Yet Ludolph must attempt to portray the prospect of love thus made available by One who loved all men incomparably more than tongue can tell.

Concord of perfect character cannot possibly be absent where each as the member of a unified body functions harmoniously with all the other organs. Even as one eye follows the other when it turns, so do Christ's members unite in a purpose and will that cannot be divergent from his own. The will that they shall exercise achieves, at last, the perfection drawn from the Omnipotent, himself. Added to this unimpaired cohesiveness will be the complete power, honor, security, and rejoicing that belong to all-pervading beatitude.

There will surely be a variety of mansions or rooms, whether in heaven or in hell. Just as there are different degrees of merit or demerit, so there will be varying recognitions of glory and dishonor affecting both bodies and souls. One house there will certainly be, just as there was one common payment to all who worked in the vineyard; but there will be differences of clarity or brightness in keeping with each individual's deserved share in the eternal beatitude. Though there will be grades of honor, no inferior will envy one who is superior, any more than a finger contends for the place of an eye in bodily organization. Ludolph closes his discussion on the heavenly community with reference to a hallowed doctrine: In this final society the defects left by fallen angels in the choir of celestial beings will be made up from the accretion of the elect destined to that joyous end.[76]

It is characteristic of the *Pricke of Conscience* that it attributes to the heavenly world those human qualities that spell enjoyment in the present life. Play, laughter, and good cheer are not beneath the delights of this world to come. The melody of the angels prevails on every hand. Loving and thanking are heard and experienced everywhere. "There is all friendship that may be, and perfect love and charity." Unity is the rule from which there are no exceptions. Perfect reverence, obedience, and virtue are everywhere observable.[77]

Nothing is to be hidden from the righteous when they see God face to face. God will be to them like a clear mirror in which all things shall be fairly seen. Realizing full well the puzzlement that enters the minds of good people, the author thinks of this new world as providing the answers to erstwhile enigmas. At last it will be evident why some died in childhood and others lived to the greatest age; why some were born in the fairest shapes and some with uncomely stature; why some were rich and some poor; why some children knew the joys of legitimate birth and others not. These and many other questions will be explained out of the open book of life.[78]

The blessed will retain no memory of their sins on earth. These will be forgotten like a wound perfectly healed. The Apostle Peter, himself, now has no shame for his dastardly betrayal of the Christ; nor has Mary Magdalene any further sense of shame for the sins in which, for some time, she delighted. The saved spend their time in praising and thanking God for his goodness in redeeming them through his mercy.[79]

Not least of the bonds which shall draw the saints together in heaven is the edifying enjoyment which they shall have in looking upon the Virgin, the angels, and all the glorious body of the redeemed. Naturally, their greatest joy shall be in the sight of the Trinity. It is in the brightness of God's face that the blessed shall see and know all things. No longer shall they see him through grace; but now face to face. The blessed Mother Mary, also, shall be in full view of the saved. She shall sit next to the Godhead, above all angels, as is right; for Christ took upon himself man's flesh and blood here

---

[76] Especially, Pars II, cap. 88; Rigollot, IV, 812-20.
[77] Morris ed., Book VII, pp. 209 ff. Ll. 7772 ff., especially 7840-44.
[78] Book VII, pp. 221-23, Ll. 8208-70.
[79] *Ibid.*, pp. 223-25, especially Ll. 8316-23, 8348-64.

below. As she sits next to the Son in a position of highest honor, her fairness may be seen by all.

Furthermore, "as the book tells," all the nine orders of angels in their celestial beauty shall be open to the gaze of all. They shall shine brighter than the sun; and in the sight of them will be great joy. The redeemed shall also see patriarchs, prophets, apostles, and evangelists "that followed none other life but Christ's." Freely to be gazed upon, also, will be many innocents slain in the name of God. Martyrs and confessors will be there likewise. Holy hermits and doctors that knew and taught Holy Writ, together with many other holy men both learned and unlearned, regular and secular, shall be in full edifying view of the elect. Here are to be seen holy virgins that have loved God and kept themselves chaste for his sake. There are others who have lived a good Christian life in the wedded state. All shall make a good glorious company to be seen and joined in heavenly rejoicing. Rightfully shall these be crowned with coronas of bliss. Their rewards won in the test of earthly life shall last forever.[80]

In contrast with that future world, the one that we know now is but a dunghill. The imagination is staggered by the attempt to conceive heaven's cosmic spaciousness and brightness. Within it might stand many thousand worlds such as we know. This bright abode of the blessed is called "sovereignty, the kingdom of God almighty." The poet thinks of it in terms of a city in which there are many dwelling places. It was in such fashion that St. John is said to have spoken:

> "I saw," he says, "the Holy City
> Of Jerusalem all new to see,
> Coming down from heaven bright,
> Of God almighty richly dight,
> As bride, made fair for her bridegroom;
> Thus says St. John he saw come.

The poem continues:

> This city is for to understand,
> Holy church that here is fighting
> Against the devil and his might,
> That it assails, both day and night;
> But that fight shall not last for aye,
> It shall last no longer than till dooms day.

[80] *Ibid.*, pp. 234-35, Ll. 8692-8751.

Then shall holy church, of fighting cease,
And be with God in rest and peace;
For it is bride, and God is bridegroom;
Then shall they both together come,
And in heaven dwell for aye together;
And all their children shall then come thither.
That to them has been obedient and true;
And that betokens the city new;
For then shall holy church that tide,
In heaven be newly glorified,
And dwell there with God Almighty,
In joy, and mirth, and melody.[81]

Such is the poet's conception of the Church militant moving toward its triumphant status in God's eternal kingdom. Holy Church sojourning in militancy here below is but gathering all Christian men of like destiny to a new home in heaven.

The writer knows well enough his own limitations. He realizes that the manner of heaven's construction is beyond his ken and that of all other mortals. That it is not made with hands, he is sure. Far from dwelling literally upon golden streets and precious stones, he thinks of these as signifying the spiritual qualities of the heavenly fatherland. Thus the streets and lanes are spiritually interpreted as referring to all holy men who dwell in heaven. The pavements are but an indication of the perfect love and endless life with peace and rest and security that shall be common to all who dwell there, eternally. The sweet music, the sweeter odors, and the concord, sweetest of all, which each shall have with his fellows in the company of angels are much more than physical realities. They betoken the ineffable experiences of multiplied thousands who shall never tire of praising God.[82]

The author is disarmingly candid in stating the objective of his long, discursive treatment of the heavenly world. Perhaps those who have read his poem may be drawn in love to the joyous society of the blessed; and repelled with edifying fear by the terrible destiny of the wicked. Fear without love is not worthy of reward. Dread should be love's brother. Love and fear should be joined together for the avoidance of hell and the winning of heaven. But God should

[81] *Ibid.*, p. 237, Ll. 8795-8800; 8801-18.
[82] *Ibid.*, pp. 238-52; Ll. 8854-9367.

not be thought of as a means to an end. He should be loved for himself alone. Only thus can men come to their proper end. The *Pricke of Conscience* is designed to make man inwardly tender and bring him to the right way. In this way lies the correction of error and the turning to the good and to the eternal.[83]

The *Ayenbite of Inwit* has many striking points of similarity with the *Pricke of Conscience*.[84] Its section on the beatitude is a much reduced, and differently phrased, interpretation of the matter with which the *Pricke of Conscience* deals. Thus the heavenly world appeared to the messenger who visited it, first of all, in the light of the majestic Trinity. On God's right hand sat the Christ, bearing in his body the wounds and signs of his passion. Next to him sat the blissful Maid and Mother ever Virgin. She it was who continued to intercede for mankind. Next came the order of blissful spirits. Prophets, patriarchs, and apostles sat upon their appropriate thrones. Countless martyrs constituted an innumerable fellowship. The visitor to heaven saw "the blessed heap of confessors, among them apostles and teachers" who contended for the faith in the Church against all enemies. There were monks shining clearer than the sun. Last of all appeared the fellowship of maidens singing the song that none other may sing.

Upon inquiry, the messenger was told of the completely blessed life of mutuality, security, and joy that these denizens of heaven forever know. Each rejoices in another's good as in his own. Invited into the Lord's bliss, they proceed wherever they will; "and the body goes where the spirit wills it." Love rules supreme; from Christ's love none is able to separate them. In the love of God all fear is dissipated. Into such loving companionship as that of the heavenly country may all the faithful come! The author bids readers remember that God made the angel as well as the little worm. One is worthy of heaven itself; the other, of earth alone. But men are worms, and of worms God makes angels. He can do what he will: Let man's heart be raised to God. Let man find bliss with him in the company of the blessed.[85]

As a fitting conclusion to this survey of early and medieval views, one may append the paraphrased convictions of a modern author. How direct the lines of communication are that lead from Christian

---

[83] *Ibid.*, pp. 255-57; Ll. 9476-9624.
[84] Morris ed. (EETS 23, London, 1866); Wells, *Manual*, pp. 345, 817.
[85] *Ibid.*, Pref., and pp. 266-71.

social thought in one era to that of another may here be clearly divined.[86]

God's judgment and grace are operative on persons; that is, on individual-collective persons. One may stand as an individual part of the human race. But he is an individual because he is of the larger human unity. Definitive personality is found only in the final community and its mutuality. There will be in the heavenly world no mystical absorption in one great "All Person." Creator and created remain differentiated from each other as persons. Creatures, too, are distinguished from one another. Together they help to make up the majestic unity of the society of God. One in Christ, they are nonetheless individuals, all. Out of their participating mutuality, their gift of themselves to one another and to God, they help to build the community which is of man and God. And this social life is supremely one of love as it is given in Christ Jesus.[87]

Such a communal experience, which in history was actualized only in its beginnings, and was always being broken, here becomes eternally realized. The "I-ness" and the "You-ness" which, in the church-of-the-world experience had always a certain foreignness about them, find their full development in an "I" and "I" relationship that is here fully consummated. The full revelation of one heart to another is now for the first time perfected in godly love. The community which was all too imperfect in its physical form now takes to itself the perfection of a spiritual oneness. Here the "I" and the "I" seek and find one another in an act of mutual giving and receiving. Actuality and supreme truth become one and the same thing.[88]

Now at last, in eternal beatitude, true personality is found. It emerges in the uniquely intimate concourse of one with the other. Here, finally, is a society that can be equated with the term "eternal salvation." Found at last is that perfect vision of eternal truth which, heretofore, was possible by faith alone. Realized now is that perfected love which is known only in the service of the spirit. God, who in his sovereignty is both King and Father, now rules free-willing spirits and has perfect companionship with them. He is, indeed, the God of living persons, not of dead beings. The objective spirit of the community becomes, actually, the Holy Spirit. There is no longer any

[86] Bonhoeffer, *Sanctorum Communio*, pp. 178-80. Cf. Althaus, *Die letzten Dinge* (5th ed., Gütersloh, 1949), Chap. 8; "Das Reich," pp. 319-65—with a critique of O. Cullmann (*Christus und die Zeit*, 1946, pp. 52 ff.), pp. 339-40.

[87] Bonhoeffer, *op. cit.*, p. 178; cf. Will, *Le Culte*, III, 93-105.

[88] Bonhoeffer, *op. cit.*, pp. 178-79.

differentiation between the corporate body of the saints in God and the true Church brought into his kingdom.[89]

Here all are one, and yet each one remains, himself, a person. They are all one in God; yet each is differentiated from the other. They are one and the same, yet not the same, in truth and love. This we may believe in the present life, even as we walk by faith rather than by full vision. But it is our Christian conviction that we shall, at last, not only see, but fully participate in, the community of God with all who love him. At long last, the kingdom of Christ will have become the kingdom of God. The ministry of Christ, the Holy Spirit, and of the Word now will have obtained its objective. Christ himself will have delivered to the Father his filial community; and God will have become all in all. No more will one speak of the Church triumphant, but rather of the kingdom of God that shall now have reached the proportions of the all-powerful and the all-pervasive. Repentance and faith will now have given way to service and light. For all of this, and unspeakably more, the Church lives in vigorous hope. For this, all present preparations and sufferings are to be gladly borne.[90]

[89] *Ibid.,* p. 179.
[90] *Ibid.,* p. 180; cf. Thielicke, *Tod und Leben,* pp. 186-99.

CHAPTER XVI

Christian Eschatology and Social Thought: Retrospect and Prospect

ONE CONVICTION OF THE MIDDLE AGES WAS MORE STUBBORNLY AND resourcefully related to everyday existence than any other. This was the Church's belief in a transcendent order that would provide ultimate judgment upon, and eventual replacement of, all temporal life. Every teaching of Christ and all emphases of Christian doctrine that the Church had since evolved were given definition and substance in relation to eschatological verities.

The modifications of eschatological thought by the Christian ages were traceable less to a changed content of belief than to the fluctuating pressures of a working commitment. Thus, the teaching and lay preaching of Francis of Assisi, for example, were not categorically different from the deliverances of theologians. His exhortations were, however, more specifically motivating and more alertly energizing for the masses than were many official pronouncements. Virtually all the incentives to Christian living in the Middle Ages were issued against the background of the eternal kingdom as already present in substance and against its foreground as an imminently impending absolute. The most persistent subliminal pressures in literature and iconography were those of approaching judgment. It is true that medieval men and women were by no means so obsessed with the thought of world's end as we sometimes picture them as being. It is even more true, however, than we can imagine today, that the anticipation of an ultimate severance between present and future worlds was an everyday postulate for every man.

This was only partly a matter of negatively dreading hell. It was chiefly a positive fear of not attaining heaven. Here, then, was the most poignant side of the longing to enter the beatitude. Such a concern was not solely, or even chiefly, the preoccupation of priests and popes. It was the *raison d'être* for the most ignorant peasant and the most devoted renunciant, alike. The simplest and the profoundest bearing of eschatology on medieval Christian life, then, was just this: Human existence on this earth, in time, had its meaning from what preceded, and would succeed, both earth and time. God made earth and man for an end beyond planets and human history. This he did with a view to man's surmounting both time and history, as well as the limits of the physical world.

In the middle period of European civilization, no considerations of ecclesiology, theology, politics, or art had an existence independent of the eschatological framework. No activity of history signified anything apart from its dedication to, and judgment by, that divine rule which transcended history.

It may be argued that the cumulative eschatological impact of medieval Christian letters and tradition was merely a tribute to the official oversimplification of human expression and to the foreclosure on freedom of thought. The inescapably historical answer to all such charges is, simply, that no other preponderant passions of which we have record meant anything aside from their eschatological perspective. This living bent was not characteristically engendered or principally described in learned volumes but was most authoritatively pronounced in the oral up-wellings and plastic symbolism of the common life.

An age such as ours is accustomed to the preservation of a token eschatology concurrent with a practicing repudiation of it. Our age, alone, could entertain any such stubborn ignorance as is ours regarding the validity and the vitality of medieval faith in ultimate end, final judgment, and eternal kingdom.

The first major proposition of Christian eschatology is that the heavenly kingdom is the society supreme and that it will have its consummate fulfillment in the beatitude. The second premise insists that the companionship of Christians on earth must be elicited, impelled, and motivated by the social dynamics of the heavenly fraternity. The genius of Christian eschatology consists in its being conscious of society primarily in terms of the heavenly *patria,* not of the earthly community. The *civitas* of earth must be defined, judged, and adapted within the limits of human, terrestrial existence, in relation to the character and customs of the celestial city. The Christian society on earth must be built on foundations established in heaven. The ultimate purchase of Christian social life, therefore, is not adaptability to human precedents but conformity with heavenly archetypes. Obviously, the eternal society is not an accretion of human, earthly innovations deemed practicable to time. It is, rather, the unified citizenship engendered and ruled by Deity itself that demands the immediate response of all Christians in the temporal order.

Here, then, is the ineluctable progression of Christian eschatology and social action. The life of Christians in human society is but a temporal response to the eternal community. The word "social" immediately loses its secular parochialism under the necessity of reproducing, in however slight a degree, the characteristics of the true, cosmic brotherhood. The terms "society" and "social" are reoriented beyond our current usage to accord with the universal connotations of basic kingdom societalism. A new, powerful sense of social thought and action eventuates from Christianity's voluntary response to this eternal *koinonia,* this eucharistic fellowship nurtured on earth, with and for the solidarity of heaven. The Christian has no choice between accommodation to established human mores and conformity with the rules of kingdom consolidation. What seemed to Greco-Roman society to be a flagrant jettisoning by Christians of hard-won human association was something quite different. It was actually a recognition by Christ's followers of superior human associativeness educed by the parent society, God's kingdom. There could be for Christians no *civitas* aside from the eternal city. Their city, the eternal commonwealth, was in heaven. They were a colony, a suburb of it, waiting full reincorporation into it. To have acknowledged any temporal society as final and authoritative would have been to give the maximum exhibition of social irresponsibility.

What the non-Christian world deemed social insensitivity was rather a superior responsiveness to ultimate sociability. The most majestic impulse in Christian life was far from being a negation of social instincts and loyalties. It was the immediate and sacrificial reinterpretation, within human limits, of working kingdom citizenship. What the Christians' enemies interpreted to be *lèse-majesté* and social lesion was in reality their probationary subscription to consummate sociality and their fullest patriotic commitment to eternal citizenship in heaven. Steadily mounting throughout this development of Christian experience was the Church's consciousness of itself as the agent of the eternal in the temporal world. The Church conceived of itself increasingly as mediating the demands of eternal sociality to temporal society. In itself the Church fostered the sense of ecclesiastical community. It acknowledged gratefully the true bond of Christian *koinonia.* Here, then, was the *pusillus grex* of the Master, the household of faith, the true soul of the body social. In the world but not of it, the twofold Church is the kingdom-dominated community living within earthly society.

Seen from this perspective, the Church is two societies in one. It derives from the perfect society of heaven the pattern and the divine energies for judging, redeeming, and—to a limited degree during history—for transforming the society of earth. The Church, then, as the ecclesiastical community, becomes the servant of the eternal kingdom in the temporal order. Apparently domesticated on earth, the Church is never wholly exiled from the *patria*. The earthly pilgrimage of the Church celebrates its liberation to an eternal society. But, even though the Church is not of the temporal order, in essence, it is resident, if only fleetingly, in a time-environed society. Accommodated, after a fashion, to the present world order, it is primarily committed to the celestial community.

The Church, according to this view, actually provides the only acceptable and accepted definition of true society. It serves as the incarnation, on earth, of society—that is, the true, eternal one. Though in a measure temporal, itself, it incorporates and exercises the empowerment of heaven.

In last analysis there was only one theory of medieval society, that of the Church. The Church defined, motivated, and actuated medieval society. It did this eschatologically, and in no other way. This was true because it, alone, not only represented, but was the agent and servant of, kingdom society in the world of men. Precisely because the Church and the Church alone could simultaneously live in history and yet proceed beyond it, medieval society gave submission to the ecclesiastical community. It was as definitely a saving incarnation of the divine society in human history as was Christ its head a saving reincarnation of Deity in the world.

Manifestly, the Church must have divinely empowered men to reincarnate a divinely established society. Increasingly significant, therefore, was the distinctive role of hierarchy and priesthood in this eschatological-social equation. The whole concept of hierarchy, whether in Pseudo-Dionysius, Bonaventura, or Thomas Aquinas, springs from the necessity of mediating eschatologically, and therefore socially, the dictates and resources of heaven to the people of earth. Just as the Church on earth is the servant of the kingdom of heaven, so also are the ordered ranks of earthly priests the instrumentation of the celestial hierarchy.

That the root concept of priesthood and hierarchy is an eschatological one is clearly shown in Gregory the Seventh's correspondence, in Hugh of St. Victor's *On the Sacraments,* in Peter Lombard's *Sentences,* in St. Bernard's *On Consideration,* and in Thomas Aquinas' *Governance of Princes.* Indeed, it is manifested throughout the whole of medieval life and letters. Furthermore, the criticisms of Roger Bacon, Raymond Lull, and others against contemporary hierarchs are actually a support for genuine priesthood and hierarchy, not a repudiation of these. The Lullian missionary passion is the outgrowth of an eschatological faith, the zeal to save souls for the eternal kingdom. This distinctively evidences Lull's faith, also, in the powers properly received and administered by such hierarchs as Pope Blanquerna, who organizes the resources of the true Church for the sacrificial evangelization, by Christians, of the infidel world. It is an eschatological mission, by way of Christian learning and informed preaching, in infidel tongues, such as Roger Bacon so enthusiastically supported.

The great medieval prophets and prophetesses such as Bernard of Clairvaux, Hildegarde of Bingen, Catherine of Siena, and Birgitta of Sweden have an eschatological goal and an eschatological leverage for social commitment. Their social presuppositions are eschatologically sustained, whether for the nerving of Christian gospelers and social critics, the call to resolute papal witness during the great schism, the appeal for a dedicated Roman hierarchy in the midst of ecclesiastical exploitation, or the clarification of Christian statesmanship under the aspect of eternity.

Virtually all of the basic treatises such as Thomas Aquinas' *Governance of Princes,* Durand of Mende's handbook on liturgical symbolics, Vincent de Beauvais's *Mirror of History,* and Humbert of Romans' book *On the Education of Preachers,* have one common concern. The teachers of Christ's Church on earth have their commission from heaven to inculcate in human society the associational principles of celestial community. The instincts and the loyalties of earthly priests must be recapitulations, under the divine empowerment, of the social predispositions moving within the heavenly orders.

The mandates of the celestial court were the instructional prototypes for the ambassadors of Christ's Church on earth. The liturgy was the hierarchical channeling of the eternal powers to temporal necessities; the means of redemptively transcending the natural with the supernatural.

Having thus summarized, briefly, the chief tenets of Christian eschatology and social thought, how may one evaluate, critically, the fundamental direction, modification, and practical implementation of these assumptions?

It is obvious, first of all, that the Church's eschatological views did not result in social paralysis but rather tended to a conscious reinvigoration of social effort. What eventuated was a kind of social moralism that threatened, ultimately, the very principle of Christian *agape*. Christ and Paul had insisted on socially effective works as the nonmeritorious expression of gratitude for God's grace freely given. Nevertheless, the sweep of Christian history subtly, but consistently, emphasized the necessity of responsible social action as a guarantee of heaven's acceptance. Medieval documents are legion in which eschatology serves to motivate and fortify the Christian's individual action out of a social kingdom context. But rarely, if ever, do these documents interpret Matthew 25:35, for instance, as identifying such ministry with the social pattern of men who react out of free *agape*. These activities are consistently viewed as the kind of social action which the returning Christ will adjudge worthy or unworthy of heavenly entrance. The effect of this is to focus Christian social action at precisely the wrong point: namely, on man's ability to merit reward by superior social acts. The emphasis mistakenly falls here, rather than on man's humble responsiveness, in grateful social ministry among fellow recipients, to the free gift which he and they have in no way earned. The Church put its weight squarely behind the very type of social activism best calculated to accrue in institutional and private resources saved up against the need for convincing God of human righteousness. This invited the whole machinery of merit-consciousness and merit-trading against which Martin Luther and others reacted so emphatically much later; even as the evangelical churches subsequently rewelcomed it under Protestant guises. Pre-Reformation history thus records the progressive loss of Jesus' revelation of kingdom *agape* and the growing substitution for it of institutional *caritas*. With this there went the hierarchically ordered dogma of supererogatory works. Instead of its being a community of those held wholly unworthy of salvation, and bound together by a common sense of gratitude for God's free gift of life, the Church became self-consciously aware of itself as a pool of merited resources, subject to loan by individuals deficient in soteriological group activity.

One signal effect of the Church's utilizing eschatological leverage for a new social moralism was its crystallization of primitive eschatological norms as a further validation of eternal verities. The clear historical tendency of the Christian Fathers was to estop creative speculation as to God's unlimited graciousness and to substitute rigidified man-made judgments of human acts now deemed beyond the reclamatory powers of God himself. Thus, for instance, Origen's stubborn faith in God's power and undefeatable will to redeem all men, ultimately, was steadily scorned as indecent naïveté. This, they felt, reflected both on man's volitional right to damn himself and on God's honorable obligation to pronounce some men too evil for salvation. The Church was faced with a clear dilemma. It could make God's graciousness sufficient to confer salvation aside from merit, even at the cost of constricting man's will to defeat God's redemptive love. Or, it might delimit, in human terms, God's ability to rescue men held free enough, but not good enough, to be saved. The Church all too readily elected the latter course. This it did in the name of a purportedly mounting revelation set forth in the Scriptures and interpreted according to ecclesiastical tradition and hierarchical absolutism. Such a repression of reverently free speculation concerning God's unhampered forgiveness poisoned the Church's faith in his resistlessly merciful love and legalized its defini-tion of God's attributes as being primarily those of primitive justice. Admission to heaven came increasingly to be interpreted as proffered by God on terms humanly stipulated. In effect, God was contractually bound to the earthly hierarch's estimate of a man's being sufficiently good to merit heaven or sufficiently bad to require hell.

This had the tragic aftermath of invoking a whole chain of un-warranted consequences. Man's salvation was defined, less and less, in terms of God's mercy freely given, all apart from the acts of merit. Man's damnation was demanded, more and more, in God's name, according to the arbitrary standards of human vengefulness. Specula-tion on the nature of God's divinely revealed heaven was stultified in favor of an unimaginative scriptural literalism determined by the hierarchical preoccupations of an institutionalized clergy. Such a ministry seldom lacked the temerity to invoke or displace the Scrip-tures precisely when and however it chose. The same clergy, how-ever, manifested a peculiar consistency in interpreting these very Scriptures in the most willfully anthropomorphic fashion, where eternal life and everlasting damnation were concerned. Doubly fate-ful was the growing tendency to establish hierarchical absolutism as a divine mandate and then to represent God's mercy toward men as being under the limitations of vindictively human judgment.

Jesus' parables on the kingdom society were strikingly suggestive of unfettered divine freedom. They were singularly divorced from human stereotypes on the spiritual economy of the community in glory. The medieval Church, on the other hand, was cumulatively sterile in spiritual imagination and correspondingly sure of God's most detailed will regarding hell and the beatitude. One might say historically that the less the institutional hierarchy thrilled to God's unpredictable surprises laid up in the beatitude, the more dogmatically they repeated themselves in man-made commonplaces about heavenly life and customs, as, also, concerning the horrors of hellish society.

As might be expected, therefore, this perversion of an eschatologically social *agape* resulted in an oversimplification of the divinely revealed beatitude. These obliquities, together, prompted, in turn, a savagely distorted focus on the character, purpose, and working details of the Last Judgment. Jesus and the Gospels had stressed the inescapably tragic consequences, individual and social, of acts oriented away from the kingdom. Jesus, himself, had not, however, fully stipulated the limits of God's grace to surmount such consequences. The medieval Church dared to explicate the fullest and most final details of God's helplessness, thereafter, to overcome tragic results thus registered. Once again the leaven of a pharisaical moralism pre-empted God's free action in the name of a humanly delineated justice.

Taking perhaps overseriously its mandate to serve as the agent of the eternal, in the temporal world, the Church came close to describing the divine initiative according to the permissive will of the temporally environed hierarchy. The priesthood commissioned to transmit the eliciting social urge of the kingdom fraternity well-nigh ended up by denaturing heaven to suit earthly circumscriptions. The Scriptures, instead of being laid hold upon as a stairway to the kingdom, were rented out as a preferential franchise by overweening patronizers of the divine love. The net effect of all this was not so much to help make earth ready for transformation by heaven as to relativize heaven and make it natural enough for earth. Here, most disastrously, is the very reverse of a major medieval claim. This was that the *Corpus Christianorum* is redeemed from the natural order by the supernatural kingdom through the graces committed into the hands of its earthly hierarchy. In actuality, medieval society was all too much palliated in its relativizing social ethics, however much it might be admonished to heavenly association by the ecclesiastical hierarchy. Thus, the monastic institution tended to become more of an eschatological substitute for social transformation than an advanced guard of an *agape*-ruled society. It supplied a powerful incentive to eschatologically motivated charity. This, however, was habitually robbed of its fully communalizing *agape* in order to provide a leverage for individual salvation by way of accommodational group merit.

Again, the doctrine of the Mystical Body and the Communion of Saints was compromised at its most crucial point. It ceased to depict in essence the very heart of a meritless society drawn together by its owing all to Christ. Instead, this doctrine gave rise to a subtly ramifying system of hierarchically rewarded, accumulating group benefits. According to it, the superior attainments of some were transferable on request to meet the needs of others. The community of humble parity under Christ's full and free provision for those equally unworthy tended increasingly to become a society of graded merit under the aegis of Christ the Judge.

Another vicious concomitant of this eschatologically elicited, social moralism was the gradual substitution of hierarchical authority for Christ's headship of the threefold Church. On earth his authority was deleted to the advantage of his reigning vicar, the head of the hierarchy. Among those of the Church suffering in purgatory his free graces were judged to be in need of supplementation. This came in part from the merits lendable by saints in glory, as also from the plus balance of good lives still on pilgrimage. In heaven, his ranks were filled up with the aid of credit loans, provided by his saints, from his celestial treasury which they helped keep solvent.

Once having proffered these punishing charges, however, we return to an even more penetrating inquiry. Was the tendency to a new Christian moralism the final and primarily corrupting fruitage of eschatology? Paradoxically enough, we must answer in the negative. Actually, the same eschatological pressures that prompted the Christian desire to seek a social warranty for kingdom entrance, provided, in a growing number of instances, a sense of helplessness to show oneself worthy. The selfsame institution that attempted refunding the human debt to the Divine proved disastrously inadequate to the task. In the institutional complexities of the medieval church there appeared an old, oft-neglected reminder: The Church on earth is but the servant of the kingdom—not its equivalent, or its inaugurator. It may be a humble service—but it is a sufficient one—that the Church is asked to supply. The Church does not confer merit by its corporate acts; it passes on free, saving grace to those left helpless to save themselves.

The same medieval Christianity that saw the pyramiding speciousness attending hierarchical nostrums of salvation, together with the grave accommodation of saints, preachers, and scholars to social moralism, also exhibited something quite different. This was the tendency to count subconsciously on a spiritual fact only half realized: namely, that God's grace really leaves nothing else to be acquired. Only gratitude in social responsiveness need be added to seal the bond of Christian association. The medieval church was to fail of spiritual renascence, not because it left too large a blot of unreformed private and social defection on the institutional record, but because it tried to reactivate a system of ecclesiastical bookkeeping as the proper means of salvation. Nonetheless, medieval ecclesiology, and soteriology, until Trent at least, had not irretrievably committed itself to the full official unalterability of such a position. The unsolicited unanimity of otherwise divergent views held by such Christians as Bernard of Clairvaux, Thomas Aquinas, John Tauler, and Nicholas of Cusa testifies to this fact. Each of these consistently upheld, in theory, the Roman doctrine of salvation by faith *and* works. Yet, all subscribed in word, as well as in deed, to the overriding elicitations of a divine love that directed human response to the divine self before it taught the soul volitional self-awareness. Any fair-minded student of such representative medieval thinkers as these must be impressed by their working acquaintance with the spirit of unprudentialized *agape*. Furthermore, he must be conscious, likewise, of categorical explications native to a doctrine of saving works illogically fostered by at least some descendants of the sixteenth-century *agape* revival. One may remark a sobering fact, not altogether without its humble efficacy, at work in the most diversified Christian soteriologies. The evangelical movements within the Reformed tradition have often acted on the basis of eschatological premises thoroughly redolent of medieval Christian societalism. The Roman Catholic communion, for its part, has frequently been no less productive of embarrassingly evangelical instincts hardly in keeping with its hierarchically rigidified ecclesiology. If it be said that Tridentine doctrine made irrevocable the Roman Catholic departure from its recurrent *agape* instincts, it may be observed with equal justice that twentieth-century Protestantism seems hardly less eager to expunge the fullest implication of salvation without works. Medieval eschatology, on its theoretical side, invited a race for moral superiority under hierarchical aegis with which to importune the divine approval. Our current Protestantism seems defensively set, in practice at least, against both the Catholic challenge to a precise eschatology and the call to a humbling community of free grace reissued by the Reformed tradition. Roman Catholic and Evangelical Protestants alike seem inclined to vie with each other for pre-eminence in group moralism; the Catholic as a consequence of eschatological rigorism, the Protestant as a gradualistic substitute for a doctrine of Last Things. Once again, as so often before, the key to a genuine recovery of historical Christian community may lie in the reappropriation of a positive eschatology sprung out of Christian *agape*. Such a recovery must not be one vitiated by competitive superciliousness, but must rather be an experience dedicated freely in the present order to the gracious mandates of the future world. This being the case, our prayer must needs be: not, "Thy kingdom come in heaven as we have made it on earth," but, "Thy kingdom-will be done on earth, as it is already regnant in heaven."

Bibliography

Key to Abbreviations

ANF: *The Ante-Nicene Fathers. Translations of the Fathers down to* A.D. *325.* 9 vols. Edited by A. Roberts and J. Donaldson. Buffalo, 1885-97.

CSEL: *Corpus scriptorum ecclesiasticorum latinorum.* Vienna, 1866 ff.

EETS: *Early English Text Society.* London, irregular years.

GCS: *Die griechischen christlichen Schriftsteller der ersten drei Jahrhunderte.* Leipzig, irregular years.

MPG: Migne, J. P. (ed.). *Patrologia Graeca.* 165 vols. Paris, 1857-66.

MPL: Migne, J. P. (ed.). *Patrologia Latina.* 221 vols. Paris, 1844-64.

NPNF: *A Select Library of Nicene and Post-Nicene Fathers of the Christian Church.* Edited by P. Schaff and H. Wace in two series: 1st Ser., 14 vols., New York, 1886-90; 2nd Ser., 14 vols., New York, 1890-1900.

NUS: *No Uncertain Sound: Sermons That Shaped the Pulpit Tradition.* Edited by Ray C. Petry. Philadelphia, 1948.

A. Primary Materials

Albert the Great. *Opera Omnia.* Ed. B. Boignet. 38 Vols. Paris, 1890.

Alexander of Hales. *Summa Theologica.* 4 Vols. Quaracchi: Ex Typographia Collegii S. Bonaventurae, 1924-48.

Ambrose of Milan. *De Officiis Ministrorum.* MPL 6.

———. *De Mysteriis. Ibid.*

———. *De Sacramentis. Ibid.*

Andrieu, M., ed. *Les "Ordines Romani" du haut moyen âge.* 2 Vols. Louvain: Spicilegium Sacrum Lovaniense, 1948.

Anselm of Canterbury. *Opera Omnia.* Vol. I, ed. F. S. Schmitt. Seecovii: Ex Officina Abbatiae Seccoviniensis in Styria, 1938. Vol. III. Edinburgh: Thomas Nelson & Sons, 1946.

———. *Méditations et prières.* Tr. D. A. Castel. Paris: Desclée, De Brouwer et Cie, 1923.

Anthony of Padua. *Sermones.* Ed. A. M. Locatelli. Padua, 1895.

The Apostolic Fathers. ANF, I.

Augustine of Hippo. *De cantico novo.* MPL 40.

———. *De Catechizandis Rudibus. Ibid.*

———. *The City of God.* NPNF, 1st Ser., II.

———. *De Civitate Dei.* CSEL, XL, 1-2.

———. *Enarrationes in Psalmos.* MPL 36-37.

———. *Enchiridion.* MPL 40.

———. *De Genesi ad Litteram.* CSEL, XVII, 1; MPL 34.

381

————. *Oeuvres.* Vol. XII. *Les révisions.* Ed. G. Bardy. Paris: Desclée, De Brouwer et Cie, 1950.

————. *Oeuvres Complètes.* Ed. M. Péronne, *et al. Sermones,* Vols. XVI-XVIII. Paris: Louis Vivès, 1872.

————. *Le plus belles homélies . . . sur les Psaumes.* Tr. G. Humeau. Paris: Beau Chesne, 1942.

————. *Sermones Post Maurinos Reperti,* in *Miscellanea Agostiniana: Testi E Studi.* Roma, 1930.

————. *Sermones.* MPL 38.

Bacon, Roger. *Opus tertium, opus minus, et compendium studii philosophiae.* Ed. J. S. Brewer. Rolls Series, 15. London, 1859.

Basil of Caesarea. *The Ascetic Works.* Tr. W. K. L. Clarke. London: S. P. C. K., 1925.

————. *Ascetical Works.* Tr. Sister M. Monica Wagner. New York: Fathers of the Church, Inc., 1950.

Bede the Venerable. *Historia Ecclesiastica Gentis Anglorum.* Ed. J. E. King in *Opera Historica,* 2 Vols. The Loeb Classical Library. New York: G. P. Putnam's Sons, 1930.

Beleth, John. *Rationale Divinorum Officiorum.* MPL 202.

Bernard of Clairvaux. *Letters.* Tr. B. S. James. London: Burns Oates and Washbourne, 1952.

————. *Oeuvres.* Tr. M.-M. Davy. 2 Vols. Paris: Aubier, 1945.

————. *On Consideration.* Tr. G. Lewis. Oxford, 1908.

————. *Sermones in Cantica.* MPL 183-84.

————. *Works.* Tr. S. J. Eales. 4 Vols. London: John Hodges, 1896.

Bernard of Morval. *De Contemptu Mundi.* Ed. H. C. Hoskier. London: Bernard Quaritch Ltd., 1929.

———— (Cluny). *Jerusalem the Golden.* Together with other pieces attributed to Bernard of Cluny. English tr. by H. Preble; ed. S. M. Jackson. Chicago: The University of Chicago Press, 1910.

Birgitta of Sweden. *Revelationes Selectae.* Ed. A. Heuser. Cologne: H. Lempertz & Co., 1851.

————. *The Revelations.* Ed. W. P. Cumming. EETS, 178. London: Milford, 1929.

Boehmer, H. and Wiegand, F. *Analekten zur Geschichte des Franciscus von Assisi.* Tübingen, 1930.

Bonaventura, *Breviloquium.* Tr. E. E. Nemmers. St. Louis: B. Herder Book Co., 1946.

————. *Oeuvres.* Ed. R. P. Valentin-M. Breton. Paris: Aubier, 1943.

————. *Opera Omnia.* 11 Vols. Quaracchi: Ex Typographia Collegii S. Bonaventurae, 1882-1902.

Bosio, G., ed. *I Padri Apostolici.* Serie Greca. Vols. I and II. Torino: Societa Editrice Internazionale, 1940-42.

Breviarium Romanum. 4 Vols (by Seasons). London: Burns Oates & Washbourne, 1946.

Butler, C. *Western Mysticism: The Teaching of SS. Augustine, Gregory and Bernard on Contemplation and the Contemplative Life.* Second edition. London: E. P. Dutton & Co., Inc., 1926.

Catherine of Siena. *Letters.* Tr. V. D. Scudder. New York: E. P. Dutton & Co., 1905.

Cavallera, F., ed. *Thesaurus Doctrinae Catholicae ex documentis Magisterii Ecclesiastici.* Paris: G. Beauchesne, 1920.

Chrysostom. *Homilies on the Gospel of St. Matthew.* NPNF, 1st Ser., X.

———. *Treatise on the Priesthood.* NPNF, 1st Ser., IX.

Coker, F. W. *Readings in Political Philosophy.* Rev. ed. New York: The Macmillan Co., 1938.

Constitutions of the Holy Apostles. ANF VII.

Cook, H. S., and Tinker, C. B. *Select Translations from Old English Prose.* Boston: Ginn & Co., 1908.

Corpus Scriptorum Ecclesiasticorum Latinorum (CSEL). Vienna: F. Tempsky.

Cursor Mundi. Pt. 4. EETS 66. Ed. R. Morris. London, 1875.

Cynewulf. *Poems.* Tr. C. W. Kennedy. London: George Routledge & Sons, Ltd., 1910.

Cyprian. *De catholicae ecclesiae unitate.* CSEL 3, Pt. 1.

———. *De lapsis. Ibid.*

Dante Alighieri. *On World Government, or De Monarchia.* Tr. H. W. Schneider. New York: The Liberal Arts Press, 1950.

———. *Tutte Le Opere.* Ed. E. Moore. Third Edition. Oxford: University Press, 1904.

Denifle, H., and Ehrle, F., eds. *Archiv für literatur-und Kirchengeschichte des Mittelalters.* Berlin, 1885-1900. I, 193-227; V, 560 ff.

Denzinger, H., ed. *Enchiridion Symbolorum.* Twenty-eighth edition by C. Rahner. Friburg i/B, 1952.

Dionysius the Areopagite, Pseudo. *Dionysiaca: Recueil donnant l'ensemble des traductions latines des ouvrages attribués au Denys de L'Aréopage.* 2 Vols. Ed. Ph. Chevallier *et al.* Paris: Desclée, De Brouwer et Cie, 1937.

———. *Mystical Theology and the Celestial Hierarchies.* Editors of the Shrine of Wisdom. N. Godalming, Surrey: The Shrine of Wisdom, 1949. See also the edition of Rolt, C. E., *Dionysius the Areopagite.* New York, 1920.

———. *Oeuvres complètes du Pseudo-Denys l'Aréopagite.* Tr. M. de Gandillac. Paris: Aubier, 1943.

Durand of Mende, Wm. *Rationale Divinorum Officiorum.* Naples: J. Dura, 1859.

———. *The Symbolism of Churches and Church Ornaments,* being the first book of the *Rationale.* Tr. J. M. Neale and B. Webb. Cambridge: T. Stevenson, 1843.

Early English Christian Poetry. Tr. C. W. Kennedy. New York: Oxford University Press, 1952.

Elucidatio in 235 Tabulas Patrologiae Latinae Auctore Cartusiensi. Rotterdam: Sumptibus et Typis Soc. Editr. De Forel, 1952.

Funk, F. X., ed. *Didascalia et Constitutiones Apostolorum.* 2 Vols. Paderborn: F. Schoeningh, 1905.

———. *Patres Apostolici.* 2 Vols. Second edition. Tübingen: H. Lanpp, 1901.

Gerson, J. *Opera Omnia.* Ed. E. Du Pin. Second edition. Hagae Comitum: P. De Hondt, 1728.

———. *Six sermons français inédits.* Ed. L. Mourin. Paris: J. Vrin, 1946.

Giles, E., ed. *Documents Illustrating Papal Authority* A.D. 96-454. London: S. P. C. K., 1952.

Godefride of Admont. *Homiliae Festivales.* MPL 174.

Goldast, M. *Monarchia sancti romani imperii; sive tractatus de iurisdictione imperiali seu regia, et pontificia.* 3 Vols. Frankfurt, 1611-14.

Gregory I. *The Book of Pastoral Rule.* Tr. J. Barmby, NPNF, 2nd Ser., XII.

——. *Dialogorum Libri IV.* MPL 77.

——. *Dialogues.* Tr. J. Zimmerman and B. R. Avery, in *Life and Miracles of St. Benedict.* Collegeville, Minnesota, 1949.

——. *Epistolae.* MPL 77.

——. *Homiliae XL In Evangelia.* MPL 76.

——. *Liber Regulae Pastoralis.* MPL 77.

——. *Morales sur Job.* Livres 1 et 2. Tr. A. De Gaudemaris. Sources Chrétiennes. Paris: Éditiones Du Cerf, 1947.

——. *Moralium Libri, sive expositio in librum B. Job.* MPL 75-76.

——. *In primum regum expositiones.* MPL 79.

——. *Registri Epistolarum Libri XIV.* MPL 77.

Grosseteste, Robert. *Sermones.* Ed. E. Brown. *Fasciculus rerum expetendarum et fugiendarum.* 2 Vols. London: Cheswell, 1690; especially II, 251-305.

Haymo of Halberstat. *De varietate librorum, sive de Amore coelestis patriae.* MPL 118.

Hilary of Poitiers. *Commentarius in Psalmos.* MPL 9.

——. *Tractatus super psalmos.* MPL 9; CSEL 22.

Hildegarde of Bingen. *Wisse die Wege, Scivias.* Ed. D. M. Boeckeler. Berlin: Sankt Augustinus Verlag, 1928.

——. *The Life and Visions.* Tr. F. M. Steele. London: Heath, Cranton, and Ousely, Ltd., 1914.

——. *Scivias.* MPL, 197.

Hincmar of Rheims. *De ordine Palatii.* Texte Latin. Tr. M. Prou. Paris: F. Vieweg, 1884.

Honorius of Autun. *Elucidarium.* MPL 172.

Hugh of St. Victor. *On the Sacraments of the Christian Faith (De Sacramentis).* Tr. R. J. Deferrari. Cambridge, Mass.: Mediaeval Academy of America, 1951.

——. *De Sacramentis.* MPL 176.

——. *Summa Sententiarum.* MPL 176.

——. *De Claustro Animae.* MPL 176.

——. *Commentariorum (Expositio) in Hierarchiam Coelestem S. Dionysii Areopagitae secundum interpretationem Joannis Scoti.* . . . MPL 175.

Humbert of Romans. *De eruditione praedicatorum.* Ed. J. J. Berthier, *Opera de vita regulari.* Vol. II. Rome: A. Befanus, 1889.

——. *De modo prompte cudendi sermones,* being Liber II of *De eruditione,* but not included in Berthier's edition. Ed. M. De La Bigne, *Maxima bibliotheca veterum patrum.* Tom. XXV. Lugduni: Apud Anissonios, 1677.

Hurlbut, S., ed. *Hortus Conclusus: A Series of Mediaeval Latin Hymns with Selected English Renderings.* Part Six: Peter Damian and Hildebert of Tours. Washington, D. C.: St. Albans Press, 1932.

——. *The Picture of the Heavenly Jerusalem in the Writings of Johannes of Fecamp, "De Contemplativa Vita,"* and in the Elizabethan Hymns. Washington, D. C.: St. Albans Press, 1943.

Innocent III. *Regestorum, sive Epistolarum continuatio.* MPL 216.

Ivo of Chartres. *Correspondance.* Tome I (1090-1098). Ed. J. Leclercq. Paris: "Les Belles Lettres," 1949.

Jacobus de Voragine. *The Golden Legend.* Tr. G. Ryan and H. Ripperger. 2 Vols. New York: Longmans, Green & Co., 1941.

Jacques de Vitry. *Sermones Selecta ex sermonibus vulgaribus.* Ed. J. B. Cardinalis Pitra, in *Analecta novissima spicilegii solesmensis altera continuatio.* Tom. II. Parisiis: Roger et Chernowitz Bibliopolis, 1888.

Jerome. *Commentaria in Ezechielem.* MPL 25.

Joachim of Flore. *De Articulis Fidei.* Ed. E. Buonaiuti, *Scritti Minori Di Gioacchino Da Fiore:* Vol. I. Roma Tipografia Del Senato, 1936.

———. *L'évangile éternel.* Vol. II. Tr. E. Aegerter. Paris: Les Éditions Rieder, 1928.

———. *Liber in Expositionem in Apocalipsam.* Venice, 1527.

John Bromyard. *Summa Praedicantium.* 2 Vols. Venice: D. Nicolinus, 1586.

John of Damascus. *Expositio Fidei orthodoxae.* MPG 94.

John of Fecamp. *The Picture of the Heavenly Jerusalem in the Writings of Johannes of Fecamp, "De Contemplativa Vita,"* and in the *Elizabethan Hymns.* Ed. S. A. Hurlbut. Washington, D. C.: St. Albans Press, 1943.

Jonas of Orléans. *De institutione regia.* Ed. J. Reviron in *Les idées politico-religieuses d' un évêque du IX⁰ siècle: Jonas d' Orléans.* Paris: J. Vrin, 1930.

———. *De institutione laicale.* MPL 106.

John of Salisbury. *Policraticus.* 2 Vols. Ed. C. C. J. Webb. Oxford: University Press, 1909.

———. *The Statesman's Book.* Being the Fourth, Fifth, and Sixth Books, and Selections from the Seventh and Eighth Books of the *Policraticus.* Tr. J. Dickinson. New York: Alfred A. Knopf, 1927.

John Scotus Erigena. *Expositiones super ierarchiam Caelestem.* MPL 122.

Julianus Pomerius. *The Contemplative Life.* Ed. M. J. Suelzer. Ancient Christian Writers, No. 4. Westminster, Md.: The Newman Bookshop, 1947.

———. *De Vita Contemplativa.* MPL 59.

Karrer, G. O. *Saint Francis of Assisi, the Legends and Lauds.* New York: Sheed and Ward, 1949.

Lactantius. *The Divine Institutes.* ANF VII.

———. *Divinae Institutiones,* etc. CSEL 19.

———. *Divinae Institutiones.* Selections edited with commentary by W. T. Radius. Grand Rapids, Mich.: Wm. B. Eerdmans Publishing Co., 1951.

———. *Epitome Institutionum Divinarum.* Ed. and Tr. E. H. Blakeney. London: S. P. C. K., 1950.

Lake, K., ed. *The Apostolic Fathers.* 2 Vols. Loeb Classical Library. Cambridge: Harvard University Press, 1948-49.

Lay Folk's Catechism. Eds. T. F. Simmons and H. E. Nolloth. EETS 111. London, 1901.

Lightfoot, J. E., ed. *The Apostolic Fathers.* Pt. 1. Vol. II. New York: The Macmillan Co., 1890.

Ludolph the Carthusian. *Vita Jesu Christi.* 4 Vols. Ed. L. M. Rigollot *et al.* Paris: V. Palmé, 1878.

Luther, M. *Predigten des Jahres 1529,* in *Werke,* XXIX. Weimar: Hermann Bohlans, 1904.

McEniry, E. C., ed. *Saint Thomas Aquinas Meditations for Everyday.* Somerset, Ohio: The Rosary Press, 1938.

Marrou, H. I., ed. *À Diognète*. Sources Chrétiennes. Paris: Éditions du Cerf, 1951.

Marsilius of Padua. *The Defensor Minor*. Ed. C. K. Brampton. Birmingham: Cornish Brothers, Ltd., 1922.

———. *Defensor Pacis*. Für Übungszwecke bearbeitet, R. Scholz. Leipzig: B. G. Teubner, 1914.

———. *Defensor Pacis*. Ed. C. W. Previté-Orton. Cambridge: University Press, 1928.

Maurice of Sully. *French Homilies*. Ed. C. A. Robson in *Maurice of Sully and the Medieval Vernacular Homily*. Oxford: Basil Blackwell, 1952.

Mechthild of Magdeburg. *The Revelations, or the Flowing Light of the Godhead*. Tr. L. Menzies. New York: Longmans, Green & Co., 1953.

Mirbt, C., ed. *Quellen zur Geschichte des Papsttums und des römischen Katholizismus*. Fourth Edition. Tübingen: J. C. B. Mohr (Paul Siebeck), 1924.

Mirk's Festial: A Collection of Homilies by Johannes Mirkus (John Mirk). Ed. T. Erbe. EETS ES 96 Pt. 1. London: Kegan Paul, Trench, Truebner & Co., Ltd., 1905.

The Missal in Latin and English. Ed. J. O'Connell *et al*. London: Burns Oates and Washbourne, 1949.

Missale Romanum. New York: Benziger Brothers, Inc., 1944.

Monumenta eucharistica et liturgica vetustissima. Part I. Ed. J. Quasten, in *Florilegium Patristicum*, VII. Eds. B. Geyer and J. Zellinger. Bonn: Sumpt. Petri Hanstein, 1935-36.

Neale, J. M., ed. *Collected Hymns, Sequences and Carols*. London: Hodder & Stoughton, 1914.

———. *Mediaeval Preachers and Mediaeval Preaching: A Series of Extracts Translated from the Sermons of the Middle Ages*. London: J. C. Mozley, 1856.

The New Missal for Every Day. Ed. Father F. X. Lasance. New York: Benziger Brothers, Inc., 1937.

Nicholas of Clemanges. *De ruina et reparacione Ecclesie*. Tr. A. Coville, *Le traité de la ruine de l'église de Nicolas de Clamanges*. . . . Paris: E. Droz, 1936.

Nicholas of Cusa. *De Concordantia*. Liber I. *Opera Omnia*, XIV. Ed. G. Kallen. Leipzig: F. Meiner, 1939. See also Schard, *De iurisdictione*. Basel, 1566, pp. 465-676, for the *De Concordantia*.

———. *Oeuvres Choisies*. Ed. M. de Gandillac. Paris: Aubier, 1942.

———. *Opera*. Ed. H. Petrus. 3 Vols. in 1. Basel: Ex Officina Henricpetrina, 1565.

———. *The Vision of God*. Tr. E. G. Salter. New York: E. P. Dutton & Co., 1928.

———. *Wichtigste Schriften* in deutscher Uebersetzung von F. N. Scharpff. Freiburg i/B: Herder, 1862.

Ockham, William. *Breviloquium de Potestate Papae*. Ed. L. Baudry. Paris, 1937.

———. *Dialogus*. Ed. Goldast, *Monarchia*.

———. *Opera Politica*, I. Ed. J. G. Sikes *et al*. Manchester: University of Manchester Press, 1940.

———. *Studies and Selections*. By S. C. Tornay. La Salle, Ill.: The Open Court Publishing Co., 1938.

Old English Homilies. Ed. R. Morris. EETS 29.1. London: N. Truebner & Co., 1868.

Optatus of Mileve. *Historia Donatistarum.* MPL 11.

——. *Libri VII Accedunt Decem Monumenta Vetera ad Donatistarum Historiam Pertinentia.* CSEL 26.

——. *De Schismate Donatistarum. Ibid.*

Ordericus Vitalis. *Historia Ecclesiastica.* MPL 188.

Origen of Alexandria. *Commentaria In Epist. Ad Rom.* MPG 14.

——. *In Jesu Nave Hom.* MPG 12.

——. *In Leviticum Hom.* GCS, VI.

——. *In Numeros Hom.* GCS VII.

——. *Werke.* Ed. in *Die griechischen christlichen Schriftsteller der ersten drei Jahrhunderte* (GCS). Leipzig: J. C. Hinrichs, 1891, etc.

Otto of Freising. *The Two Cities: A Chronicle of Universal History to the Year 1146 A.D.* Tr. C. C. Mierow. New York: Columbia University Press, 1928.

Patrologia Latina (MPL). 221 Vols. Ed. J. P. Migne. Paris: Migne, 1844-64.

Patrologia Graeca (MPG). 165 Vols. Ed. J. P. Migne. Paris: Migne, 1857-66.

Peter of Blois. *Opera Omnia.* Vol. I. *Epistolae.* Ed. J. H. Giles. Oxford: Parker, 1847.

——. *Epistolae* and *Sermones.* MPL 207.

Peter Lombard. *Libri IV Sententiarum.* Ed. P. P. Collegii S. Bonaventurae. 2 Vols. Second edition. Quaracchi: Ex Typographia Collegii S. Bonaventurae, 1916.

Petry, R. C., ed. *No Uncertain Sound: Sermons That Shaped the Pulpit Tradition* (NUS). Philadelphia: Westminster Press, 1948.

Phillip of Harveng. *De Institutione clericorum.* MPL 203.

The Pricke of Conscience (Stimulus Conscientiae). Ed. R. Morris. Berlin: A. Asher & Co., 1863.

Prosper of Aquitaine. *Expositio Psalmorum.* MPL 51.

Raoul Glaber. *Chronicon.* MPL 142.

Richardson, C. C., ed. *Early Christian Fathers.* Library of Christian Classics, I. Philadelphia: Westminster Press, 1953.

Robert de Basevorn. *Forma praedicandi,* in Th.-M. Charland, *Artes praedicandi.* Ottawa, 1936.

Robert de Sorbon. *De Consciencia et de Tribus Dietis.* Ed. F. Chambon. Paris: A. Picard et Fils, 1902.

The Roman Breviary: Reformed by order of the Holy Oecumenical Council of Trent. . . . Tr. John, Marquess of Bute (Summer). Edinburgh: William Blackwood and Sons, 1879.

Ross, J. B., and McLaughlin, M. M., eds. *The Portable Medieval Reader.* New York: The Viking Press, 1949.

Rupert of Deutz. *De glorificatione Trinitatis.* MPL 169.

Ruysbroeck, John of. *The Adornment of the Spiritual Marriage; The Sparkling Stone; The Book of Supreme Truth.* Tr. C. A. Wynschenk Dom. London: John M. Watkins, 1916.

——. *The Spiritual Espousals.* Tr. E. Colledge. London: Faber and Faber, Ltd., 1952.

Schard, S. *De iurisdictione, auctoritate et praeeminentia imperiali ac potestate ecclesiastica.* . . . Basel, 1566.

Stephen of Tornai. *Summa . . . über das Decretum Gratiani.* Ed. J. F. von Schulte. Giessen: E. Roth, 1891.

The Teaching of the Twelve Apostles, ANF VII.

Tertullian. *Ad nationes.* CSEL 20. Pt. 1.

Theodulph of Orleans. *Capitula ad presbyteros parochiae suae.* MPL 105.

Théry, G. *Études Dionysiennes.* 2 Vols. Paris, 1932-37.

Thomas Aquinas. *The Religious State, the Episcopate, and the Priestly Office.* Tr. Father Procter. St. Louis: B. Herder Book Co., 1902.

———. *On the Governance of Rulers.* Tr. G. B. Phelan, London: Sheed and Ward, 1937. Revised by I. Th. Eschmann, as *On Kingship: To the King of Cyprus.* Toronto: Pontifical Institute of Mediaeval Studies, 1949.

———. *Compendium of Theology.* Tr. C. Vollert. St. Louis: B. Herder Book Co., 1952.

———. *Catechetical Instructions.* Tr. J. B. Collins. New York: Joseph F. Wagner, Inc., 1939.

———. *Summa Theologiae.* Ed. Institute of Medieval Studies of Ottawa. 4 Vols. Ottawa: College Dominicain d'Ottawa, 1941.

The "Summa Theologica" of St. Thomas Aquinas. Translated by the Fathers of the English Dominican Province. London: Burns, Oates and Washbourne.

———. *In Librum Beati Dionysii de Divinis Nominibus Commentaria. Opera Omnia,* XV. Parma Edition. New York: Musurgia Publishers, 1950.

———. *De Humanitate Jesu Christi Domini Nostri. Op. Om.* Parma, XVII.

———. *De Regimine Principum ad Regem Cypri. Op. Om.* Parma, XVI.

———. *Sermones Festivi. Op. Om.* Parma, XV.

———. *Expositio in Omnes S. Paul Epistolas. Op. Om.* Parma, XIII.

———. *Compendium Theologiae ad Fratrem Reginaldum. Op. Om.* Parma, XVI.

Thomas Cisterciensis. *Commentarium in Cantica Canticorum.* MPL 206.

Thomas Waleys. *De modo componendi sermones cum documentis.* Ed. Th.-M. Charland, *Artes Praedicandi.* Ottawa, 1936.

The Towneley Plays. Ed. G. England and A. W. Pollard. EETS, ES: 71. London: Kegan Paul, Trench, Truebner & Co., 1897.

Vincent de Beauvais. *De eruditione filiorum nobilium.* Ed. A. Steiner. Cambridge, 1938.

Walafrid Strabo. *Glossa Ordinaria.* MPL 113.

Wells, H. W., and Loomis, R. S., eds. *Representative Medieval and Tudor Plays.* New York: Sheed & Ward, 1942.

West, R. C. *Western Liturgies.* London: S. P. C. K., 1938.

William le Maire. *Liber Guillelmi Majoris.* Ed. M. Célestin Port, in *Mélanges Historiques,* II. Paris: Imprimerie Nationale, 1877.

Wyclif, J. *Opus evangelicum.* Vols. I and II. Ed. J. Loserth. London: Truebner & Co., 1895.

———. *Select English Works.* Ed. T. Arnold. 3 Vols. Oxford: The Clarendon Press, 1869-70.

———. *Select English Writings.* Ed. H. E. Winn. London: Milford, 1929.

———. *Sermones.* Vol. I. Ed. J. Loserth. London: Truebner & Co., 1887.

——. *Tractatus De Blasphemia*. Ed. M. H. Dziewicke. London: Truebner & Co., 1893.

——. *De veritate sacrae scripturae*. Ed. R. Buddensieg. 3 Vols. London: Truebner & Co., 1905-7.

B. Secondary Works

Aegerter, E., ed. *Joachim de Flore, L'évangile éternel: Première traduction française précédée d'une biographie*. 2 Vols. Paris: Rieder, 1928.

Aigrain, A. *Liturgia*. Paris: Bloud et Gay, 1931.

Altaner, B. *Patrologie*. Third edition. Freiburg: Herder, 1951.

Althaus, P. *Die letzen Dinge*. Fifth edition. Gütersloh: C. Bertelsmann, 1949.

Ancelet-Hustache, J. *Mechtilde de Magdebourg 1207-1282; Étude de psychologie religieuse*. Paris: Librairie Ancienne Honoré Champion, 1926.

Anderson, G. K. *The Literature of the Anglo-Saxons*. Princeton: Princeton University Press, 1949.

Anger, Abbé. *The Doctrine of the Mystical Body of Christ According to the Principles of the Theology of St. Thomas*. Tr. J. J. Burke. New York: Benziger Brothers, Inc., 1931.

Bacon, B. W. *Studies in Matthew*. New York: Henry Holt & Co., 1930.

Baillie, J. *And the Life Everlasting*. New York: Charles Scribner's Sons, 1933.

Bardenhewer, O. *Geschichte der altkirchlichen Literatur*. Vols. II and III. Friburg i/B, 1914, 1912.

Batiffol, C. *Leçons sur le Messe*. Paris: Victor Lecoffre, 1927.

Baumann, J. J. *Die Staatslehre des Hl. Thomas von Aquino*. Leipzig, 1873.

Bennett, J. *Social Salvation*. New York: Charles Scribner's Sons, 1935.

Benz, E. *Ecclesia spiritualis*. Stuttgart: W. Kohlhammer, 1934.

Berlière, N. *L'ordre monastique des origines au XII* siècle*. Paris: Librairie P. Lethielloux, 1924.

Bett, H. *Joachim of Flora*. London: Methuen & Co., Ltd., 1931.

Bevan, E. R. *Hellenism and Christianity*. London: G. Allen & Unwin, Ltd., 1921.

Bicknell, E. J. *The First and Second Epistles to the Thessalonians*. London: Methuen & Co., Ltd., 1932.

Bohatec, J. *Calvins Lehre von Staat und Kirche mit besonderer Berücksichtigung des Organismusgedankens*. Breslau: M & H. Marcus, 1937.

Bonhoeffer, D. *Sanctorum Communio: eine dogmatische Untersuchung zur Soziologie der Kirche*. Berlin: Trowitzsch & Sohn, 1930.

Bosworth, E. I. *The Life and Teaching of Jesus*. New York: The Macmillan Co., 1929.

Bréhier, L. *L'art chrétien: son développement iconographique des origines à nos jours*. Paris: Laurens, 1928.

Breton, Valentin-M. *The Communion of Saints: History—Dogma—Devotion*. St. Louis, B. Herder Book Co., 1934.

Brillant, M. *Eucharistia*. Paris: Bloud et Gay, 1934.

Carlyle, R. W., and Carlyle, A. J. *A History of Medieval Political Theory in the West*. 5 Vols. London: W. Blackwood and Sons, 1903—.

Case, S. J. *The Social Triumph of the Ancient Church*. New York: Harper & Bros., 1933.

Cayré, A. A. *Patrologie et histoire de la théologie*. 3 Vols. Fourth edition. Paris: Desclée et Cie, 1947.

Chappuis, P. G. *La destinée de l'homme, de l'influence du Stoicisme sur la pensée chrétienne primitive.* Paris: Fischbacher, 1926.

Charland, Th.-M. *Artes praedicandi.* Ottawa: Inst. d'études médiévales, 1936.

Charles, R. H. *A Critical History of the Doctrine of a Future Life in Israel, in Judaism, and in Christianity.* Second edition. London: Adam and Charles Black, 1913.

Clair, C. *Le Dies Irae: histoire, traduction, commentaire.* Paris: Librairie de Féchoz et Letouzey, 1881.

Clark, K. W. "Realized Eschatology," *Journal of Biblical Literature,* LIX, 3 (1940), 367-83.

Cochrane, C. N. *Christianity and Classical Culture.* Oxford: Clarendon Press, 1940.

Connolly, J. L. *John Gerson: Reformer and Mystic.* Louvain: Librairie Universitaire, 1928.

Coulton, G. G. *Five Centuries of Religion.* Vols. I-IV. Cambridge: University Press, 1923-50.

Cranz, F. E. "*De Civitate Dei,* XV, 2 and Augustine's Idea of the Christian Society," *Speculum,* XXV, 2 (April, 1950), 215-25.

Cullmann, O. *Christus und die Zeit.* Zurich: A. G. Zollikon, 1946.

———. *Christ et le temps.* Neuchâtel: Delachaux et Niestlé, S. A., 1947.

———. *Christ and Time.* Tr. F. W. Filson. Philadelphia: Westminster Press, 1948.

———. *Le retour du Christ.* Neuchâtel: Delachaux et Niestlé, S. A., 1945.

Cushman, R. E. "Greek and Christian Views of Time," *Journal of Religion,* XXXIII, 4 (Oct, 1953), 254-65.

Dalman, G. D. *The Words of Jesus.* Edinburgh: T. & T. Clark, 1902.

———. *Die Worte Jesu.* Leipzig: J. C. Hinrichs, 1930.

Davies, W. D. *Paul and Rabbinic Judaism: Some Rabbinic Elements in Pauline Theology.* London: S. P. C. K., 1948.

Dempf, A. *Sacrum Imperium: Geschichts-und Staatsphilosophie des Mittelalters und der politischen Renaissance.* Munich: R. Oldenbourg, 1929.

Diekamp, F. *Theologiae Dogmaticae Manuale. . . .* Vol. IV. Rome: Desclée & Sociorum, 1946.

Dodd, C. H. *The Apostolic Preaching and Its Developments.* Second edition. New York: Harper & Bros., 1944.

———. *The Coming of Christ.* Cambridge: University Press, 1951.

———. *The Parables of the Kingdom.* New York: Charles Scribner's Sons, 1936.

Dondaine, H. F. "Les 'Expositiones super Ierarchiam Caelestem' de Jean Scot Érigène: texte inédit, d'après *Douai 202,*" *Archives d'hist. doctr. et litt. du moyen âge,* XVIII (1950-51), 245-302.

Dubois, M. M. *Les éléments latins dans la poésie religieuse de Cynewulf.* Paris: E. Droz, 1943.

Duckett, E. S. *Anglo-Saxon Saints and Scholars.* New York: The Macmillan Co., 1947.

———. *Alcuin, Friend of Charlemagne.* New York: The Macmillan Co., 1951.

Easton, B. S. T. *The Apostolic Tradition of Hippolytus.* Cambridge: University Press, 1934.

Ebert, A. *Histoire Générale de la littérature du moyen âge en occident.* 2 Vols. Paris: Ernest Leroux, 1883.

Ellul, J. *Le fondement théologique du droit*. Neuchâtel: Delachaux and Niestlé, S. A., 1946.

Emerton, E. *The Defensor Pacis of Marsiglio of Padua, A Critical Study*. Cambridge: Harvard University Press, 1920.

Enlart, C. *Manuel d'archéologie française depuis les temps mérovingiens jusqu'à la renaissance*. 3 Vols. Paris, 1902-16.

Faye, E. de. *Origène: sa vie, son oeuvre, sa pensée*. Vol. III, Paris: Librairie Ernest Leroux, 1928.

Fenton, J. "The Communion of Saints and the Mystical Body," *The American Ecclesiastical Review*, CX, 5 (May, 1944), 378-89.

――――. "Scholastic Definitions of the Catholic Church," *Ibid*. CXI, 1 (July, 1944), 59-61.

Flew, R. N. *Jesus and His Church*. New York: The Abingdon Press, 1938.

Froom, Le Roy E. *The Prophetic Faith of Our Fathers*, Vols. I and II. Washington, D. C.: Review and Herald, 1950, 1948.

Galbraith, G. R. *The Constitution of the Dominican Order*. Manchester: University Press, 1925.

Garrigou-Lagrange, R. *L'éternelle vie et la profondeur de l'âme*. Paris: Desclée, De Brouwer et Cie, 1945.

Gavin, F. S. B. *Seven Centuries of the Problem of Church and State*. Princeton: Princeton University Press, 1938.

Ghellinck, J. de. *L'essor de la littérature latine au XII* siècle*. 2 Vols. Paris: Desclée, De Brouwer et Cie, 1946.

――――. *Le mouvement théologique du XII* siècle*. Paris: Desclée, De Brouwer et Cie, 1948.

Gierke, O. *Political Theories of the Middle Age*. Tr. F. W. Maitland. Cambridge: University Press, 1900.

Gihr, N. *The Holy Sacrifice of the Mass, Dogmatically, Liturgically and Ascetically Explained*. St. Louis: B. Herder Book Co., 1941.

Gilson, E. *Introduction à l'étude de Saint Augustin*. Third edition. Paiis: Librairie Philosophique J. Vrin, 1949.

Glorieux, P. "La vie et les oeuvres de Gerson: Essai chronologique," *Archives d' histoire doctrinale et littéraire du moyen âge*, XVIII (1950-51), 149-92.

Goguel, M. *Jésus*. Second edition. Paris: Payot, 1950.

――――. "Pneumatisme et eschatologie dans le christianisme primitif," *Revue de l'histoire des religions*, CXXXII, 1-3 (Juil.-Dec., 1946), 124-69; CXXXIII, 1-3 Jan.-Juin, 1947-48), 103-61.

Gonse, L. *L'art gothique*. Paris, N. D.

Gougaud, L. *Gaelic Pioneers of Christianity*. Dublin: M. H. Gill and Son, Ltd., 1923.

Gourmont, R. de. *Le Latin mystique*. Paris: Mercure de France, 1892.

Grandmaison, R. P. Leonce de. *Jésus Christ*. 2 Vols. Paris: Gabriel Beauchesne, 1929.

Grant, F. C. *The Earliest Gospel*. New York and Nashville: Abingdon Press, 1943.

Guignebert, C. *Jésus*. Paris, 1933.

Guy, H. A. *The New Testament Doctrine of the "Last Things": A Study of Eschatology*. London: Oxford University Press, 1948.

Hammann, P. *La doctrin de l'église et de l'état chez Occam*. Paris, 1942.

Héring, J., *Le royaume de Dieu et sa venue: étude sur l'espérance de Jésus et de L'Apotre Paul.* Paris: Librairie Felix Alcan, 1937.

Holland, H. S. *The Real Problem of Eschatology.* London: Longmans, Green & Co., 1916.

Huber, R. M. *St. Anthony of Padua.* Milwaukee: Bruce, 1948.

Huegel, F. von. *Eternal Life.* Edinburgh: T. & T. Clark, 1913.

———. *Essays and Addresses on the Philosophy of Religion.* New York: E. P. Dutton & Co., Inc., 1928.

Hurter, H. *Medulla Theologiae Dogmaticae.* Third edition: Oeniponte: Libraria Academica Wagneriana, 1889.

———. *Nomenclator literarius theologiae Catholicae.* Third edition. Vols. I and II. Oeniponte: Libraria Academica Wagneriana, 1903-6.

Jacob, E. F. "Nicholas of Cusa," in *The Social and Political Ideas of Some Great Thinkers of the Renaissance and the Reformation.* Ed. F. J. C. Hearnshaw. New York: Brentanos, N. D.

———. *Essays in the Conciliar Epoch.* Second edition. Manchester, 1953.

———. "Political Thought," in C. G. Crump and C. F. Jacob, *The Legacy of the Middle Ages.* Oxford: The Clarendon Press, 1926.

Jarrett, B. *Social Theories of the Middle Ages.* London: E. Benn, Ltd., 1926.

Jost, K. *Wulfstanstudien.* Bern: A. Francke, 1950.

Jungmann, J. A. *Missarum Sollemnia: explication génétique de la Messe romaine.* 2 Vols. Paris: Aubier, 1951-52.

Kennedy, H. A. A. *St. Paul's Conceptions of the Last Things.* Second edition. London: Hodder and Stoughton, Ltd., 1905.

Kirk, K. E., ed. *The Study of Theology.* London: Hodder and Stoughton, Ltd., 1939.

Knox, R. *The Epistles and Gospels for Sundays and Holydays: Translation and Commentary.* New York: Sheed & Ward, 1946.

Kraus, J. B. *Scholastik, Puritanismus und Kapitalismus.* Munich: Duncker & Humblot, 1930.

Kunzelmann, A. "Die Chronologie der Sermones des Hl. Augustinus," in *Miscellanea Agostiniana,* II, 417-520.

Lagarde, G. *La naissance de l'esprit laique au déclin du moyen âge:* II Marsile de Padue. Wien, 1934.

Leclercq, J. *Saint Bernard Mystique.* Paris: Desclée, De Brouwer et Cie, 1948.

Lietzmann, H. *The Beginnings of the Christian Church.* London: Ivan Nicholson and Watson, Ltd., 1937.

———. *Handbuch zum Neuen Testament.* Tübingen: J. C. B. Mohr (Paul Siebeck); *Das Johannesevangelium,* eds. D. W. Bauer, 1925; *Das Matthausevangelium,* ed. E. Klostermann, 1927; *Lukasevangelium,* ed. H. Gressmann and E. Klostermann, 1919.

Littel, F. H. *The Anabaptist View of the Church.* Berne, Ind.: American Society of Church History, 1952.

Loewith, K. *Meaning in History.* Chicago: University of Chicago Press, 1949.

Loisy, A. *L'évangile et l'église.* Third edition. Bellevue: Chez l'auteur, 1901.

———. *Le quatrième évangile.* Paris: A. Picard et Fils, 1903.

Lossky, V. "La notion des 'analogies' chez Denys le Pseudo-Aréopagite," *Archives d'hist. doctrinale et littéraire du moyen âge.* Paris, 1930.

Lubac, H. de. *Catholicisme: les aspects sociaux du dogme.* Fourth edition. Paris: Éditions du Cerf, 1947.

MacCulloch, J. A. *Medieval Faith and Fable.* Boston: Marshall Jones Co., 1932.

McNeill, J. T. *Christian Hope for World Society.* New York: Willett, Clark & Co., 1937.

———. *A History of the Cure of Souls.* New York: Harper & Bros., 1951.

Major, H. D. A., Manson, T. W., and Wright, C. J. *The Mission and Message of Jesus: An Exposition of the Gospels in the Light of Modern Research.* London: Ivan Nicholson & Watson, Ltd., 1937.

Mâle, E. *L'art religieux du XIII° siècle en France.* Fourth edition. Paris: Librairie Armand Colin, 1919.

———. *L'art religieux du XII° siècle en France.* Third edition. Paris: Librairie Amand Colin, 1928.

Mandonnet, P. *Saint Dominique.* 2 Vols. Paris: Desclée, De Brouwer et Cie, 1937.

Manitius, M. *Geschichte der lateinischen Literatur des Mittelalters.* 3 Vols. Munich: C. H. Beck'sche, 1911-31.

Manson, T. W. *The Teaching of Jesus: Studies of Its Form and Content.* Second edition. Cambridge: University Press, 1935.

Manson, W. *The Gospel of Luke.* The Moffatt New Testament Commentary. New York: Harper & Bros., 1930.

Mario Dal Pra. *Scoti Eriugena.* Second edition. Milan, 1951.

Merrill, W. A. *Latin Hymns.* Boston: Sanborn, 1904.

Mersch, É. *Le corps mystique du Christ.* 2 Vols. Second edition. Paris: Desclée, De Brouwer et Cie, 1936.

———. *The Whole Christ.* Translation from the French, by J. R. Kelly. Milwaukee, Wis.: Bruce Publishing Co., 1938.

Miscellanea Liturgica. . . L. C. Mohlberg. 2 Vols. Rome: Edizioni Liturgiche, 1948.

Moehlman, C. H. *Protestantism's Challenge.* New York: Harper & Bros., 1939.

Monod, V. *Dieu dans l'univers.* Paris: Librairie Fischbacher, 1933.

Moorman, J. R. H. *Church Life in England in the Thirteenth Century.* Cambridge: University Press, 1946.

Morey, C. R. *Mediaeval Art.* New York: W. W. Norton & Co., Inc., 1942.

Mourin, L. *Jean Gerson: Prédicateur français.* Bruges: Tempelhof, 1952.

Mueller, K. *Kirchengeschichte.* Third edition. Vol. I, Pt. 1. Tübingen: J. C. B. Mohr (Paul Siebeck), 1938.

Muilenburg, J. *The Literary Relations of the Epistle of Barnabas and the Teaching of the Twelve Apostles.* Marburg, 1929.

Muller, W. "Der Staat in seinen Beziehungen zur sittlichen Ordnung bei Thomas von Aquin," in *Beiträge zur Geschichte der Philosophie des Mittelalters.* . . . Ed. C. Baeumker, XIX, 1 (Münster, 1916) , 45 ff.

Nichols, J. H. *Primer for Protestants.* New York: Association Press, 1950.

Niebuhr, H. R. *The Kingdom of God in America.* Chicago: Willett, Clark & Co., 1937.

———. *Christ and Culture.* New York: Harper & Bros., 1951.

Niebuhr, R. *Faith and History.* New York: Charles Scribner's Sons, 1949.

Nygren, A. *Agape and Eros.* Part I. New York, 1932.

Osborne, C. E. *Christian Ideas in Political History.* London: J. Murray, 1929.

Otto, R. *The Kingdom of God and the Son of Man.* Tr. F. V. Filson and B. L. Woolf. London: The Lutterworth Press, 1938.

Owst, G. R. *Literature and Pulpit in Medieval England.* Cambridge: University Press, 1933.

Patch, H. R. *The Other World According to Descriptions in Medieval Literature.* Cambridge, Mass.: Harvard University Press, 1950.

Petry, R. C. *Francis of Assisi: Apostle of Poverty.* Durham, N. C.: Duke University Press, 1941.

————, ed. *No Uncertain Sound: Sermons That Shaped the Pulpit Tradition.* Philadelphia: Westminster Press, 1948.

————. *Preaching in the Great Tradition: Neglected Chapters in the History of Preaching.* Philadelphia: Westminster Press, 1950.

————. "Emphasis on the Gospel and Christian Reform in Late Medieval Preaching," *Church History,* XVI, 2 (June, 1947), 75-91.

————. "Medieval Eschatology and St. Francis of Assisi," *Church History,* IX, (March, 1940), 54-69.

————. "The Social Character of Heavenly Beatitude According to the Thought of St. Thomas Aquinas," *The Thomist,* VII, 1 (Jan., 1944), 65-79.

————. "Mediaeval Eschatology and Social Responsibility in Bernard of Morval's *De Contemptu Mundi,*" *Speculum,* XXIV, 2 (April, 1949), 207-17.

Plumpe, J. C. *Mater Ecclesia: An Inquiry into the Concept of the Church as Mother in Early Christianity.* Washington, D. C.: The Catholic University of America Press, 1943.

Pohle, J. *Eschatology or the Catholic Doctrine of the Last Things: a Dogmatic Treatise.* St Louis: B. Herder Book Co., 1945.

Pontet, M. *L'exégèse de S. Augustin Prédicateur.* Paris, 1944.

Preger, W. *Geschichte der deutschen Mystik im Mittelalter.* Leipzig: Dörffling und Franke, 1874.

Puech, A. *Histoire de la littérature Grecque Chrétienne.* Vols. II & III. Paris: Les Belles Lettres, 1928-30.

Quasten, J. *Patrology.* Westminster, Md.: Newman Press, 1950.

Rogers, E. F. *Peter Lombard and the Sacramental System.* New York, 1917.

Rohr, L. R. *The Use of Sacred Scripture in the Sermons of St. Anthony of Padua.* Washington, D. C.: Catholic University of America Press, 1948.

Rondet, H. *et al. Études Augustiniennes.* Paris: Aubier, 1953.

Roques, R. "La notion de hiérarchie selon le Pseudo-Denys," *Archives d'histoire doctrinale et littéraire du moyen âge,* XVII (1949), 183-222, and XVIII (1950-51), 5-44.

Sabatier, P. *Études inédites sur S. François d' Assise.* Paris: Fishbacher, 1932.

Salvemini, G. *Historian and Scientist: An Essay on the Nature of History and the Social Sciences.* Cambridge: Harvard University Press, 1939.

Schilling, O. *Die Staats-und Soziallehre des Heiligen Thomas von Aquin.* Second edition. Munich: Max Hueber, 1930.

Schmitz, P. *Histoire de l'ordre de Saint-Benoît.* 6 Vols. Second edition. Maredsous: Les Éditions de Maredsous, 1948.

Schnuerer, G. *Kirche und Kultur im Mittelalter.* 3 Vols. Paderborn: F. Schoningh, 1924-26.

Schwab, J. B. *Johannes Gerson.* Wurzburg: Verlag der Stahel'schen Buchhandlung, 1858.

Scott. E. F. *The Book of Revelation.* Second edition. London: S. C. M. Press, 1940.

Seeberg, R. *Lehrbuch der Dogmengeschichte.* 4 Vols. Leipzig: Deichert, 1922.

————. *Textbook of the History of Doctrines.* Revised edition. Translated by C. E. Hay. Grand Rapids, Mich.: Baker Book House, 1952.

Seymour, St. John D. *Irish Visions of the Other World.* London: S. P. C. K., 1930.

Shepherd, M. H. *The Living Liturgy.* New York: Oxford University Press, 1946.

Shinn, R. *Christianity and the Problem of History.* New York: Charles Scribner's Sons, 1953.

Slosser, G. J. *The Communion of Saints.* New York: Harper & Bros., 1937.

Spicq, C. *Esquisse d'une histoire de l'exégèse latine au moyen âge.* Paris: J. Vrin, 1944.

Stapper, R., and Baier, D. *Catholic Liturgics.* Revised edition. Paterson, N. J.: St. Anthony Guild Press, 1938.

Steidle, B. *Patrologia.* Friburg i/B: Herder & Co., 1937.

Streeter, B. H. *The Four Gospels.* New York: The Macmillan Co., 1925.

Sullivan, W. L. *Under Orders.* W. Rindge, N. H.: Richard R. Smith, Publisher, Inc., 1944.

Swete, H. B. *The Holy Catholic Church: The Communion of Saints.* London: Macmillan and Co., Ltd., 1915 (1919).

Taubes, J. *Abendlandische Eschatologie.* Bern: A. Francke, 1947.

Taylor, A. E. *The Christian Hope of Immortality.* Second edition. London: The Century Press, 1939.

Thielicke, H. *Tod und Leben.* Tübingen: J. C. B. Mohr (Paul Siebeck), 1946.

Thamin, R. *St. Ambrose et la morale chrétienne au IV⁰ siècle.* Paris, 1895.

Troeltsch, E. *The Social Teaching of the Christian Churches.* Tr. by O. Wyon. 2 Vols. New York: The Macmillan Co., 1931.

————. "Eschatologie," *Religion in Geschichte und Gegenwart,* II, 622 ff.

Van der Meer, F. *Augustinus der Seelsorger.* Cologne, 1951.

Vansteenberghe, E. *Le cardinal Nicolas de Cues 1401-1464 . . . l'action, la pensée.* Paris: Champion, 1920.

Visser t'Hooft, W. A., and Oldham, J. H. *The Church and Its Function in Society.* London: George Allen & Unwin, Ltd., 1937.

Wadstein, E. *Die eschatologische Ideengruppe: Antichrist, Weltsabbat, Weltende und Weltgericht.* Leipzig: O. T. Reisland, 1896.

Walz, P. A. *Compendium historiae Ordinis Praedicatorum.* Rome: Pontificum Athenaeum Angelicum, 1948.

Webb, C. C. J. *John of Salisbury.* London: Methuen & Co., Ltd., 1932.

Weiss, J. *Die Predigt Jesu vom Reiche Gottes.* Göttingen, 1900.

Weisweiler, H. "Die Ps:-Dionysiuskommentare 'In Coelestem Hierarchiam' des Skotus Eriugena und Hugo von St. Viktor," . . . *Recherches de théol. anc. et méd.,* XIX (Jan.-Juin, 1952), 26-47.

Wells, J. E. *A Manual of the Writings in Middle English 1050-1400.* New Haven, 1926.

Welter, J. T. *L'exemplum dans la littérature religieuse et didactique du moyen âge.* Paris: E. H. Guitard, 1927.

Wendland, H. D. *Die Eschatologie des Reiches Gottes bei Jesus.* Gütersloh, 1931.

Wilder, A., *Eschatology and Ethics in the Teaching of Jesus.* Revised edition. New York: Harper & Bros., 1950.

Will, R. *Le Culte: ètude d'histoire et de philosophie religieuses.* 3 Vols. Paris: Librairie Felix Alcan, 1935.

Wilmart, A., ed. *Auteurs spirituels et texts dévots du moyen âge latin: études d'histoire littéraire.* Paris: Librairie Bloud et Gay, 1932.

Workman, H. B. *John Wyclif.* 2 Vols. Oxford: Clarendon Press, 1926.

Young, K. *The Drama of the Medieval Church.* 2 Vols. Oxford: University Press, 1933.

Index

411

415